Reinhard Gieselmann

Reinhard Gieselmann
On the Search of Style
Auf der Suche nach Stil

with an essay by
mit einem Essay von

Gerhard Kabierske

Edition Axel Menges

© 2007 Edition Axel Menges, Stuttgart / London
ISBN 978-3-932565-55-7

Printing and binding/Druck und Bindearbeiten:
Everbest Printing Co., Ltd., China

Translation into English/Übersetzung ins Englische:
Ilze Klavina, Portland, Oregon
Design: Axel Menges

Contents

Inhalt

Gerhard Kabierske

»They wanted function – I, however, wanted structure and atmosphere.« On the life and work of Reinhard Gieselmann

A built manifesto

Even passersby who otherwise didn't have an eye for architecture became aware of the house that sprang up at the foot of Turmberg in Karlsruhe-Durlach in 1964. Whether they disapproved of the obviously avant-garde building or felt enthusiastic about it, all those who saw it probably agreed that this was a house that had nothing in common with the often costly yet unimpressive, run-of-the-mill, assembly-line buildings that appeared everywhere in the »better« neighborhoods during those years of the German »economic miracle«.

At the sight of this unconventional style, those familiar with the local scene rightly suspected that Reinhard Gieselmann, who was not even forty years old at the time, was at work in this house on the slope. He had settled in the town only a few years earlier and had already drawn attention to himself on several occasions. In this case he was involved in the project not only as the architect who designed the building, but also as its owner, planning to use it for purposes of personal demonstration. It was to be a real architect's house, a manifesto of his own standards, his own ideas, and his own skill. Even the design – living space for himself and his family, work space for his office, and additional living facilities for staff members – emphasized, by the close spatial connection between home and workplace, and the way the employer and his employees lived together in intentionally neighborly proximity that the architect hoped to realize particular ambitions with this project.

The blueprints were ready soon after Gieselmann and his wife purchased the building site, located in the section of a valley, in 1960.[1] However, because of problems with building regulations, the actual work did not start until three years later. In

1. Reinhard Gieselmann, Gieselmann multi-family house and studio, Karlsruhe, 1960–65. View from the south.
2. Reinhard Gieselmann, Gieselmann multi-family house and studio, Karlsruhe, 1960–65. View from the south-east.
3. Reinhard Gieselmann, Gieselmann multi-family house and studio, Karlsruhe, 1960–65. Section.
4. Reinhard Gieselmann, Gieselmann multi-family house and studio, Karlsruhe, 1960–65. Plan of the 2nd floor.

1. Reinhard Gieselmann, Wohn- und Atelierhaus Gieselmann, Karlsruhe, 1960–65. Ansicht von Süden.
2. Reinhard Gieselmann, Wohn- und Atelierhaus Gieselmann, Karlsruhe, 1960–65. Ansicht von Südosten.
3. Reinhard Gieselmann, Wohn- und Atelierhaus Gieselmann, Karlsruhe, 1960–65. Schnitt.
4. Reinhard Gieselmann, Wohn- und Atelierhaus Gieselmann, Karlsruhe, 1960–65. Grundriß des 2. Obergeschosses.

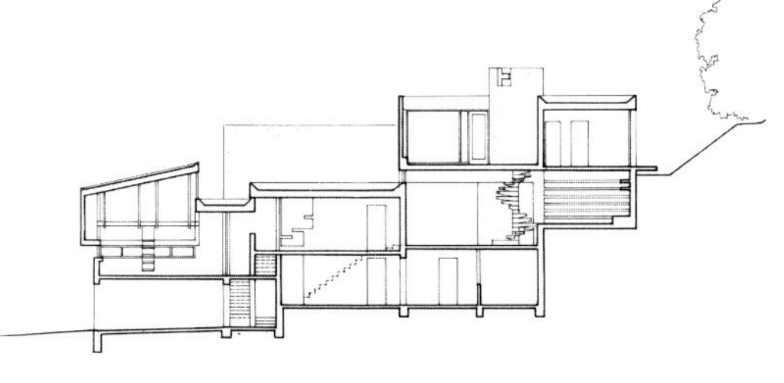

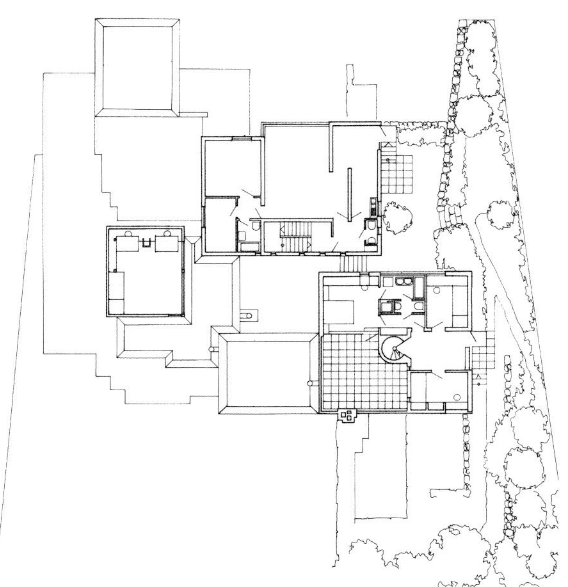

Gerhard Kabierske
»Sie wollten Funktion – ich: Struktur und Atmosphäre.« Zu Leben und Werk von Reinhard Gieselmann

Ein gebautes Manifest

Sogar Passanten, die sonst keinen Blick für Architektur hatten, wurden auf das Wohnhaus aufmerksam, das 1964 am Fuße des Turmbergs in Karlsruhe-Durlach aus dem Boden wuchs. Doch einerlei, ob man dem offensichtlich avantgardistischen Gebäude ablehnend gegenüberstand oder sich dafür zu begeistern vermochte, alle Betrachter dürften sich einig gewesen sein, daß hier ein Haus entstand, das nichts zu tun hatte mit den oftmals kostspieligen und dennoch belanglosen Allerweltsbauten von der Stange, die sich in diesen Jahren des Wirtschaftswunders überall in den »besseren« Wohngegenden breitmachten.

Kenner der lokalen Szene vermuteten angesichts der eigenwilligen Handschrift zu Recht, daß bei diesem Haus am Hang der damals noch nicht vierzigjährige Reinhard Gieselmann am Werk war. Er hatte sich erst wenige Jahre zuvor in der Stadt niedergelassen und bereits mehrfach für Aufmerksamkeit gesorgt. In diesem Fall stand er nicht nur als entwerfender Architekt, sondern auch selbst als Bauherr hinter dem Vorhaben, das er zu einer persönlichen Demonstration nutzen wollte. Ein wirkliches Architektenhaus sollte es werden, ein Manifest des eigenen Anspruchs, der eigenen Ideen und des eigenen Könnens. Bereits das Programm – Wohnung für sich und seine Familie, Arbeitsräume für sein Architekturbüro sowie weitere Wohnmöglichkeiten für Mitarbeiter – unterstrich in der engen räumlichen Verbindung von Eigenheim und Arbeitstätte und dem bewußt nachbarschaftlichen Zusammenleben von Chef und Angestellten die besonderen Ambitionen, die der Architekt mit diesem Projekt verband.

Schon bald nachdem Gieselmann und seine Frau 1960 den in einem Taleinschnitt gelegenen Bauplatz erworben hatten, stand der Entwurf.[1] Wegen baurechtlicher Probleme konnte allerdings erst drei Jahre später mit den eigentlichen Arbeiten begonnen werden, 1965 war das Anwesen schließlich bezugsfertig.

Obwohl der Bau inzwischen fast völlig hinter wuchernder Vegetation verschwindet und trotz einiger unglücklicher Veränderungen in Details durch spätere Bewohner, kann man vor Ort den überraschenden Gesamteindruck, den die Aufnahmen aus der Zeit unmittelbar nach der Fertigstellung dokumentieren, auch heute noch nacherleben:[2] Ein komplex gegliederter Baukörper von plastischer Wucht erhebt sich an einem Hang, der in seinem unteren Bereich flach, nach oben immer steiler ansteigt. Kantige Kuben unterschiedlichsten Zuschnitts scheinen übereinander getürmt, nebeneinander gestellt und ineinander geschoben, wobei der einheitlich weiße Rauhputzüberzug den Kontrast zur umgebenden Natur hervorhebt. Ein Solitär baut sich hier burgenartig vor dem Betrachter auf, dem sich beim Nähern und Umschreiten immer neue Perspektiven eröffnen. Ständig wechselt mit dem Standort auch das Erscheinungsbild. Von der nach Süden, talseitig gelegenen Straße wirkt das Gebäude klar und einfach gegliedert, während vor allem an der öst-

lichen Hangseite die Baumasse durch Kleinteiligkeit, Staffelung und Durchdringung völlig in Bewegung gerät. Der Architekt selbst hat diese expressive Wirkung metaphorisch zu umschreiben versucht: »Beim Herumgehen zeigen die Formen ihr Temperament. Barbarisch und aggressiv beim diagonalen, lagerhaft ruhig dagegen beim orthogonalen Blickwinkel des Betrachters. (...) Das Haus ist wie ein Lebewesen an den Hang gelegt. Keine Ecke gleicht der anderen. Es scheint ein Aufstand stattzufinden. Gegen die Perfektion des unmenschlichen Rechtecks protestieren hier versehrte und verzahnte Flächen. Wie individuelle Menschen eine Familie bilden können, bilden die Einzelformen schließlich das ganze Haus.«[3]

Das ausgeklügelte Spiel mit Kontrasten und Widersprüchen läßt sich auch an anderer Stelle verfolgen. Unterschiedlichste Fenster perforieren die Kuben und lösen sie in ihrer Stereometrie auf. Die schwarz gestrichenen, optisch zurücktretenden Fensterrahmen und Türen lassen die Öffnungen wie Löcher erscheinen, wodurch der skulpturale Charakter der Architektur verstärkt wird. So massiv und schwer die Volumina auch wirken, der ebenfalls schwarz gestrichene, zurücktretende Sockel, der sich dem Terrain folgend vielfach abgetreppt wie eine Schattenfuge unter den Bau legt, läßt die Baumasse dennoch gleichsam schwerelos über der Erde schweben. Hat man sich allerdings daran gewöhnt, Schwarz als Farbe zu erkennen, welche die Elemente hinter der Ebene der weißen Rauhputzflächen charakterisiert, so wird man beim schwarzen Kubus, der die Mitte der Talansicht akzentuiert, wiederum eines Besseren belehrt. Hier ist das Prinzip ins Gegenteil verkehrt: Der holzverschalte Kasten springt vor die Flucht und über die Trauflinie, sein pultartig ansteigendes Dach negiert außerdem die sonst streng eingehaltene Rechtwinkligkeit, laut Gieselmann eine bewußte »pubertäre Störform« innerhalb der »Familie« der stereometrischen Körper.[4]

Dem komplexen äußeren Erscheinungsbild entspricht die innere Disposition. Selbst einem Fachmann dürfte es schwerfallen, sich angesichts der Grundrisse rasch Klarheit über die Räumlichkeiten zu verschaffen, gibt es doch vom untersten Niveau der talseitigen Garagen bis hinauf zur Plattform des turmartigen Dachaufbaus nicht weniger als neun verschiedene Ebenen. Die Verhältnisse scheinen labyrinthisch. Bei der näheren Analyse, dem Vergleich von Grundrissen, Schnitten und Ansichten, schälen sich jedoch klare Gliederungsprinzipien heraus. Das Gebäude gibt sich als Konglomerat dreier zusammengeschobener, in sich weitgehend unabhängiger Baukörper zu erkennen. Jeweils eigenständig erschlossen, erfüllen sie die verschiedenen Funktionen des Programms: Bergseitig liegen versetzt nebeneinander, nach Osten orientiert das Wohnhaus des Architekten, nach Westen der Gebäudeteil, der drei Wohnungen für Mitarbeiter aufnimmt. Das Büro ist beiden talseits vorgelagert, im Innern über das Sekretariat mit dem Wohnteil des Architekten verbunden, im Äußeren schon von weitem erkennbar durch den schwarzen Holzaufbau. Dieser steht mit seiner Dachschräge nicht nur formal und materiell in Opposition zu den weißen Putzkuben, das ansteigende Dach hat auch eine funktionale Bedeutung: Es erweist sich als Shed mit einem Fensterband nach Norden, über das gleichmäßiges Nordlicht in das Atelier gelangt.

1965, the property finally was ready for occupation.

Since then, the building has almost become hidden behind proliferating vegetation. In spite of a few unfortunate detail changes by later residents, it is possible even today to reexperience the unexpected overall impression documented by photographs taken right after its completion:[2] A complexly structured edifice, three-dimensional and powerful, rises on a slope that ascends gently in its lower section and more and more steeply toward the top. Angular cubes, each of a different size, seem to be piled one on top of the other, placed next to each other, and pushed inside each other, and the uniformly white roughcast plastering underlines the contrast with the surrounding countryside. Castle-like, a solitaire building appears before observers, who discover ever new perspectives as they approach and walk around the building. Its appearance changes constantly as one shifts one's position. From the road on the south or valley side, the building appears to be clearly and simply organized, while on the eastern or slope side, it is all set in motion because it is divided into small sections that are gradated and penetrate each other. The architect himself tried to state this expressive effect in metaphorical terms: »When you walk around, the forms show their temperament. They're barbaric and aggressive when the observer's angle of vision is diagonal, and layered and restful when it is orthogonal. (...) The house is placed on the slope like a living creature. Not one corner is like another. A rebellion seems to be taking place. Here, imperfect and dovetailed areas protest against the perfection of the inhuman rectangle. Just as individual human beings can form a family, the individual forms finally create the entire house.«[3]

This ingenious playing with contrasts and contradictions can be observed elsewhere as well. Many different windows perforate the cubes and dissolve their solid geometry. Because they are painted black and recede visually, the window frames and doors make the openings look like holes, intensifying the sculptural character of the architecture. Though the volumes seem massive and heavy, the receding base, which is also painted black and follows the terrain in many steps, is laid under the building like a shadowy joint and gives the structure the appearance of floating weightlessly above the ground. Admittedly, once one gets used to recognizing black as the color that characterizes the elements behind the plane of white roughcast areas, one is forced to reconsider the sight of the black cube accentuating the midpoint of the valley panorama. Here the principle becomes its opposite: The wood-paneled box projects in front of the alignment and above the line of the eaves; moreover, its roof, rising like a lectern, negates the strictly maintained use of right angles elsewhere in the structure. To quote Gieselmann, this was a deliberate »adolescent intrusion« in the family of stereometric bodies.[4]

The inside layout corresponds to the complex outside appearance. Even for a professional architect it might be difficult to get a clear and immediate idea of the rooms inside merely from looking at the projection, since from the lowest level – the garages on the valley side – up to the platform of the towerlike roof structure there are no less than nine different levels. The situation seems labyrinthine. Clear structural principles emerge, however, upon closer analysis and a comparison of the projections, elevations, and sectional drawings. The building looks like a conglomerate of three structures pushed together and largely independent per se. Developed autonomously, they fulfill the various functions of the design: Staggered next to each other on the hill side are the architect's home, orientated towards the east, and the section that contains the three apartments for staff members, orientated towards the west. The office is on the valley side, placed in front of the other two structures. Inside it is connected to the architect's residence by means of the secretary's office. On the outside it can be recognized from afar by the black wooden structure. With its sloping roof, it is not only formally and materially the opposite of the white roughcast cubes, but its ascending roof also has a functional significance: It proves to be a shed roof with a horizontal row of windows facing north, by which constant north light enters the studio.

Halfway down the slope the parts of the building surround an inner courtyard. Similar to an atrium, it is attached to the home of the architect, but can also be accessed from the slope. In summer this is a place where the house residents and the office employees could meet in the evening – like a village square. The trough of a fountain where the rain water from the flat roofs collects forms the integrating central point of the courtyard and the entire complex. The lateral orientation of the apartments towards the sides of the slope is an ingenious way to keep sounds from one apartment from reaching another. Here, seven of a total of nine levels were orientated in accordance with the terrain. In each case large openings lead to ground-level terraces. These are the terraces of former vineyards that were sensitively integrated together with their old, picturesque retaining walls made of red sandstone quarried close by. Thus the new building is skillfully linked with its immediate surroundings.

In the individual residential units, the main rooms are always located in the center of the floor plan. In the Gieselmann house, this area is particularly spacious and versatile in design, almost like a hall, multileveled, with an open kitchen, fireplace, and a freestanding spiral staircase that gives an astoundingly three-dimensional effect. On the other hand, all the rest of the rooms, which are grouped around it and the shaftlike one-flight stairs are intentionally less spacious, and full of nooks and crannies. In terms of space, as with the exterior, this creates a stage setting that is full of tension. This effect is sustained by means of deliberate lighting almost reminding one of baroque dramaturgy, and also by the use of contrasting and totally frugal materials such as exposed concrete, terrazzo, clinker bricks, and wood. Terracotta and sandstone historical relics set in here and there – fragmentary parts of the former Heinrich Hübsch-built court theater of Karlsruhe that was gutted by fire in the war and demolished after heated discussions demanding that it be preserved and rebuilt – contrast with the angular stylistic idiom and are constant reminders in an everyday setting of history and transience.

The importance of the house, the quality of its design, and its role in contemporary architecture

5. Reinhard Gieselmann, Gieselmann multi-family house and studio, Karlsruhe, 1960–65. Living area.
6. Reinhard Gieselmann, Gieselmann multi-family house and studio, Karlsruhe, 1960–65. View of the open kitchen from the living room.
7. Reinhard Gieselmann, Gieselmann multi-family house and studio, Karlsruhe, 1960–65. East side with old vineyard walls.
8. Egon Eiermann, Eiermann house, Baden-Baden, 1959–61.

5. Reinhard Gieselmann, Wohn- und Atelierhaus Gieselmann, Karlsruhe, 1960–65. Wohnbereich.
6. Reinhard Gieselmann, Wohn- und Atelierhaus Gieselmann, Karlsruhe, 1960–65. Blick vom Wohnraum in die offene Küche.
7. Reinhard Gieselmann, Wohn- und Atelierhaus Gieselmann, Karlsruhe, 1960–65. Ostseite mit alten Weinbergmauern.
8. Egon Eiermann, Haus Eiermann, Baden-Baden, 1959–61.

Die Bauteile nehmen auf halber Hanglage einen Innenhof in ihre Mitte, der atriumartig der Wohnung des Architekten zugeordnet ist, aber auch einen Zugang von der Hangseite her besitzt. Im Sommer war er abendlicher Treffpunkt von Hausbewohnern und Büromitgliedern, wie der Dorfplatz einer kleinen Siedlung. Ein Brunnentrog, in dem sich das Regenwasser der Flachdächer sammelt, bildet den integrierenden Mittelpunkt des Hofes und der gesamten Anlage. Die Orientierung der Wohnungen nach den seitlichen Hangseiten verhindert geschickt gegenseitige Störung. Sieben der insgesamt neun Ebenen des Hauses wurden hier nach dem vorgefundenen Terrain ausgerichtet. Große Öffnungen führen jeweils ebenerdig hinaus auf Terrassen. Es sind ehemalige Weinbergterrassen, die mitsamt ihren alten malerischen Stützmauern aus rotem, ganz in der Nähe gebrochenem Sandstein einfühlsam integriert wurden und den Neubau geschickt mit seiner unmittelbaren Umgebung verklammern.

In den einzelnen Wohneinheiten befinden sich die Hauptwohnräume jeweils im Zentrum des Grundrisses. Im Haus Gieselmann präsentiert sich dieser Bereich besonders großzügig geschnitten und abwechslungsreich gestaltet, fast hallenartig, mit verschiedenen Ebenen, offener Küche, Kamin und einer frei im Raum stehenden, sich nach oben schraubenden Wendeltreppe von stupend plastischer Wirkung. Die übrigen sich darum gruppierenden Räume sowie die schachtartigen einläufigen Treppen sind dagegen überall absichtlich knapp bemessen und verwinkelt. Auch in räumlicher Hinsicht entsteht so wie beim Äußeren eine spannungsreiche Inszenierung. Durch die gezielte, in ihren Effekten geradezu an barocke Dramaturgie erinnernde Lichtregie, aber auch durch die Verwendung kontrastreicher und durchweg karger Materialien wie Sichtbeton, Terrazzo, Klinker und Holz wird diese Wirkung unterstützt. Hier und da eingelassene Spolien aus Terrakotta und Sandstein, fragmentarische Bauglieder des ehemaligen Karlsruher Hoftheaters von Heinrich Hübsch, dessen im Krieg ausgebrannter Torso 1963 nach hitzigen Diskussionen um Erhalt und Wiederaufbau doch der Spitzhacke zum Opfer fiel, kontrastieren mit der kantigen Formensprache und erinnern im alltäglichen Umfeld immer wieder an Geschichte und Vergänglichkeit.

Die Bedeutung des Hauses, seine gestalterische Qualität und sein Stellenwert im zeitgenössischen Bauen der frühen sechziger Jahre wurde schon damals erkannt. Zahlreiche Publikationen, selbst in internationalen Fachzeitschriften, etwa im italienischen *Zodiac* oder in der französischen *L'Architecture d'Aujourd'hui*, belegen das besondere Interesse, welches das Gebäude auch über die Grenzen Deutschlands hinaus erfuhr. In Günther Feuersteins amerikanischer Publikation *New Directions in German Architecture* von 1968 fand das Haus genauso Beachtung wie in Wolfgang Pehnts 1970 erschienener, noch heute gültiger Anthologie *Neue deutsche Architektur 3*, worin der Bau als eines von zehn vorbildlichen Beispielen moderner Wohnhäuser der sechziger Jahre aufgenommen wurde.[5]

In Karlsruhe indes fiel der Beifall der Kollegen eher verhalten aus. Zu sehr stand die regionale Architekturszene Mitte der sechziger Jahre unter dem Einfluß Egon Eiermanns, jener zentralen Figur des Bauens der bundesrepublikanischen Nachkriegszeit. Wenngleich Eiermann selbst keines seiner Schlüsselwerke in der Stadt hatte realisieren können, so prägte er doch seit 1947 als charismatischer Lehrer an der Technischen Hochschule, die er zu einer der führenden Architekturschulen in Deutschland gemacht hatte, das Baugeschehen über die große Zahl seiner Schüler.[6] Reinhard Gieselmann war einer von ihnen gewesen, sogar einer der ersten unmittelbar nach Eiermanns Berufung, und damit eigentlich jener Generation zugehörig, die der Meister nach den Kriegserlebnissen besonders eng an sich zu binden wußte. Wie sehr dieser frühere Schüler sich in den sechziger Jahren jedoch von seinem Lehrer entfernt, ja ihm entfremdet hatte, mag ein vergleichender Blick auf Egon Eiermanns eigenes Wohnhaus in Baden-Baden belegen, das ebenso wie das Haus Gieselmann programmatisch die persönlichen Intentionen des Architekten umsetzt. 1959–62 errichtet und damit nur wenig älter als das Haus Gieselmann, zeigt es eine fundamental andere Auffassung von Architektur: Ein von den Möglichkeiten der Konstruktion und den Eigenschaften der Materialien ausgehender Entwurfsansatz, die Addition gleicher Elemente in Grundriß und Aufriß, eine an Auszehrung heranreichende Reduktion von Masse, fließende Übergänge zwischen innen und außen samt den für Eiermann so charakteristischen Umgängen mit ihren leichten Gestängen, aber auch Proportionen von feinfühligster Ästhetik ohne spektakuläre Effekte – all dies sucht man bei Gieselmanns spannungsreicher, körperhaft komponierter Anordnung vergebens. Niemals hätte Eiermann ein Haus als massives plastisches Gebilde verstanden, und niemals hätte er es verputzen lassen, sollten doch seiner Meinung nach sogar Backsteine als kleinste Elemente eines gefügten Ganzen einzeln ablesbar bleiben. »Gott sieht alles«, rief er 1963 in einer Vorlesung über die »Wahrheit in der Architektur« den Studenten zu, um ihnen zu verdeutlichen, daß es einem Architekten niemals gestattet sei, verschiedene Baustoffe unter einem alles kaschierenden Putzüberzug zu verstecken.[7]

Kein Wunder, daß das Haus Gieselmann als ausgesprochener Gegenentwurf zur damaligen Karlsruher Schule betrachtet wurde. Die Kollegen im Fahrwasser Eiermanns gingen auf Distanz. Pointiert zugespitzt schildert Gieselmann in seinen Lebenserinnerungen den Besuch einiger Karlsruher Werkbund-Mitglieder, denen er sein Werk präsentierte: »Sie kamen, das neue Haus des Außenseiters zu sehen, stellten ihre Autos an den Rand der ansteigenden Straße, umkreisten es neugierig von außen und traten durch die schwarze Haustür mit den senkrechten Glasstreifen. Sie legten ab in der kleinen Diele, stiegen die Treppenflucht hoch und standen im hohen Teil des vielfältigen Raumes mit der schwarzen Treppe zur Bibliothek mit den weißen Betonregalen, und zum Geschoß darüber. (...) Sie standen herum, starrten ins Kaminfeuer, Brote und Rotweingläser in der Hand, und begannen zu diskutieren. Müßte ein Haus nicht flexibel sein, um in vielfacher Weise dienen zu können? Darf sich der individuelle Geschmack so manifestieren, daß spätere Bewohner darauf fixiert sind? (...) Sie standen auf Mies van der Rohes breiten Schultern und verabscheuten die Festlegung einer Form. (...) Ich war mir klar; die Opposition lag mir mehr als die Anpassung. Nicht einmal Koalition wollte ich, zu weit war ich von der Karlsruher Ideo-

of the early 1960s were recognized at the time of its construction. Many publications, even in international professional journals such as the Italian *Zodiac* or the French *L'Architecture d'Aujourd'hui* are evidence that the building was greeted with exceptional interest even outside Germany. In Günther Feuerstein's 1968 American publication *New Directions in German Architecture*, the house received just as much attention as it did in Wolfgang Pehnt's 1970 anthology *Neue deutsche Architektur 3*, still authoritative today, where the building is regarded as one of the ten exemplary modern homes of the 1960s.[5]

In Karlsruhe, meanwhile, Gieselmann's colleagues gave somewhat guarded approval. Egon Eiermann, a central figure in Federal German architecture during the postwar period, had too much influence over the regional architecture scene in the mid-sixties. Although Eiermann himself had not been able to construct any of his key buildings in the town, he had since 1947 been a charismatic teacher at the Technische Hochschule. He had made the school into one of Germany's leading schools of architecture and because he had a large number of students left his mark on German architecture.[6] Reinhard Gieselmann had been one of them, in fact one of the first directly after Eiermann's appointment, and thus actually belonged to the generation with whom the master had formed a special bond due to their shared wartime experiences. Later the former student distanced himself from his teacher, indeed became alienated from him. A comparison with Egon Eiermann's own house in Baden-Baden, which like the Gieselmann house programmatically expresses the architect's personal intentions, shows to what extent the two architects divergBuilt between 1959 and 1962, and thus only a little older than the Gieselmann house, it shows a fundamentally different concept of architecture: The design attempts to exploit construction capabilities and the characteristics of materials. It combines similar elements in the floor plan and elevation; it severely reduces mass. It provides fluid transitions between interior and exterior, together with the light strutted circular passages so characteristic of Eiermann. In addition the proportions show the most sensitive aesthetics without spectacular effects – features not found in Gieselmann's tension-filled, corporeally composed arrangements. Eiermann would never have regarded a house as a massive three-dimensional object and would never have had it roughcast, since in his opinion even bricks as the smallest elements of an assembled whole should remain individually identifiable. »God sees everything«, he told the students in a 1963 lecture about »truth in architecture« in order to make it clear to them that an architect is never permitted to hide various types of building materials under a layer of roughcast that conceals everything.[7]

No wonder the Gieselmann house was regarded as the distinct counter-design to the former school of Karlsruhe. The colleagues who followed in Eiermann's wake tended to distance themselves. In his memoirs, Gieselmann describes with pithy exaggeration the visit of several members of the Karlsruhe Werkbund to whom he presented his work: »They came to see the outsider's new house, parked their cars on the shoulder of the ascending road, circled around it curiously and entered through the black door with its vertical glass strips. They took off their coats and hats in the little entryway, went up a flight of stairs, and stood in the high part of the multi-purpose room where the black stairs lead to the library with its white concrete shelves, and to the floor above. (...) They stood around, stared into the fire as they held open-faced sandwiches and wine, and began to discuss: Shouldn't a house be flexible so as to serve a large number of purposes? Is it permissible for individual taste to manifest itself in such a way that later residents are locked into it? (...) They stood on Mies van der Rohe's broad shoulders and detested fixed forms. (...) It was clear to me that the opposition appealed to me more than the conformity. I didn't even want coalition, I was too far removed from the Karlsruhe ideology. They wanted slick, obvious boxes, or at best boxes structured by a skeleton framework – while I wanted three-dimensional bodies. They wanted simple rooms – I wanted mysterious interpenetrations. They wanted visibility at a glance and distinctly discernible elements – I wanted individualization above all. They wanted the rooms to be equal and interchangeable – I wanted a hierarchical arrangement. They wanted the rooms to be lined up along the corridor – I wanted the centripetal middle. They wanted function – I, however, wanted structure and atmosphere.«[8]

Premises, 1925–1955

The path Reinhard Gieselmann took to reach so central a work as his first personal house was long but direct. One of the earliest memories of the architect, born in 1925 in Münster, Westphalia, was the sensual experience of his built environment.[9] In his hometown and from his artistically inclined parents, he absorbed values related to history and culture. Early in life, the boy's attention was drawn explicitly to modern architecture. A white cube of a house with a flat roof and stair tower, a rare evidence of the New Architecture, built in 1931 in Münster for a Jewish businessman, made him realize – he was not even ten at the time – that architecture could be something provocative, scandalous.[10] At the same time young Reinhard developed a special talent for drawing. This was encouraged by his open-minded parents. Later, while at school in the »Paulinum«, a tradition-rich grammar school in Münster, the boy spent school holidays working for a cabinetmaker, and took watercolor lessons from a painter, thus acquiring additional practical and artistic skills.

Most young men who graduated from a German secondary school in 1943 would be »sent off to the slaughter« at one of the collapsing front lines of the world war. At first Reinhard Gieselmann seemed to be lucky. His health was not very stable, he tended to be a loner, and disliked military drill. A positive side effect of a childhood stomach disorder that had reappeared with unpleasant consequences during the »labor service« digging peat in Emsland was that he was exempted from military service. In the winter semester of 1943/44 he was therefore granted the privilege of enrolling at the Technische Hochschule Danzig as an architecture student. In view of the destruction wrought by the bombs in Münster, he firmly re-

9. Reinhard Gieselmann, Kriegszerstörungen an
der Petrikirche, Münster, Juli 1944.
10. Reinhard Gieselmann, »Mein Bett«, 1945/46.
Entstanden im britischen Kriegsgefangenenlager
in Belgien.

logie entfernt. Sie wollten glatte, klare, allenfalls durch ein Skelett gegliederte Kästen – ich wollte plastische Körper. Sie wollten einfache Räume – ich wollte geheimnisvolle Durchdringungen. Sie wollten Überschaubarkeit und Elementierung – ich wollte vor allem Individualisierung. Sie wollten Gleichschaltung der Räume – ich wollte ihre Hierarchie. Sie wollten den Ablauf der Räume am Flur – ich wollte die zentripedale Mitte. Sie wollten Funktion – ich: Struktur und Atmosphäre.«[8]

Voraussetzungen, 1925–1955

Reinhard Gieselmanns Weg hin zu einem solch zentralen Werk wie dem ersten eigenen Wohnhaus war lang, aber geradlinig. Noch heute zählt die sinnliche Erfahrung des gebauten Lebensumfeldes zu den frühesten Erinnerungen des 1925 im westfälischen Münster geborenen Architekten.[9] Die Heimatstadt vermittelte Werte von Geschichte und Kultur, die auch von den musisch veranlagten Eltern getragen wurden. Es war aber auch schon früh explizit moderne Architektur, welche die Aufmerksamkeit des Jungen auf sich zog. Ein weißer Hauskubus mit Flachdach und Treppenturm, 1931 als eines der wenigen Zeugnisse Neuen Bauens in Münster für einen jüdischen Kaufmann errichtet und von der konservativen Einwohnerschaft ebenso argwöhnisch beäugt wie von den Nationalsozialisten, ließ ihn – keine zehn Jahre alt – bereits erkennen, daß Architektur etwas Provozierendes, Anstößiges sein konnte.[10] Parallel dazu entwickelte der junge Reinhard ein besonderes Zeichentalent, das von den aufgeschlossenen Eltern gefördert wurde. Später, während der Schulzeit am »Paulinum«, Münsters traditionsreichem humanistischem Gymnasium, sorgten Ferienarbeit bei einem Tischler und Aquarellstunden bei einem Kunstmaler für weitere praktische und künstlerische Fertigkeiten.

Zum Abiturjahrgang 1943 zu gehören, bedeutete für die meisten jungen Männer im damaligen Deutschland, an einer der zusammenbrechenden Fronten des Weltkriegs »verheizt« zu werden. Reinhard Gieselmann schien zunächst Glück zu haben. Gesundheitlich wenig stabil, eher einzelgängerisch veranlagt und militärischem Drill abgeneigt, brachte ein seit Kindertagen vorhandenes Magenleiden, das sich während des »Arbeitsdienstes« beim Torfstechen im Emsland wieder unangenehm bemerkbar gemacht hatte, den positiven Nebeneffekt der Freistellung vom Kriegsdienst. Im Wintersemester 1943/44 war es ihm deshalb vergönnt, sich als Architekturstudent an der Technischen Hochschule Danzig einzuschreiben. Angesichts der Bombenzerstörung von Münster war er nun fest entschlossen, Denkmalpfleger zu werden. Das beschauliche Leben im bis dahin vom Krieg noch kaum tangierten Danzig und der Einstieg in ein äußerst traditionell orientiertes Studium sollten indes nicht lange währen. In einer Nachuntersuchung wurde Gieselmann 1944 doch für tauglich befunden. Er mußte einrücken, um dann in den Endkämpfen in der Eifel und am Niederrhein die Schrecken des Krieges bis zum bitteren Ende am eigenen Leib zu erfahren. Immerhin überlebte er das Inferno im Unterschied zu vielen seiner gleichaltrigen Kameraden.

Nach der Entlassung aus der Kriegsgefangenschaft, abgemagert und geprägt von traumatischen Erfahrungen, aber auch hochmotiviert, eine bessere Zukunft mitzugestalten, wollte Gieselmann so schnell wie möglich sein Studium fortsetzen. Zunächst absolvierte er in Münster ein Baupraktikum in einer Zimmerei und bewarb sich gleichzeitig an verschiedenen Technischen Hochschulen. Auch wenn er eigentlich lieber nach München gegangen wäre, es war die Technische Hochschule in Karlsruhe, die ihm die Zulassung erteilte.

Im Herbst 1946 zog der Westfale nach Baden und kam in eine Stadt, die ebenso wie Münster schwer vom Krieg gezeichnet war. Das halb zerstörte Architekturgebäude der Hochschule war nur notdürftig hergerichtet, als zum Wintersemester die Lehrtätigkeit wieder aufgenommen wurde. Immerhin standen mit Professoren wie Otto Ernst Schweizer, Heinrich Müller oder Otto Haupt Lehrer bereit, die Qualität versprachen und sich im Nationalsozialismus nicht allzu sehr mit den Machthabern eingelassen hatten. Mit der einhellig ausgesprochenen Berufung von Egon Eiermann wurden Anfang 1947 die Weichen gestellt für eine modern-progressive Entwicklung der Architekturfakultät. Reinhard Gieselmanns Karlsruher Studienzeit sollte in diese, von anderen Schülern später geradezu verklärte Phase des Neuanfangs fallen.

Auch auf den gerade zweiundzwanzigjährigen Studenten Gieselmann übte Egon Eiermanns Persönlichkeit zunächst eine suggestive Wirkung aus. Vor allem die stets überfüllten Vorlesungen vermittelten Erlebnisse besonderer Art. Mit seinem legeren Habitus, der spontanen Rede und ungebremsten Vitalität entsprach dieser Lehrer von 43 Jahren so gar nicht dem gewohnten Professorenbild.[11] Als engagierter Vertreter eines modernen Bauens hatte er nach 1933 den Spagat vollbracht, nicht zu emigrieren und dennoch seinen Idealen treu zu bleiben. Vor allem aber schien das Grauen der letzten Jahre keinerlei Spuren bei ihm hinterlassen zu haben. Nach den persönlichen Erfahrungen am Rande des Abgrunds mußte dies einem Reinhard Gieselmann ebenso imponieren wie seinen Kommilitonen. Indes wahrte er im Unterschied zu vielen seiner Generation eine deutliche innere Distanz. Mit Eiermanns mitreißender, jedoch äußerst plakativer Schwarzweißmalerei, seiner Vorstellung des allein richtigen Bauens ausschließlich mittels konstruktiver, funktionaler und technischer Kriterien ohne Rücksicht auf Traditionen konnte und mochte sich Gieselmann schon damals nicht voll identifizieren. Er hatte ja erst Denkmalpfleger werden wollen und stand zu seiner humanistischen Bildung. Warum sollte deshalb ein Blick auf die Baugeschichte so verwerflich sein? Warum spielte in Eiermanns Lehre die gebaute Nachbarschaft als Bezugspunkt für Neues überhaupt keine Rolle? Und wo blieben soziale Überlegungen? Belesen in Literatur und Philosophie, aber auch geprägt vom westfälischen Katholizismus, schienen sie ihm Grundbedingung für menschliches Zusammenleben und damit auch Grundlage für eine menschliche Architektur schlechthin.

Reinhard Gieselmanns heute noch erhaltenen Studienarbeiten sind vor allem bei Heinrich Müller entstanden. Beim Diplom, das er im Frühjahr 1950 nach sieben Semestern in Karlsruhe ablegte, suchte er hingegen die Herausforderung, sich dem zweifellos profiliertesten der Karlsruher Architekturprofessoren zu stellen, auch auf die Gefahr

solved to become a curator of historical monuments. The quiet life in a Danzig that had so far hardly been touched by the war, and the studies in an extremely traditionally oriented field were short-lived. In a 1944 follow-up medical examination, Gieselmann was found to be fit after all. He had to report for duty and personally experience the horrors of war to the bitter end in the final battles in the Eifel and the Lower Rhine regions. At least he survived the inferno unlike many of his contemporaries.

After he was released from captivity, emaciated and marked by traumatic experiences but also highly motivated to help create a better future, Gieselmann wanted to continue his studies as quickly as possible. At first he completed a practical course in construction at a Münster carpenter's shop, and simultaneously applied for admission at a number of technical colleges. Alhough he would actually have preferred to go to Munich, it was the Technische Hochschule of Karlsruhe that admitted him as a student.

In the fall of 1946 the Westphalian moved to Baden which, like Münster, had been badly damaged by the war. The half destroyed architecture building of the college had been only provisionally repaired when teaching was resumed in the winter semester. Still, professors such as Otto Ernst Schweizer, Heinrich Müller, or Otto Haupt promised to be quality teachers and had not been too involved with the National Socialist dictatorship. With Egon Eiermann's unanimous appointment at the beginning of 1947 the course was set for a modern, progressive development of the department of architecture. Reinhard Gieselmann's period of study in Karlsruhe coincided with this new beginning, which was later almost glorified by other students.

Initially Egon Eiermann's personality had a suggestive effect on the student Gieselmann, who had just turned 22. The constantly overcrowded lectures, especially, were very special experiences. With his casual bearing, spontaneous manner of speaking, and unbridled vitality, this forty-three-year-old teacher did not fit the customary stereotype of a professor.[11] As a committed advocate of modern architecture, he had after 1933 managed the difficult balancing act of not emigrating, yet remaining true to his ideals. Above all, however, the horror of the last years seemed not to have affected him. After their personal experiences at the edge of the abyss, this must have impressed someone like Reinhard Gieselmann as much as it did his fellow students. However, unlike many of his generation, he kept a distinct inward distance. Even then he was unable and unwilling to identify fully with Eiermann's infectious, but extremely flashy black-and-white presentations, his idea that the only correct building design should be ruled by constructive, functional, and technical criteria without regard for traditions. Of course, Gieselmann had initially wanted to be a curator of monuments, and he stood by his humanistic education. Then why should a look at the history of architecture be so reprehensible? In Eiermann's doctrine, why did the built neighborhood play absolutely no role as a point of reference for new buildings? And what about social considerations? Well-read in literature and philosophy, but also formed by Westphalian Catholicism, Gieselmann felt social concerns were a basic condition for community living,

and thus also the basis for a humane architecture as such.

Those of Reinhard Gieselmann's student projects still preserved today were work he did largely with Heinrich Müller. On the other hand, when he submitted the work for his diploma, which he attained in spring 1950 after seven semesters in Karlsruhe, he sought the challenge of working with the unquestionably most prominent of the Karlsruhe architecture professors, even at the risk of having to pull his punches. His diploma project, »Motel at the autobahn«, proves that the student had understood the teacher's lessons and had adopted the latter's maxims of function, logically consistent construction, and reduction of material in conjunction with an aesthetics of lightness. His approach started out from a strict modular design that permitted variants in arranging the buildings depending on location and topographic situation. In addition to solitaire buildings for a restaurant and gas station, the complex was to be an additive sequence of cubelike building units, each consisting of two rooms and plumbing units. Bearing in mind Eiermann's directives, Gieselmann paid particular attention to a method of building using a wood frame with a board partition. Down to the last detail, the design was constructively thought through. The buildings were meant to float above the site on eight slender steel pillars and be accessed by an open flight of stairs. Vehicles would have had a sheltered parking space underneath.

Eiermann gave the project a grade of »very good«. Gieselmann made an impression on him. Doubtlessly he had expectations regarding this talented student, with whom he continued to remain in contact. Initially the young architect did not free himself from his teacher's influence. Like other capable Eiermann graduates, he found his first job with Lange & Mitzlaff in Mannheim, one of the few architectural firms in southwest Germany that stood up to Eiermann's strict judgement.[12] The firm maintained a relationship with the Karlsruhe professor, since Poelzig's student Albrecht Lange had himself worked with Eiermann in Berlin for a few years before the war.

While the firm offered young Reinhard Gieselmann an opportunity to work relatively independently on a design for a sanatorium project in Heidelberg that was never implemented, he felt the sober working atmosphere was rather uninspiring. »Convinced of the validity of their forms as justified by purpose and functional development, my employers created buildings that lacked expression and form. They called this ›decent‹ architecture; they did not demand anything like style«[13], Gieselmann later criticized. Soon he tried to continue his personal search for »style« somewhere else. A coincidence helped him do so. The recommendation of a Swiss professor living in Gieselmann's parents' Münster neighborhood brought him a position in Switzerland. Only six years after the lost war, he was thus given an opportunity that at the time would not have been automatically offered to a young German. According to the doyen of Swiss modernism Alfred Roth, Gieselmann's new employer in Basel, Otto Senn, was an »intellectual cosmopolitan« with »universal interests« and a special love for all the arts.[14] This was what Gieselmann had missed so much in Karlsruhe and Mannheim. In Senn's firm it was

11. Reinhard Gieselmann, motel at the autobahn, 1950, project submitted for a diploma. Axonometric view of a building unit.
12. Otto Senn, development of the Gellert-Areal, Basel, 1950/51, project. Model photo.
13. Otto Senn, Reformist Gellert-Kirche, Basel, 1950/51, project. Plan of the gallery level.

11. Reinhard Gieselmann, Motel an der Autobahn, 1950, Diplomarbeit. Axonometrie einer Baueinheit.
12. Otto Senn, Bebauung des Gellert-Areals, Basel, 1950/51, Projekt. Modellphoto.
13. Otto Senn, Reformierte Gellert-Kirche, Basel, 1950/51, Projekt. Grundriß der Emporenebene.

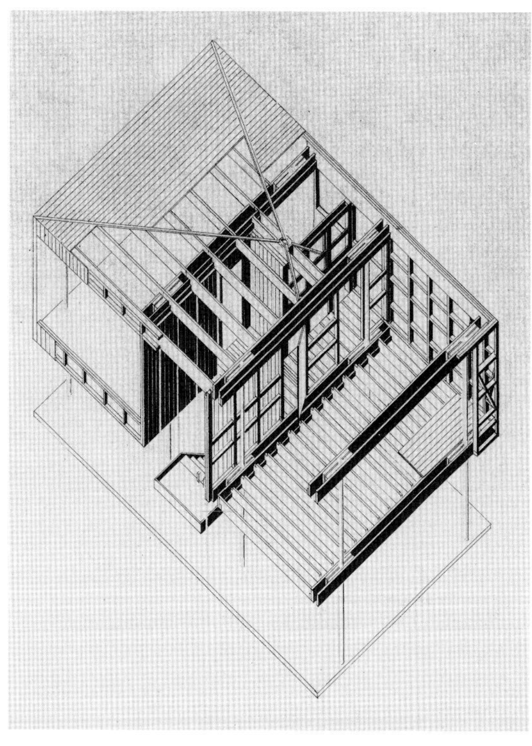

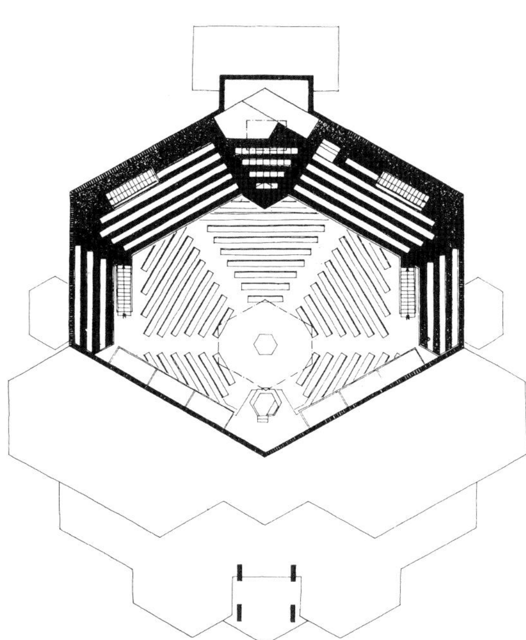

hin, sich selbst zurücknehmen zu müssen. Die Diplomarbeit »Motel an der Autobahn« belegt, daß der Schüler die Lektionen des Lehrers verstanden und sich dessen Maximen von Funktion, konsequenter Konstruktion sowie Reduktion von Material in Verbindung mit einer Ästhetik der Leichtigkeit zu eigen gemacht hatte. Sein Ansatz ging von einem strengen Baukastensystem aus, das je nach Standort und topographischer Situation Varianten bei der Anordnung der Bauten erlaubt hätte. Neben Solitären für Restaurant und Tankstelle sollte die Anlage aus einer additiven Reihung kubusartiger Gebäudeeinheiten bestehen, die jeweils zwei Zimmer mit Naßzellen beherbergen. Der Bauweise als Holzskelett mit Bretterverschalung widmete sich der Diplomand, Eiermanns Direktiven Rechnung tragend, besonders intensiv. Bis in die Details ist der Entwurf konstruktiv durchdacht. Die Gebäude sollten auf acht dünnen Stahlstützen über dem Gelände schweben und durch einen offenen Treppenlauf erschlossen werden. Darunter hätten die Fahrzeuge einen geschützten Parkplatz gefunden.

Eiermann bewertete die Arbeit mit »sehr gut«. Der Name Gieselmann prägte sich ihm ein, und er dürfte sich von diesem talentierten Schüler, mit dem er weiterhin Kontakt hielt, einiges erwartet haben. Zunächst befreite sich der angehende Architekt auch noch nicht vom Einfluß des Lehrers. Er fand wie andere fähige Eiermann-Absolventen erste Arbeit bei Lange & Mitzlaff in Mannheim, einem der wenigen Architekturbüros im deutschen Südwesten, das dem strengen Urteil Eiermanns standhielt.[12] Dort pflegte man die Beziehung zu dem Karlsruher Professor, war doch der Poelzig-Schüler Albrecht Lange in der Vorkriegszeit selbst einige Jahre bei Eiermann in Berlin tätig gewesen.

Das Büro bot dem jungen Reinhard Gieselmann zwar die Möglichkeit, relativ selbständig den Entwurf für ein nie realisiertes Sanatoriumsprojekt in Heidelberg zu bearbeiten. Er empfand die von Nüchternheit geprägte Abeitsatmosphäre indes als wenig inspirierend. »Überzeugt von der Gültigkeit ihrer vom Zweck und funktionellen Ablauf her begründeten Formen schufen meine Chefs ausdrucks- und formarme Bauten. Sie nannten das ›anständige‹ Architektur; Anspruch auf etwas wie Stil wurde nicht gestellt«[13], so Gieselmanns spätere Kritik. Bald versuchte er, seine persönliche Suche nach »Stil« anderswo fortzusetzen. Ein Zufall half dabei weiter. Die Vermittlung eines eidgenössischen Professors, der in der Nachbarschaft der Eltern in Münster wohnte, bescherte ihm eine Anstellung in der Schweiz. Nur sechs Jahre nach dem verlorenen Krieg erhielt er damit eine Chance, die damals nicht selbstverständlich war für einen jungen Deutschen.

In Basel erwartete Gieselmann 1951 mit Otto Senn ein Chef, dem Alfred Roth, der Doyen der Schweizer Moderne, »geistige Weltoffenheit«, »Universalität seiner Interessiertheit« und eine besondere Liebe zu allen Künsten attestierte.[14] Das war es, was Gieselmann in Karlsruhe und Mannheim bislang so sehr vermißt hatte. Im Büro Senn wurde ein grundsätzlicher Diskurs über das moderne Bauen und seine Bedingungen gepflegt, weitblickend neue Tendenzen in Frankreich, Skandinavien und den USA wahrgenommen sowie bei eigenen Projekten, gerade was Typologien anging, offen experimentiert. In der Bibliothek stand Literatur, die in Deutschland unter den Nazis verpönt gewesen war. Das Bauhaus, Le Corbusier, Frank Lloyd Wright und Alvar Aalto, aber auch Mondrian gab es hier zu entdecken, und Gieselmann wußte das interessante Angebot zur Erweiterung seines Horizonts zu nutzen.

Otto Senn, geboren 1902, hatte sich bereits Mitte der dreißiger Jahre als eigenwilliger Kopf profiliert. Innovation und unorthodoxes Denken waren auch Anfang der fünfziger Jahre Motor seines Schaffens. Nicht nur die Basler überraschte er mit seinen der Zeit vorauseilenden Vorschlägen für das Gellert-Areal, das man aus heutiger Sicht eher einer Stadtplanung um 1965 zurechnen möchte. Er projektierte für dieses Neubauquartier eine komplexe Anordnung mit niedrigen Reihenhäusern, Punkthochhäusern auf polygonalem Grundriß und – besonders auffällig – bandartigen, raupenartig sich windenden Wohnhauszeilen. Durch ihre vielfältigen Räume und abwechslungsreichen Ansichten hob sich diese Konzeption deutlich ab vom zeitgenössischen Leitbild eines Städtebaus, der wohlgeordnete, auf dem Zeichenbrett schematisch nach der Besonnung ausgerichtete, parallel stehende Häuserzeilen, eingebettet in öffentliches Grün, propagierte – jene Richtung, die auch Otto Ernst Schweizer an der Karlsruher Hochschule vertrat. Reinhard Gieselmann war an dieser nicht realisierten Planung beteiligt, und sie gab ihm in dem auf Raumwirkung zielenden Ansatz wichtige Anregungen für sein späteres Werk.

Daneben hatte er noch an einem weiteren Projekt Senns, das für ihn Folgen haben sollte, Anteil. Als Mittelpunkt des Gellert-Viertels war eine reformierte Kirche vorgesehen, die trotz mehrerer Überarbeitungen und jahrelanger Diskussionen ebenfalls auf dem Papier blieb. Das Modell, das den Planungsstand von 1951 dokumentiert, überrascht durch die ungewöhnliche Form eines gedrückten Sechsecks und einen Haupteingang über Eck. Die Außenwände sind rundum rasterartig durchbrochen von sechseckigen Lichtöffnungen. Typologisch setzt sich der Entwurf zwar mit der Tradition des protestantischen Predigtraums mit zentraler Anordnung von Altar und Kanzel sowie großen Emporen auseinander, formal kommt er jedoch in der wabenartigen Struktur von Baukörper und angeschlossenen Nebengebäuden sowie einem eher profanen Erscheinungsbild den damaligen Erwartungen der Öffentlichkeit nicht entgegen. Gieselmann mußte im Zuge einer Überarbeitung des Entwurfs prüfen, auf welche Weise das unregelmäßige sechseckige Innere mit einer Betonkuppel überspannt werden konnte. Im Umfeld Eiermanns hätte man solche Überlegungen schlichtweg als formale Spielerei und üblen Verstoß gegen konstruktive Folgerichtigkeit abgetan. Bei Senn galt experimentelles, künstlerisches Ausprobieren hingegen als Tugend, der sich der junge Mitarbeiter gerne anschloß.

Mangels Aufträgen war an ein längeres Verbleiben in diesem anregenden Umfeld allerdings nicht zu denken. Nach einem Intermezzo bei Walter Senn, Ottos Bruder, der im gleichen Haus ein eigenes Architekturbüro betrieb und damals einen Wohnblock mit Arbeiterwohnungen zu errichten hatte, blieb Reinhard Gieselmann nichts anderes übrig, als im Sommer 1952 zu Lange & Mitzlaff zurückzukehren, die in Basel angefragt hatten, ob er dort entbehrlich sei. Aus der Routine, die sich im nun noch grauer empfundenen Mannheimer

customary to discuss modern architecture and its requirements, to be aware of farsighted new trends in France, Scandinavia, and the US, and to experiment openly in personal projects particularly with regard to typologies. The library included literature that had been frowned upon in Germany under the Nazis. There was much to discover: the Bauhaus, Le Corbusier, Frank Lloyd Wright, and Alvar Aalto, but also Mondrian. Gieselmann used the interesting job offer to widen his horizons.

Born in 1902, Otto Senn had made a name for himself as early as the mid-1930s as a man who had a mind of his own. Innovation and unorthodox thinking were still the driving force behind his creative work in the '50s. He surprised the Basel citizens with his proposals for the Gellert district, so far ahead of their time that from today's perspective one might think they were the work of urban planners around 1965. For the new housing development he projected a complex arrangement with low row houses, high-rises on a polygonal ground plan, and – something that was particularly striking – ribbonlike snaking rows of houses. With its manifold spaces and diverse perspectives this concept was distinctly different from the contemporary model of urban planning, with its orderly parallel rows of houses, orientated mechanically on the drawing board in accordance with available sunlight, and embedded in public green spaces – a direction that Otto Ernst Schweizer at the Karlsruhe college also advocated. Reinhard Gieselmann was involved in this planning – which was never implemented – and it gave him important ideas for his later work in that it was an attempt to produce three-dimensional effects.

In addition he participated in another Senn project that would have consequences for him. A Reformed church was planned as the central point for the Gellert district. Despite several revisions and years of discussion, it too was never implemented. The model that is documented by the 1951 plans is surprising because of its unusual form, a compressed hexagon, and a main entrance at an angle. The exterior walls all have a grid of hexagonal light openings. While typologically the design takes a critical look at the tradition of the Protestant sanctuary, where the altar and the pulpit are placed in the center, formally it did not meet the public's expectations at the time because of the honeycomb structure of the church and its attached buildings and because of its secular appearance. In the course of revising the design Gieselmann had to study how the irregular hexagonal interior could be spanned with a concrete dome. Eiermann and his supporters would have dismissed such considerations as mere toying with form, and a severe violation against constructional logical consistency. In Senn's firm, experimental, artistic innovation was considered to be a virtue, and the young staff member was glad to go along.

Because of a lack of clients, a longer stay in this stimulating environment was out of the question. After an intermezzo with Walter Senn, Otto's brother, who ran his own architectural firm in the same house and had at the time been commissioned to design an apartment house for blue-collar workers, Reinhard Gieselmann had no choice but to return to Lange & Mitzlaff in the summer of 1952. They had inquired in Basel whether the firm

could spare him. He kept trying to escape the routine that once again awaited him in the daily grind of Mannheim, which now felt even more dreary. Launching his academic career and incorporating his Basel impressions, he began on weekends and holidays a paper about »church architecture in our time«, which was accepted as a dissertation in Aachen in 1955. He won over Hans Schwippert and Rudolf Steinbach as advisers. They were former associates of Rudolf Schwarz and Otto Bartning respectively, two prominent personalities in German church architecture. Even though it would take quite some time until he could build his first church, an important foundation stone was thus laid for tackling this task.

September 1953 brought another experience that would have consequences – a trip to Finland that Gieselmann took together with a friend, a Ludwigshafen architect. They traveled north on a Vespa to look at buildings by Alvar Aalto to which Otto Senn had specifically referred. A detailed account of the journey, published in 1954 in *Bauen und Wohnen*, still conveys the enthusiasm that filled the young architect as he viewed not only Scandinavian architecture but also the Nordic landscape.[15]

Important modernist works in Denmark and Sweden marked the beginning of the journey to Finland. In the course of the long tour, the friends chiefly viewed buildings by Aalto. The »master of a synthetic architecture«[16] welcomed the travelers in his Helsinki home and particularly invited them to see his recently completed town hall in Säynätsalo. The visit there became a key experience. To Gieselmann, the complex layout – carefully set in its natural environment and arranged around a raised inner courtyard, with a conference hall, offices, apartments, a community library, and several stores –, the sculptured quality of the volumes, the contrast of materials used, such as klinker bricks, wood, and glass, and the differentiated interior rooms seemed the epitome of successful artistic and architectural creative expression. »Here the walls were not just slabs but three-dimensional devices for enclosing space and forming corners. Materials and areas were not separated, but harmoniously linked«, said Gieselmann in retrospect.[17] »For us this was a completely new kind of modernism – conceived neither in accordance with the ascetic nor the aesthetic rules familiar to us, but freely, expressively, sensually, asymmetrically, sinuously, playing with the light, and with reference to nature – in its details, an individual achievement that seemed far more human than our scanty vocabulary.«

The travelers were just as enthusiastic about Aalto's summerhouse on Muuratsalo Island, where the two were invited to spend the night. Gieselmann captured its characteristic form in a simple sketch. The angled residential part with Aalto's typical shed roofs slanting outward and creating rooms of varying heights combines with an open courtyard to form a rectangle. Windows of various sizes create different types of connection between inside and outside while a fireplace marks the center of the courtyard. Large openings cut into the exterior walls of the courtyard give framed views of the largely untouched countryside – rocks, forest, and lake. »I realized«, writes Gieselmann, »that this way of building would become

14. Alvar Aalto, city hall in Säynätsalo, 1949–52.
15. Alvar Aalto, holyday house in Muuratsalo, 1952/1953. Drawing by Reinhard Gieselmann, 1953.
16. Reinhard Gieselmann, Werner Aebli, Theo Manz and Beppo Merkle, panel from the »gril CIAM«, 1953.

14. Alvar Aalto, Rathaus in Säynätsalo, 1949–52.
15. Alvar Aalto, Ferienhaus in Muuratsalo, 1952/53. Zeichnung von Reinhard Gieselmann, 1953.
16. Reinhard Gieselmann, Werner Aebli, Theo Manz und Beppo Merkle, Tafel aus dem »gril CIAM«, 1953.

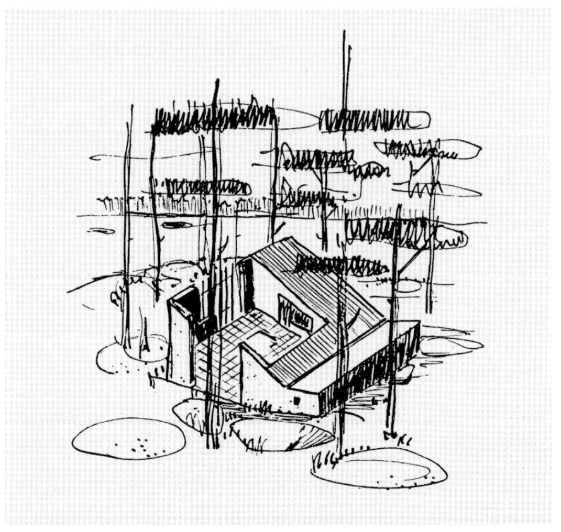

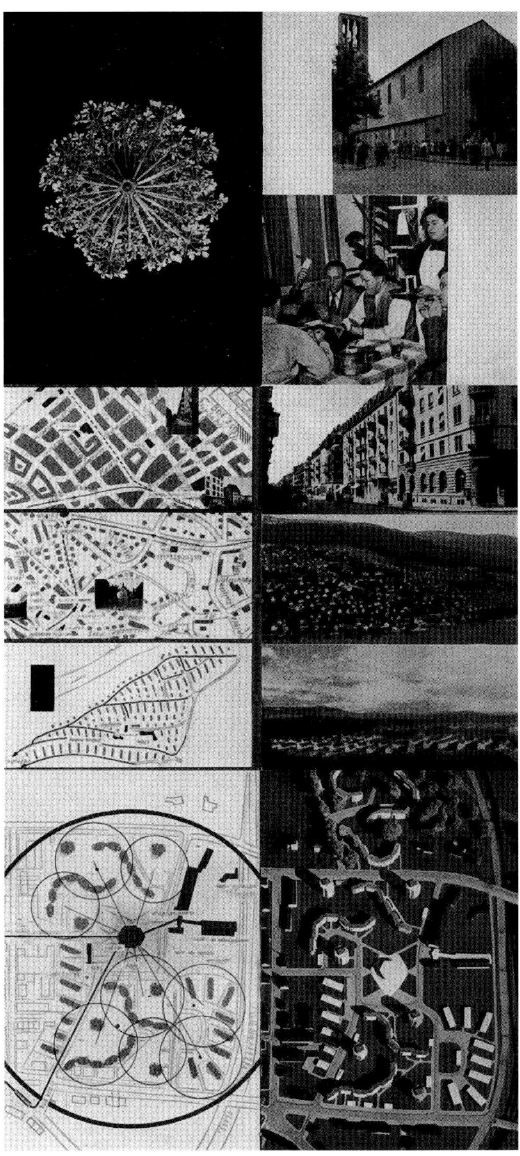

Alltag erneut einstellte, versuchte er immer wieder auszubrechen. Seinen akademischen Anspruch postulierend und die Basler Eindrücke aufnehmend, begann er an Feierabenden und Wochenenden mit einer Arbeit über den »Kirchenbau unserer Zeit«, die 1955 als Dissertation in Aachen angenommen wurde. Als Betreuer hatte er Hans Schwippert und Rudolf Steinbach gewonnen, die früheren Mitarbeiter von Rudolf Schwarz bzw. Otto Bartning, beide herausragende Persönlichkeiten des deutschen Kirchenbaus. Auch wenn es noch geraume Zeit dauern sollte, bis er seine erste Kirche bauen konnte, so war doch damit ein wichtiger Grundstein für die Auseinandersetzung mit dieser Aufgabe gelegt.

Der September 1953 brachte ein weiteres Erlebnis mit Auswirkungen, eine Reise nach Finnland, die Gieselmann zusammen mit einem befreundeten Ludwigshafener Architekten unternahm. Auf einer Vespa machten sie sich auf den Weg nach Norden, um Bauten Alvar Aaltos zu besichtigen, auf die Otto Senn besonders hingewiesen hatte. Ein ausführlicher Reisebericht, 1954 in *Bauen und Wohnen* abgedruckt, läßt wie die Textpassagen in den Lebenserinnerungen auch heute noch etwas von der Begeisterung spüren, die den jungen Architekten angesichts der Baukunst Skandinaviens, aber auch angesichts der nordischen Landschaft erfaßte.[15]

Wichtige Werke der Moderne in Dänemark und Schweden markierten erste Etappen auf dem Weg nach Finnland. Auf einer großen Rundfahrt wurden hauptsächlich Bauten von Aalto besichtigt. Der »Meister einer synthetischen Architektur«,[16] der die Reisenden in seinem Haus in Helsinki empfing, wies sie vor allem auf sein soeben vollendetes Rathaus in Säynätsalo hin. Der Besuch dort wurde zu einem Schlüsselerlebnis. Die sorgsam in die umgebende Natur eingebettete, um einen erhöhten Innenhof angeordnete Gebäudegruppe mit Sitzungssaal, Büros, Wohnungen, einer Gemeindebibliothek und einigen Läden erschien Gieselmann in seiner komplexen Disposition, der Plastizität der Volumen, dem Kontrast der verwendeten Materialien wie Klinker, Holz und Glas und der differenzierten Innenräume als Inbegriff gelungenen künstlerisch-architektonischen Gestaltens. »Hier waren Wände nicht mehr nur Scheiben, sondern raumumschließende, eckenbildende, plastische Mittel. Materialien und Bereiche waren nicht getrennt, sondern in harmonischer Weise verknüpft«, so Reinhard Gieselmann in der Rückschau.[17] »Es war für uns eine ganz neue Art Moderne – weder nach den uns geläufigen asketischen noch auch nach den ästhetischen Regeln konzipiert, sondern frei, gefühlvoll, sinnlich, asymmetrisch, gekurvt, im Spiel mit dem Licht, in der Einbeziehung der Natur – in den Details eine individuelle Leistung, die mir insgesamt menschlicher vorkam als unser karges Vokabular.«

Den gleichen Enthusiasmus entfachte Aaltos Sommerhaus auf der Insel Muuratsalo, in dem die beiden Reisenden sogar übernachten durften. Gieselmann hat dessen charakteristische Form in einer einfachen Skizze festgehalten. Der winkelförmige Wohnteil mit jenen für Aalto typischen, nach außen ansteigenden Pultdächern, die im Inneren Räume unterschiedlicher Höhe schaffen, wird durch einen offenen Hof zum Rechteck ergänzt. Fenster verschiedener Größe vermitteln differenziert zwischen innen und außen, eine Feuer-

stelle markiert die Hofmitte. Große eingeschnittene Öffnungen in den äußeren Hofmauern erlauben gerahmte Ausblicke auf die weitgehend unberührt bleibende Natur der Umgebung mit Felsen, Wald und See. »Mir wurde klar«, so Gieselmann, »daß diese Art zu bauen auch mein Weg werden würde. Diese Architektur würde brauchbarer und langlebiger sein als funktionalistische Glaskästen, sie stand in Übereinstimmung mit den Naturgesetzen.« Zurück bei Lange & Mitzlaff holte ihn die Realität schnell wieder ein: »Ich zeichnete lustlos (an einem Bürobau) herum und fand das Leben banal. Mein Funktionalismus war schon 1953 zu Ende. (...) Aber Aalto und seine Bauten habe ich nie vergessen.«

Lange sollte es Gieselmann indes nicht mehr in Mannheim aushalten. Der Wunsch, in die Schweiz zurückzukehren, war groß. Gemeinsam mit Werner Aebli, einem nahezu gleichaltrigen Schweizer Kollegen, mit dem er sich im Büro Senn angefreundet hatte, wagte er es, 1953 in Basel ein eigenes Büro zu eröffnen. Da Aufträge ausblieben oder Projekte in der ersten Planungsphase steckenblieben, war dem Unternehmen kein Glück beschieden. Um so bedeutender war das einzige konkrete Ergebnis der kurzzeitigen Zusammenarbeit. Gemeinsam mit dem Architekten Theo Manz und dem Photographen Beppo Merkle gründeten sie eine Basler Sektion der »Congrès Internationaux d'Architecture Moderne« und bearbeiteten einen »gril CIAM«, eine Folge von Schautafeln nach dem von Le Corbusier entwickelten System für eine klar strukturierte, einheitliche Präsentation von Ideen und Projekten. Stark soziologisch ausgerichtet, didaktisch gut vermittelt und in aktueller graphischer Gestaltung vorgestellt, untersuchte die Studie das Verhältnis des einzelnen, der Familie, der Haus-, Quartiers- und Stadtbewohner zu ihrem jeweiligen Lebensumfeld. Ziel war es, modernen Städtebau nicht nur als formale Angelegenheit, sondern in einem komplexen Zusammenhang mit den alltäglichen Lebensabläufen zu verstehen. Menschliche Gesellschaft baue sich nicht auf aus einer Addition von einzelnen, sondern aus Gruppen, die in komplexen Verhältnissen zueinander stünden. Jedweder Raum müsse auf einen Mittelpunkt bezogen sein, egal ob in der Wohnung, im Haus, Stadtteil oder in der Stadt – das war die zentrale Botschaft, die der anspruchsvolle »Beitrag zur Abklärung des Habitat« propagierte. Ausgangspunkt waren dabei ganz offensichtlich die theoretischen Überlegungen, die Otto Senn – selbst seit Mitte der dreißiger Jahre CIAM-Mitglied und mehrfach aktiver Kongreßteilnehmer – im Zusammenhang mit seiner Planung für das Gellert-Quartier bei seinen jungen Mitarbeitern angestoßen hatte. Beim IX. CIAM-Kongreß im Juni 1953 in Aix-en-Provence konnte die Gruppe ihren »gril« der internationalen Fachöffentlichkeit vorstellen, die Schweizer Zeitschrift *Werk* publizierte ihn Anfang 1954.[18]

Der Aufenthalt in Aix, die Begegnung mit Architekturgrößen der Moderne – »Gropius kam herbei und interessierte sich für Details«[19] –, aber nicht zuletzt auch der Kontakt mit anderen jungen Kräften wie Aldo van Eyck oder Alison und Peter Smithson, die gleichfalls mit soziologischen Ansätzen gegen die reine Lehre des Funktionalismus opponierten, beflügelten Reinhard Gieselmann. Am nachhaltigsten war freilich die Besichtigung der gerade fertiggestellten Unité d'habitation in

mine as well. This architecture would be more useful and long-lived than functionalist glass boxes – it was in harmony with the laws of nature.« Back with Lange & Mitzlaff, reality quickly caught up with him again: »I listlessly drafted (an office building) and found life banal. My functionalism was all over by 1953. (...) But I've never forgotten Aalto and his buildings.«

Gieselmann could not stand Mannheim much longer. He longed to return to Switzerland. In 1953, he took the plunge and opened his own office in Basel together with Werner Aebli, a Swiss colleague almost the same age as himself who had become his friend in Senn's office. Since commissions failed to materialize or projects did not progress beyond the initial planning phase, the venture was not successful. All the more important was the only concrete result of the short collaboration: Together with the architect Theo Manz and the photographer Beppo Merkle, they founded a Basel section of the »Congrès Internationaux d'Architecture Moderne« and worked on a »gril CIAM«, a series of visual aids modeled on a system developed by Le Corbusier for a clearly structured, uniform presentation of ideas and projects. Very sociologically oriented, didactically well communicated, and presented in an up-to-date graphic form, the project examined the relationship of the individual, the family, the residents of a house, district, and town to their environment. Its goal was to understand modern urban planning not only as a formal matter, but to see its complex connection with everyday lives. Human society, claimed the authors, is not just an aggregate of individuals but of groups existing in complex relationships with each other. Every space, whether in an apartment, in a house, part of town, or a city must refer to a central point – that was the central message that the ambitious »Beitrag zur Abklärung des Habitat« (Contribution to clarifying the habitat) wished to convey. Obviously, the point of departure of the study were the theoretical reflections that Otto Senn – himself a CIAM member since the mid-thirties and often an active participant in its conventions – had set in motion among his young staff members with his plans for the Gellert district. At the ninth CIAM congress in June 1953 in Aix-en-Provence, the group was able to introduce its »gril« to an international professional public. The Swiss periodical *Werk* published it in early 1954.[18]

The stay in Aix, his meetings with architectural greats of the modern age – »Gropius dropped in and was interested in details«[19] – but especially the contact with other young professionals like Aldo van Eyck or Alison and Peter Smithson who also opposed the pure doctrine of functionalism from a sociological point of view, inspired Reinhard Gieselmann. Of course, what impressed him most profoundly was a visit to the recently completed Unité d'habitation in Marseille, where Le Corbusier invited guests to a party on the famous roof terrace. Even though he was fascinated by Le Corbusier, who gave the Basel group a personal tour, Gieselmann regarded the »machine à habiter« with mixed feelings. He was »impressed by the monumentality and the three-dimensional details«, but was also taken aback by the huge number of apartments.

At the congress in Aix, Reinhard Gieselmann ran into a former fellow student from Karlsruhe,

Oswald Mathias Ungers, who had attracted his attention three years earlier in one of Otto Ernst Schweizer's seminars. There, Ungers had dared to disregard in his urban planning project the only principles of the professor that mattered. Unger's unconcealed rebellion against conventions made Gieselmann curious; they began talking and discovered they agreed on many issues. They had a great deal to talk about – particularly their shared ambivalence toward Eiermann and the theoretical writings they had both read, such as Wilhelm Worringer's book *Abstraktion und Einfühlung*, which preoccupied them intensively, as Gieselmann remembers.[20] A lifelong friendship developed, and particularly in the 1950s and early 1960s the friends were often in touch and worked on joint projects. In 1954 they visited the Biennale in Venice and the Triennale in Milan – a report they wrote together appeared in the periodical *Baukunst und Werkform*.[21] In 1955 they viewed the recently dedicated Ronchamp chapel, Le Corbusier's momentous masterpiece, an impressive experience for them. Egon Eiermann also made his way to Ronchamp at this time. Admittedly he did not come to join the chorus of admirers. Rather, he wanted to convince the students he brought with him that this structure was not architecture but an accessible three-dimensional sculpture that broke all the rules of tectonics. By knocking he demonstrated how hollow Le Corbusier's famous wall of windows, seemingly 2.50 meters thick, really is – for him this was nothing more than evidence of deception for the sake of cheap effects, and thus at most movie-set architecture.[22] In 1953 Eiermann had offered Reinhard Gieselmann the chance to join his staff, which Gieselmann refused in spite of his difficult financial situation, believing that »it would have been a step backwards.«[23]

First assignments, 1950–1957

During his apprenticeship years around 1950 Reinhard Gieselmann theoretically came to terms with contemporary architecture to an extent many of his fellow students surely did not. However, this did not mean he did not feel the urge to begin practicing architecture. He had already showed a pragmatic side before he got his diploma when he provided his landlady with a design for a modest little house and a chicken coop, which were actually built. Also, with student friends, he had participated in a number of competitions after 1950.

The first building for which Gieselmann had sole responsibility was the Roth house in Ludwigshafen (1952/53), combining a residence and studio. This simple house, for which only limited funds were available, is conceived as a light building with a flat, sloped corrugated asbestos cement roof without an overhang. The façades come to life from the alternating generously glazed, well-proportioned openings with mullioned windows, and solid sections of wall. For the last time, Eiermann's influence is apparent here: There is an unmistakable similarity to his 1930s Berlin apartment houses. In the interior, however, the prospective architect was already introducing his own ideas, which went beyond those of his teacher. The living, dining, and bedroom are combined with the studio into one open area without doors. The freestanding brick fireplace functions

17. Reinhard Gieselmann, Roth house and studio, Ludwigshafen, 1952/53. View from the street.
18. Reinhard Gieselmann, Roth house and studio, Ludwigshafen, 1952/53. View of the living area with freestanding fireplace from the studio.
19. Reinhard Gieselmann, sports hall of the Marienschule, Krefeld, 1954. View from the street.

17. Reinhard Gieselmann, Wohn- und Atelierhaus Roth, Ludwigshafen, 1952/53. Straßenansicht.
18. Reinhard Gieselmann, Wohn- und Atelierhaus Roth, Ludwigshafen, 1952/53. Blick vom Atelier in den Wohnbereich mit frei stehendem Kamin.
19. Reinhard Gieselmann, Turnhalle der Marienschule, Krefeld, 1954. Straßenansicht.

Marseille, wohin Le Corbusier zu einem Fest auf die berühmte Dachterrasse geladen hatte. So sehr ihm die Persönlichkeit Le Corbusiers, der die Basler Gruppe persönlich herumführte, auch faszinierte, die »machine à habiter« betrachtete er mit gemischten Gefühlen, einerseits »beeindruckt von der Monumentalität und den plastischen Details«, andererseits befremdet von der gigantischen Anhäufung von Wohnungen.

Auf dem Kongreß in Aix traf Reinhard Gieselmann auch einen ehemaligen Studienkollegen aus Karlsruhe wieder, Oswald Mathias Ungers, der ihm drei Jahre zuvor in einem Seminar von Otto Ernst Schweizer aufgefallen war. Dort hatte Ungers gewagt, in seinem städtebaulichen Entwurf die allein maßgeblichen Prinzipien des Professors zu mißachten. Ungers unverhohlene Rebellion gegen Konventionen machte Gieselmann neugierig, man kam ins Gespräch, entdeckte übereinstimmende Ansichten. Vor allem die von beiden geteilte Ambivalenz gegenüber Eiermann sorgte für Gesprächsstoff, aber auch die gemeinsame Lektüre von theoretischen Schriften, etwa Wilhelm Worringers Buch *Abstraktion und Einfühlung*, das sie intensiv beschäftigte, wie sich Gieselmann erinnert.[20] Eine lebenslange Freundschaft sollte sich entwickeln, die sich vor allem in den fünfziger und frühen sechziger Jahren in häufigem Kontakt und gemeinsamen Unternehmungen manifestierte. 1954 besuchten sie die Biennale in Venedig und die Triennale in Mailand, ein miteinander verfaßter Bericht erschien in der Zeitschrift *Baukunst und Werkform*.[21] 1955 besichtigten sie die gerade eingeweihte Kapelle von Ronchamp, das epochale Meisterwerk von Le Corbusier, für sie ein eindrückliches Erlebnis. Auch Egon Eiermann fand zu dieser Zeit den Weg nach Ronchamp. Er kam allerdings nicht, um in den Chor der Bewunderer einzustimmen. Vielmehr wollte er die Studenten, die er mitbrachte, davon überzeugen, daß dieses Bauwerk keine Architektur sei, sondern eine begehbare Plastik, die alle Spielregeln der Tektonik verletze. Durch Klopfen führte er vor, wie hohl Le Corbusiers berühmte Fensterwand von scheinbar 2,50 Meter Dicke ist – für ihn nichts anderes als ein Zeugnis der Täuschung um der Effekte willen und damit allenfalls Kinoarchitektur.[22] 1953 hatte er Reinhard Gieselmann angeboten, sein Mitarbeiter zu werden, was dieser trotz der schwierigen finanziellen Lage, in der er sich befand, ablehnte, denn, so sein Urteil: »Es wäre ein Rückschritt gewesen.«[23]

Erste Tätigkeit, 1950–1957

Reinhard Gieselmann setzte sich in seinen Lehrjahren um 1950 in einem Maße theoretisch mit zeitgenössischer Architektur auseinander, wie dies sicherlich nicht viele seiner Kommilitonen taten. Das bedeutete jedoch keineswegs, daß es ihn nicht danach drängte, auch praktisch tätig zu werden. Pragmatismus hatte er bereits vor dem Diplom an den Tag gelegt, als er seiner Karlsruher Zimmerwirtin den Entwurf für ein anspruchloses Stadtrandhäuschen mit Hühnerstall lieferte, das sogar ausgeführt wurde. Daneben beteiligte er sich seit 1950 gemeinsam mit Studienfreunden an einigen Wettbewerben.

Das Wohn- und Atelierhaus Roth in Ludwigshafen sollte 1952/53 der erste Bau werden, den Gieselmann in alleiniger Verantwortung errichtete. Das einfache Haus, für das nur sehr beschränkte Mittel zur Verfügung standen, ist als leichter Bau mit flach geneigtem Welleternitdach ohne Überstand konzipiert. Die Fassaden leben vom Wechsel großzügig verglaster, gut proportionierter Öffnungen mit feinsprossigen Fenstern und geschlossenen Wandabschnitten. Ein letztes Mal ist hier Eiermanns Einfluß zu spüren, unverkennbar die Verwandtschaft mit dessen Berliner Wohnhäusern der dreißiger Jahre. Beim Inneren war der angehende Architekt allerdings bereits dabei, eigene Ideen einzubringen, die über den Lehrer hinausführten. Wohn-, Eß- und Schlafzimmer sind mit dem Atelier zu einem offenen Bereich ohne Türen zusammengezogen. Als Raumteiler fungiert der aus Backsteinen gemauerte frei stehende Kamin, der zusammen mit einem mächtigen, im rechten Winkel dazu stehenden Wandstück sowie einem horizontal schwebenden Element und der flach geneigten Decke darüber eine spannungsreiche, räumlich-plastische Komposition bildet. Frank Lloyd Wrights Idee vom Kamin als Mittelpunkt des Wohnens war hier ein wichtiges Vorbild. Erst beim genaueren Hinsehen enthüllt sich, daß das horizontale Element sogar eine Funktion erfüllt: Bei Bedarf kann die leichte, mit Papier bespannte Rahmenkonstruktion um eine Querachse in eine vertikale Position geschwenkt werden. Als »japanische Wand« trennt sie dann das Atelier vom Eßbereich.

Nachdem sich 1953 mangels Aufträgen die kurzzeitige Bürogemeinschaft mit Werner Aebli in Basel zerschlagen hatte, kam das Angebot des Architekten Franz Schlüter-Padberg, eines Verwandten von Reinhard Gieselmann, gerade zur rechten Zeit. Für etwa ein Jahr war er nun als dessen Mitarbeiter in Krefeld tätig. Viel Entwurfsarbeit wartete dort auf ihn, da der Onkel sich vor allem als Gutachter betätigte und daher auch bereit war, dem kreativen Neffen freie Hand zu lassen. Kurz hintereinander entstand eine Reihe heute nur noch namentlich überlieferter Projekte. Realisiert wurde neben dem eigenen Wohnhaus von Schlüter-Padberg, das sich durch eine ungewöhnliche, das Dach durchstoßende Gaubenlösung auszeichnet, sowie einem Kindergarten nur die Turnhalle der Marienschule in Krefeld, ein Auftrag der Schwestern des Ursulinenordens. Dieses erste größere Gebäude kann als Markstein in Gieselmanns Entwicklung gelten, fand der nun neunundzwanzigjährige Architekt doch hier zu einer persönlichen Handschrift, die charakteristisch für ihn werden sollte.

Der Betonskelettbau mit einer Verkleidung aus groben Backsteinen, auf der Hofseite überdies mit großen Flächen aus Glasbausteinen ausgefacht, hat nichts Leichtes mehr. Die auf Filigranes und Transparentes zielende Ästhetik Eiermanns, die im Wohnhaus Roth noch offensichtlich war, ist endgültig überwunden. Der Baukörper gibt sich schwer und geschlossen, nüchtern und kantig. In kompromißloser Weise wirkt das Gebäude nur durch seine plastische Präsenz, seine Materialien und Proportionen. Dabei macht sich jedoch keine Langeweile breit. Trotz aller Reduktion sind intelligente Details zu erkennen, die den Bau zum Kunstwerk machen: Die wenigen Öffnungen – hauptsächlich schmale Fensterbänder über dem Boden und unter dem Flachdach – ziehen sich nicht schematisch um den gesamten Bau, son-

as a room divider; together with a massive piece of wall and a horizontally suspended element, and the flat sloped ceiling above it, it forms a tension-filled, spatially three-dimensional composition. Frank Lloyd Wright's idea that the fireplace is the central point of living space was an important model here. Not until we look more carefully do we realize that the horizontal element actually fulfills a function: When necessary, the light, paper-covered frame construction can be swiveled around a transverse axis into a vertical position. As a »Japanese wall« it then separates the studio from the dining area.

In 1953, after the short-term collaboration with Werner Aebli in Basel was dissolved for lack of commissions, Reinhard Gieselmann received an offer from a relative, the architect Franz Schlüter-Padberg, which came in the nick of time. Gieselmann worked with Schlüter-Padberg for about a year in Krefeld. There was much design work to be done there since his uncle was mainly busy as a consultant and therefore willing to let his creative nephew have free rein. It was shortly after this that Gieselmann completed a series of projects only known by their names today. The only designs that were built other than Schlüter-Padberg's own house, characterized by its unusual solution for the dormer windows of breaking through the roof, were a kindergarten and the gym of Marienschule, a school in Krefeld, commissioned by Ursuline Sisters. This first large building may be regarded as a milestone in Gieselmann's development since the twenty-nine-year-old architect now found a personal style that would soon become characteristic of him.

There is nothing light about the concrete skeleton building faced with rough bricks and with large surfaces on the courtyard side where glass bricks fill in the interstices in the skeleton. Gieselmann had finally overcome Eiermann's aesthetics, which aimed for a filigree effect and transparency – still evident in the Roth house. The gym seems heavy and closed, sober and angular. Uncompromisingly, the building is effective only through its three-dimensional presence, its materials and proportions. It is not boring, however. In spite of all the trimming down, intelligent details make the structure into a work of art: The small number of openings – mainly narrow rows of windows above the ground and below the flat roof – do not extend schematically around the entire building but bring tension into the composition by means of surprising interruptions. The concrete frame appears on the exterior in some places while in others it is covered by the brick facing. The resulting layering – the concrete frame in a back plane, the bricks as a cladding in front of it – becomes an artificial theme, enriched by the fact that narrow concrete lintels lie above the lower rows of windows not on the plane of the concrete frame but in front of it on that of the masonry. Moreover, the edge of the eaves at the corner of the building is built somewhat higher, breaking through the rigid right angle and making the building dynamic.

No doubt it was because he was inspired by Alvar Aalto that Gieselmann was in a position to use such forms in a building. Less than two years earlier, in the town hall of Säynätsalo, he had seen plasticity, materiality, and expressive gestures, but also detail forms such as the row of windows or the raising of the edge of the roof at the corner. In

an Aalto building, however, the architecture would not have seemed as meager. In this respect Gieselmann deliberately went farther than the Finnish master, and thus became a very early representative of Brutalism in Germany, a style developed in Great Britain in the early 1950s and whose eloquent advocates were the prolific designers Alison and Peter Smithson. As was previously mentioned, Gieselmann had met them a few months earlier at the Ninth CIAM Congress, where the »beton brut« of Le Corbusier's Unité also made such a strong impression on him.

From today's perspective, we can understand why the Ursulines of Krefeld had difficulty befriending their new building. The superior of the congregation asked a question recorded by the architect: »When will the windows finally come?«,[24] clearly demonstrating that this gym in 1954 broke with traditional visual habits. It conformed neither with conservative traditional construction nor with trends that were considered to be modern in the era of the kidney-shaped table. But Reinhard Gieselmann was so sure of his mission – to proclaim a pure architectural language – that he refused at least to soften by means of »Kunst am Bau« (art on architecture) the hermetic street façade about which there had been the most complaints. No wonder the congregation refused to use the firm of Schlüter-Padberg for additional, already planned phases of construction in the school's expansion. Soon thereafter Gieselmann, whose rebellious or ironic letters to the editor in professional journals repeatedly proposed breaking up functionalist thought patterns,[25] was in turn fired by his uncle. Schlüter-Padberg realized that the ideas of prospective Krefeld clients could hardly be brought into line with his nephew's architectural ambitions.

Now that he had been fired, Gieselmann took the risk of becoming self-employed. His attempt was successful, though initially he needed to improvise. The Roth family in Ludwigshafen, who commissioned his first house, allowed him to stay in their guest room until he could move into a converted garage in the neighborhood that also served him as an office. In the mid-1950s, the architect surprisingly quickly found clients who were willing to trust him, even though in some cases he had to make concessions. A commission for a production plant inside the BASF (Baden Aniline and Soda Factory) surely was not exactly near to his heart, but it did result in two houses for BASF employees in Ludwigshafen. Through his father, Gieselmann got commissions for renovating the offices of the Münster chamber of industry and commerce and for building a house for Josef Höffner, then a professor of theology and later the cardinal of Cologne. In Markgröningen, Württemberg, he built a duplex, and in Mannheim he designed an exhibition initiated by the German Werkbund, »Möbel, billig und schön« – all projects that show Gieselmann's innovative standards both typologically and formally.

But the principal work from 1954 to 1957, and not just because of its size, is the Frey building, an apartment and commercial building in Mundenheim, a district of Ludwigshafen. Young furniture store owners with high design standards dared to entrust the then-thirty-year-old architect with their large new building that would house the

20. Reinhard Gieselmann, Frey residential and commercial building, Ludwigshafen, 1954–57.
21. Oswald Mathias Ungers, residential building in Köln-Nippes, 1955–59.
22. Reinhard Gieselmann (to the left) and Oswald Mathias Ungers visiting the building site of a reservoir in the Sauerland, 1958.

20. Reinhard Gieselmann, Mehrfamilien- und Geschäftshaus Frey, Ludwigshafen, 1954–57.
21. Oswald Mathias Ungers, Mehrfamilienhaus in Köln-Nippes, 1955–59.
22. Reinhard Gieselmann (links) und Oswald Mathias Ungers bei der Besichtigung der Baustelle eines Stausees im Sauerland, 1958.

dern bringen durch überraschende Unterbrechungen Spannung in die Komposition. Das Betonskelett tritt im Äußeren an einigen Stellen in Erscheinung, an anderen wird es wieder von der Backsteinvormauerung verdeckt. Die entstehende Schichtung – das Betonskelett in einer hinteren Ebene, die Backsteine als Mantel davor – wird zum artifiziellen Thema gemacht, das noch dadurch bereichert wird, daß schmale Betonstürze über den unteren Bandfenstern nicht auf der Ebene des Betonskeletts, sondern davor auf jener des Mauerwerks liegen. Zudem ist die Traufkante an der Gebäudeecke leicht höher gezogen, was den strengen rechten Winkel durchbricht und dem Bau Dynamik verleiht.

Zweifellos war es der Impuls Alvar Aaltos, der Gieselmann in die Lage versetzte, ein Gebäude in solchen Formen zu bauen. Plastizität, Materialität und ausdrucksstarke Gestik, aber auch Detailformen wie das Fensterband oder das Hochziehen der Dachkante zur Ecke hin hatte er keine zwei Jahre zuvor beim Rathaus in Säynätsalo in durchaus vergleichbarer Weise gesehen. Bei einem Werk Aaltos hätte die Architektur allerdings nicht einen derart kargen Ausdruck vermittelt. Gieselmann ging in dieser Hinsicht bewußt weiter als der finnische Meister, und er wurde damit zu einem sehr frühen Vertreter des Brutalismus in Deutschland, jenem Stil, der sich in den frühen fünfziger Jahren in Großbritannien herausgebildet und in Alison und Peter Smithson seine ebenso entwurfsstarken wie wortgewandten Vermittler gefunden hatte. Gieselmann war ihnen, wie bereits erwähnt, wenige Monate zuvor beim IX. CIAM-Kongreß begegnet, wo ihm ja auch der »beton brut« von Le Corbusiers Unité einen starken Eindruck hinterlassen hatte.

Es ist aus heutiger Sicht durchaus nachzuvollziehen, weshalb sich die Krefelder Ordensschwestern nicht mit ihrem Neubau anzufreunden vermochten. Die vom Architekten überlieferte Frage der Oberin, wann denn nun endlich die Fenster kämen,[24] belegt nur zu gut, daß diese Turnhalle im Jahr 1954 mit herkömmlichen Sehgewohnheiten brach. Sie entsprach weder konservativ-traditionellem Bauen noch dem, was in jener Zeit des Nierentischs als modern galt. Doch Reinhard Gieselmann war von seiner Mission, eine reine Architektursprache verkünden zu müssen, derart überzeugt, daß er sich weigerte, wenigstens die besonders beanstandete hermetische Straßenfassade durch »Kunst am Bau« aufzulockern. Kein Wunder, daß der Orden das Büro Schlüter-Padberg nicht mehr für weitere, bereits in Aussicht gestellte Bauabschnitte der Schulerweiterung heranziehen wollte. Und kurz darauf sah sich Gieselmann, der in Fachzeitschriften immer wieder mit aufmüpfigen oder ironischen Leserbeiträgen für ein Aufbrechen funktionalistischer Denkschemata Position bezog,[25] seinerseits mit der Kündigung durch den Onkel konfrontiert. Schlüter-Padberg war zu der Erkenntnis gelangt, daß sich die Vorstellungen potentieller Krefelder Kunden nur schwer mit den baukünstlerischen Ambitionen seines Neffen in Einklang bringen ließen.

Der auf die Straße Gesetzte wagte den Sprung in die Selbständigkeit. Der Versuch gelang, wenn auch anfangs Improvisation gefragt war. Familie Roth in Ludwigshafen, die Auftraggeber seines ersten Hauses, stellte Gieselmann als Bleibe ihr Gastzimmer zur Verfügung, bevor er in eine aus-

gebaute Garage in der Nachbarschaft umziehen konnte, die gleichzeitig als Büro diente. Überraschend schnell fand der Architekt Mitte der fünfziger Jahre Bauherren, die bereit waren, ihm zu vertrauen, wobei er in dem einen oder anderen Fall auch Konzessionen machen mußte. Ein Auftrag für eine Produktionsanlage innerhalb der BASF war sicherlich keine Herzensangelegenheit, hatte aber zwei Wohnhäuser für Angestellte in Ludwigshafen zur Folge. Auf Vermittlung des Vaters waren in Münster Büroräume der Industrie- und Handelskammer neu auszustatten und ein Wohnhaus für den damaligen Theologieprofessor und späteren Kölner Kardinal Josef Höffner zu bauen. Im württembergischen Markgröningen entstand ein Zweifamilienhaus und in Mannheim die vom Deutschen Werkbund initiierte Ausstellung »Möbel, billig und schön« – allesamt Arbeiten, die typologisch und formal Gieselmanns innovativen Anspruch zeigen.

Das Hauptwerk jener Jahre zwischen 1954 und 1957 ist jedoch nicht nur wegen seiner Größe das Mehrfamilien- und Geschäftshaus Frey im Ludwigshafener Stadtteil Mundenheim. Die jungen Inhaber eines Möbelhauses mit gestalterischem Anspruch hatten es gewagt, dem gerade dreißigjährigen Architekten ihren großen Neubau anzuvertrauen, der in Unter- und Erdgeschoß die Geschäftsräume der Firma, in den Obergeschossen, über drei Treppenhäuser erschlossen, Wohnungen beherbergt. Ähnlich wie die Krefelder Turnhalle mit Sichtbeton und grober Klinkerverkleidung von rauher Materialität gestaltet, steigert sich das winkelförmige Gebäude an seiner Ecke zu kraftvollem Ausdruck, wie man ihn seit dem Expressionismus der zwanziger Jahre nicht mehr gesehen hatte. Der viergeschossige Trakt an der Hauptstraße ist hier mit dem um eine Etage niedrigeren Bauteil entlang einer Nebenstraße auf komplexe Weise verzahnt und gestaffelt. Die Blicke der Passanten auf der Hauptstraße werden durch die Rücksprünge in die Tiefe der Nebenflucht und zu weiteren Schaufenstern gelenkt – plastische Form ergänzt sich mit räumlicher Wirkung zu einer ungemein eindrucksvollen Inszenierung, wobei sich für den Vorübergehenden die Perspektiven mit jedem Schritt verändern.

Obwohl eher abseits in einem von dörflichen Strukturen und Industrie geprägten Vorort gelegen, fand das Gebäude Aufnahme in eine beachtliche Zahl von Fachzeitschriften. Bemerkenswert ist, daß dies überwiegend erst einige Jahre nach Fertigstellung des Baues nach 1960 geschah. Tatsächlich würde man ihn heute auch in die frühen sechziger Jahre datieren, wüßte man nicht um sein deutlich früheres Entstehungsdatum. Zweifellos war der Urheber seiner Zeit voraus, und es gab damals im bundesdeutschen Vergleich nur einen Architekten, dem ein ähnliches Gebäude zuzutrauen war – Gieselmanns Freund und Weggefährten Oswald Mathias Ungers, dessen Frühwerk erstaunlich viele Parallelen zeigt. Auch Ungers hatte sich in der ersten Hälfte der fünfziger Jahre allmählich vom Einfluß seines Lehrers Eiermann freigemacht, um eine persönliche Ausprägung des Brutalismus zu finden, der in rauhen Fassaden aus Backstein und Sichtbeton sowie in kantigen Volumen artikulierte. Selbst Gieselmanns Ludwigshafener Motiv der expressiven Staffelung und Eckbetonung findet sich in Ungers' frühen Kölner Häusern. Ein genauer Vergleich der

company's business in the basement and on the ground floor, and apartments on the upper floors, accessed by three stairwells. Designed like the Krefeld gym using the coarse materials of exposed concrete and rough brick facing, the angular building at the corner of the block is powerfully imaginative. Nothing like it had been seen since the expressionism of the twenties. Here the four-storey section along the main street is staggered and dovetailed in a complex way with the three-storey section of the building along a side street. Recesses direct the eye of the main street passersby into the depth of the side alignment and toward more store windows – three-dimensional form combines with spatial effect to create an uncommonly impressive setting, where a pedestrian's perspective changes with every step.

Although located somewhat off the beaten path in a suburb characterized by village structures and industry, the building was critiqued in a significant number of professional periodicals. It is noteworthy that for the most part this did not happen until after 1960, a few years after the building was completed. As a matter of fact, today one would also date it to the early 1960s if one did not know that it was built much earlier. Without a doubt Gieselmann was ahead of his time, and there was only one architect in West Germany at the time who could be credited with a similar building – Gieselmann's friend and companion Oswald Mathias Ungers, whose early work shows an amazing number of parallels. Ungers had also gradually liberated himself from the influence of his teacher Eiermann in the first half of the 1950s. He developed a personal expression of Brutalism, articulated in rough façades of brick and exposed concrete, and in angular volumes. Even Gieselmann's Ludwigshafen motif of expressive staggering and an accentuation of corners is found in Ungers' early Cologne houses. An exact comparison of dates shows that chronologically the development of both architects was completely parallel and that we can completely rule out a purely one-way influence of one on the other.[26] The close personal contact between Gieselmann and Ungers that had existed since 1953, their joint travels, and their common goal of understanding architecture as art again led to their having a very similar stylistic idiom for a period of time. However, Reinhard Gieselmann never shared Ungers' rigorism or his tendency towards the absolute and towards principles – which would chiefly characterize his later work – defined by the square – but that could already initially be detected in the 1950s. Gieselmann looked for his solutions mainly in the conditions of the locale and the purpose in question, and not in the intention to stick to a formal plan rigidly.

The Karlsruhe years, 1957–1969

By 1957, Reinhard Gieselmann had succeeded in finding his own position in the creative field of tension of Eiermann, Senn, Aalto, Le Corbusier, and in the exchange of ideas with his friends Aebli and Ungers, and in implementing his concepts in his first buildings. The ensuing phase of his work up to the late 1960s was a time of most fertile productivity: This is when, from a statistical viewpoint, a large part of his oeuvre came into being – no less than 36 implemented building schemes and 40 projects. During this part of his life the architect achieved the most recognition.

He owed this not only to his buildings, which architecture critics regarded as highly as those of the likes of Gottfried Böhm, but also to *Manifest zu einer neuen Architektur* (Manifesto on a new architecture) which he wrote in 1960 together with Oswald Mathias Ungers. *Manifest*, published in full for the first time in 1963, was widely disseminated largely because it was included in Ulrich Conrads' 1964 anthology *Programme und Manifeste zur Architektur des 20. Jahrhunderts*.[27] The twenty theses with which Gieselmann and Ungers programmatically »address all those who (...) strive for a renewal of European architecture« postulate the credo of »subjective persons« »who doubt what is calculable and at the same time believe in intuition«: »Architecture is partial creation. But every creative process is art. It deserves the highest intellectual standing. (...) Technology is the application of knowledge and experience. Technology and construction are aids in implementation. Technology is not art. Form is an expression of the intellectual content. (...) The concern of architecture is to search for the perfect expression of the content. Architecture is vital penetration into a multilayered, mysterious, organically evolved, and shaped environment. Its creative mission is making the task visible, integration with what already exists, accentuation and heightening of place. Architecture always recognizes the genius loci from which it develops. Architecture is no longer a two-dimensional impression, but becomes an experience of the corporeal and spatial, through circling around and penetrating them.«[28] The authors' settling of accounts with Egon Eiermann's functionalist doctrine could not have been clearer. But the tone of the manifesto also addressed a generation of young architects in search of an expressionistic subjectivism that questioned the ironbound models of the »fathers of the modern era«.

It is one of the coincidences of life that Karlsruhe, a planned city with a rational layout, a place he did not really love, turned out to be the center of Reinhard Gieselmann's creative life. The reasons were personal. In 1955, Gieselmann had married Maria Verena Fischer, a former colleague at the Mannheim office of Lange & Mitzlaff. After earning her diploma with Egon Eiermann, she traveled on a grant in the United States, where she saw the contemporary architecture of Mies van der Rohe, Richard Neutra, and Frank Lloyd Wright, meeting almost all the architects personally. Upon her return she worked independently in Karlsruhe. After her marriage and the birth of her son in 1956, she mainly devoted her time to taking care of her young family in Ludwigshafen. Her father Alfred Fischer was one of the architects of the 1929 Karlsruhe–Dammerstock housing development. After WWII, he worked for the state building administration until his retirement in 1954. He was already seventy years old in 1957 when new commissions materialized after his successful participation in a competition to develop the Waldstadt district of Karlsruhe.[29] His idea of partnering with his daughter and son-in-law proved advantageous for all especially in the initial period after the young couple's 1957 move to Karlsruhe. Alfred Fischer's local connections ensured commissions, while he left the blueprints up to his gifted son-in-

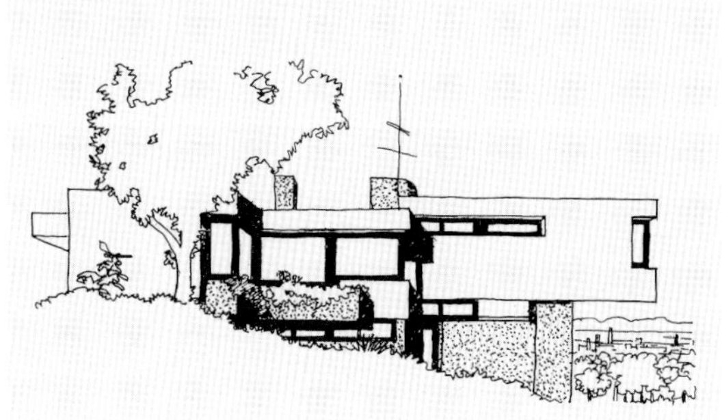

23. Reinhard Gieselmann, Becker house, Karlsruhe, 1957–59.
24. Reinhard Gieselmann, Hanfmann/Herzer house, Karlsruhe, 1959–61.
25. Reinhard Gieselmann, Lankheit house, Karlsruhe, 1964/65.
26. Reinhard Gieselmann, Z. house, Karlsruhe, 1964–67.

23. Reinhard Gieselmann, Haus Becker, Karlsruhe, 1957–59.
24. Reinhard Gieselmann, Haus Hanfmann/Herzer, Karlsruhe, 1959–61.
25. Reinhard Gieselmann, Haus Lankheit, Karlsruhe, 1964/65.
26. Reinhard Gieselmann, Haus Z., Karlsruhe, 1964–67.

Datierungen zeigt, daß die Entwicklung der beiden zeitlich völlig parallel verlief und eine einseitige Rezeption des einen vom anderen ausgeschlossen werden kann.[26] Der enge persönliche Kontakt zwischen Gieselmann und Ungers, wie er seit 1953 bestand, die gemeinsamen Reisen und das beide einende Ziel, Architektur wieder als Kunst zu verstehen, mündeten in einer für eine gewisse Zeit recht ähnlichen Formensprache. Ungers' Rigorismus, sein Hang zum Absoluten und Prinzipiellen, wie es vor allem sein späteres, vom Quadrat bestimmtes Werk auszeichnen wird, aber in Ansätzen schon in den fünfziger Jahren zu beobachten ist, teilte Reinhard Gieselmann indes nie. Seine Lösungen suchte er vor allem in den Bedingungen des jeweiligen Ortes und des Zwecks und nicht in der Absicht, ein formales Schema durchzuhalten.

Karlsruher Jahre, 1957–1969

Bis 1957 war es Reinhard Gieselmann gelungen, im kreativen Spannungsfeld von Eiermann, Senn, Aalto, Le Corbusier und im gegenseitigen Austausch mit den Freunden Aebli und Ungers einen eigenen Standort zu finden und seine Vorstellungen in ersten Bauten zu verwirklichen. Die sich anschließende Werkphase bis zum Ende der sechziger Jahre sollte die Zeitspanne fruchtbarster Produktivität werden: Jetzt entstand, statistisch gesehen, ein großer Teil des Gesamtwerks, nicht weniger als 36 realisierte Bauvorhaben und 40 Projekte. Es war der Lebensabschnitt, in dem der Architekt die größte Anerkennung erzielen konnte.

Dazu trugen nicht nur seine Bauten bei, die von der Architekturkritik etwa neben die eines Gottfried Böhm gestellt wurden, sondern auch das 1960 gemeinsam mit Oswald Mathias Ungers verfaßte *Manifest zu einer neuen Architektur*, das – 1963 erstmals im vollen Wortlaut veröffentlicht – vor allem durch seine Aufnahme in Ulrich Conrads' 1964 erschiener Sammlung *Programme und Manifeste zur Architektur des 20. Jahrhunderts* große Verbreitung fand.[27] Die zwanzig Thesen, mit denen sich Gieselmann und Ungers programmatisch »an alle wenden, die (...) eine Erneuerung der europäischen Architektur anstreben«, postulieren das Credo der »Subjektiven«, »die ihre Zweifel an der Berechenbarkeit mit dem Glauben an die Intuition verbinden«: »Architektur ist partielle Schöpfung. Jeder schöpferische Vorgang aber ist Kunst. Ihm gebührt der höchste geistige Rang. (...) Technik ist Anwendung von Wissen und Erfahrung. Technik und Konstruktion sind Hilfsmittel der Verwirklichung. Technik ist nicht Kunst. Form ist Ausdruck des geistigen Gehaltes. (...) Das Anliegen der Architektur ist die Suche nach vollkommenem Ausdruck des Inhalts. Architektur ist vitales Eindringen in eine vielschichtige, geheimnisvolle, gewachsene und geprägte Umwelt. Ihr schöpferischer Auftrag ist Sichtbarmachung der Aufgabe, Einordnung in das Vorhandene, Akzentuierung und Überhöhung des Ortes. Sie ist immer Erkennen des genius loci, aus dem sie erwächst. Architektur ist nicht mehr zweidimensionaler Eindruck, sondern wird Erlebnis des Körperhaften und Räumlichen, durch Umschreiten und Eindringen.«[28] Deutlicher hätte die Abrechnung mit dem, was Egon Eiermanns funktionalistische Lehre ausmachte, nicht ausfallen kön-

nen. Der Ton sprach aber auch eine junge Architektengeneration an, die auf der Suche war nach einem expressionistischen Subjektivismus, der die erstarrten Leitbilder der »Väter der Moderne« in Frage stellte.

Es gehört zu den Zufällen des Lebens, daß ausgerechnet das von ihm nicht unbedingt geliebte Karlsruhe, die rational angelegte Planstadt, zum Zentrum von Reinhard Gieselmanns Wirken werden sollte. Persönliche Gründe waren dafür verantwortlich. 1955 hatte Gieselmann Maria Verena Fischer geheiratet, eine frühere Kollegin im Mannheimer Büro Lange & Mitzlaff. Nach ihrem Diplom bei Egon Eiermann war sie 1951 als Stipendiatin durch die USA gereist, wo sie aktuelle Architektur, etwa die Bauten von Mies van der Rohe, Richard Neutra und Frank Lloyd Wright gesehen und die Meister fast alle auch persönlich kennengelernt hatte. Nach der Rückkehr arbeitete sie selbständig in Karlsruhe, bis sie sich nach Heirat und Geburt des Sohnes 1956 vor allem um ihre junge Familie in Ludwigshafen kümmerte. Ihr Vater Alfred Fischer, 1929 einer der Architekten der Karlsruher Dammerstock-Siedlung und nach dem Zweiten Weltkrieg bis zu seiner Pensionierung 1954 in der staatlichen Bauverwaltung tätig, war 1957 schon fast siebzig Jahre alt, als sich für ihn nach einem Erfolg im Wettbewerb um die Bebauung der Karlsruher Waldstadt neue Aufträge abzeichneten.[29] Seine Idee, eine Büropartnerschaft mit Tochter und Schwiegersohn zu bilden, sollte sich gerade in der Anfangszeit nach der Übersiedlung des Ehepaars Gieselmann nach Karlsruhe im Jahr 1957 für alle Beteiligten als vorteilhaft erweisen: Alfred Fischers örtliche Beziehungen sorgten für Aufträge, während er den Entwurf seinem begabten Schwiegersohn überließ. Darüber hinaus kamen Maria Verena Gieselmanns ausgesprochen organisatorische Fähigkeiten nicht nur der wachsenden Familie, sondern auch dem wachsenden Bürobetrieb zugute.[30]

Schon eines der ersten Projekte der Karlsruher Jahre, das 1959 bezogene Wohnhaus Becker in Karlsruhe-Durlach, geriet zu einem virtuosen Meisterwerk. All die Charakteristika, die eingangs am Beispiel des etwas jüngeren ersten eigenen Hauses beschrieben wurden, finden sich bereits hier: plastische Wirkung durch phantasievolle Verschränkung strenger Baukörper, Kontraste von geschlossenen Flächen und scharfkantig eingeschnittenen Öffnungen, durchdachte Einbettung des Gebäudes in das umgebende Terrain, der um einen zentralen Wohnraum herum organisierte Grundriß sowie komplexe Räumlichkeiten, teils nach innen gekehrt, teils sich weit nach außen in den Garten öffnend.

Nicht nur Bauzeitschriften wurden auf das Werk aufmerksam und publizierten es. In Ulrich Conrads' Sammelband *Neue deutsche Architektur 2* stand es 1962 neben Ungers' berühmt gewordenem Wohnhaus in Köln-Müngersdorf exemplarisch für die im gemeinsamen Manifest geforderte, auf expressive Gebärde zielende Architektur.[31] Daneben mußten sich selbst namhafte Beispiele der damals relevanten Mies-Rezeption geradezu langweilig ausnehmen. Aber nicht nur in der Fachwelt fand das Haus Anklang. Auch unter badischen Bauherren gab es in den folgenden Jahren eine interessierte Klientel, fast durchweg Wissenschaftler, Ärzte und Künstler, die in einem dieser nicht alltäglichen Häuser leben wollten. Außer sei-

law. In addition, Maria Verena Gieselmann's organizational skills benefited not only the growing family but also the growing business.[30]

Even one of the initial projects during the Karlsruhe years, the Becker house in Karlsruhe-Durlach, occupied since 1959, turned out to be a virtuoso masterpiece. All the characteristics described earlier using the architect's somewhat later first personal home as an example are already present here: a three-dimensional effect by the imaginative interlacing of rigid volumes, contrasts of closed surfaces and sharp-edged cut openings, a carefully thought-out embedding of the building in the surrounding terrain, a floor plan organized around a central living area, as well as complex rooms, partly turned inward, partly opening far toward the outside into the garden.

The work received attention and was publicized not only by architectural journals. In Ulrich Conrads' anthology *Neue deutsche Architektur 2* the Becker house, as well as Ungers' famous residence in Köln-Müngersdorf, represented in exemplary fashion an architecture aimed at expressive gesture demanded by their joint manifesto.[31] Next to this, even well-known examples of architecture by followers of Mies, important at the time, sound almost boring. But it was not only the professionals who acclaimed the house. In the years that followed, clients in Baden were interested as well – almost exclusively scientists, doctors, and artists who wanted to live in one of these unusual houses. By 1969 Gieselmann was able to build more than a dozen more residences in addition to his own house. Indeed, he even presumed to reject enquiries by professors after a rift between him and one of his academic clients. Evidence of his overflowing creativity is the fact that in spite of many similar projects he always found individual, sophisticated solutions regardless of whether funds were ample, as in the case of the luxurious »Z. house« for a prominent physician, or funds were limited, as in the case of the house for art historian Klaus Lankheit. While their styles and the materials used were different, developed for a unique topography and created in response to the often complex wishes of the clients, they always reveal the originator and his preference for staggered sections, angled windows, open fireplaces, and cruciform ground floor typologies, the latter a conscious homage to Frank Lloyd Wright.[32]

Alfred Fischer's successful participation in the Karlsruhe-Waldstadt competition resulted in a commission to develop part of the new satellite town. The available area was enclosed by streets on three sides. Gieselmann's urban planning ambitions, awakened in Otto Senn's firm in Basel, would take shape here in 1957–61 as part of the plan of a building and loan association. The architect placed twenty single-family homes along the street, preserving the forest between them as a green center. However economically the individual houses had to be built, their design – a staggered row and gable roofs whose incline is picked up by the masonry garden walls – is as carefully thought out as it is formally sophisticated. Here it is obvious that Gieselmann's buildings were modeled on Scandinavian architecture, and particularly Aalto's summerhouse with its tilted roof and the orientation of inside rooms towards the surrounding landscape. An innovative feature was the fact that the architect allowed future residents, who bought the houses ready for occupancy, to take part in the planning process. Ten years before participation became a catchword, prospective residents were able not only to choose between three basic types but also to have floor plans and furnishings changed according to their needs.

A second housing development was built slightly later, in 1959–62, in the Nordweststadt district of Karlsruhe, though here a completely different concept was operative. Here, as a remarkably early example in Germany and elsewhere, Gieselmann developed a group of »compact, low buildings«, a type that would later become almost synonymous with 1960s modern architecture. Only a little later, the Swiss Atelier 5 with its Halen housing development in Bern supplied the most important model of this new style.

The development, a so-called »carpet-type« development, fits together a dozen one-storey U-shaped flat-roof bungalows and their garden yards in a very confined space. The units are arranged in such a way that neighbors have complete privacy. Narrow lanes provide access to the buildings, and a small central square, strictly framed by walls, provides public spaces. These have an unmistakable identity when compared to the anonymity of the surrounding new housing development – even though the architecture, with its reduced cubes and surfaces of exposed concrete and sand-lime brick, deliberately allows no associations with the kind of cozy idyll linked with traditional garden cities.[33]

Reinhard Gieselmann was now able to address another subject constantly on his mind: the building of churches. Gathering examples from history and from the present, analyzing and interpreting, he had already examined the topic in 1951 while working for Otto Senn, again in his 1955 dissertation, and finally in professional articles, lectures, and a book entitled *Der Kirchenbau*, published together with Werner Aebli in 1960.[34] This theoretical preoccupation was now followed by practice. After the appropriate archiepiscopal building authorities became aware of the book, he received – without competition – a direct commission for the church of St. Jakobus in Sinsheim. The job was just made for him. He had concrete ideas of Christian community, combining his Westphalian Catholic roots and his interest in modern sociology. Discussions involving liturgy reform and its architectural consequences that would soon characterize the Second Vatican Council were already in the air. Also, at this time in history, a true architectural artist willing to work as an independent designer probably could not fulfill himself as completely in any other type of building as in building churches. Church architecture had become a sort of playing field where architects could forget the growing focus on efficiency and standardization of everyday life.

Gieselmann's Sinsheim contribution is an example of many churches in the 1950s and 1960s whose planners took a critical look at the chapel of Ronchamp. This is no surprise, considering his existential experience when he first visited this central work by Le Corbusier in 1955. Both there and in Sinsheim, curved wall shells, rolled inward in the floor plan, coated with roughcast, define the interior. Familiar motifs from Ronchamp can be found in Sinsheim: separate chapels, confession-

27. Reinhard Gieselmann, Wüstenrot housing development, Karlsruhe-Waldstadt, 1957–61.
28. Reinhard Gieselmann, »carpet-type« housing development in Karlsruhe, 1959–62.
29. Reinhard Gieselmann, St. Jakobus, Sinsheim, 1961–67. Plan.
30. Le Corbusier, Notre-Dame-du-Haut, Ronchamp, 1951–55. Plan.

27. Reinhard Gieselmann, Siedlung Wüstenrot, Karlsruhe-Waldstadt, 1957–61.
28. Reinhard Gieselmann, Teppichsiedlung in Karlsruhe, 1959–62.
29. Reinhard Gieselmann, St. Jakobus, Sinsheim, 1961–67. Grundriß.
30. Le Corbusier, Notre-Dame-du-Haut, Ronchamp, 1951–55. Grundriß.

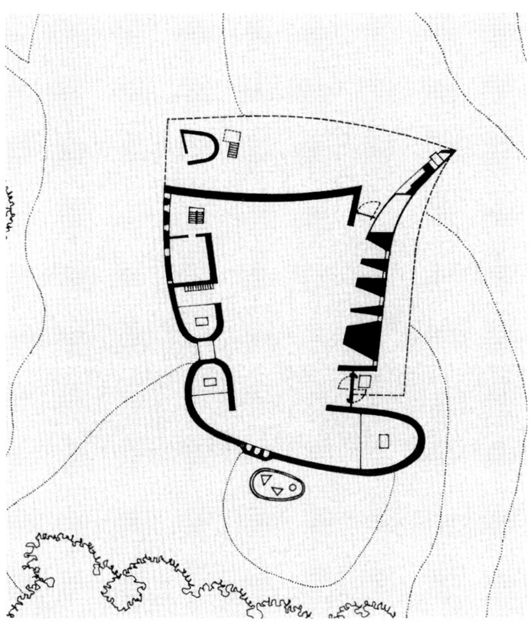

nem eigenen konnte Gieselmann bis 1969 mehr als ein Dutzend weiterer Wohnhäuser errichten, ja er erlaubte sich sogar, Anfragen von Professoren abzulehnen, nachdem es mit einem der akademischen Bauherren zum Bruch gekommen war. Es zeugt von seiner überbordenden Kreativität jener Jahre, daß er trotz der Vielzahl gleicher Aufgaben immer individuelle, anspruchsvolle Lösungen fand, einerlei, ob beispielsweise beim luxuriösen »Haus Z.« für einen Chefarzt mehr oder beim Haus des Kunsthistorikers Klaus Lankheit weniger Mittel zur Verfügung standen. In ihrem Typus und ihrer Materialität verschieden, aus der jeweiligen Topographie entwickelt und den oft komplexen Wünschen der Auftraggeber Rechnung tragend, lassen sie doch immer den Urheber erkennen und dessen Vorlieben für gestaffelte Körper, übereck gezogene Fenster, offene Kamine und kreuzförmige Grundrißtypologien, letztere eine bewußte Reverenz an Frank Lloyd Wright.[32]

Aus der erfolgreichen Teilnahme Alfred Fischers am Karlsruher Waldstadt-Wettbewerb resultierte der Auftrag für die Bebauung eines Teilbereichs der neuen Trabantenstadt. Zur Verfügung stand ein auf drei Seiten von Straßen umschlossenes Areal. Gieselmanns städtebauliche Ambitionen, die bei Otto Senn in Basel geweckt worden waren, konnten hier 1957–61 im Rahmen des Vorhabens einer Bausparkasse Gestalt annehmen. Der Architekt plazierte zwanzig Einfamilienhäuser entlang der Straße, um dazwischen den bestehenden Wald als grüne Mitte zu bewahren. So kostengünstig die einzelnen Häuser auch gebaut werden mußten, in der Gestaltung sind sie in ihrer gestaffelten Reihung und mit den Satteldächern, deren Neigung von den gemauerten Garteneinfriedungen aufgenommen wird, ebenso durchdacht wie formal anspruchsvoll. Hier ist das Vorbild skandinavischer Architektur, insbesondere die Rezeption von Aaltos Sommerhaus mit seinen Dachschrägen und der Orientierung der Innenräume zur umgebenden Natur, augenfällig. Neuartig war, daß der Architekt künftige Bewohner, welche die Häuser schlüsselfertig kauften, am Planungsprozeß teilhaben ließ. Schon zehn Jahre, bevor Partizipation zum Schlagwort wurde, konnten Interessenten nicht nur zwischen drei Grundtypen wählen, sondern auch Grundrisse und Ausstattung nach ihren Bedürfnissen variieren lassen.

Eine zweite Siedlung entstand nur wenig später 1959–62 in der Karlsruher Nordweststadt, allerdings nach einer völlig anderen Konzeption. Als ein bemerkenswert frühes Beispiel nicht nur in Deutschland entwickelte Gieselmann hier eine Gebäudegruppe in »verdichtetem Flachbau«, einem Typus, der geradezu Synonym für die moderne Architektur der sechziger Jahre werden sollte. Das Schweizer Atelier 5 lieferte erst wenig später mit der Siedlung Halen in Bern das wichtigste Leitbild dieser neuen Bauweise.

Die »Teppichsiedlung« fügt auf engstem Raum ein Dutzend eingeschossige U-förmige Flachdachbungalows mit zugehörigen Gartenhöfen aneinander. Die Einheiten sind dabei so geordnet, daß eine gegenseitige Störung ausgeschlossen ist. Schmale Gassen, die die Anlage erschließen, und ein kleiner zentraler Platz bilden, von Mauern streng gefaßt, öffentliche Räume, die der Anonymität des umgebenden Neubauviertels eine unverwechselbare Identität entgegenstellen – und das, obwohl die Architektur in ihren reduzierten Kuben

und Oberflächen aus Sichtbeton und Kalksandsteinen eine traute Idylle im Sinne traditioneller Gartenstädte bewußt nicht aufkommen lassen will.[33]

Ein weiteres Thema, das Reinhard Gieselmann immer wieder umtrieb, konnte nun endlich auch Gestalt annehmen: der Kirchenbau. Beispiele aus Geschichte und Gegenwart sammelnd, analysierend und interpretierend, hatte er sich damit bereits 1951 bei Otto Senn, dann in seiner Dissertation von 1955, schließlich in Fachartikeln, Vorträgen und 1960 in einem gemeinsam mit Werner Aebli herausgegebenen Buch gleichen Titels auseinandergesetzt.[34] Der theoretischen Beschäftigung folgte jetzt die Praxis. Nachdem das zuständige Erzbischöfliche Bauamt auf das Buch aufmerksam geworden war, bekam er ohne vorherigen Wettbewerb 1961 den Direktauftrag für die Kirche St. Jakobus in Sinsheim. Es war eine Aufgabe wie geschaffen für ihn. Einerseits hatte er konkrete Vorstellungen von christlicher Gemeinschaft, in denen sich die westfälisch-katholischen Wurzeln mit dem Interesse an moderner Soziologie verbanden. Die Diskussionen um die Liturgiereform und ihre baulichen Folgen, die wenig später das Zweite Vatikanische Konzil bestimmen sollten, lagen bereits in der Luft. Andererseits konnte man sich als ausgesprochener Baukünstler mit dem Willen zur freien Gestaltung in der damaligen Zeit wohl bei keinem anderen Gebäudetypus so verwirklichen wie beim Kirchenbau. Er war zu einer Art Spielwiese geworden, auf der man die um sich greifende Rationalisierung und Normierung des Alltags vergessen konnte.

Gieselmanns Sinsheimer Beitrag ist jenen zahlreichen Kirchenbeispielen zuzuordnen, die sich in den fünfziger und sechziger Jahren mit der Kapelle von Ronchamp auseinandersetzten. Vor dem biographischen Hintergrund des existentiellen Erlebnisses beim ersten Besuch dieses zentralen Werkes von Le Corbusier 1955 mag dies nicht weiter verwundern. Gekurvte, im Grundriß nach innen gerollte Wandschalen, von Rauhputz überzogen, umgrenzen hier wie dort den Innenraum. Ebenso findet man in Sinsheim aus Ronchamp bekannte Motive wie separate Kapellen, in die Wand eingelassene Beichtstühle oder jene typischen Wasserspeier, die ihr Naß gezielt in ein gefaßtes Becken am Boden entleeren. Dennoch muß man St. Jakobus in seiner Größe, dem frei stehenden Turm, der deutlicheren Längsausrichtung sowie der Ausbildung einer Chorrundung als durchaus eigenständige Leistung würdigen, welche die Herausforderung annimmt, die »organische« Architektur der isoliert auf einem Berg sich erhebenden Wallfahrtskapelle den Anforderungen einer in der Stadt gelegenen Hauptpfarrkirche anzupassen. Die archaische Wirkung, die von Ronchamp ausgeht, strahlt St. Jakobus nicht aus. Der Hinweis des Architekten, er habe in Sinsheim auch die auf einer Spanienreise erlebte Formenwelt eines Antoni Gaudí verarbeitet, ist durchaus nachvollziehbar.[35] Die unregelmäßig gewölbten Deckenkompartimente mit ihren teilenden Graten – eine technisch höchst komplizierte Rohrmattenputz-Konstruktion – und die in sie einschneidenden dynamisch-verzogenen Bogenfenster erinnern ebenso an den Jugendstil wie das graphische Muster der leider entfernten ursprünglichen Glasfenster oder die floral-dekorativen Linien im Bodenbelag der Außenbereiche.

als let into the wall, or those typical gargoyles that empty into a curbed basin on the ground. Yet one must appreciate St. Jakobus as a completely independent achievement because of the size, the freestanding tower, the clearer longitudinal alignment, and the formation of a curved choir. The architect has accepted the challenge of adapting the »organic« architecture of a pilgrimage chapel that rises isolated on a mountain to the requirements of the main parish church located in town. St. Jakobus does not radiate the archaic effect that emanates from Ronchamp. We can understand the architect's remark that in Sinsheim he also assimilated the world of forms of someone like Antoni Gaudí, which he had experienced on a trip to Spain.[35] The irregularly arched ceiling compartments with the hips that divide them – a technically highly complicated reed-mat plaster construction – and the dynamically distorted bow windows cut into them are reminiscent of Art Nouveau, as is the graphic pattern of the original glass windows, which unfortunately have been removed, and the floral decorative pattern of lines in the floor covering of the outside areas.

The Ronchamp chapter of Gieselmann's life was closed – he would not return to it. His next church, St. Stephanus in Filderstadt-Bernhausen, which he erected in three stages from 1965 to 1975 after winning a competition, has a different point of departure. Here he acknowledged extensive specifications requiring a kindergarten, a community hall, and a larger presbytery with apartments in addition to the church, and designed a self-contained community center that stands out like a rocky island, a compact unit of urban development among its insignificant architectural neighborhood. Cubes of buildings are staggered one behind the other, as was the case with the residential houses; individual elements, and particularly the church, are added diagonally in the ground plan. A walkway, overcoming various levels by means of stairs, leads between squat outbuildings to the blocklike church with a steep campanile towering over it. In the interior the path to the altar is consistently emphasized and behind the altar the eyes are drawn upward through slit-like windows high above it to the light. The interior walls are roughcast and painted white; outside, however, the group of buildings is massive and heavy, and monolithically poured in concrete.

Gieselmann had also used exposed concrete in its roughest form in another important work, the Red Cross old-age home in Karlsruhe built in 1962–67. The very three-dimensionally formed street façade with its balconies receding in an irregular rhythm, projecting bay windows, and a fireplace placed in the outside alignment caused a sensation. With his formal Brutalism, the architect enriched not some desolate new development on the outskirts of town but showed the building off demonstratively on a site along a classicistic street. Even within the family the building touched off discussions, since Alfred Fischer, now retired from the partnership for several reasons including his age, did not want to lend his support to such an ostentatious solution. As for Gieselmann, he justified himself by citing the neighboring façade of the massive gate building leading to Balschstrasse that Hermann Billing – whose assistant the father-in-law had been in the 1920s – had erected soon after 1900, the most important example of Baden

Art Nouveau style. In spite of all the differences, there is something apt about the comparison: Three-dimensionality, expressiveness and monumentality, the interplay of regularity and disruption, as well as a certain pleasure in provoking the observer were characteristics present in Hermann Billing, and it is no surprise that Reinhard Gieselmann wrote one of the first articles paying homage to this long-forgotten architect.[36]

Professor in Vienna, 1969–1992

With his doctorate and numerous contributions to professional periodicals, an academic career was also a possibility for Reinhard Gieselmann. Admittedly, there seemed to be no prospect of a successful career at Karlsruhe University, since up to his death in 1970 Egon Eiermann had a decisive influence on the hiring for the department of architecture. It is obvious how critically Eiermann regarded this former student when we read that in his lectures he bluntly denounced »Mr. G's« new buildings as examples of inadmissible artistic liberties.[37] There was no room for Reinhard Gieselmann at this school, nor could the architect count on the support of his former teacher even when there were openings at other universities. However, Eiermann's influence did not reach as far as Vienna. In 1968, Gieselmann received an invitation to accept a chair for residential building and design from the Technische Hochschule there. He was glad to accept it, seeing this as an opportunity to risk another new beginning at 44.

Getting used to the completely new surroundings was not simple. The family had to exchange a Karlsruhe house tailored for them for a plain Viennese apartment. The mentality of the Viennese and their singular manners were another source of many a misunderstanding. Even after he had lived in the Austrian capital for a dozen years, the Westphalian smugly explained in a »Bericht eines Deutschen aus Wien« (Report of a German from Vienna) how many things still seemed strange to him there.[38]

A great deal of work awaited the new professor after the fall of 1969. It was a challenge, especially in those years of student unrest, to set up his institute with no less than six assistants. So was teaching – something new for him – with lectures, seminars, field trips, talks, and later research projects and his own demanding periodical *Prolegomena*.[39] Early on Gieselmann realized that the atmosphere was inflamed in Vienna as well. The Viennese architect Ottokar Uhl, himself involved in residential and church architecture and – by an ironic twist of history – Egon Eiermann's successor after 1973 to the position in Karlsruhe, attacked him directly in an article, obviously because he was embittered by his own failed ambitions and also because he was the avowed opponent of Gieselmann's self-conception as an artist. In late 1960s jargon he reproached the newly appointed professor as a candidate of the university's ruling establishment for his lack of understanding for »the new development of society and architecture« and accused him of being a »reactionary«.[40] In his position statement, Gieselmann countered with a pun (on the German version of the English proverb »One man's meat is another man's poison«, transl.) that alluded to the tolerant

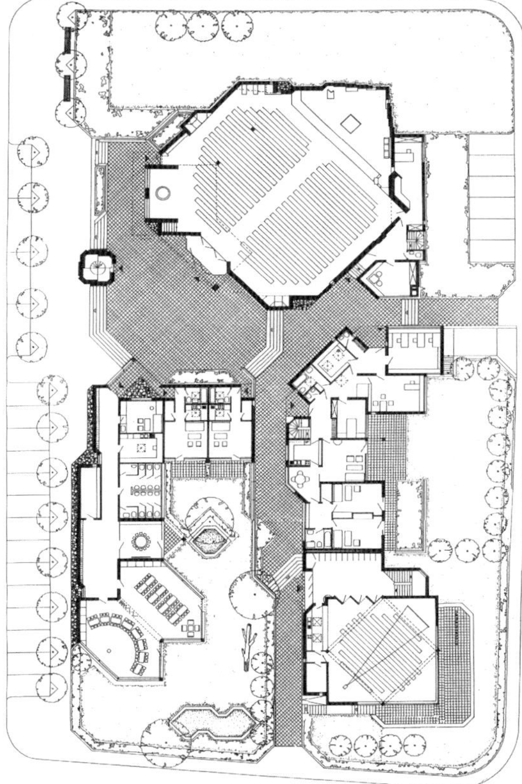

31. Reinhard Gieselmann, St. Stephanus parish center, Filderstadt-Bernhausen, 1965–75. View of the church from the community center.
32. Reinhard Gieselmann, St. Stephanus parish center, Filderstadt-Bernhausen, 1965–75. Plan of the whole complex.
33. Reinhard Gieselmann, old-age home of the Deutsches Rotes Kreuz, Karlsruhe, 1962–67. View from the street.
34. Hermann Billing, Baischstraße development, Karlsruhe, 1900–03. Façade at Stephanienstrasse.

31. Reinhard Gieselmann, Kirchengemeindezentrum St. Stephanus, Filderstadt-Bernhausen, 1965 bis 1975. Blick vom Gemeindezentrum auf die Kirche.
32. Reinhard Gieselmann, Kirchengemeindezentrum St. Stephanus, Filderstadt-Bernhausen, 1965 bis 1975. Grundriß der Gesamtanlage.
33. Reinhard Gieselmann, Altenheim des Deutschen Roten Kreuzes, Karlsruhe, 1962–67. Straßenansicht.
34. Hermann Billing, Bebauung der Baischstraße, Karlsruhe, 1900–03. Fassade an der Stephanienstraße.

Reinhard Gieselmann wird das Kapitel Ronchamp später nicht mehr aufschlagen. Seine nächste Kirche, St. Stephanus in Filderstadt-Bernhausen, nach einem gewonnenen Wettbewerb in drei Abschnitten 1965–75 errichtet, geht von einem anderen Ansatz aus. Hier nutzte er das umfangreiche Programm, das neben der Kirche auch einen Kindergarten, einen Gemeindesaal und ein größeres Pfarrhaus mit Wohnungen verlangte, zur Anlage eines geschlossenen Gemeindezentrums, das sich wie eine Felseninsel als kompakte städtebauliche Einheit aus ihrer belanglosen baulichen Nachbarschaft in der Nähe des Stuttgarter Flughafens herauszuheben sucht. Baukuben sind, wie von den Wohnhäusern her bekannt, hintereinander gestaffelt, einzelne Elemente, vor allem die Kirche, im Grundriß diagonal dazu gesetzt. Ein Weg führt, verschiedene Niveaus mit Treppen überwindend, zwischen den sich duckenden Nebengebäuden hin zum Block der Kirche, der seinerseits vom steil emporschießenden Campanile überragt wird. Im Inneren ist der Weg zum Altar konsequent betont, die Blicke werden dahinter durch hoch angeordnete schlitzartige Fenster nach oben, zum Licht, gezogen. Die Innenwände sind mit weiß gestrichenem Rauhputz versehen, außen zeigt sich die Anlage dagegen monolithisch in Beton gegossen, mächtig und schwer.

Sichtbeton in seiner rohesten Form hatte Gieselmann auch bei einem anderen Hauptwerk verwendet, dem 1962–67 errichteten Altersheim des Roten Kreuzes in Karlsruhe. Die stark plastisch ausgeformte Straßenfassade mit ihren im unregelmäßigen Rhythmus zurückspringenden Loggien und vortretenden Erkern sowie dem in die Außenflucht gestellten Kamin sorgte für Aufsehen. Hier bereicherte der Architekt mit seinem Formbrutalismus nicht irgendein ödes Neubauviertel am Stadtrand, sondern setzte ihn demonstrativ auf einem Grundstück in der Flucht einer klassizistischen Straße zur Schau. Selbst innerhalb der Familie sorgte dieser Bau für Diskussionen, da Alfred Fischer, der sich damals auch altersbedingt aus der Partnerschaft zurückzog, eine solch ostentative Lösung nicht mittragen wollte. Gieselmann selbst rechtfertigte sich mit dem Blick auf die benachbarte Fassade des mächtigen Torgebäudes zur Baischstraße, das Hermann Billing – der Schwiegervater war in den zwanziger Jahren noch sein Assistent gewesen – gleich nach 1900 als Hauptwerk des badischen Jugendstils errichtet hatte. Der Vergleich hat bei allen Unterschieden durchaus etwas Schlagendes: Plastizität, expressiver Ausdruck und Monumentalität, das Spiel von Regelmaß und Störung sowie eine gewisse Freude an der Provokation des Betrachters scheinen bei Hermann Billing vorgeprägt, und es ist nicht verwunderlich, daß Reinhard Gieselmann diesem damals völlig vergessenen Baukünstler einen ersten würdigenden Artikel widmete.[36]

Professor in Wien, 1969–1992

Mit seinem Doktorgrad und den zahlreichen Textbeiträgen in Fachzeitschriften stand Reinhard Gieselmann auch die Möglichkeit einer akademischen Laufbahn offen. An der Karlsruher Universität zu reüssieren, schien freilich aussichtslos, nahm doch Egon Eiermann noch bis zu seinem Tod 1970 entscheidenden Einfluß auf die Berufungspolitik der Architekturfakultät. Und wie kritisch Eiermann diesem früheren Schüler gegenüberstand, zeigte sich schon darin, daß er in Vorlesungen die Neubauten »des Herrn G.« unverblümt als Exempel unzulässiger künstlerischer Freiheiten brandmarkte.[37] Für Reinhard Gieselmann war an dieser Schule kein Platz, und sogar bei Vakanzen an anderen Hochschulen konnte der Architekt nicht mit der Unterstützung seines ehemaligen Lehrers rechnen. Bis nach Wien sollte der Einfluß Eiermanns hingegen nicht reichen. Von der dortigen Technischen Hochschule erreichte Gieselmann 1968 den Ruf auf einen Lehrstuhl für Wohnbau und Entwerfen. Er nahm ihn gerne an, sah er doch darin die Chance, mit 44 Jahren noch einen Neubeginn zu wagen.

Die Eingewöhnung in die so gänzlich andere Umgebung war nicht einfach, nicht nur deshalb, weil die Familie das auf sie zugeschnittene Haus in Karlsruhe zunächst gegen eine schlichte Wiener Mietwohnung eintauschen mußte. Auch die Mentalität der Wiener und ihre speziellen Umgangsformen sorgten für manche Irritation. Als er schon über ein Dutzend Jahre in der österreichischen Hauptstadt lebte, setzte sich der Westfale in einem »Bericht eines Deutschen aus Wien« in der *Bauwelt* süffisant damit auseinander, was ihm hier immer noch fremd geblieben war.[38]

Viel Arbeit wartete ab Herbst 1969 auf den neuen Lehrstuhlinhaber. Der Aufbau seines Instituts mit nicht weniger als sechs Assistenten sowie die für ihn neue Lehrtätigkeit mit Vorlesungen, Seminaren, Exkursionen und Vorträgen, später auch mit Forschungsprojekten und der anspruchsvollen eigenen Zeitschrift *Prolegomena*, waren eine Herausforderung, gerade in jener Zeit der Studentenunruhen.[39] Daß auch in Wien die Atmosphäre aufgeheizt war, bekam Gieselmann gleich am Anfang zu spüren. Der Wiener Architekt Ottokar Uhl, selbst auf den Gebieten des Wohn- und Kirchenbaus engagiert sowie – Ironie der Geschichte – von 1973 an Nachfolger auf dem Lehrstuhl Eiermann in Karlsruhe, trat offensichtlich aus Verbitterung über gescheiterte eigene Ambitionen und nicht zuletzt als erklärter Gegner des von Gieselmann vertretenen Künstlerselbstverständnisses in einem Zeitschriftenartikel zum Direktangriff an. Im Jargon der späten sechziger Jahre warf er dem Neuberufenen als einem Kandidaten der »Herrschenden« an der Hochschule Unverständnis gegenüber »der neuen Entwicklung der Gesellschaft und der Architektur« vor und bezichtigte ihn der Rückschrittlichkeit.[40] Der Attackierte konterte in einer Stellungnahme geschickt mit einer Redewendung, die auf die tolerante Einstellung seiner bisherigen Heimat anspielte: »Was dem einen sein Uhl, ist dem andern sein Gieselmann.«[41] Die Zielsetzung seiner Lehre, die er nun für mehr als zwei Jahrzehnte mit Engagement in Wien betreiben sollte, resümierte er in seiner Antrittsvorlesung folgendermaßen: »Das Ergebnis muß Gestalt sein. (...) Gestalt ist in vielfacher Hinsicht Orientierungshilfe, Wegweiser, Identifikator, Zeitgeber.« Wenn die Erscheinungsbilder der Architektur es fertigbrächten, »unsere psychischen Bedürfnisse nach Identifikation zu befriedigen ohne ideologische Krücken und mystische Prothesen, aber mit Technik und Poesie, dann können wir sie als die architektonische Kunst unserer Zeit bezeichnen«.[42]

Trotz des neuen universitären Tätigkeitsfeldes wollte Reinhard Gieselmann auch weiterhin ent-

attitude of his former homeland: »One man's Uhl (owl) is another man's Gieselmann (nightingale).«[41] He summed up his teaching, which he was to pursue with deep commitment in Vienna for more than two decades, as follows in his inaugural lecture: »The result must be form (*Gestalt*). (...) Form is in many respects a help in orientation, a signpost, an identifier.« If the images of architecture manage to »satisfy our psychic needs for identification without ideological crutches and mystical prostheses, but with technology and poetry«, he went on, »then we can refer to them as the architectural art of our time«.[42]

In spite of his new career at the, Reinhard Gieselmann wanted to continue his work designing and building. He tried to continue running the Karlsruhe office and opened a second one in Vienna, a demanding balancing act between two distant cities that he was able to sustain only for a limited time. After about 1973 he merged his two offices to one in Vienna, housed in the *sala terrena* of the baroque Palais Coburg. Right at the beginning he was able to design and build a group of buildings with apartments for professors, a commission connected with his university appointment. After that, at first, there were no more commissions. Gieselmann's almost utopian-sounding competition designs for a redevelopment of the Karlsruhe Old Town and the huge urban plan for Wien-Süd in 1970/71 led nowhere. Projects he completed in 1972 for large housing complexes in southwest Germany also remained on paper after the client, an entrepreneur who built apartment houses, became insolvent. This may not have been such a bad thing, for some of these plans would have become evidence of the giantism that characterized urban planning around 1970. The Märkisches Viertel in Berlin, for instance – highly praised at first – soon fell into disrepute, an example of the trend at the time towards extremely densely built-up areas or towards those megastructures that were supposed to overspread a »world of tomorrow«. This undiminished trust in the future was reflected primarily in the buildings of Expo 1970 in Osaka, which Gieselmann specifically traveled to see with his assistants.[43]

One of Gieselmann's disappointments in the first half of the 70s was the rejection of three large-scale model plans completed on behalf of the municipality of Vienna to restructure Viennese suburban districts of the postwar period. He wanted to condense and upgrade the existing desolate rows of dilapidated, prefab public housing into spatially extremely tension-rich urban landscapes, trying to substantiate his concepts theoretically as well as examples of »relative architecture«.[44] His plan was diverse and complementary: low houses built around an open court, various kinds of extensions of existing rows, buildings on the edges of blocks that would complete them, and tall high-rises. Obviously the force behind this – apart from the sensational buildings of someone like Lucien Kroll – was Otto Senn's 1951 urban planning project for the Gellert district of Basel. Even the caterpillar-shaped rows of houses would have materialized again in Gieselmann's plans, though extremely condensed and intensified for expressive spatial effect. Admittedly the residents of the Viennese districts slated for urban renewal were not enthusiastic about the planned drastic changes, or the fact that they would have

to move closer together with new neighbors, or the noise and dirt that could be expected when construction began. They vented their discontent at civic rallies, and all these projects fell through for political reasons.

However, Reinhard Gieselmann had not lost his artistic flair during this time of giant-size urban renewal projects. He proved it in 1971–74 by building his own new house-cum-studio in Wien-Neustift, a way of compensating for the separation from the Karlsruhe house he had built a decade earlier and of putting down permanent roots in Vienna. Once again, he showed off his exceptional experience to advantage. The compact building, whose flat shed roof follows the ascending slope, is located in the foothills of the Wienerwald in the best of locations on the Vienna outskirts. In comparison to the earlier examples, the exterior looks extremely simple. Looking from the outside at the window rows on the hill and valley sides, and at the small openings facing the adjacent lots on the sides, one would not suspect the complex structure inside: six different levels, differentiated spatial effects, and ingenious play with the incidence of light. This work was also publicized in professional periodicals, but unfortunately it was to be Gieselmann's only single-family home in Vienna if one omits the renovation of a neighbor's house.

The 1973 oil crisis, which impressively showed the limits of growth, caused a radical rethinking of economic, political, and social issues. Architecture was also affected to a large degree. The future-oriented mentality of the 60s which believed that architecturally and economically everything was feasible and that only the very latest was appropriate for the people of this new world was to turn into its opposite. Discontent with the inhospitable feel of reconstructed cities sacrificed to private transport, and shock at what were in the end unsatisfactory architectural accomplishments of the recent past were manifested in many ways: spontaneous spray-painted slogans on walls, such as »Too bad concrete doesn't burn«, or organized events, such as the successful 1975 campaign in the year of the protection of historical monuments (*Denkmalschutzjahr*). The public at large, including architects and urban planners, again became aware of the qualities of European cities. The repair of cities was the new motto. This meant renovation of buildings rather than extensive demolition, a careful closing of gaps, and an architecture that would turn away from one-sided functionalistic thinking and be an art again.

Reinhard Gieselmann had always known the models of the postmodern era – the somewhat too pithy expression under which the new views were soon subsumed – since he had always supported architecture as art, while the consideration of the location, and the intellectual examination of tradition were central concepts in his 1960 manifesto. In it, however, he had also stated that »creative art« must »shatter« existing form »in order to find a pure expression of its own period«.[45] Up to that point this postulate, borrowed from Italian Futurism, had characterized the architect's stylistic idiom, intent on contrast. Now he wanted to distance himself from it explicitly.

The key year for the formal reorientation of Reinhard Gieselmann was 1977. The apartment complex project in Wien-Ottakring was the foundation stone for extensive activity in apartment

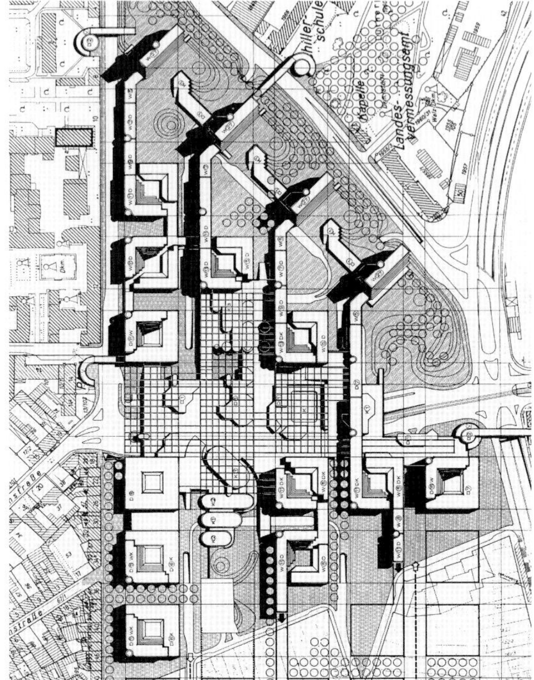

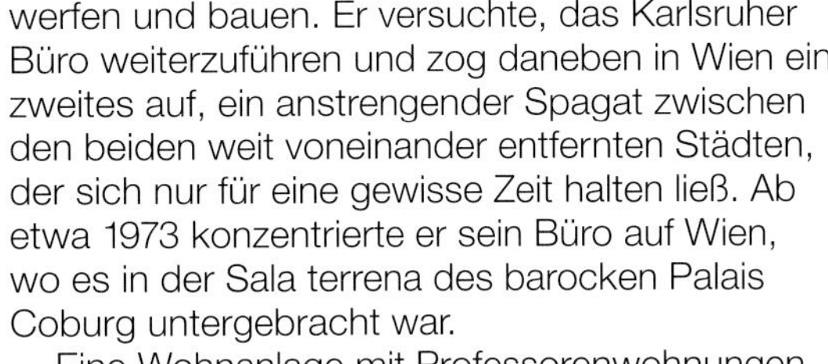

35. Reinhard Gieselmann, urban redevelopment of the old part of Karlsruhe, 1970/71, competition project. Site plan.
36. Reinhard Gieselmann, urban redevelopment at Eipeldauerstrasse, Vienna, 1974/75, project. Model photo.
37. Reinhard Gieselmann, Gieselmann house and studio, Vienna, 1971–74. Axonometric view.

35. Reinhard Gieselmann, Sanierung der Karlsruher Altstadt, 1970/71, Wettbewerbsentwurf. Lageplan.
36. Reinhard Gieselmann, Stadterneuerung an der Eipeldauerstraße, Wien, 1974/75, Projekt. Modellphoto.
37. Reinhard Gieselmann, Wohn- und Atelierhaus Gieselmann, Wien, 1971–74. Axonometrie.

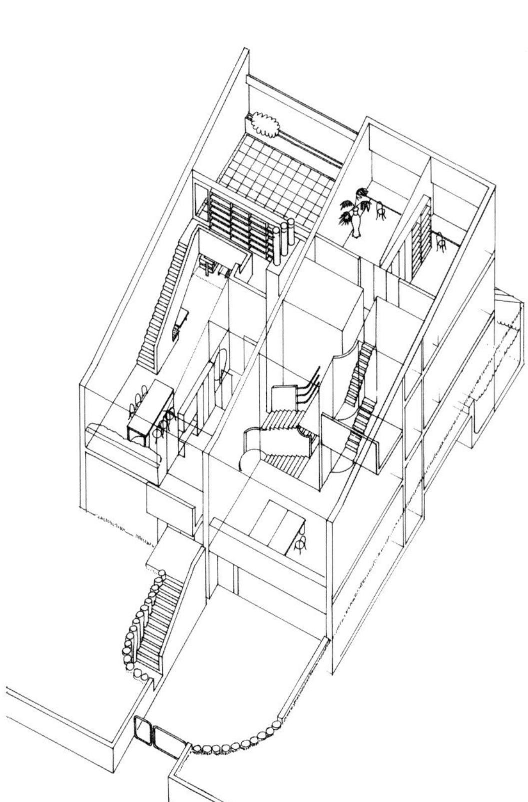

werfen und bauen. Er versuchte, das Karlsruher Büro weiterzuführen und zog daneben in Wien ein zweites auf, ein anstrengender Spagat zwischen den beiden weit voneinander entfernten Städten, der sich nur für eine gewisse Zeit halten ließ. Ab etwa 1973 konzentrierte er sein Büro auf Wien, wo es in der Sala terrena des barocken Palais Coburg untergebracht war.

Eine Wohnanlage mit Professorenwohnungen, ein Auftrag in Zusammenhang mit seiner Berufung, konnte er gleich zu Beginn realisieren. Danach wollten sich allerdings erst einmal keine Folgeaufträge einstellen. Gieselmanns geradezu utopisch anmutende Wettbewerbsentwürfe zur Neuüberbauung der Karlsruher Altstadt sowie die städtebauliche Riesenplanung für Wien-Süd von 1970/71 führten nicht weiter. 1972 erarbeitete Projekte für große Wohnanlagen in Südwestdeutschland blieben ebenfalls auf dem Papier, nachdem der Auftraggeber, ein Wohnbauunternehmer, zahlungsunfähig geworden war. Heute kann man darüber nicht allzu unglücklich sein, denn einige dieser Vorhaben wären Zeugnisse jenes Gigantismus geworden, der Planungen um 1970 generell zu eigen war. Erinnert sei nur an das zunächst hochgelobte und bald in Verruf geratene Märkische Viertel in Berlin als Beispiel des damaligen Trends zu extremer Verdichtung oder an jene Megastrukturen, mit denen eine »Welt von morgen« geradezu überkrustet werden sollte. Die ungebrochene Zukunftsgläubigkeit hatte vor allem in den Bauten der Expo 1970 in Osaka ihren Niederschlag gefunden, zu der Gieselmann mit seinen Assistenten eigens nach Japan gereist war.[43]

Zu Gieselmanns Enttäuschungen der ersten Hälfte der siebziger Jahre gehörte auch die Ablehnung von drei groß angelegten Musterplanungen zur Umstrukturierung von Wiener Vorstadtquartieren aus der Nachkriegszeit, die er im Auftrag der Gemeinde Wien erarbeitet hatte. Die vorgefundenen öden Aufreihungen heruntergekommener Fertigteilzeilen des sozialen Wohnungsbaus wollte er zu räumlich äußerst spannungsreichen Stadtlandschaften verdichten und aufwerten, was er als Exempel »relativer Architektur« auch theoretisch zu untermauern suchte.[44] Geplant war dafür eine vielfältige ergänzende Bebauung: flache Atriumhäuser, unterschiedlichste Anbauten an die vorhandenen Zeilen, blockschließende Randgebäude und steil aufragende Hochhäuser. Pate stand dabei – neben den aktuell für Aufsehen sorgenden Baustrukturen eines Lucien Kroll – ganz offensichtlich auch Otto Senns städtebaulicher Ansatz für das Basler Gellert-Quartier von 1951. Selbst die raupenförmigen Häuserzeilen hätten bei Gieselmann noch einmal Gestalt angenommen, freilich extrem verdichtet und zu expressiver Raumwirkung gesteigert. Die Bewohner der zum Umbau vorgesehenen Wiener Viertel waren allerdings von den geplanten einschneidenden Veränderungen, dem notwendigen Zusammenrücken mit neuen Nachbarn und dem zu erwartenden Baulärm und Bauschmutz nicht begeistert. Sie machten ihrem Mißmut auf Bürgerversammlungen Luft und brachten all diese Projekte politisch zum Scheitern.

Reinhard Gieselmann hatte in dieser Zeit überzogener Maßstäblichkeit sein künstlerisches Fingerspitzengefühl jedoch nicht verloren. Er bewies es mit dem Bau des neuen eigenen Wohn- und Atelierhauses in Wien-Neustift von 1971–74, mit

dem er die Trennung von dem ein Jahrzehnt zuvor errichteten Karlsruher Haus wettmachen und endgültig in Wien Wurzeln schlagen wollte. Noch einmal brachte er seine besonderen Erfahrungen mit dieser Bauaufgabe zur Geltung. In bester Stadtrandlage, in den Ausläufern des Wienerwaldes gelegen, erhebt sich das Gebäude als kompakter Baukörper, dessen flaches Pultdach dem ansteigenden Hang folgt. Im Vergleich zu den früheren Beispielen wirkt das Äußere überraschend einfach. Bandartige Fenster an Berg- und Talseite sowie kleine Öffnungen zu den angrenzenden Parzellen an den Flanken lassen von außen das komplexe Gefüge des Innern nicht vermuten: sechs verschiedene Ebenen, differenzierte Raumwirkungen und ein ausgeklügeltes Spiel mit dem Lichteinfall. Auch dieses Werk wurde in Fachzeitschriften publiziert, doch leider blieb es Gieselmanns einziges Einfamilienhaus in Wien, sieht man ab vom Umbau eines Nachbarhauses.

Die Ölkrise von 1973, die eindrücklich die Grenzen des Wachstums aufzeigte, bewirkte nicht nur in Wirtschaft, Politik und Gesellschaft ein grundsätzliches Umdenken. Auch das Bauen war in starkem Maße davon betroffen. Die zukunftsorientierte Vorstellung der sechziger Jahre, daß architektonisch und ökonomisch alles machbar und nur das Neue dem neuen Menschen adäquat sei, sollte sich ins Gegenteil verkehren. Das Unbehagen an der Unwirtlichkeit der wiederaufgebauten und dem Individualverkehr geopferten Städte sowie das Erschrecken über die letztlich unbefriedigenden architektonischen Leistungen der jüngsten Vergangenheit manifestierten sich auf vielfältige Weise: spontan mit auf Wänden gesprühten Parolen wie »Schade, daß Beton nicht brennt« oder organisiert in der erfolgreichen Kampagne des Denkmalschutzjahres 1975. Qualitäten traditioneller europäischer Städte rückten wieder ins Bewußtsein einer größeren Öffentlichkeit, auch bei Architekten und Stadtplanern. Stadtreparatur war das neue Schlagwort, und es bedeutete Objektsanierung statt Flächenabbruch, behutsames Schließen von Lücken, und eine Architektur, die in Abkehr von einseitig funktionalistischem Denken auch wieder Kunst sein sollte.

Die Leitbilder der Postmoderne, so der etwas allzu griffige Ausdruck, unter dem die neuen Anschauungen bald subsumiert wurden, waren Reinhard Gieselmann nie fremd gewesen, hatte er sich doch immer zur Architektur als Kunst, zum Eingehen auf den Ort und zur geistigen Auseinandersetzung mit der Tradition bekannt – zentrale Begriffe im Manifest von 1960. Dort stand jedoch auch, daß »schöpferische Kunst« bestehende Form »zertrümmern« müsse, »um reinen Ausdruck ihrer eigenen Zeit finden zu können«.[45] Dieses vom italienischen Futurismus übernommene Postulat hatte die bisherige, auf Kontrast bedachte Formensprache des Architekten bestimmt. Jetzt wollte er sich deutlich davon distanzieren.

1977 wurde zum Schlüsseljahr der formalen Neuorientierung Reinhard Gieselmanns. Das Projekt für eine Wohnanlage in Wien-Ottakring legte den Grundstein für eine umfangreiche Tätigkeit im Geschoßwohnungsbau, der zuvor nur eine marginale Rolle gespielt hatte. Bis 1985 realisierte Gieselmann und sein Büro als Teil dieser Quartierssanierung nicht weniger als 114 Neubauwohnungen, die sich auf zwei Parzellen einer Baulückenschließung verteilen. Die Fassaden zeigen nun nicht

house construction, which had previously played only a marginal role. By 1985, as part of this district redevelopment, Gieselmann and his office implemented the construction of no less than 114 new apartments distributed over two lots in an infill project between buildings. The façades now no longer stand out from the neighborhood in an expressive gesture or function as clamorous dominant features – with all their autonomy and precisely because their design is three-dimensional they are integrated in the existing historically developed context. Gieselmann here interprets the familiar 19th century theme of emphasizing the house corners at intersections in an independent, ironic manner characteristic of the postmodern era: As conspicuous »art in public space« a huge naturalistically sculptured arm powerfully props up the roof cornice, a reference to the neighborhood tradition as a working-class district.

Urban apartment construction now became a subject that occupied Gieselmann on an ongoing basis. Until the mid-1990s, after successful competitions, more than half a dozen additional projects followed, some of them very large. These were all developed within the framework of the tradition-rich Viennese housing authority, whose administration had come to regard the architect's competence and reliability very highly. A traditionally Viennese type of building, the apartment block with a central courtyard, was used for the most part, whether projects involved individual complementary buildings in historical districts such as the Karmelitenviertel, or urban expansions in the open countryside, such as the Leberberg one. The plans also attempt to do justice to each site and specific task in terms of scale, material, and form, despite a lack of scope due to limited funds and strict municipal building regulations.

In Gieselmann's late work, church buildings stand out particularly. Here, too, 1977 opened new productive directions for the then fifty-two-year-old architect. From Vienna he successfully participated in a competition based in Markgröningen, Württemberg, where earlier, in the mid-1950s, he had built a house for friends. The task he was commissioned to implement was out of the ordinary. A new nave had to be built on to the rudimentary late Gothic Heilig-Geist-Kirche (Church of the Holy Spirit) originally built by the master builder Bär. It was a former almshouse chapel of which nothing was left after early 19th century demolition but the choir, the flanking tower of the choir, and the sacristy. Although little space was available because the historical Old Town was cramped, the new church was intended to be a spacious sanctuary for the fast-growing Catholic diaspora community. Consecrated in 1981, the building met the high expectations set by the design submitted for the competition. Gieselmann walked the tightrope, keeping in mind the desired specifications while also linking the old and the new – without currying favor and without obscuring the historical substance with the newly built-on sections.

The topic of old and new had preoccupied Gieselmann for a long time. In 1961, he converted an old mill in the Eifel into a weekend house in what was then an extremely unconventional rustic manner. In 1962/63, when few modern architects were interested in such a commission, he undertook the job of adding a floor to the late classical Rees house and used the opportunity to make it a de-sign happening. And in his first years in Vienna he proposed the enlargement of several baroque and historical townhouses by adding a floor, although these designs were not implemented. In accordance with his principles at the time, the new sections in all these projects stood out pointedly from the rest of the buildings. The contrasts were staged particularly sharply. But in the Heilig-Geist-Kirche, in the context of the postmodern era, the architect found a more balanced solution that was received positively by lay people and professionals alike and is still convincing today.

The success of the widely noted church of Markgröningen was to bear fruit for Reinhard Gieselmann. In the coming years, he received other commissions with similar types of problems. In 1982/83 he had the opportunity of building the new presbytery in Petronell, ancient Carnuntum, near the Austro-Hungarian border. Here, not only did part of the dilapidated old building, a large vaulted cellar that possibly dated back to Roman times, have to be incorporated in the new structure, but also the old outlines of the building had to be included and the new building had to fit in with the picturesque townscape. In the Lower Austrian town of Landschach in 1986–90, a small village church needed to be enlarged to more than double its previous size for a larger congregation, and in 1989–93 the convent church of St. Georg in Maselheim-Heggbach, Upper Swabia, had to be adapted to the needs of a nursing home for the handicapped. In both cases, unlike Markgröningen, important modifications of the historical structure were necessary. Additions were made and even the orientation of the sanctuaries was altered. Gieselmann very successfully did justice to the old medieval and baroque components and furnishings, combining the new architecture harmoniously with the old. Between 1994 and 1998, his church-building activities ended with the renovation of St. Martinus in Schwaigern, Württemberg, and the inner-city church of St. Michael zu den Wengen in Ulm, both post-WWII period buildings.

Epilogue

After twenty-three years of teaching in Vienna interrupted only by guest professorships in Raleigh, NC, in 1979 and in Kyoto and Tokyo in 1983, Reinhard Gieselmann retired from his academic chair at the age of sixty-seven in 1992. He implemented projects such as the last apartment building for the municipality of Vienna in the new district of Leberberg, and the churches in Maselheim-Heggbach, Schwaigern, and Ulm with the help of his Viennese firm, subsequently dissolved, or, respectively, in partnership with Anna Stern and Franz Zeyer, both of Stuttgart. His decades-long practical and theoretical preoccupation with house building now found expression in longer book projects.[46] Since 1995 the now over eighty-year-old architect and his wife have again been living in Karlsruhe, where he once was a student and where in 1957 he began the main phase of his creative work. And he has not stopped working as an artist: Recently, he illustrated a new edition of the fairy tales of Oscar Wilde.

38. Reinhard Gieselmann, housing estate of the city of Vienna in Wien-Ottakring, 1978–85.
39. Reinhard Gieselmann, urban renewal in the Karmeliterviertel, Vienna, 1984/85, competition project.
40. Reinhard Gieselmann, Heilig-Geist-Kirche, Markgröningen, 1977–81. View of the historic tower and the newly added part.
41. Reinhard Gieselmann, St. Valentin am Forst, Landschach, Lower Austria, 1986–90. Interior with old and new parts.

38. Reinhard Gieselmann, Wohnanlage der Gemeinde Wien in Wien-Ottakring, 1978–85.
39. Reinhard Gieselmann, Stadterneuerung im Karmeliterviertel, Wien, 1984/85, Wettbewerbsentwurf.
40. Reinhard Gieselmann, Heilig-Geist-Kirche, Markgröningen, 1977–81. Blick auf den historischen Turm und den neu hinzugefügten Bauteil.
41. Reinhard Gieselmann, St. Valentin am Forst, Landschach, Niederösterreich, 1986–90. Innenraum mit alten und neuen Bauteilen.

mehr das Anliegen, sich in expressiver Geste von der Nachbarschaft zu unterscheiden und lautstarke Dominanten zu setzen, sondern sind bei aller Eigenständigkeit gerade in ihrer dreidimensionalen Durchbildung in den vorgefundenen, historisch gewachsenen Kontext integriert. Das aus dem 19. Jahrhundert bekannte Motiv der Eckbetonung von Häusern an Straßenkreuzungen interpretiert Gieselmann hier in einer für die Postmoderne charakteristischen, eigenständig-ironischen Weise: Als auffällige »Kunst am Bau« stützt ein riesiger, naturalistisch dargestellter Arm kraftvoll das Dachgesims, Hinweis auf die Tradition des Ortes als Arbeiterviertel.

Der städtische Mietwohnungsbau wurde nun zu einem Thema, mit dem sich Gieselmann fortlaufend beschäftigte. Bis zur Mitte der neunziger Jahre folgte nach Wettbewerbserfolgen mehr als ein halbes Dutzend weiterer, teilweise recht großer Projekte. Sie entstanden durchweg im Rahmen des traditionsreichen Wiener Gemeindebaus, dessen Administration die Kompetenz und Verläßlichkeit des Architekten schätzen gelernt hatte. Ob es sich um einzelne Ergänzungsbauten in historischen Quartieren wie dem Karmeliterviertel handelte oder um Stadterweiterungen auf der grünen Wiese wie am Leberberg – meist wurde der Typus der traditionell-wienerischen Blockrandbebauung aufgenommen. Zudem zeigen die Planungen den Versuch, in Maßstäblichkeit, Material und Form dem jeweiligen Ort und der Aufgabe gerecht zu werden, trotz des beschränkten Spielraums, den die finanziellen Mittel und die strikten Vorschriften des kommunalen Bauwesens vorgaben.

Besondere Glanzpunkte im Spätwerk Gieselmanns setzte der Kirchenbau. Auch hier eröffnete das Jahr 1977 dem damals Zweiundfünfzigjährigen neue Wege produktiven Schaffens. Von Wien aus hatte er erfolgreich an einem Wettbewerb im württembergischen Markgröningen teilgenommen, wo er bereits Mitte der fünfziger Jahre für Freunde ein Haus gebaut hatte. Die Aufgabe, für deren Realisierung er den Auftrag erhielt, war nicht alltäglich. Es galt, an die rudimentäre spätgotische Heilig-Geist-Kirche des Baumeisters Bär, eine ehemalige Spitalkirche, von der nach Abbrüchen des frühen 19. Jahrhunderts nur noch Chor, Chorflankenturm und Sakristei erhalten geblieben waren, ein neues Schiff anzubauen. Obwohl aufgrund der beengten Verhältnisse in der historischen Altstadt nur wenig Platz zur Verfügung stand, sollte hier wieder ein geräumiges Gotteshaus für die rasch wachsende katholische Diasporagemeinde entstehen. Der 1981 eingeweihte Bau erfüllte die hohen Erwartungen, die der Wettbewerbsentwurf geweckt hatte. Gieselmann gelang die Gratwanderung, das gewünschte Programm zu berücksichtigen sowie das Alte mit dem Neuen zu verbinden – ohne Anbiederung, aber auch ohne die historische Substanz durch die Neubauteile zu verunklären.

Das Thema Alt-Neu beschäftigte Gieselmann schon lange. 1961 hatte er auf damals äußerst unkonventionell-rustikale Weise eine alte Mühle in der Eifel zum Wochenendhaus umgebaut. 1962/63, als sich kaum ein moderner Architekt für einen solchen Auftrag interessierte, nahm er die Aufstockung des spätklassizistischen Hauses Rees in Karlsruhe zum Anlaß, daraus ein gestalterisches Ereignis zu machen. Und in den ersten Wiener Jahren schlug er sogar in einigen unausgeführt gebliebenen Entwürfen Erweiterungen barocker und historistischer Stadthäuser mittels Aufstockungen vor. Gemäß seinen damaligen Prinzipien hoben sich die Neubauteile in all diesen Projekten pointiert vom Bestand ab. Die Kontraste waren bewußt hart inszeniert. Bei der Heilig-Geist-Kirche fand der Architekt unter dem Vorzeichen der Postmoderne dann eine ausgewogenere Lösung, die unter Laien wie Fachleuten positiv aufgenommen wurde und auch heute noch zu überzeugen vermag.

Der Erfolg der weithin beachteten Markgröninger Kirche sollte für Reinhard Gieselmann Früchte tragen. Über Jahre schlossen sich weitere Aufträge mit ähnlichen Aufgabenstellungen an. 1982/83 konnte er den neuen Pfarrhof in Petronell, dem antiken Carnuntum, nahe der österreichisch-ungarischen Grenze errichten. Hier war vom baufälligen Vorgängerbau nicht nur ein großer, möglicherweise bis auf die Römerzeit zurückgehender Gewölbekeller zu übernehmen, sondern es mußten auch die alten Gebäudeumrisse aufgenommen und der Neubau dem malerischen Ortsbild eingefügt werden. Im niederösterreichischen Landschach sollte 1986–90 eine kleine Dorfkirche für eine deutlich gewachsene Gemeinde um mehr als das Doppelte vergrößert und 1989–93 die Klosterkirche St. Georg am Hang im oberschwäbischen Maselheim-Heggbach den Bedürfnissen einer Pflegeanstalt für Behinderte angepaßt werden. In beiden Fällen wurden, anders als in Markgröningen, starke Eingriffe in die historische Bausubstanz notwendig, es wurde angebaut und sogar die Orientierung der Kirchenräume geändert. Auf durchaus gelungene Art versuchte Gieselmann jedoch, den alten Bauteilen und Ausstattungsgegenständen aus Mittelalter und Barock gerecht zu werden und die neue Architektur harmonisch mit dem Alten zu verbinden. Mit den Umbauten von St. Martinus im württembergischen Schwaigern und der Innenstadtkirche St. Michael zu den Wengen in Ulm, beides Bauten aus der Nachkriegszeit, fand seine Tätigkeit im Kirchenbau zwischen 1994 und 1998 ihren Abschluß.

Epilog

Nach 23 Jahren Lehrtätigkeit in Wien, die lediglich von Gastprofessuren in Raleigh, NC, im Jahr 1979 sowie in Kyoto und Tokyo im Jahr 1983 unterbrochen worden war, wurde Reinhard Gieselmann 1992 im Alter von 67 Jahren emeritiert. Projekte wie der letzte Wohnblock für die Gemeinde Wien im Neubauquartier Leberberg und die Kirchen in Maselheim-Heggbach, Schwaigern und Ulm realisierte er mit Hilfe seines anschließend aufgelösten Wiener Büros bzw. in Partnerschaft mit Anna Stern und Franz Zeyer aus Stuttgart. Die jahrzehntelange praktische und theoretische Beschäftigung mit dem Wohnungsbau schlug sich nun in größeren Buchprojekten nieder.[46] Seit 1995 lebt der heute über Achtzigjährige gemeinsam mit seiner Frau wieder in Karlsruhe, dort wo er studiert und 1957 seine Hauptschaffensphase begonnen hatte. Und er hat nicht aufgehört, künstlerisch zu arbeiten: Zuletzt illustrierte er eine Neuausgabe der Märchen von Oscar Wilde.

[1] Plans and construction files for this building, like the major part of Reinhard Gieselmann's work archive, are kept at the Südwestdeutsches Archiv für Architektur und Ingenieurbau, Universität Karlsruhe (saai).

[2] The house, which is basically well preserved but has been damaged particularly by interior changes, was declared a cultural monument a few years ago

[3] Reinhard Gieselmann, *Die Geschichte eines Hauses*, unpublished MS, Vienna 1976, no page number.

[4] See fn. 3.

[5] Cf. *Zodiac*, 1964, no. 12, p. 193; *L'Architecture d'Aujourd'hui*, 1968, no. 136, pp. 104/105; Günther Feuerstein, *New Directions in German Architecture*, New York 1968, pp. 78–80; Wolfgang Pehnt, *Neue deutsche Architektur 3*, Stuttgart 1970, pp. 62/63.

[6] Cf. Gerhard Kabierske: »Eiermann als Lehrer«, in: Annemarie Jaeggi (ed.), *Egon Eiermann 1904 to 1970. Die Kontinuität der Moderne*, exhibition catalogue, Ostfildern 2004, pp. 40–49.

[7] Tape recording of the lecture in the Egon Eiermann literary estate at the Südwestdeutsches Archiv für Architektur und Ingenieurbau, Universität Karlsruhe (saai).

[8] Reinhard Gieselmann, *Architektenleben, Memoiren eines Unruhigen*, n.p. 2005 (privately printed), pp. 127/128.

[9] Biographical data from conversations with Reinhard Gieselmann and from his privately printed memoirs, see fn. 8.

[10] This is the Wiedemann house, Münzstraße 9, built by the Münster architects Franz Möning and Peter Strupp. Cf. Jost Schäfer, »Neues Bauen in Westfalen. Wohnhäuser der 20er Jahre«, *Westfalen. Hefte für Geschichte, Kunst, Volkskunde*, vol. 72, Münster 1994, p. 505.

[11] Cf. Kabierske 2004 (see fn. 6).

[12] Among Gieselmann's fellow staffers at the firm were Carlfried Mutschler, Peter Haupt, and Gieselmann's later wife Maria Verena Fischer, all of whom took their diploma with Eiermann.

[13] Gieselmann 2005 (see fn. 8), p. 99.

[14] Otto Senn, *Raum als Form*, exhibition catalogue, Basel 1990, p. 29.

[15] *Bauen und Wohnen*, 9, 1954, no. 3, pp. 119–124; Gieselmann 2005 (see fn. 8), pp. 109–117.

[16] *Bauen und Wohnen*, 9, 1954, no. 3, p. 124.

[17] This and the following quotations Gieselmann 2005 (see fn. 8), pp. 112–117.

[18] Cf. *Werk*, 41, 1951, no. 1, p. 8–14.

[19] Gieselmann 2005 (see fn. 8), p. 119.

[20] Worringer's work, subtitled »Ein Beitrag zur Stilpsychologie«, originally published in 1908 in Munich, was reprinted in 1948.

[21] Cf. *Baukunst und Werkform*, 7, 1954, no. 10, pp. 589–595.

[22] Cf. Kabierske 2004 (see fn. 6), p. 47.

[23] Gieselmann 2005 (see fn. 8), p. 99.

[24] Cf. Gieselmann 2005 (see fn. 8), p. 122.

[25] Cf. *Baukunst und Werkform*, 5, 1952, no. 6/7, pp. 82/83; 6, 1953, no. 9, pp. 447/448; 7, 1954, no. 6, p. 323.

[26] Cf. *Oswald Mathias Ungers, Architektur 1951 bis 1990*, Stuttgart 1991.

[27] Written in 1960, the manifesto was mentioned in 1962 publications by Ulrich Conrads and Ulrich von Altenstadt, and was first printed in full in 1963 in the cultural periodical *Der Monat*. Gieselmann had asked for it in a letter to the editor in response to Ulrich von Altenstadt's article where the latter had

conjured up a future determined by technology. Cf. Jörg Stabenow, *Architekten wohnen. Ihre Domizile im 20. Jahrhundert*. Berlin 2000, p. 192–193.

[28] Gieselmann in *Der Monat*, no. 174, March 1963, p. 96.

[29] On Alfred Fischer (1889–1969) cf. Anna Schairer, »Der Architekt Alfred Fischer«, in: *Bauen in Baden, Architektur in Karlsruhe 1920–30*, Karlsruhe 2006, pp. 189–193. Documents on his personal life and work in the Südwestdeutsches Archiv für Architektur und Ingenieurbau Karlsruhe.

[30] After their son Moritz (b. 1956) a daughter, Sibylle, was born in 1958.

[31] Cf. *Neue deutsche Architektur 2*, Stuttgart 1962, pp. 26/27.

[32] On the residential houses cf. the brochure published as a result of a seminar, *gewohnt plastisch. Häuser von Reinhard Gieselmann*, ed. by Universität Karlsruhe, Institut für Baugestaltung, Professor Peter Fierz, Karlsruhe 2006. An important contemporary article about Gieselmann and his residential houses by Wolfgang Pehnt appeared in *Zodiac*, 1964, no. 12, pp. 192–199.

[33] In the Waldstadt development and in the »carpet-type« development such major modifications have been carried out on individual homes in recent years that their appearance has been seriously impaired, and having them declared cultural monuments hardly seems possible.

[34] Cf. Reinhard Gieselmann, »Nieuwe Kerksbouw in Duitsland«, *Steven*, 1955, no. 11/12, pp. 430–436; Reinhard Gieselmann/Werner Aebli, *Kirchenbau*, Zürich 1960; Reinhard Gieselmann, *Neue Kirchen*, Stuttgart 1972.

[35] Cf. *Baumeister*, 1967, no. 12, p. 1522.

[36] Cf. Reinhard Gieselmann, »Hommage à Billing«, *Bauen und Wohnen*, 24, 1969, no. 7, pp. VII 3–4; on Hermann Billing cf. Gerhard Kabierske, *Der Architekt Hermann Billing (1867–1946). Leben und Werk*, Karlsruhe 1996.

[37] Information kindly provided by Hildegund Brandenburg, Dr.-Ing., Karlsruhe. a former student.

[38] Cf. *Bauwelt*, 73, 1982, no. 3, pp. 92–93.

[39] Under the serial title *Prolegomena, Arbeitsblätter des Instituts für Wohnbau und Entwerfen an der Technischen Universität Wien*, a total of 60 issues and three extra issues were published in 1972–92.

[40] Cf. Ottokar Uhl, »Lebenslänglich für Wien?«, *Bau*, 1969, no. 6, p. 123; on Uhl cf. *Ottokar Uhl* (ed.), Architekturzentrum Wien, Salzburg 2005.

[41] *Bau*, 1969, no. 6, p. 132.

[42] Reinhard Gieselmann, »Die Identifikation von Räumen«, *Antrittsvorlesungen der Technischen Hochschule in Wien*, 9, Vienna 1969, pp. 20/21.

[43] Cf. Gieselmann's travel report »Bauten der Weltausstellung in Osaka«, *Detail*, 1970, no.5, pp. 1019 to 1023.

[44] Cf. Reinhard Gieselmann, »Relative Architektur«, *Prolegomena*, no. 15, 1975, pp. 4–7.

[45] *Der Monat*, no. 174, March 1963, p. 96.

[46] Reinhard Gieselmann, Anna Stern, and Franz Zeyer (eds.), *Sanierhandbuch Wohnungsbau. Probleme, Lösungen, Kosten*, Düsseldorf 1994; Reinhard Gieselmann, *Wohnbau, Entwicklungen. Wohnen, Wohnung, Wohnhaus, Wohnungsbau*, ed. by Anna Stern, Düsseldorf 1998.

42. The Gieselmann studio in the house of the architect in Karlsruhe.
43. The Gieselmann studio in the in sala terrena of the Palais Coburg, Vienna.
44. Reinhard Gieselmann, building sign, used on a building site in the 1960s.

42. Das Büro Gieselmann im Wohnhaus des Architekten in Karlsruhe.
43. Das Büro Gieselmann in der Sala terrena des Palais Coburg, Wien.
44. Reinhard Gieselmann, Bauschild, verwendet auf einer Baustelle in den 1960er Jahren.

[1] Pläne und Bauakten zu diesem Bau werden wie ein Großteil des Werkarchivs von Reinhard Gieselmann aufbewahrt im Südwestdeutschen Archiv für Architektur und Ingenieurbau an der Universität Karlsruhe (saai).

[2] Das Haus, das in seiner Grundsubstanz gut erhalten ist, aber vor allem im Innern durch Veränderungen gelitten hat, ist seit einigen Jahren als Kulturdenkmal ausgewiesen.

[3] Reinhard Gieselmann, *Die Geschichte eines Hauses*, ungedrucktes Manuskript, Wien 1976, o. S.

[4] Wie Anm. 3.

[5] Vgl. *Zodiac*, 1964, Nr. 12, S. 193; *L'Architecture d'Aujourd'hui*, 1968, Nr. 136, S. 104/105; Günther Feuerstein, *New Directions in German Architecture*, New York 1968, S. 78–80; Wolfgang Pehnt, *Neue deutsche Architektur 3*, Stuttgart 1970, S. 62/63.

[6] Vgl. Gerhard Kabierske: »Eiermann als Lehrer«, in: Annemarie Jaeggi (Hrsg.), *Egon Eiermann 1904 bis 1970. Die Kontinuität der Moderne*, Ausstellungskatalog, Ostfildern 2004, S. 40–49.

[7] Tonbandaufnahme der Vorlesung im Nachlaß von Egon Eiermann im Südwestdeutschen Archiv für Architektur und Ingenieurbau an der Universität Karlsruhe (saai).

[8] Reinhard Gieselmann, *Architektenleben, Memoiren eines Unruhigen*, o. O. 2005 (Privatdruck), S. 127/128.

[9] Biographische Angaben aus Gesprächen mit Reinhard Gieselmann sowie aus seinen im Privatdruck erschienenen Lebenserinnerungen, wie Anm. 8.

[10] Es handelt sich um das Wohnhaus Wiedemann, Münzstraße 9, erbaut von den Münsteraner Architekten Franz Möning und Peter Strupp. Vgl. Jost Schäfer, »Neues Bauen in Westfalen. Wohnhäuser der 20er Jahre«, *Westfalen. Hefte für Geschichte, Kunst, Volkskunde*, 72. Bd., Münster 1994, S. 505.

[11] Vgl. Kabierske 2004 (wie Anm. 6).

[12] Gieselmanns damalige Bürokollegen waren unter anderen Carlfried Mutschler, Peter Haupt und seine spätere Frau Maria Verena Fischer, allesamt Eiermann-Diplomanden.

[13] Gieselmann 2005 (wie Anm. 8), S. 99.

[14] Otto Senn, *Raum als Form*, Ausstellungskatalog, Basel 1990, S. 29.

[15] *Bauen und Wohnen*, 9, 1954, Nr. 3, S. 119–124; Gieselmann 2005 (wie Anm. 8), S. 109–117.

[16] *Bauen und Wohnen*, 9, 1954, Nr. 3, S. 124.

[17] Dieses und die folgenden Zitate Gieselmann 2005 (wie Anm. 8), S. 112–117.

[18] Vgl. *Werk*, 41, 1951, Nr. 1, S. 8–14.

[19] Gieselmann 2005 (wie Anm. 8), S. 119.

[20] Worringers Werk mit dem Untertitel »Ein Beitrag zur Stilpsychologie«, erstmals 1908 in München erschienen, war 1948 neu aufgelegt worden.

[21] Vgl. *Baukunst und Werkform*, 7, 1954, Nr. 10, S. 589–595.

[22] Vgl. Kabierske 2004 (wie Anm. 6), S. 47.

[23] Gieselmann 2005 (wie Anm. 8), S. 119.

[24] Vgl. Gieselmann 2005 (wie Anm. 8), S. 122.

[25] Vgl. *Baukunst und Werkform*, 5, 1952, Nr. 6/7, S. 82/83; 6, 1953, Nr. 9, S. 447/448; 7, 1954, Nr. 6, S. 323.

[26] Vgl. *Oswald Mathias Ungers, Architektur 1951 bis 1990*, Stuttgart 1991.

[27] 1960 geschrieben, wurde das Manifest 1962 in Veröffentlichungen von Ulrich Conrads und Ulrich von Altenstadt erwähnt und vollständig erstmals 1963 in der Kulturzeitschrift *Der Monat* abgedruckt. Gieselmann hatte darum in einem Leserbrief als Erwiderung auf den Artikel von Ulrich von Altenstadt gebeten, der in seinem Aufsatz eine von der Technik bestimmte Zukunft beschworen hatte. Vgl. auch Jörg Stabenow, *Architekten wohnen. Ihre Domizile im 20. Jahrhundert*. Berlin 2000, S. 192/193.

[28] Gieselmann in *Der Monat*, Nr. 174, März 1963, S. 96.

[29] Zu Alfred Fischer (1889–1969) vgl. Anna Schairer, »Der Architekt Alfred Fischer«, in: *Bauen in Baden, Architektur in Karlsruhe 1920–30*, Karlsruhe 2006, S. 189–193. Unterlagen zu seiner Person und seinem Schaffen im Südwestdeutschen Archiv für Architektur und Ingenieurbau Karlsruhe.

[30] Nach dem Sohn Moritz 1956 kam 1958 Tochter Sibylle zur Welt.

[31] Vgl. *Neue deutsche Architektur 2*, Stuttgart 1962, S. 26–27.

[32] Zu den Wohnhäusern vgl. die als Ergebnis eines Seminars erschienene Broschüre *gewohnt plastisch. Häuser von Reinhard Gieselmann*, hrsg. von der Universität Karlsruhe, Institut für Baugestaltung, Professor Peter Fierz, Karlsruhe 2006. Ein wichtiger zeitgenössischer Artikel über Gieselmann und seine Wohnhäuser von Wolfgang Pehnt in *Zodiac*, 1964, Nr. 12, S. 192–199.

[33] Bei der Siedlung in der Waldstadt wie auch bei der Teppichsiedlung wurden in den letzten Jahren derart starke Veränderungen an Einzelhäusern vorgenommen, daß das Erscheinungsbild stark gelitten hat und eine Einstufung als Kulturdenkmale kaum mehr in Frage kommt.

[34] Vgl. Reinhard Gieselmann, »Nieuwe Kerksbouw in Duitsland«, *Steven*, 1955, Nr. 11/12, S. 430–436; Reinhard Gieselmann / Werner Aebli, *Kirchenbau*, Zürich 1960; Reinhard Gieselmann, *Neue Kirchen*, Stuttgart 1972.

[35] Vgl. *Baumeister*, 1967, Nr. 12, S. 1522.

[36] Vgl. Reinhard Gieselmann, »Hommage à Billing«, *Bauen und Wohnen*, 24, 1969, Nr. 7, S. VII 3–4; zu Hermann Billing vgl. Gerhard Kabierske, *Der Architekt Hermann Billing (1867–1946). Leben und Werk*, Karlsruhe 1996.

[37] Freundliche Auskunft von Frau Dr.-Ing. Hildegund Brandenburg, Karlsruhe, einer damaligen Studentin.

[38] Vgl. *Bauwelt*, 73, 1982, Nr. 3, S. 92/93.

[39] Unter dem Reihentitel *Prolegomena, Arbeitsblätter des Instituts für Wohnbau und Entwerfen an der Technischen Universität Wien*, erschienen 1972–92 insgesamt 60 Hefte und drei Extrahefte.

[40] Vgl. Ottokar Uhl, »Lebenslänglich für Wien?«, *Bau*, 1969, Nr. 6, S. 123; zu Uhl vgl. *Ottokar Uhl*, hrsg. vom Architekturzentrum Wien, Salzburg 2005.

[41] *Bau*, 1969, Nr. 6, S. 132.

[42] Reinhard Gieselmann, »Die Identifikation von Räumen«, *Antrittsvorlesungen der Technischen Hochschule in Wien*, 9, Wien 1969, S. 20/21.

[43] Vgl. den Reisebericht Gieselmanns »Bauten der Weltausstellung in Osaka«, *Detail*, 1970, Nr. 5, S. 1019–1023.

[44] Vgl. Reinhard Gieselmann, »Relative Architektur«, *Prolegomena*, Nr. 15, 1975, S. 4–7.

[45] *Der Monat*, Nr. 174, März 1963, S. 96.

[46] Reinhard Gieselmann, Anna Stern und Franz Zeyer (Hrsg.), *Sanierungshandbuch Wohnungsbau. Probleme, Lösungen, Kosten*, Düsseldorf 1994; Reinhard Gieselmann, *Wohnbau, Entwicklungen. Wohnen, Wohnung, Wohnhaus, Wohnungsbau*, hrsg. von Anna Stern, Düsseldorf 1998.

Roth house, Ludwigshafen-Gartenstadt, 1952/53

A house from a different era. In those days, standards were much less stringent than today. That is why I was asked to design a house that the client, an artist who had become disabled in the war, together with his father, could build largely on their own for himself, his wife (a dressmaker) and a child. They had purchased some land in the suburbs, sloping gently up to the garden.

It was possible to increase the gentle slope of the building site by means of excavation, so that the dressmaker's studio and the guest room could be located in the well-lit lower floor, which faced east towards the street, and on the upper floor a spatial flow for the living area and a large studio could be created. It begins with the sleeping area on the east side and continues – separated only by a curtain – through the living area on the west side around a freestanding fireplace. The fireplace defines the dining area, around which the spatial flow pours fully into the studio with a detour onto the terrace – if the light partition of laths and Japan paper, which lifts up, is not closed. On the opposite – east – side are the utility rooms and the staircase, and next door is the nursery, at a distance that promotes the children's emancipation. The gradients of the easily installed gable roof – a frame of joists (glue laminated beams), with insulation between them, corrugated fiber-reinforced cement (Eternit) over them, and reed mat plaster under them – are visible in the interior as a third dimension that creates space. The pine window elements were replaced by aluminum ones forty-five years later.

Haus Roth, Ludwigshafen-Gartenstadt, 1952/53

Ein Haus aus einer anderen Zeit. Die Ansprüche waren damals weitaus niedriger als heute. Daher war ein Haus zu entwerfen, das der Bauherr, ein kriegsbeschädigter Künstler, mit seinem Vater – für sich, seine Frau (Schneiderin) und ein Kind – größtenteils selbst bauen konnte. Sie hatten ein Vorstadtgrundstück, sanft zum Garten ansteigend, erworben.

Diese leichte Hanglage des Grundstücks ließ sich durch den Aushub verstärken, so daß Schneideratelier und Gastzimmer nach Osten zur Straße im gut belichteten Untergeschoß Platz finden, und im Obergeschoß ein Raumfluß für den Wohnbereich und ein großes Atelier entstehen konnten. Er beginnt mit dem Schlafteil im Osten und setzt sich – nur mit Vorhangtrennung – über den Wohnteil im Westen um den freistehenden Kamin fort. Der fixiert den Eßplatz, um den sich der Raumfluß mit einer Abzweigung auf die Terrasse voll ins Atelier ergießt – wenn die leichte Hebewand aus Latten und Japanpapier nicht geschlossen ist. Gegenüber auf der Ostseite liegen die Naßräume und die Treppe, daneben in emanzipationsförderndem Abstand das Kinderzimmer. Die Neigungen des leicht montierbaren Satteldachs – eine Balkenlage (Leimbinder), dazwischen Wärmedämmung, darauf Welleternit, darunter Rohrmattenputz – sind im Innern als dritte Dimension raumbildend sichtbar. Die Fensterelemente aus Kiefernholz wurden nach 45 Jahren durch solche aus Aluminium ersetzt.

1, 2. Floor plans (lower floor, upper floor).
3. View from the garden.

1, 2. Grundrisse (Untergeschoß, Obergeschoß).
3. Ansicht vom Garten.

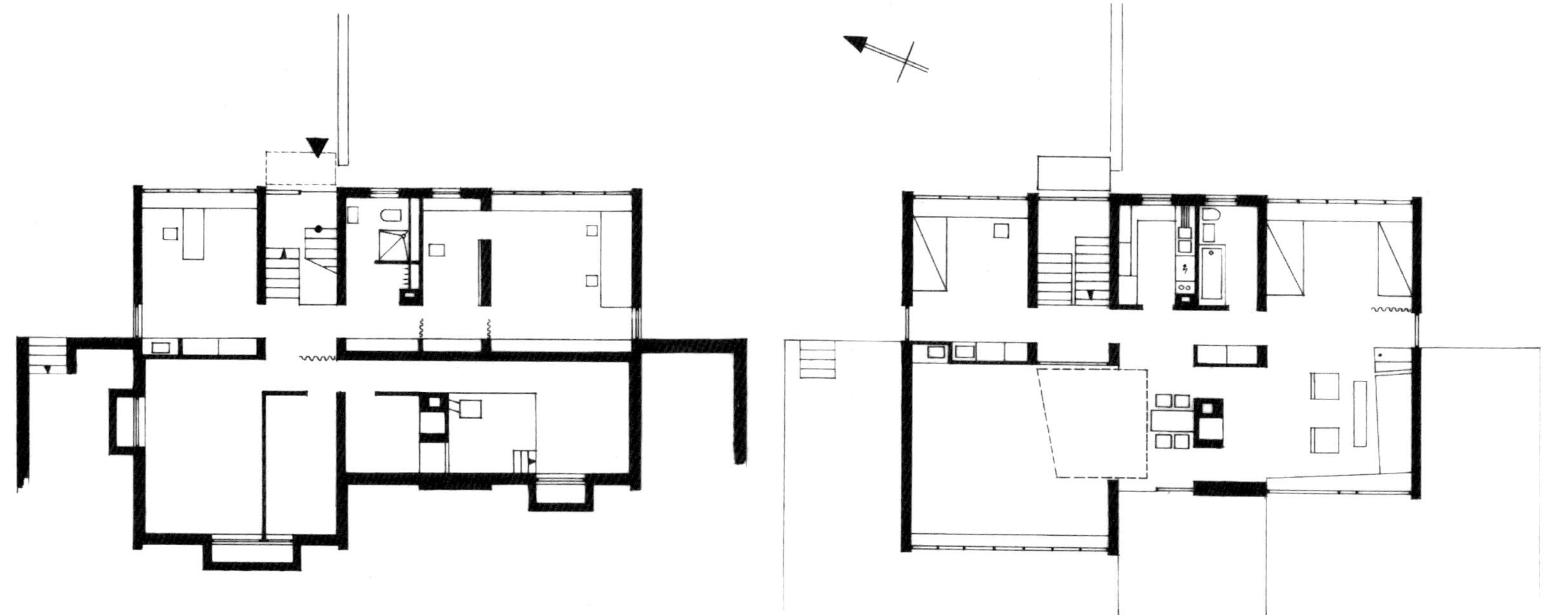

4. Sitting area in front of the fireplace. In the
background is the studio.
5. Section through the building.
6. Sleeping area.
7. Living area.

4. Sitzplatz vor dem offenem Kamin. Im Hintergrund liegt das Atelier.
5. Schnitt durch das Gebäude.
6. Schlafbereich.
7. Wohnbereich.

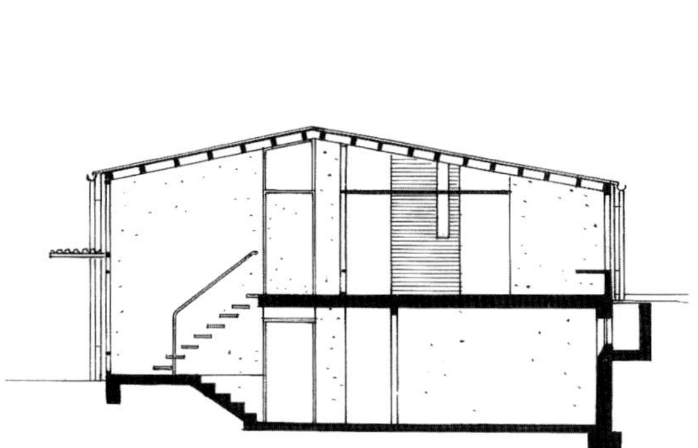

Becker house, Karlsruhe-Durlach, 1957–59

The site has a pronounced slope down toward the street and a lovely view of the mountains. Only the garage is at street level. Walking under the branches of an old apple tree you go up a staircase to the entrance emphasized by a chimney.

A small entryway is the prelude to the sequence of spaces of this one-storey semi-atrium style house. The central living room opens in its full width to the garden courtyard with an adjacent covered terrace on one side. A strong accent between the two is formed by a freestanding open brick fireplace, one of whose walls stands in the rainwater basin (thus uniting the elements of air, fire, and water). In front of this is the fourth increasing sequence of spaces, the part of the garden that is at ground level, and the swimming pool. The shored-up, higher second garden level – with tall plants along the edge – brings to a close the sequence of garden spaces. On the east side the living area is framed by the bedrooms, on the north and west side by the kitchen, side entrance, guest room, and the most secluded room of the house, the home office.

Haus Becker, Karlsruhe-Durlach, 1957–59

Das Grundstück hat ein starkes Gefälle zur Straße und eine schöne Aussicht auf die Berge. Auf Straßenhöhe steht nur die Garage. Unter den Zweigen eines alten Apfelbaums gelangt man über die Treppe zu dem vom Heizungskamin betonten Eingang.

Ein kleiner Vorraum ist der Auftakt für die Steigerung der Räume des eingeschossigen Semiatriumhauses. Dessen zentraler Wohnraum öffnet sich in voller Breite zum Gartenhof mit seitlich anschließender, überdeckter Terrasse. Einen starken Akzent zwischen beiden bildet ein frei- und mit einer Wand im Regenwasserbecken stehender offener Kamin aus Backsteinen (der so die Elemente Luft, Feuer und Wasser vereinigt). Davor eröffnet sich die vierte Raumsteigerung, der ebenerdige Gartenteil mit Schwimmbad. Die abgestützte, höhere zweite Gartenebene – mit hoher Randbepflanzung – schließt die Außenraumfolge ab. Auf der Ostseite wird die Wohnzone von den Schlafzimmern, auf der Nord- und Westseite von Küche, Nebeneingang, Gast- und – in der einsamsten Lage – Studierzimmer des Hausherrn gerahmt.

1. Floor plan.
2. View from the street.
3. View from the garden.

1. Grundriß.
2. Ansicht von der Straße.
3. Ansicht vom Garten.

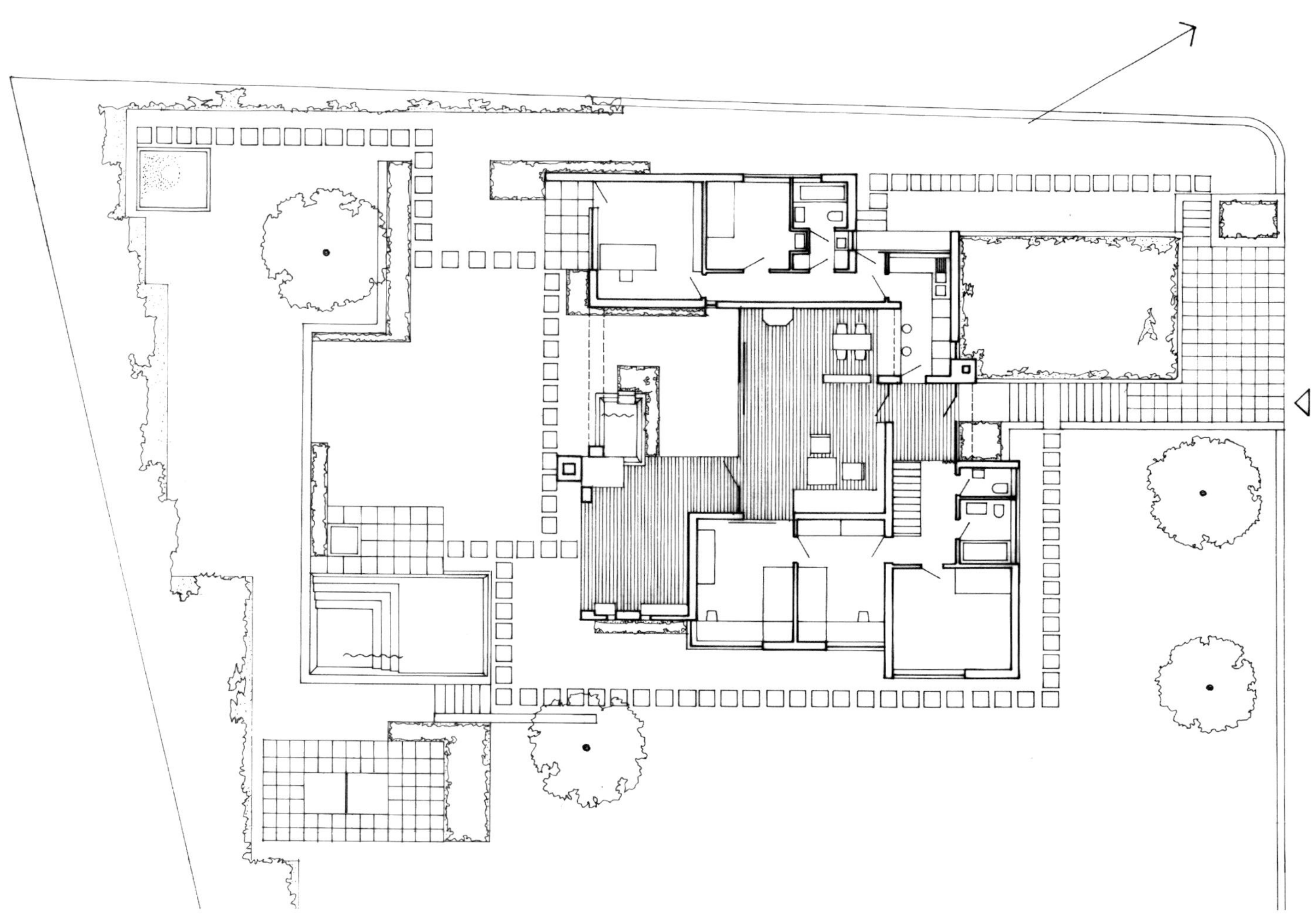

Hanfmann/Herzer house, Karlsruhe-Durlach, 1959–61

A solid walkout basement of locally manufactured dark-brown exposed aggregate concrete, which was also used for the two fireplaces, supports the elegantly contrasted white roughcast cubes of the staggered split-level main floor. The guest rooms are located in the semi-basement next to the staircase. The basement adjoins the semi-basement a little lower down. The half-stairs end on a landing with the kitchen on the east side and – across from the kitchen – a door to a pergola-covered path into the garden and to the children's sandbox at its end. Opposite the stairs to the bedrooms is the entrance to the dining area, made more intimate by the open fireplace, with access to the study on the upper level and to the sunken living room two steps down. The glazed southwest corner of the living room, and the terrace, are screened by a wide projecting roof. The slope adjoining the house on the south side was leveled somewhat, so that the swimming pool and – a little above it – a grassy playground could be laid out in the resulting sunny hollow. There is a contrast between this intimacy of living in the sunshine and the floor with the bedrooms, six steps higher, with its far-ranging view. The floor plan of the bedrooms – unlike the loose arrangement of the living area – is concentrated in a solid square and corbels outwards far over the foundation. It appears to be trying to span the valley that lies before it, and offers a magnificent view, from the slopes of the northern Black Forest to the mountains of the Palatinate.

Haus Hanfmann/Herzer, Karlsruhe-Durlach, 1959–61

Ein solides Sockelgeschoß aus örtlich hergestelltem dunkelbraunem Waschbeton, aus dem auch die beiden Kamine hergestellt wurden, trägt die eher elegant kontrastierenden weiß verputzten Kuben des in sich halbgeschossig versetzten Hauptgeschosses. Im Sockel sind neben der Treppe die Gasträume untergebracht. Etwas tiefer schließt sich der Keller an. Die halbe Treppe endet an einem Vorplatz mit der Küche auf der Ostseite und – ihr gegenüber – einem Ausgang zu einem pergolaüberdeckten Weg in den Garten und zum Kindersandkasten am Ende. Gegenüber den Stufen zu den Schlafzimmern liegt der Eingang zu dem durch den offenen Kamin intimisierten Eßplatz mit Zugang zum Arbeitszimmer auf dem oberen Niveau und zur zwei Stufen tieferen Wohngrube. Deren verglaste Südwestecke und die Terrasse sind mit einem weiten Dachvorsprung abgeschirmt. Der im Süden anschließende Hang wurde ein wenig abgetragen, um in der entstandenen Sonnenmulde das Schwimmbad und – etwas höher – eine Spielwiese anlegen zu können. Zu dieser Intimität des Wohnens an der Sonne kontrastiert das sechs Stufen höhere Schlafgeschoß mit der Sicht in die Weite. Dessen Grundriß ist in einem strengen Quadrat zusammengefaßt – im Gegensatz zu der aufgelockerten Anordnung des Wohnteils – und kragt weit über den Sockel aus. Er scheint das vor ihm liegende Tal überspringen zu wollen und bietet eine großartige Aussicht von den Hängen des Nordschwarzwalds bis zu den Pfälzer Bergen.

1. View from the south.
2, 3. Floor plans (lower floor, upper floor).

1. Ansicht von Süden.
2, 3. Grundrisse (Untergeschoß, Obergeschoß).

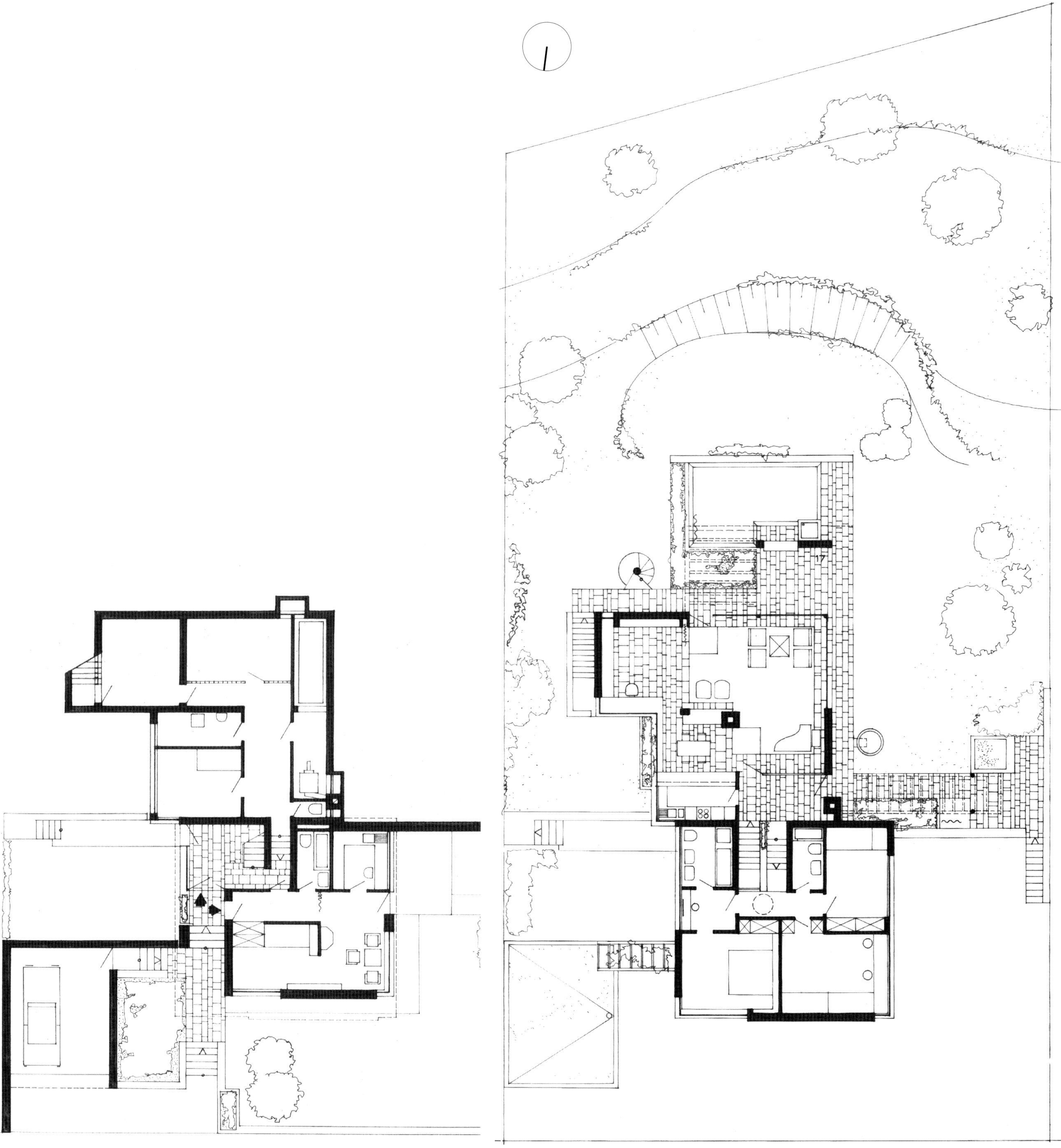

4. View from the east.
5. North–south section through the building.
6. View from the west.
4. Ansicht von Osten.
5. Nord–Süd-Schnitt durch das Gebäude.
6. Ansicht von Westen.

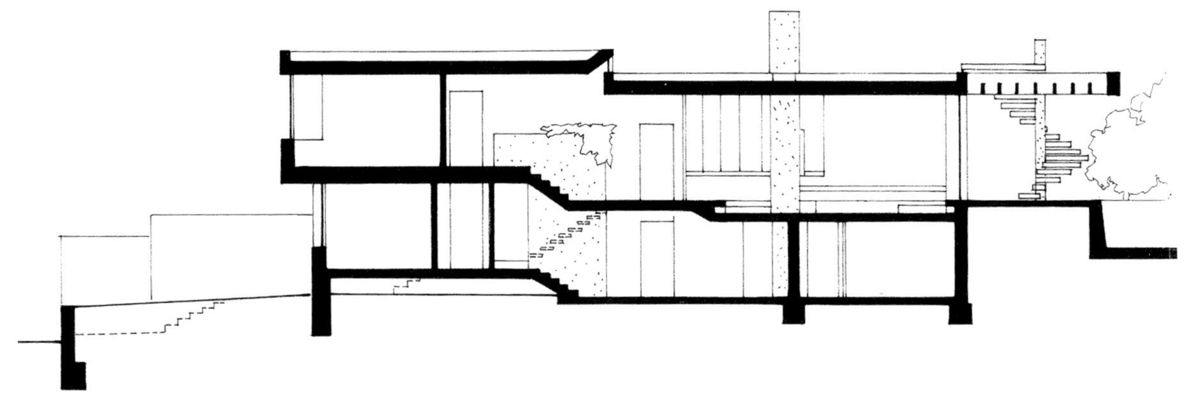

Nees house, Karlsruhe, 1962–64

This fixed point at a street corner was the result
of a large-scale project for a small site. Closest to
the corner is the entrance to the office of the general practitioner. Three steps up is the entrance to
the stair tower and to the private apartment, set
apart somewhat by a projecting structure. Only
the kitchen and the two-storey dining area of the
main apartment are located on the ground floor.
The dining area and the staircase connect the dining area to the living room on the first floor via a
two-storey space. Going down three steps, one
reaches the doctor's office from the dining area.
The location of the living room and the terrace in
front of it was due not only to the fact that the
available building site was narrow, but also to the
westward view of the city and landscape. The parents' and children's bedrooms are on the same
level, but face east. On the third floor there is an
independent apartment for relatives, which also
has a large terrace.

   The house was bought by an architect who
insulated the exterior walls and used the office
space for his four children.

**Haus Nees, Karlsruhe-Grötzingen, 1962
to 1964**

Ergebnis eines großen Programms für ein kleines
Grundstück war dieser Festpunkt an der Stra-
ßenecke. Ihr am nächsten liegt der Zugang zur
Praxis des praktischen Arztes. Drei Stufen höher
ist der Eingang zum Treppenturm und zur Privat-
wohnung durch einen Baukörpervorsprung ein
wenig abgesondert. Im Erdgeschoß liegen nur die
Küche und der zweigeschossige Eßraum der
Hauptwohnung. Der Luftraum des Eßraums und
die Treppe verbinden diesen mit dem Wohnraum
im ersten Obergeschoß. Über drei Stufen nach
unten kommt man vom Eßplatz in die Praxis. Die
Lage des Wohnraums mit der vorgelagerten Terrasse ergab sich nicht nur aus der Enge des zur
Verfügung stehenden Grundstücks, sondern vor
allem wegen der Aussicht nach Westen auf Stadt
und Landschaft. Die Eltern- und Kinderschlafzim-
mer liegen auf derselben Ebene, aber nach Osten
orientiert. In einem weiteren Geschoß ist eine
unabhängige Wohnung für Verwandte untergebracht, der ebenfalls eine große Terrassenfläche
zugeordnet wurde.

   Ein Architekt kaufte das Haus, isolierte die Außenwände und verwendete die Praxis für seine
vier Kinder.

3. View from the east.
4–7. East–west section and floor plans (ground
floor, 1st floor, 2nd floor).

3. Ansicht von Osten.
4–7. Ost–West-Schnitt und Grundrisse (Erdgeschoß, 1. Obergeschoß, 2. Obergeschoß).

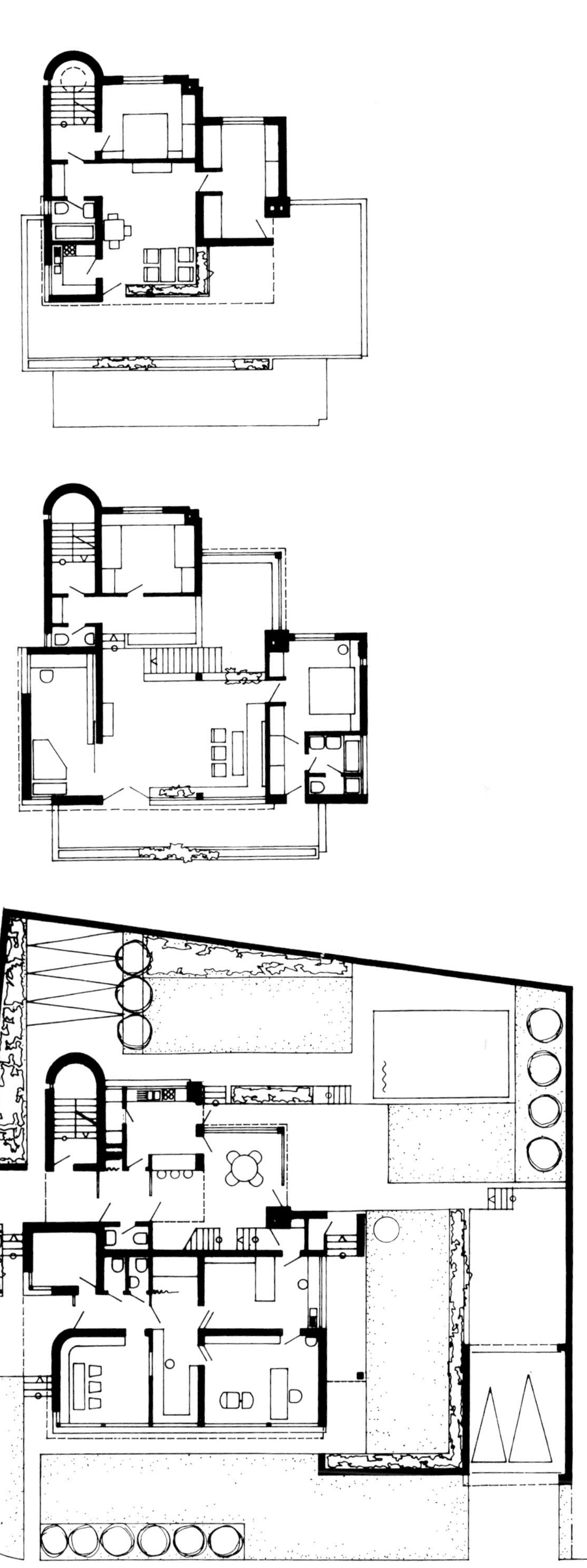

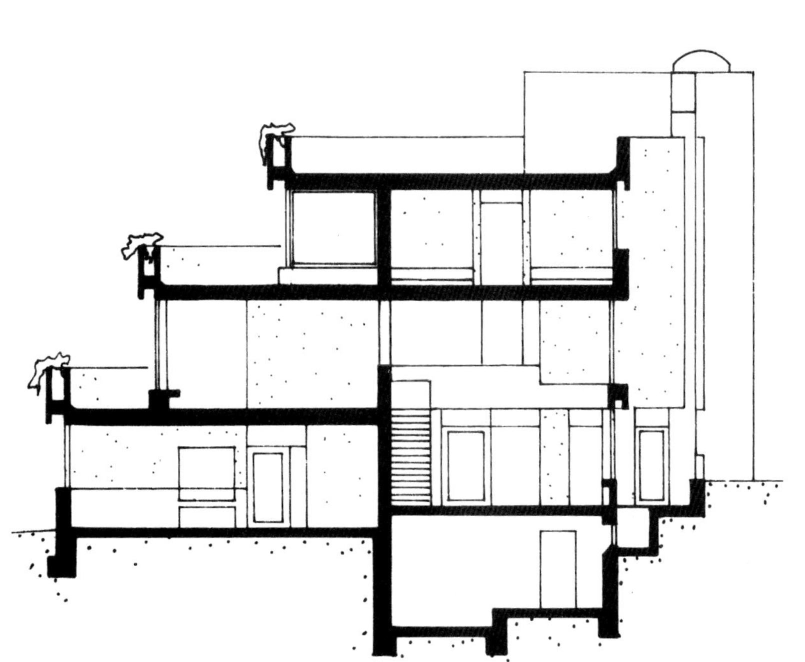

Schulte-Frohlinde house, Karlsruhe-Grötzingen, 1963–66, 1977–80, 1983–85

Thirty steps above the street and garage, the site becomes suitable for building purposes. The stair tower marks the corner of the angular projection that encloses the level surface of the building site. The living room – which has an open fireplace and is fully glazed on the south and west sides – together with the adjoining, secluded study and the partiallly covered terrace forms one side of the angle, which is directly adjoined on the south side by the dining area next to the kitchen. Here there is a door to the hallway leading to the bedrooms, which widens into the children's play area with a terrace in front of it.

The common areas were covered with a higher, flat, wooden roof, stained brown. The rest of the rooms are roughcast lower masonry cubes with a flat concrete roof which are partly »pushed« under the higher wooden roof. This was meant to parallel the contrast between intimate experience and the experience of community on a spatial level as well – quite apart from the fact that such spatial proportions are hardly ever used in the building of homes anymore. After the house was sold, this structure was expanded without problems by adding a bedroom and an enlarged play area.

In the basement, in addition to the cellar rooms, extra space has been planned next to the entrance for adding on a two-room apartment.

Haus Schulte-Frohlinde, Karlsruhe-Grötzingen, 1963–66, 1977–80, 1983–85

Dreißig Stufen über Straße und Garage wird das Grundstück bebaubar. Der Treppenturm markiert die Ecke des Winkelgrundrisses, der die ebene Grundstücksfläche umschließt. Der Wohnraum – mit offenem Kamin und voll verglast nach Süden und Westen – bildet mit dem anschließenden, abgelegenen Arbeitszimmer und der teilüberdeckten Terrasse den einen Schenkel, an den sich nach Süden direkt der Eßplatz neben der Küche anschließt. Hier erschließt eine Tür den Schlafzimmerflur, der sich zum Kinderspielplatz mit davorliegender Terrasse erweitert.

Die gemeinschaftlichen Flächen wurden mit einem höheren, braun imprägnierten Holzflachdach überdeckt, die übrigen Räume sind gemauerte und verputzte niedrigere Kuben mit Betonflachdach, die teilweise unter das höhere Holzdach »geschoben« sind. Damit sollte der Kontrast zwischen dem Intimerlebnis und dem Gemeinschaftserlebnis auch räumlich nachvollzogen werden – ganz abgesehen von den im Wohnungsbau kaum mehr geübten Raumproportionen. Diese Struktur wurde nach dem Verkauf ohne Probleme um ein Schlafzimmer und einen vergrößerten Spielflur erweitert.

Im Untergeschoß wurde außer den Kellerräumen neben dem Eingang eine Reserverfläche für den Ausbau einer Zweizimmerwohnung vorgesehen.

1, 2. Floor plans (lower floor, upper floor).
3. View from the west.

1, 2. Grundrisse (Untergeschoß, Obergeschoß).
2. Ansicht von Westen.

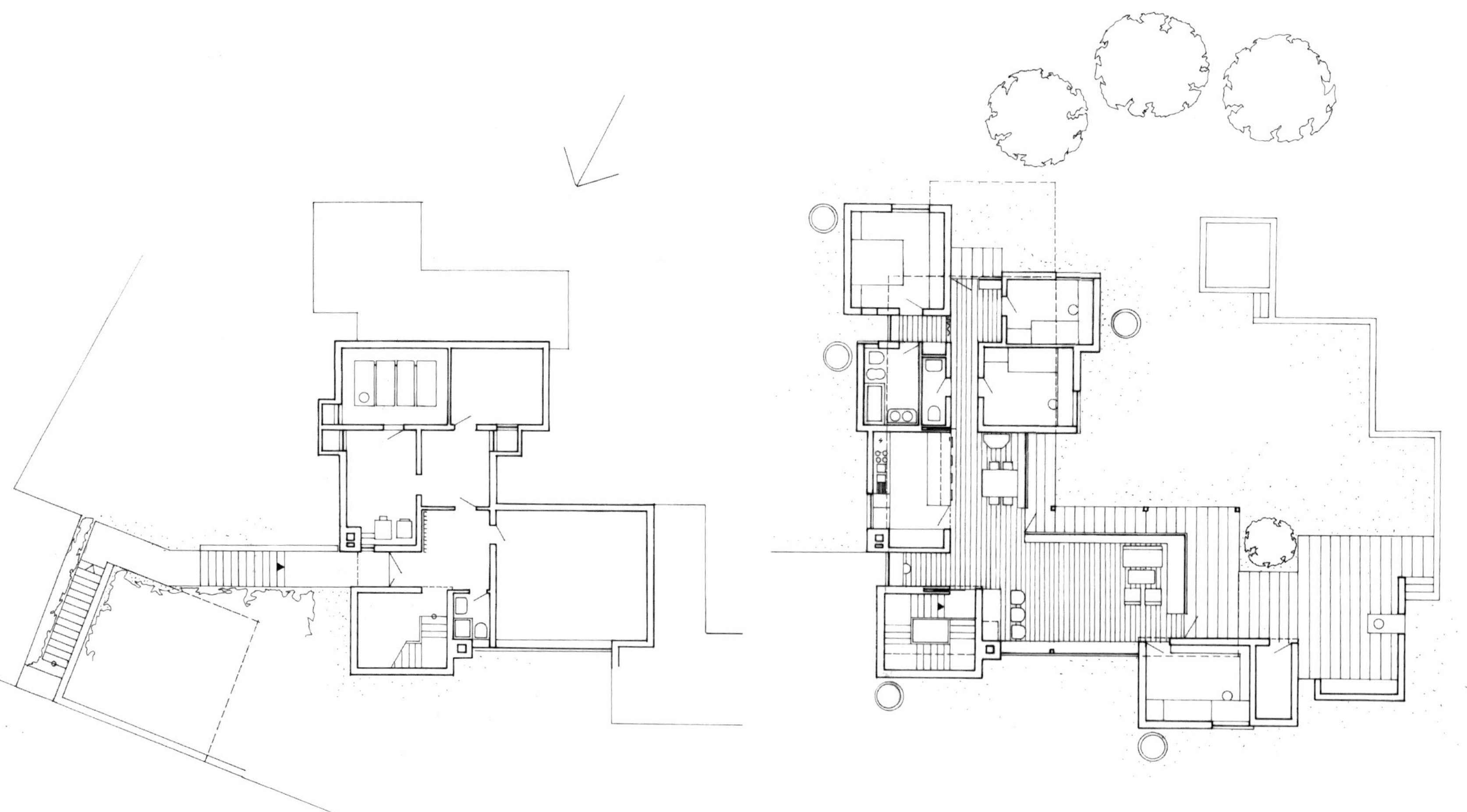

4. View from the south-west.
5. Living room with fireplace.
6. Kitchen with dining bar.

4. Ansicht von Südwesten.
5. Wohnraum mit offenem Kamin.
6. Küche mit Eßbar.

Häfele house, Karlsruhe, 1963–66

The land slopes with a 40 percent gradient, yet
opposite it there is a vineyard with ever-changing
colors, and in the west there is a view of the
mountainous scenery of the Palatinate. This was
to be the new home of a scientist, his wife, and
three children. The goal was to show that the
house belonged in the landscape (as far as possible without using bulldozers that would do vio-
lence to the locality) – and this was achieved by
placing the building parallel to the upper road and
by having the slope of the roof parallel to the gradient of the way. Each of the children got one of
the rectangular rooms with the staggered windows that looked out on the vineyard; adjoining
these is the study, the same size, but looking out
over the valley and the town – at the same level,
but not as high as the large protruding five-cornered living room, which in turn has a somewhat
different view and a window that faces east,
receiving the first ray of the sun, which shines
through the entire building as far as the parents'
bedroom at the other end. The latter has a window for watching the sunset over the valley, while
the bathroom has one for watching the sunrise.
The living room overhangs the entrance as well as
the kitchen and the dining area, plus a large part
of the built-out terrace. Under the bedrooms is the
basement, which has windows and can be used
as a play area and for other purposes. Below the
basement, its claws dug into the hill, is the foundation frame. A serpentine road winds down to
the garage – buried in the hill, yet at the end of a
street.

Haus Häfele, Karlsruhe-Durlach, 1963–66

Ein Hang mit 40 Prozent Gefälle, doch gegenüber
liegt ein Weinberg mit wechselnden Farben, und
nach Westen bietet sich die Aussicht auf das Pfälzer Bergland. Für die Familie eines Wissenschaftlers mit drei Kindern sollte dieses Haus zur neuen
Heimat werden. Also war die Zugehörigkeit zum
Ort sichtbar zu machen (möglichst ohne den Ort
vergewaltigende Bulldozer) – versucht durch die
Einordnung des Baukörpers parallel zum oberen
Weg und durch die Dachneigung parallel zur Weg-
steigung. Jedes Kind bekam einen der rechteckigen Räume mit den gestaffelten, auf den Weinberg ausgerichteten Fenstern; im Anschluß daran
das Arbeitszimmer, genauso groß, aber mit Blick
ins Tal mit der Stadt – auf gleicher Höhe, aber
nicht so hoch wie der dicke Kopf des fünfeckigen
Wohnraums, der wieder eine etwas andere Aussicht hat, dazu ein Fenster nach Osten zum ersten
Sonnenstrahl, der durch den ganzen Bau geht bis
zum Elternschlafzimmer am anderen Ende. Dieses
hat ein Fenster zum Sonnenuntergang über dem
Tal und eines zum Sonnenaufgang. Der Wohnraum überdeckt auskragend den Eingang, dazu
die Küche und den Eßplatz und einen Großteil der
vorgebauten Terrasse. Unter den Schlafzimmern
liegt der bespiel- und sonstig nutzbare, befenster-
te Keller, darunter – verkrallt in den Berg der Fun-
damentrahmen. Ein Serpentinenweg führt nach
unten zur Garage – vergraben im Berg, doch am
Ende einer Straße.

1. Site plan with sight line to the town.
2. View from the north.

1. Lageplan mit Sichtlinie zur Stadt.
2. Ansicht von Norden.

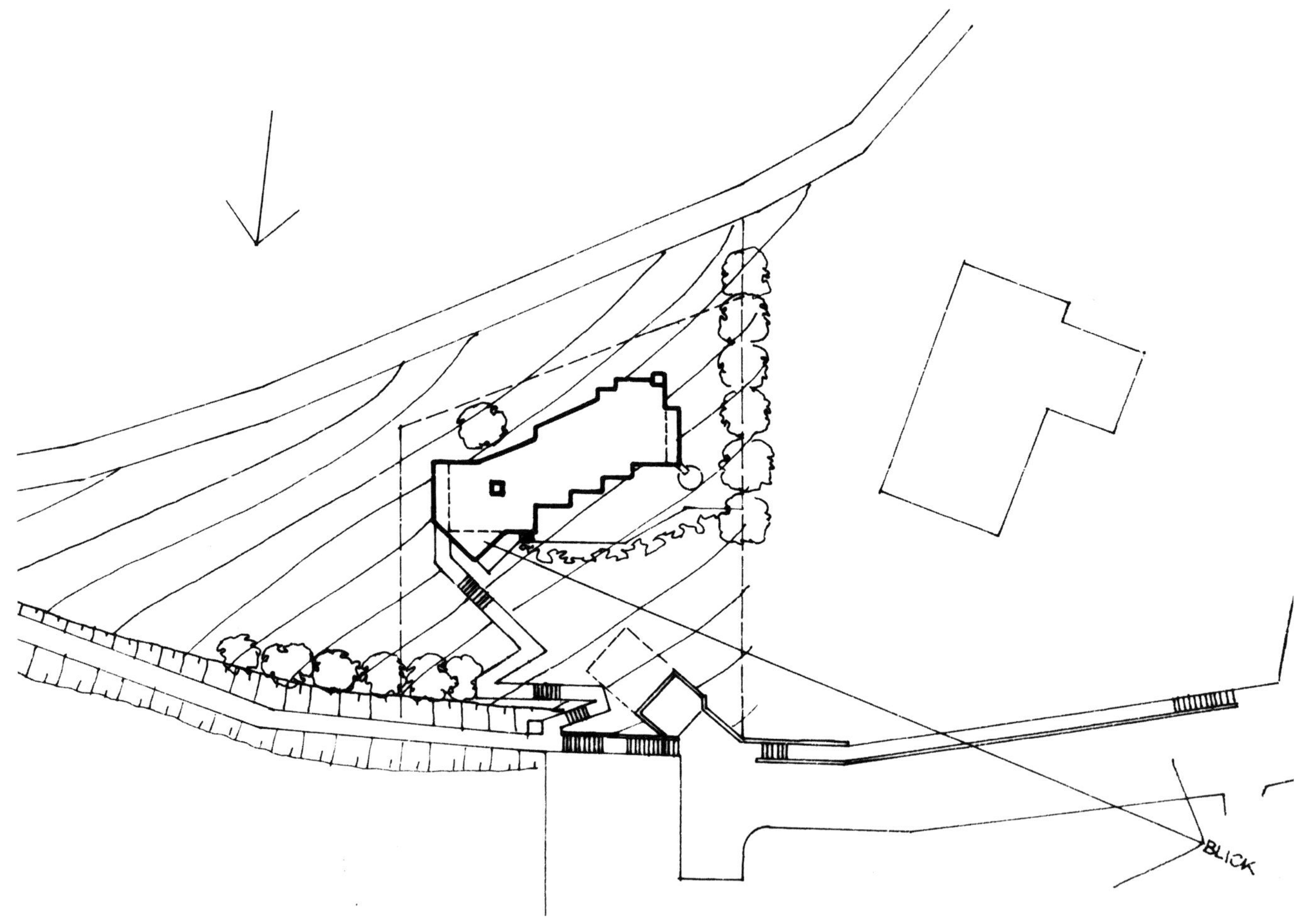

3. View from the east.
4. View from the south-east.
5–7. Floor plans (lower floor, upper floor) and
north–south section.

3. Ansicht von Osten.
4. Ansicht von Südosten.
5–7. Grundrisse (Untergeschoß, Obergeschoß)
und Nord–Süd-Schnitt.

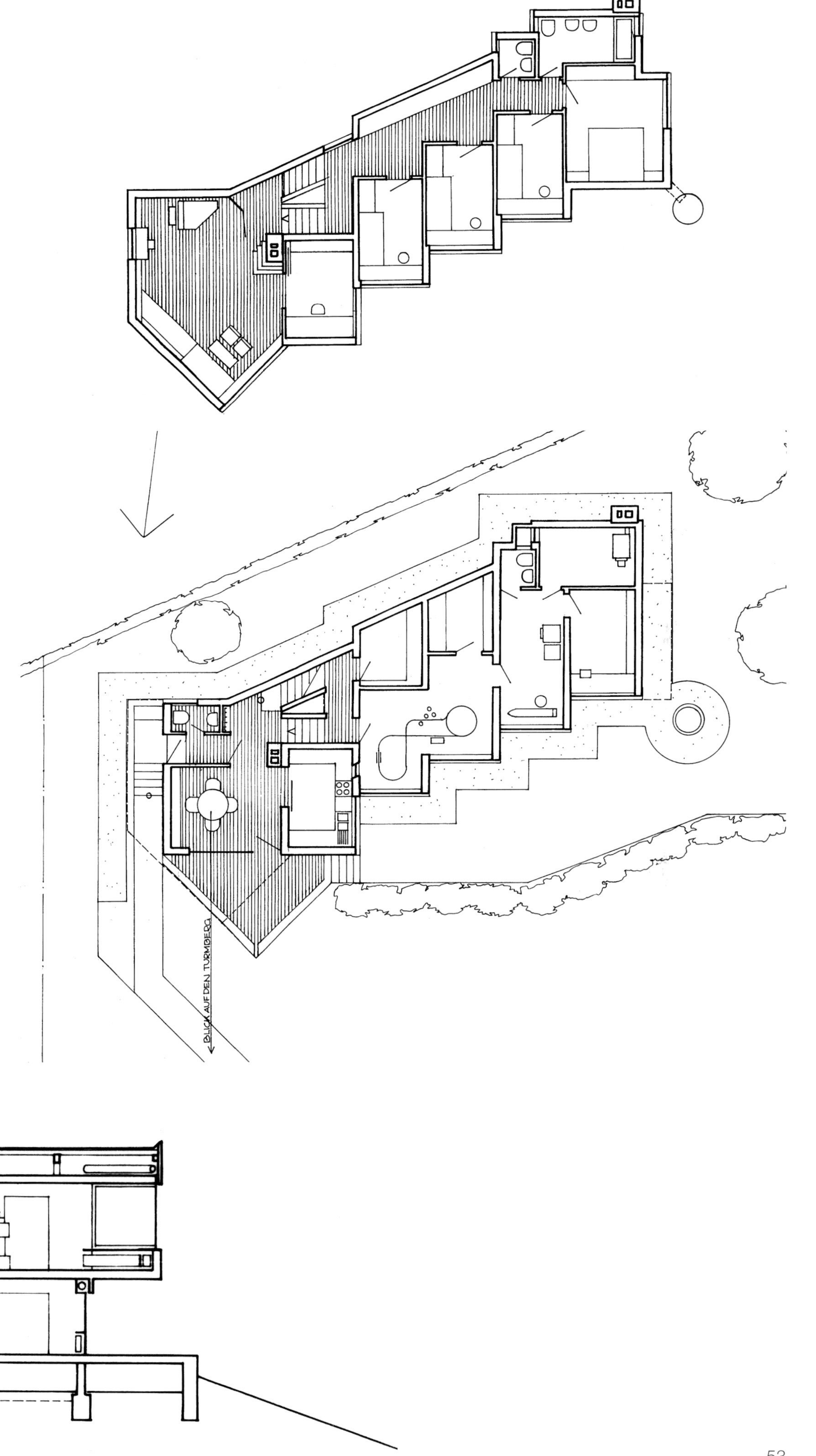

BLICK AUF DEN TURMBERG

Lankheit house, Karlsruhe-Durlach, 1964/65

This house, built on a long, narrow site, has a cruciform floor plan. At the point of intersection of one axis (entrance–garden gate) and the other axis (nursery hallway– living room) upstairs and the parents' suite below is the gathering point of the family in the center: the dining area. The latter can easily be moved outside by opening the door to the roofed terrace. The terrace in turn is located in the longitudinal center point of the narrow garden. So much for the influence of the architect on the life of the family ...

The sloping site, which drops away from the street, is counteracted by the surface of the roof, which slopes the other way. The roof rises without interruption over the entire longitudinal direction of the house. This is how the best vantage position was achieved for the split-level living room, located above the main level and giving a north view of the town and across the Rhine. Next to the living room, somewhat secluded, is the scientist's study, with a view of the mountains in the east. Below this level there is the parents' bedroom suite with its own bath and ground level exit into the garden. At the south end of the staggered hallway with the children's rooms, there is direct access to the play area and a hobby and craft courtyard next to the garage.

Building materials used were dark brown clinker bricks for the walls and pinewood for ceiling work and eaves.

Haus Lankheit, Karlsruhe-Durlach, 1964/65

Dieses Haus auf einem langen, schmalen Grundstück hat einen Kreuzgrundriß. Im Schnittpunkt von der einen Achse Eingang–Gartenausgang und der anderen Achse Kinderzimmerflur–Wohnraum oben und Elternappartement darunter liegt in der Mitte der Sammelpunkt der Familie: der Eßplatz. Diesen kann man leicht durch Türöffnung im Sommer nach draußen auf die überdeckte Terrasse verlegen. Sie ihrereseits liegt im Längsmittelpunkt des schmalen Gartens. Soweit der Einfluß des Architekten auf das Familienleben ...

Das von der Straße abfallende Hanggrundstück wird durch die gegengeneigte Dachfläche konterkariert. Sie steigt über die ganze Längsrichtung des Hauses ohne Unterbrechung an. Dadurch wurde die beste Aussichtsposition für den Wohnraum erreicht, der halbgeschossig über der Hauptebene liegt und den Blick nach Norden auf die Stadt bis über den Rhein freigibt. Neben dem Wohnraum liegt – etwas abgesondert – das Arbeitszimmer des Wissenschaftlers mit Blick nach Osten auf das Gebirge. Unter dieser Ebene ist das Schlafappartement der Eltern mit eigenem Bad und ebenerdigem Ausgang zum Garten angeordnet. Am Südende des gestaffelten Kinderzimmerflurs kann man direkt den Spiel- und Bastelhof neben der Garage betreten.

Als Baumaterialien wurden dunkelbraune Klinker für Wände und Kiefernholz für Deckenschalungen und Dachvorsprünge verwendet.

1. View from the east with the brick façade originally unplastered.
2. View from the west with the brick façade covered with plaster today.

1. Ansicht von Osten mit der ursprünglich unverputzten Backsteinfassade.
2. Ansicht von Westen mit der heute verputzten Backsteinfassade.

3, 4. View of the dining space from the living room in a drawing by the architect and in its present state.
5–7. Floor plans (lower floor, upper floor) and section.

3, 4. Blick vom Wohnraum auf den Eßplatz in einer Zeichnung des Architekten und im heutigen Zustand.
5–7. Grundrisse (Untergeschoß, Obergeschoß) und Schnitt.

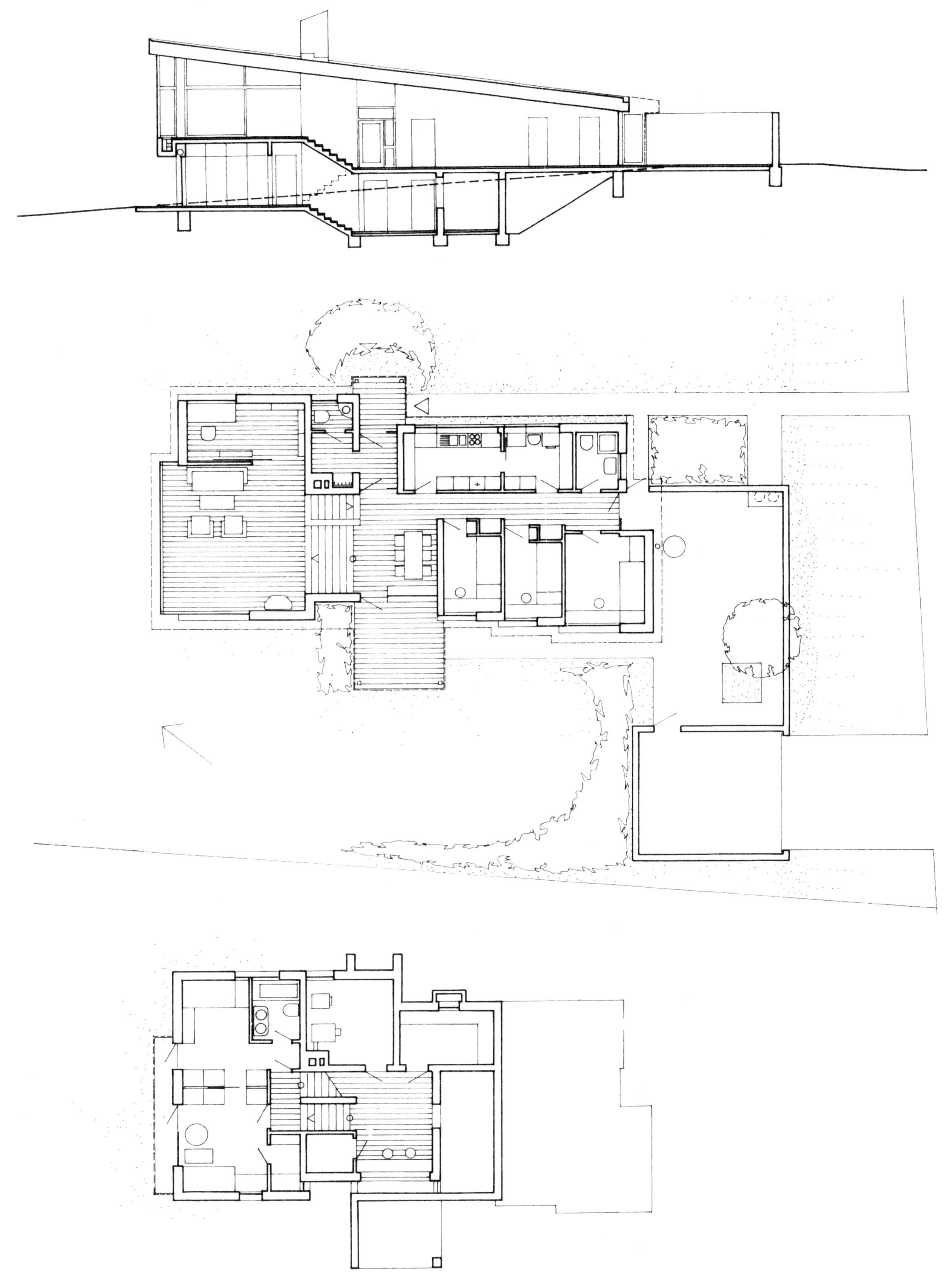

Z. house, Karlsruhe, 1964–67

At the point of intersection of the cruciform floor plan is the empty center, where one has to decide: whether to choose a wide-open space, the living room, which looks out on a panoramic landscape, with its grand piano and books, a door to the terrace, a fireplace, and the study of the master of the house – or the space of intimacy: the dining area which looks out into the walled courtyard or – opposite – the space of distance: the gallery hallway, which grows perspectively narrower between the bedrooms, after which one can look at the collection of paintings and then go down the staircase to the garden, or else enter the normal corridor between the housekeeping rooms and the guest rooms.

The walls are sand-lime bricks which are insulated and plastered on the outside and faced on the inside; the concrete ceilings are paneled with wood from below, the floors are granite, and the swimming pool, which is at garden level, is tiled. A sun deck of wood block paving is placed in front of the swimming pool. The open fireplace paraphrases the style of the house.

The garden was designed by Gunnar Martinsson. The house is dedicated to Frank Lloyd Wright. It was he who invented the cruciform floor plan, but – in contrast to this house – put the the open fireplace in the center of the house.

Haus Z., Karlsruhe-Durlach, 1964–67

Im Schnittpunkt des Kreuzgrundrisses liegt die leere Mitte, wo man sich entscheiden muß: ob man den großen Raum der Weite wählt, den zum Landschaftspanorama geöffneten Wohnraum mit dem Flügel und den Büchern, dem Ausgang zur Terrasse mit Kamin und dem Arbeitszimmer des Hausherrn – oder den Raum der Nähe: den zum ummauerten Hof orientierten Eßplatz oder – gegenüber diesem – den Raum der Ferne: den zwischen den Schlafzimmern perspektivisch sich verengenden Galerieflur, um die Bildersammlung anzuschauen und dann die Treppe zum Garten hinabzusteigen oder aber den Normalflur zwischen den Haushaltsräumen und den Gastzimmern zu betreten.

Die Wände sind außen gedämmte und verputzte und innen sichtgemauerte Kalksandsteine, die Betondecken sind von unten holzverschalt, die Böden aus Granit, das Schwimmbad, das auf Gartenhöhe liegt, wurde verfliest. Eine Sonnenterrasse aus Holzpflaster ist dem Schwimmbad vorgelagert. Der offene Kamin ist eine Paraphrase auf den Stil des Hauses.

Den Garten gestaltete Gunnar Martinsson. Das Haus ist Frank Lloyd Wright gewidmet. Er hat den Kreuzgrundriß erfunden, aber die Mitte – im Gegensatz zu diesem Haus – mit dem offenen Kamin akzentuiert.

1. View from the south.
2. Detailed view from the north-west of the terrace with fireplace and the living room to the right.

1. Ansicht von Süden.
2. Detailansicht von Nordwesten auf die Terrasse mit offenem Kamin und den Wohnraum zur Rechten.

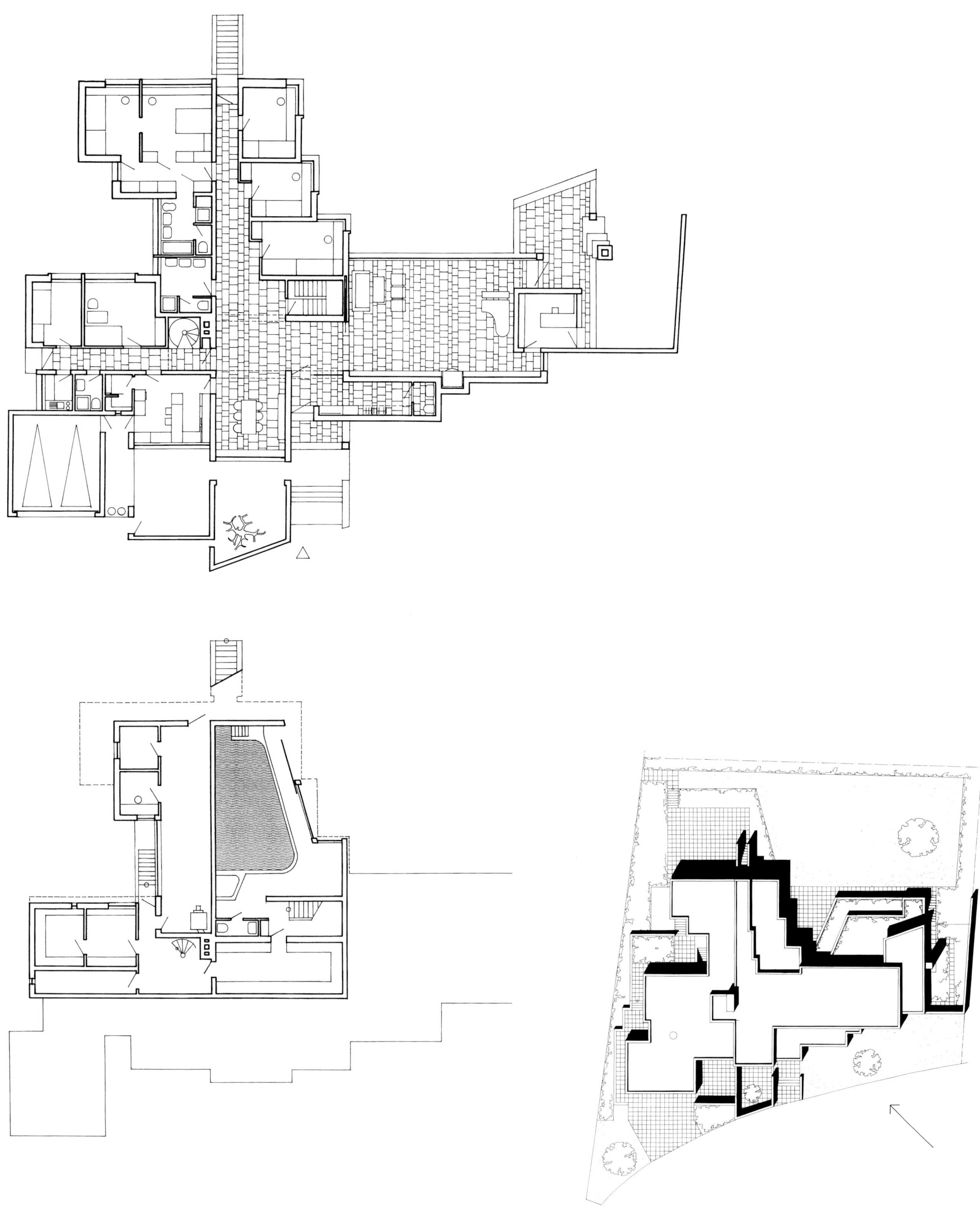

3–5. Floor plans (lower floor, upper floor) and site plan.
6. View from the north-east with the living room in the center and the terrace with the open fireplace to the left.

3–5. Grundrisse (Untergeschoß, Obergeschoß) und Lageplan.
6. Ansicht von Nordosten mit dem Wohnraum im Zentrum und der Terrasse mit offenem Kamin auf der linken Seite.

7. Living room looking towards the kitchen
and bedroom wing.
8. Swimming pool on the lower floor.
9. Corridor in the bedroom wing.

7. Wohnraum in Richtung Küchen- und Schlafraumtrakt.
8. Schwimmbad im Untergeschoß.
9. Flur im Schlafraumtrakt.

Rödiger house, Umkirch, 1968–71, project

Here – from an architect's perspective – the right
angle, which was de rigueur among the first rep-
resentatives of modernism, including the de Stijl
group, is contrasted with the quadrant. The round
»corner« here is given the task of livening up spatial compositions, leading visitors inside, toning
things down, and making the building more
vibrant.

Visitors enter the one-storey house between
the guiding wall of the garage and the curve, are
encouraged by the wardrobe to enter the guest
room that is next to it or go past another guiding
curve into the west- and south-facing living room,
which has a writing space and an open fireplace –
that can also be fueled from the terrace in front of
it. The swinging door to the left of the aforemen-
tioned visually leading curve takes visitors into the
dining room and kitchen, then around the corner
of the swimming pool, which is lit and heated by a
large glass roof, and along the pool to the hallway
with bedrooms that face east. At the end of the
hallway is the parents' bedroom suite with access
to the covered terrace in front of the living room.

The plans for this house, which were fully
accepted by the client – planned for a level site
between other houses – was doomed to remain
just a (beautiful) dream.

Haus Rödiger, Umkirch, 1968–71, Projekt

Hier ist – architektonisch gesehen – der rechte
Winkel, welcher nicht nur bei den ersten Modernen der De-Stijl-Gruppe Absolutheit beanspruch-
te, in Kontrast zu einem Viertelkreis gesetzt. Die
runde »Ecke« bekommt hier die Aufgabe, Leben
in die Raumkompositionen zu bringen, verbindlich
Leitgesten zu übernehmen, entschärfend zu wirken und den Bau lebendiger zu machen.

Der Besucher betritt das eingeschossige Haus
zwischen Garagenleitwand und Kurve, wird von
der Garderobe animiert, das daneben liegende
Gastzimmer zu betreten, oder kommt an einer
zweiten Leitkurve vorbei in den nach Westen und
Süden orientierten Wohnraum mit Schreibplatz
und offenem Kamin – der auch von der davor liegenden Terrasse aus zu befeuern ist. Hätte er die
Pendeltür links von der erwähnten Leitkurve ge-
öffnet, wäre er in den Eßraum und die Küche ge-
kommem und um die Ecke des Schwimmbads
herum, das durch ein Glasdach belichtet und
erwärmt wird, und an ihm entlang in den Schlafzimmerflur mit den Zimmern nach Osten. Am
Ende liegt das Schlafappartement der Eltern mit
Zugang zu der überdeckten Terrasse vor dem
Wohnraum.

Der von der Bauherrnschaft voll akzeptierte
Hausentwurf – zwischen anderen Häusern auf
einem ebenen Grundstück geplant – blieb leider
ein (schöner) Traum.

1. Roof plan.
2. Floor plan.
3. Garden elevation.

1. Dachaufsicht.
2. Grundriß.
3. Aufriß der Gartenseite.

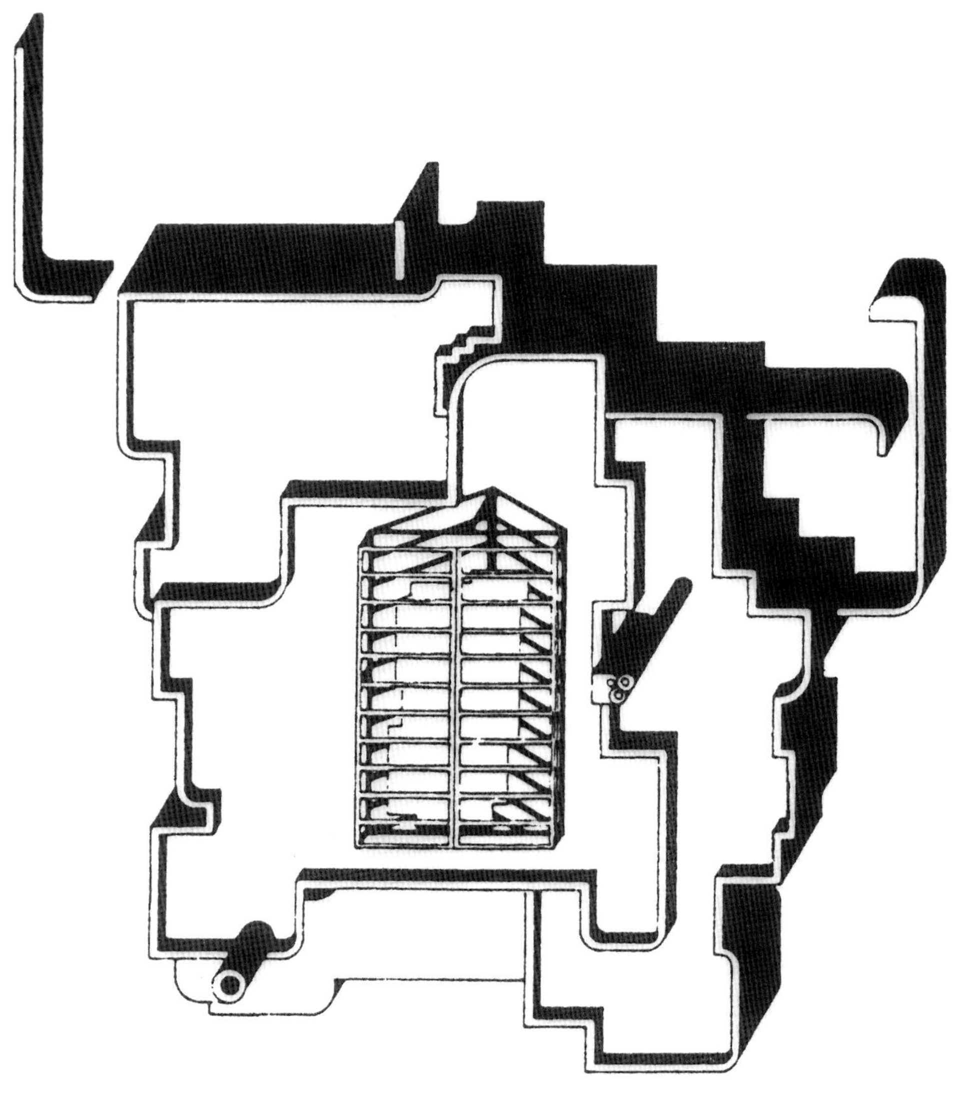

Strasse
Sträucher
Sträucher
Parkplatz
Bodendecker
Magnolie
Hecke
Baugrenze
Haupteingang
Bodendecker
5.80
Gartengeräte
Grube
BA
Garage
Müll
Küche
BA
Bad-G
Gard.
Diele
Esszimmer
Besen
Hausarbeitsraum
Küchenhof
Gast
BA
Küchenflur
Nebeneingang
Schreibplatz
Öltankentlüft. u. Einfüllst.
BA
WC
Gästedusche
Bad-M
BA
Mädchen
S
Baugrenze
Liegebank
FS
BA
BA
Kind 1
Wohnraum
BA
Bad-K.
Schwimmhalle
Kind 2
Grundstücksgrenze
Kamin
Bad-E.
BA
Überdachte Terrasse
Eltern
Grundstücksgrenze
Baugrenze
Baugrenze
Wendeltreppe zum Dach

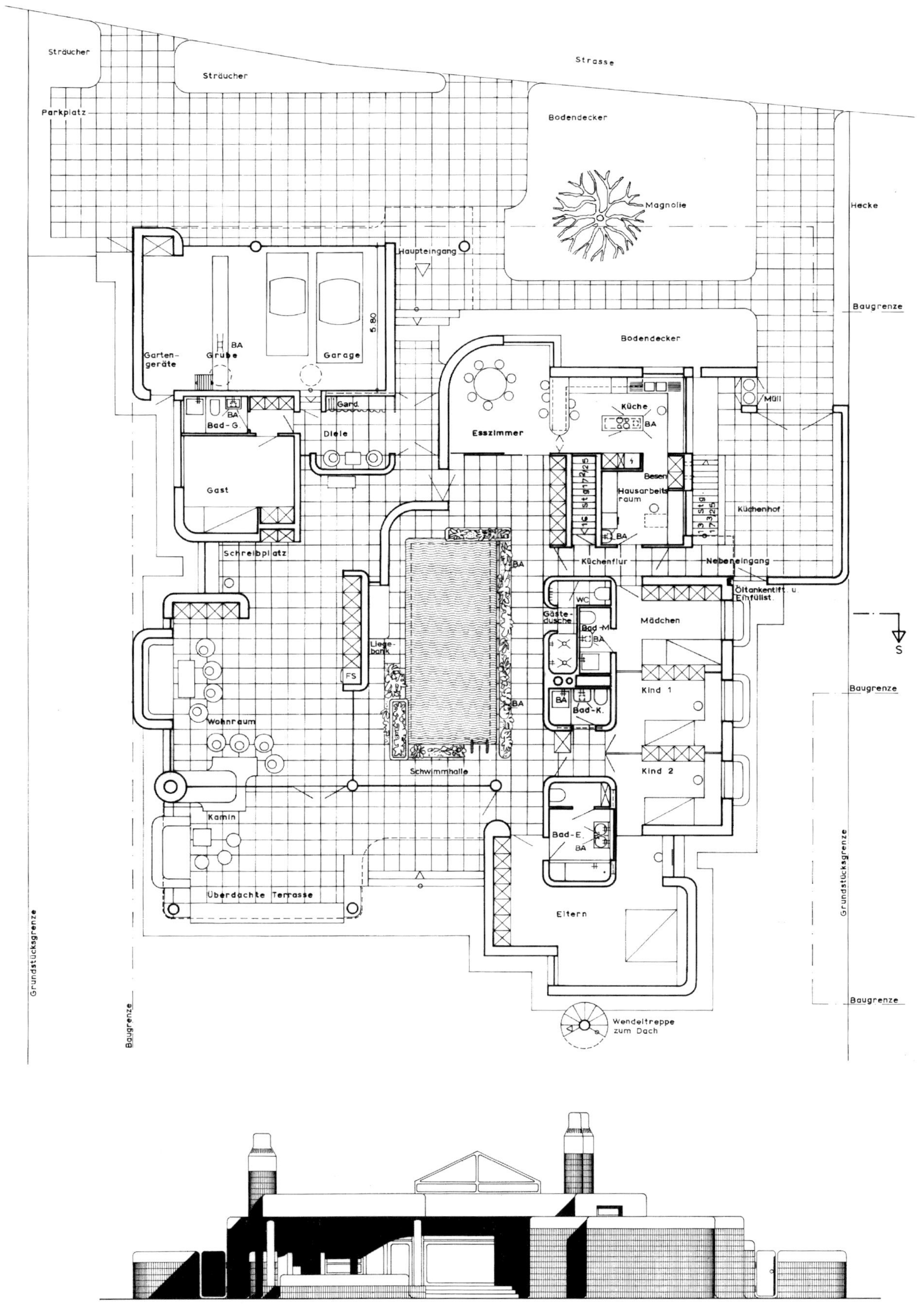

Gieselmann residence and studio, Wien-Neustift, 1971–74

The house differs from the other houses because its form is compact – the square floor plan was a result of the narrow site. Because it is located on a slope, it is constructed on six levels. The entrance hall also opens into the guest and basement rooms. At its end it receives light through the swimming pool, which has a glass roof and is built in front of the garden frontage. Halfway up is the spacious, high-ceilinged studio and a small writing gallery. The main level consists of a kitchen, dining area with stairs to the library gallery, living room, parents' bedroom suite with stairs to the studio and a ladder to the swimming pool (in the closet) and the adjacent rooms on the closet corridor, with an exit door to the garden. In front of the living room there is a basin for goldfish and toads. The terrace next to it, paved with flagstones, is walled off against the slope with a low retaining wall. The garden with a larger pond for frogs and salamanders is on a rising slope and is bordered by the edge of the Wienerwald. To give the children more freedom, access to the children's floor is from the main stairway and from the living room by way of the library.

The blue guiding wall of the stairs, which curves into the entryway, the cylindrical blue fireplace between the living and dining room, and the alternation of high- and low-ceilinged rooms with horizontal and sloping ceilings are part of the irrational mix of the building's rational potential.

Wohn- und Atelierhaus Gieselmann, Wien-Neustift, 1971–74

Das Haus unterscheidet sich von den anderen Häusern durch seine kompakte Form – der quadratische Grundriß ergab sich durch das enge Grundstück. Es ist wegen der Hanglage in sechs Ebenen angelegt. Die Eingangshalle erschließt auch die Gast- und Kellerräume. An ihrem Ende bekommt sie Licht durch das mit einem Glasdach vor die Gartenfront gebaute Schwimmbad. Auf halber Höhe liegt das hohe Atelier mit einer kleinen Schreibgalerie. Die Hauptebene besteht aus Küche, Eßplatz mit Treppe zu Bibliotheksgalerie, Wohnraum, Elternappartement mit Treppe zum Atelier und Leiter zum Schwimmbad (im Schrank) und den Nebenräumen am Schrankflur mit Gartenausgang. Vor dem Wohnraum liegt ein Wasserbecken für Goldfische und Kröten. Die anschließende, mit Pflastersteinen belegte Terrasse ist mit einer niedrigen Stützmauer gegen den Hang abgegrenzt. Der Garten mit größerem Teich für Frösche und Molche steigt an und wird vom Saum des Wienerwalds begrenzt. Emanzipationshalber ist das Kindergeschoß von der Haupttreppe und vom Wohnraum über die Bibliothek erreichbar.

Die in die Eingangshalle gebogene, blaue Treppenleitwand, der zylindrische blaue Kamin zwischen Wohn- und Eßraum und der Wechsel von hohen und niedrigen Räumen mit waagerechten und schrägen Decken gehört zur irrationalen Aufmischung des rationalen Potentials.

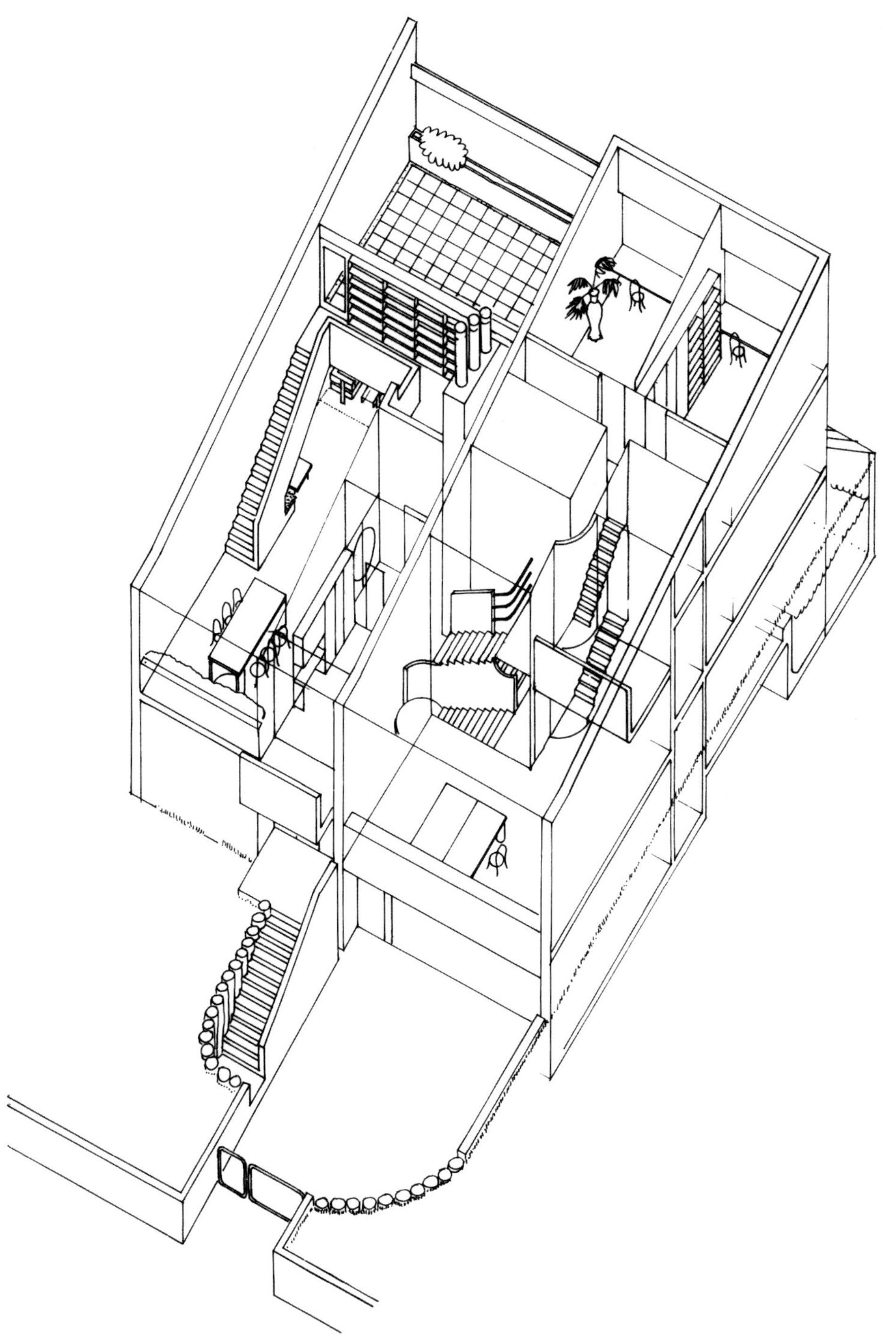

1. Axonometric view.
2. View from the street.
3. View from the garden.

1. Axonometrie.
2. Ansicht von der Straße.
3. Ansicht vom Garten.

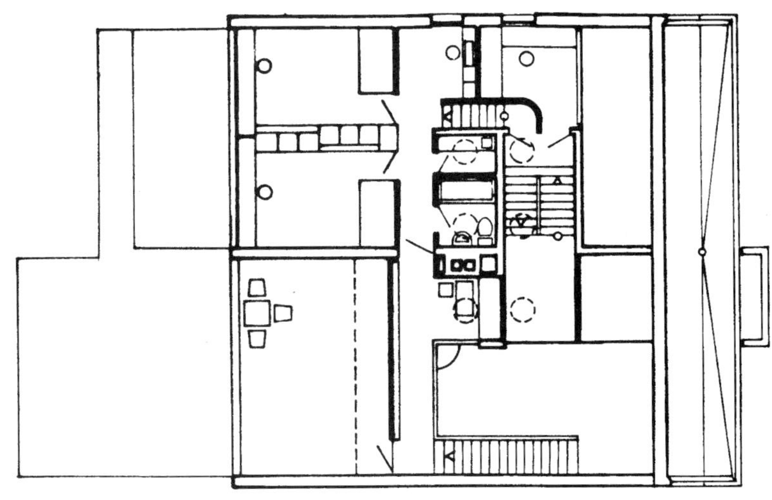

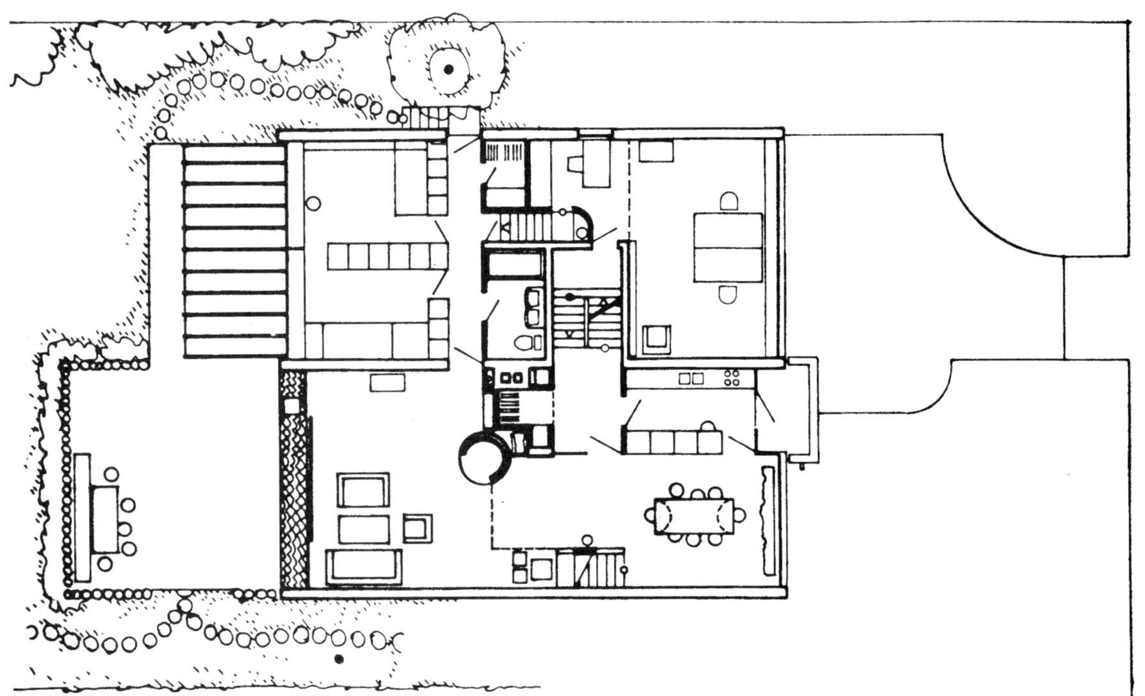

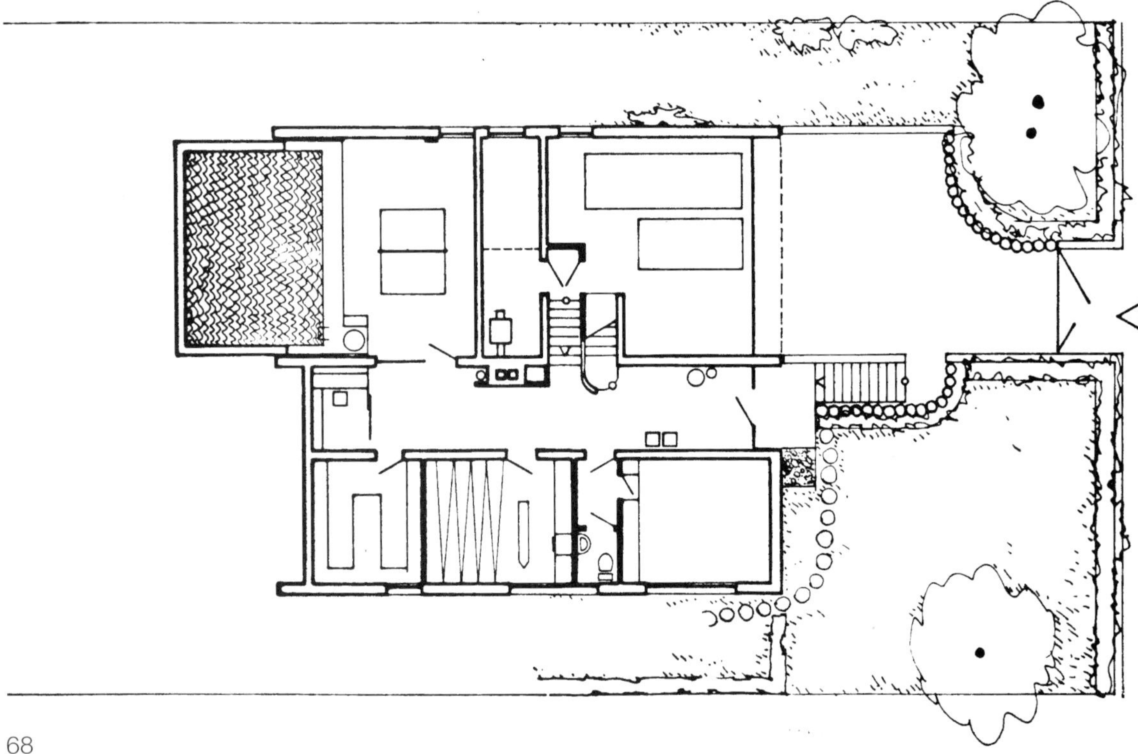

4–6. Floor plans (ground floor, 1st floor, 2nd floor).
7. View of the living room and the library above from the dining space.

4–6. Grundrisse (Erdgeschoß, 1. Obergeschoß, 2. Obergeschoß).
7. Blick vom Eßplatz auf den Wohnraum und die darüber liegende Bibliothek.

8. Swimming pool on the ground floor.
9. Section through the building.
10. Library on the 1st floor.

8. Schwimmbad im Erdgeschoß.
9. Schnitt durch das Gebäude.
10. Bibliothek im 1. Obergeschoß.

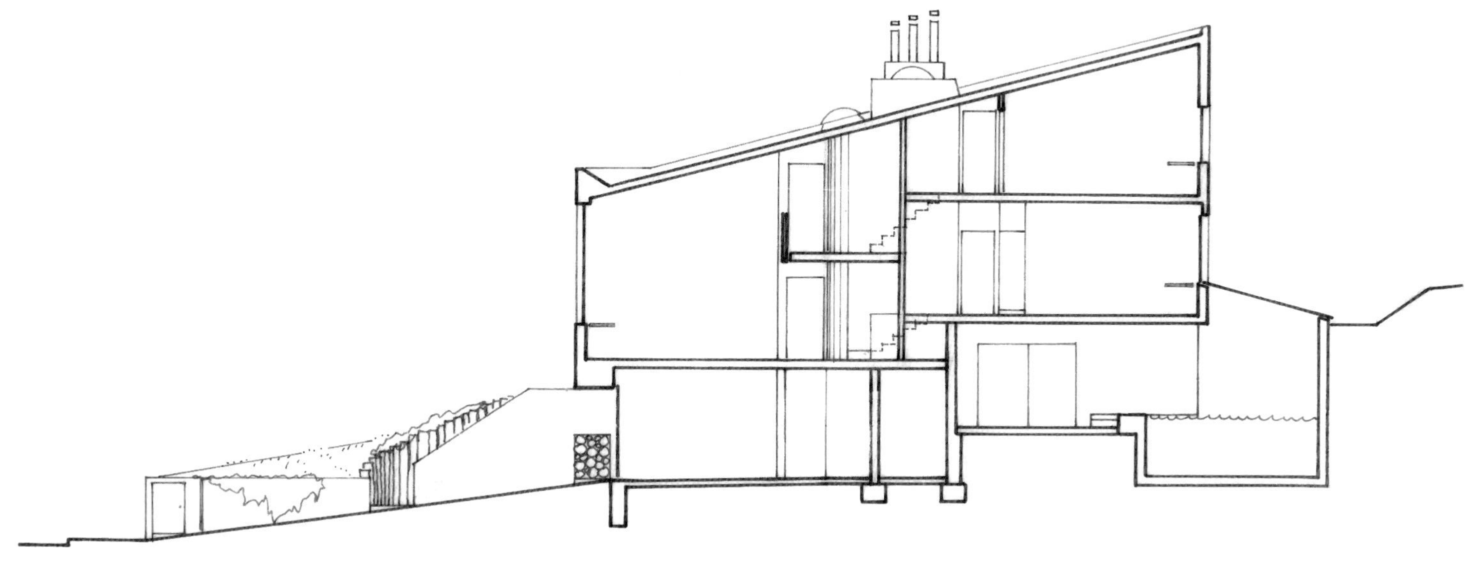

Garden of the Cardinal Höffner residence, Cologne, 1978/79

The project was to enhance the meager experiential world of a cardinal living in the middle of a large city by designing a big garden for his house (relatively big for a garden located in the city center). What was there was a somewhat monotonous path along the edge of the big lawn – beginning and ending at the terrace in front of the living room of the episcopal residence. In addition to a number of other trees there was also a beautiful old copper beech. It was quite obvious that it ought to be possible to provide stronger stimuli for the perpatetic cardinal!

At first a network of paths with flower beds alongside them was created, connected with the preexisting border path – thus increasing various path options fifteenfold.

A number of intellectual, spiritual, and natural stimuli were added as well.

The intellect is affected by three basic geometric forms. In the garden they appear as a circle (the form of the small rock garden, created from blocks of quarrystone), a square (the shape of the fish pool, built from clinker bricks, at seat height), and as a triangle (the tetrahedron-shaped hill sown with grass in three different shades of green).

The spiritual element, on the other hand, comes from three sculptured figures from the cardinal's own history: a column personally dedicated by the pope that reminds the cardinal of his years of study in Rome, a statue of the Virgin from his own diocese for meditation, and a tower pinnacle from Cologne Cathedral, recalling the varied construction history of the church, which points heavenward and at the same time takes one back to the terra firma of factual reality.

Lastly, three stimuli from natural creation play a role in the garden. They include two new almond trees that give the effect of a gate leading into the network of paths from the terrace, the copper beech mentioned above that provides shelter when it rains and under which one can sit down on the edge of the fish pool to pet and feed the animals, and finally the new pergola, made from semicircular bent steel tubes over the big curve in the path – with red climbing roses above and blue vinca minors below.

Garten der Residenz von Kardinal Höffner, Köln, 1978/79

Die karge Erlebniswelt eines inmitten der Großstadt residierenden Kardinals sollte durch Gestaltung des zum Haus gehörenden, für die Stadtmitte relativ großen Gartens bereichert werden. Vorhanden waren ein etwas eintöniger Weg am Rand der großen Rasenfläche – beginnend und endend an der dem Wohnraum des bischöflichen Hauses vorgelagerten Terrasse –, dazu neben anderen Bäumen eine alte, schöne Blutbuche. Da sollten für den geistlichen Peripatetiker stärkere Anregungen möglich sein!

Zunächst wurde ein in den vorhandenen langen Randweg mit Begleitbeeten eingesponnenes Wegenetz geschaffen – was die Wegvarianten gegenüber dem bisherigen Zustand um das Fünfzehnfache vermehrte.

Hinzu kamen weitere Anregungen verstandesmäßiger, übersinnlicher und natürlicher Art.

Der Verstand wird durch drei geometrische Grundformen angerührt. Sie manifestieren sich in dem Kreis, der die Form des kleinen Alpinums aus Bruchsteinen bestimmt, in dem Quadrat in Gestalt des aus Klinkern gemauerten Fischbeckens (auf Sitzhöhe) und als Dreieck in Gestalt eines tetraedrischen Hügels, der mit drei verschieden grünen Grassorten besät wurde.

Das Übersinnliche dagegen kommt von drei plastischen Gestalten aus der Umwelt des Kardinals: einer vom Papst persönlich dedizierten Säule, die den Kardinal an seine Studienzeit in Rom erinnert, einer Marienstatue aus dem eigenen Bistum für die Meditation und einer Turmfiale des Kölner Doms, die an die wechselvolle Baugeschichte der himmelweisenden bischöflichen Kirche erinnert und damit auch wieder auf den Boden der Tatsachen zurückführt.

Schließlich wirken auch drei Anregungen aus der natürlichen Schöpfung mit. Dazu gehören zwei neue Mandelbäumchen mit Torwirkung, indem sie das Wegenetz von der Terrasse aus eröffnen, die schon erwähnte Blutbuche mit beschützender Wirkung bei Regen, unter der man sich auf dem Fischbecken zum Streicheln und Füttern der Tiere niedersetzen kann, und schließlich die neue Pergola aus halbkreisförmig gebogenen Rohren über der großen Wegkurve – mit den roten Rankrosen über sich und den Blausternen am Boden unter sich.

1. Plan of the former garden.
2. Plan of the converted garden.

1. Plan des früheren Gartens.
2. Plan des umgestalteten Gartens.

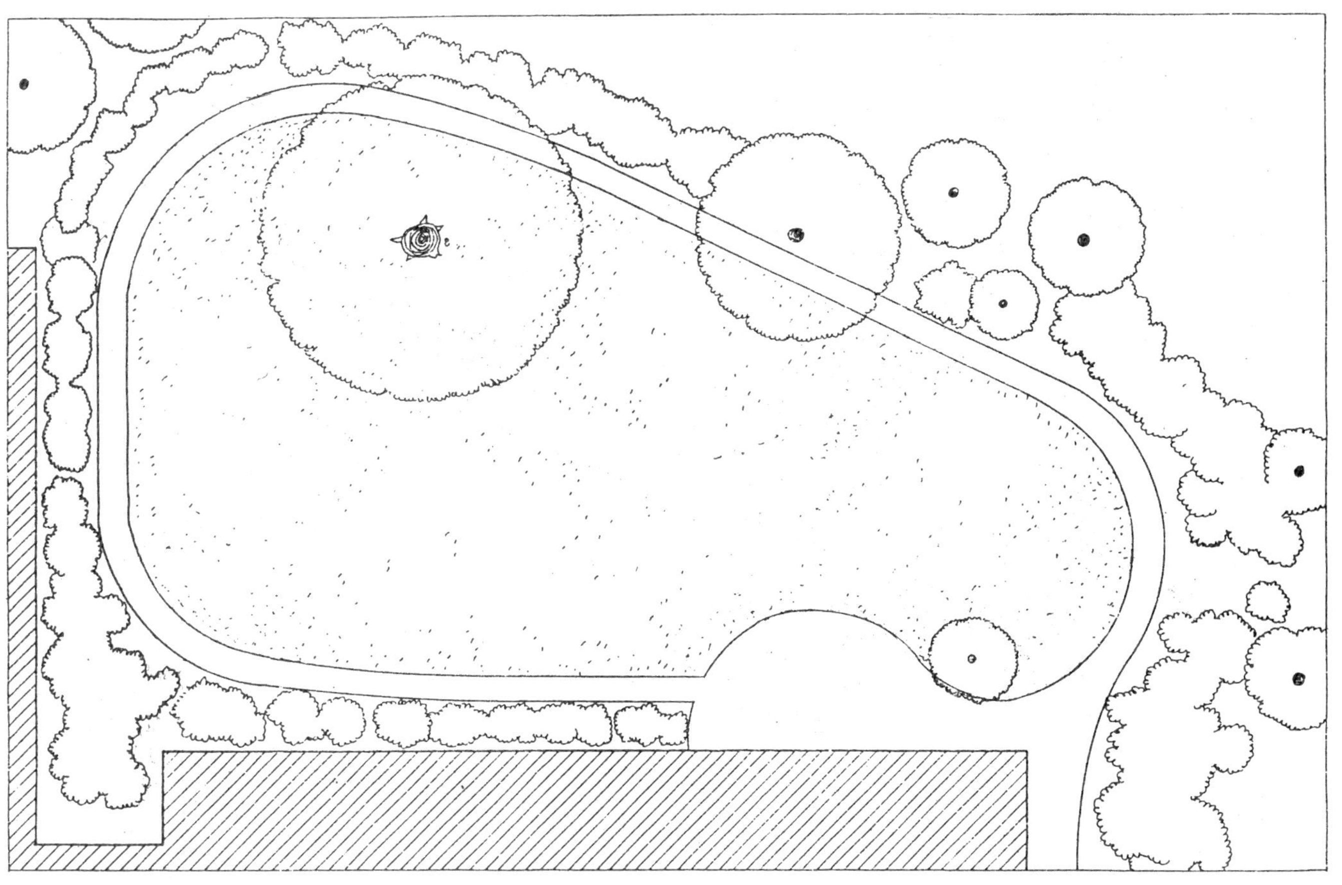

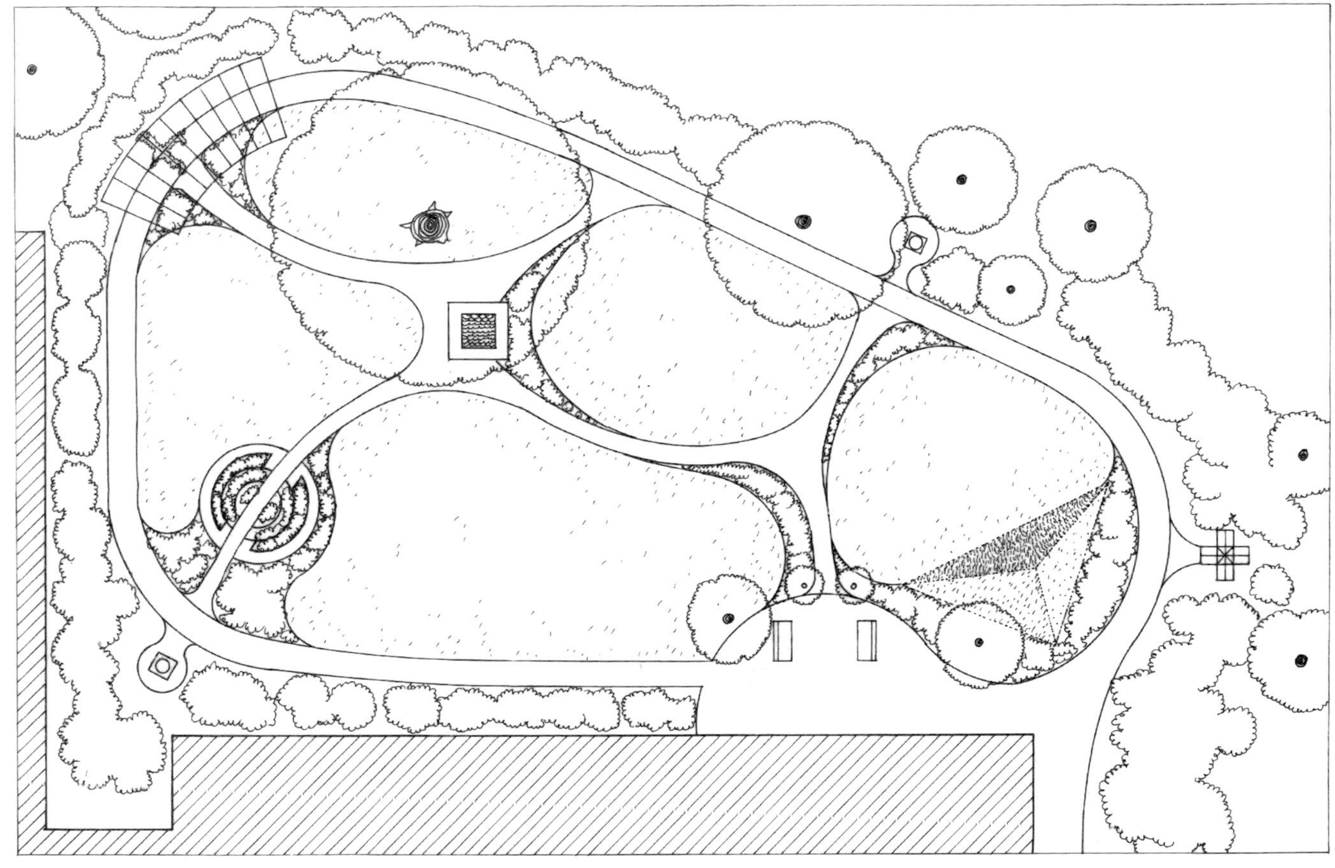

3. Path to the Madonna.
4. Path through the circular stone bed.

3. Weg zur Madonna.
4. Weg durch das kreisförmige Steinbeet.

5. Tower pinnacle from Cologne Cathedral.
6. Creeper scaffold for red roses.

5. Turmfiale des Kölner Doms.
6. Rankgerüst für rote Rosen.

Parish house in Petronell-Carnuntum, Lower Austria, 1982/83

For centuries, the parish house had formed the third side of the sloping square between church and town hall. The demolition of the desolate old building, classified as a historical monument, was finally authorized – though under the condition that the building that replaced it would be erected within its old contours, and that an ancient (Roman?) cellar would be preserved. The width of the cellar gave rise to the fundamental concept of having three naves, supported by four longitudinal beams, which remain exposed throughout the entire house. The course of the floor plan starts with the public zone of the parish offices and the round conference room, and then increasingly moves into more private space through the living room with the book gallery and, expandable, to the dining room (though the parish priest wished for a window in the glass oriel for conversations with passersby, in order not to exclude the public altogether even when he was in the living room); the bedrooms that follow, and a study, are completely private space. There is a short adjoining flight of stairs leading to the garage.

The old cellar and an additional basement, which have a separate entrance, are used by the young people of the parish. A glass dormer window emphasizes the roof both in the east-facing guest room with a view of the church and in the housekeeper's west-facing room with a view of the village. The fact that the traditional basic form is pierced by the three glass surfaces, a modern feature, was not only tolerated, but was awarded an architecture prize.

The representation of the symbolic lamb above the entrance is by the architect.

Pfarrhof in Petronell-Carnuntum, Niederösterreich, 1982/83

Seit Jahrhunderten bildete der Pfarrhof die dritte Seite zwischen Kirche und Rathaus. Der unter Denkmalschutz stehende, desolate Altbau wurde zum Abriß freigegeben – allerdings unter der Bedingung, daß der Neubau in dessen Konturen entstehen und ein uralter (römischer?) Keller erhalten würde. Des Kellers Breite ergab das dreischiffige Grundkonzept, getragen durch vier Längsbalken, die im ganzen Haus sichtbar bleiben. Der Grundrißablauf beginnt mit der öffentlichen Zone der Pfarrbüros und des runden Besprechungszimmers und nimmt im weiteren Verlauf durch den Wohnraum mit Büchergalerie und erweiterbar zum Eßzimmer an Privatheit zu (wobei der Pfarrer, um auch im Wohnraum Öffentlichkeit nicht ganz auszuschließen, sich ein Fenster im Glaserker für ein Gespräch mit einem Passanten wünschte); privatissime wird der Ablauf dann mit den folgenden Schlafzimmern und einem Arbeitsraum. An diese schließt sich ein Treppchen zur Garage an.

Der alte und ein weiterer Keller stehen – mit eigenem Eingang – der Jugend zur Verfügung. Das Dach wurde für den Gastraum nach Osten zur Kirche und für das Haushälterinnenzimmer nach Westen zum Dorf durch je eine Glasgaube betont. Die Durchdringung der traditionellen Grundform des Gebäudes durch die drei Glaskörper als Beitrag unserer Zeit wurde nicht nur toleriert, sondern mit einem Architekturpreis gewürdigt.

Die Darstellung des Lammsymbols über dem Eingang stammt vom Architekten.

1. Main entrance with symbolic lamb above the door designed by the architect.
2, 3. Floor plans (ground floor, 1st floor).

1. Haupteingang mit vom Architekten entworfenem Lammsymbol über der Tür.
2, 3. Grundrisse (Erdgeschoß, 1. Obergeschoß).

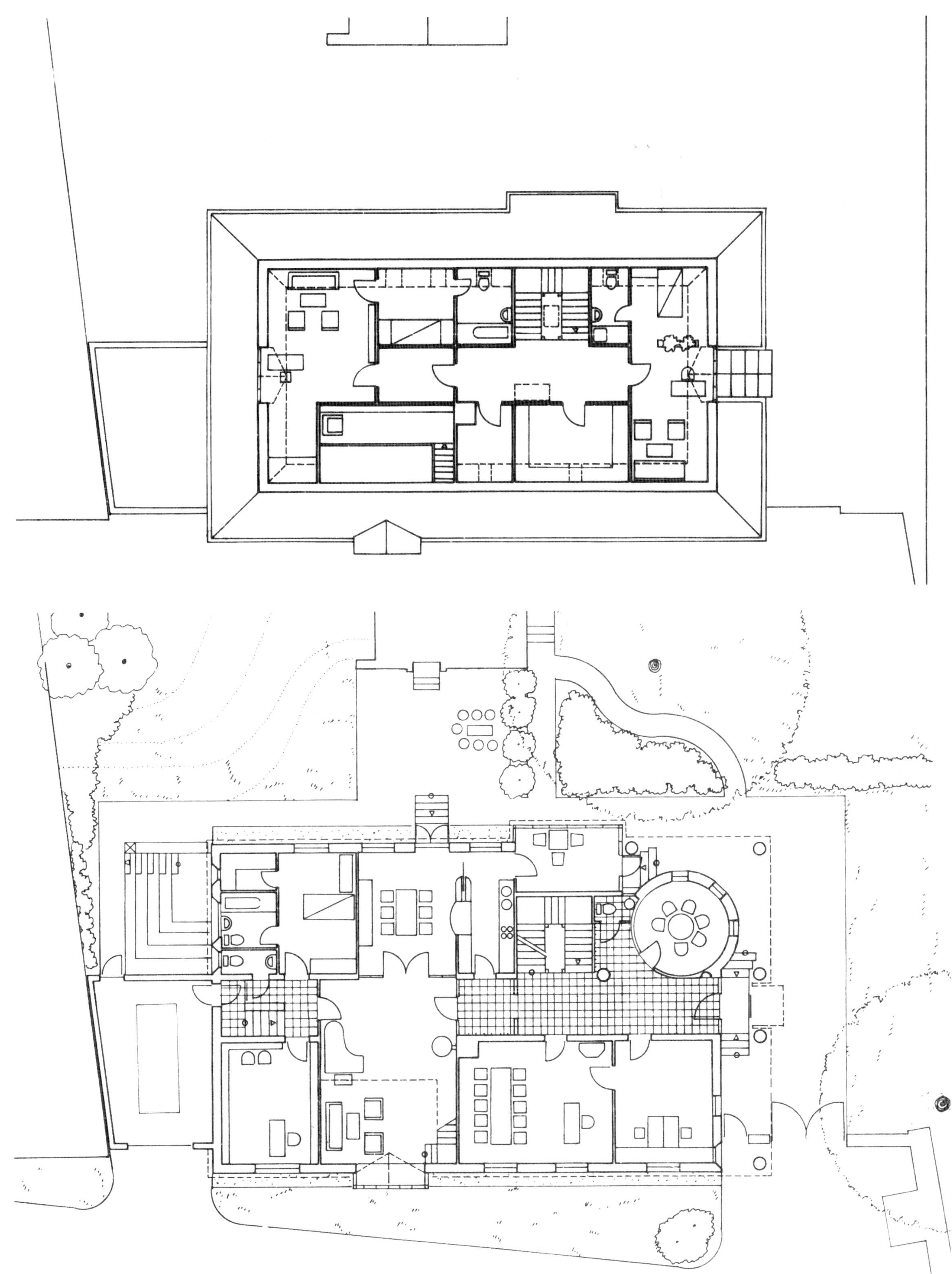

4. View from the village green.
5. View from the garden.
6. Corridor on the ground floor looking towards
the main entrance.
7. Cellar with own entrance.

4. Ansicht vom Dorfplatz.
5. Ansicht vom Garten.
6. Flur im Erdgeschoß in Richtung Haupteingang.
7. Keller mit eigenem Eingang.

Frey residential and commercial building, Ludwigshafen-Mundenheim, 1954–57

The goal was to add a four-storey building to an existing old building with its staircase on the main street; three floors of the addition could be expanded beginning with the corner on the side street. The entire ground floor and the basement were to house a furniture store, while apartments that could be adapted as exhibition areas would be planned for the rest of the floors. Two of the apartments were to be remodeled for the owners.

The corner proved to be a formal problem of social function: While potential shoppers like to look at the shop windows on the main street, it is apparent that they are less inclined to go look at those on the side street (from which all the wartime rubble had not yet been removed). Hence the concept of a staggered and projecting corner, which could entice interested shoppers into the side street even when it rained. Because variability was necessary, only concrete was used, with yellow clinker brick cladding for the upper floors.

One of the owners had wife and child, and chose the 3rd-floor corner apartment in the part of the building facing the main street. As a result, a roof terrace with an open fireplace was created on the three-floor part of the building; the terrace was shielded from view by a wooden fence and a movie projection screen.

Wohn- und Geschäftshaus Frey, Ludwigshafen-Mundenheim, 1954–57

An einen Altbau mit Treppe an der Hauptstraße war ein viergeschossiges Gebäude anzuschließen, das sich ab der Ecke in der Nebenstraße dreigeschossig erweitern ließ. Das gesamte Erdgeschoß und der Keller sollten ein Möbelgeschäft aufnehmen, während für die übrigen Geschosse Wohnungen zu planen waren, die als Ausstellungsflächen adaptierbar sein sollten. Zwei davon waren für die Inhaber auszubauen.

Als sozial-funktional-formales Thema ergab sich die Ecke: Während potentielle Käufer gern die Schaufenster an der Hauptstraße anschauen, gehen sie sicherlich weniger gern an denen der Nebenstraße entlang (in der noch nicht alle Trümmer aus Kriegszeiten beseitigt waren). Daher das Konzept einer gestaffelten und überkragenden Ecke, die die Kaufinteressenten sogar bei Regen in die Nebenstraße locken könnte. Wegen der notwendigen Variabilität entstand ein reiner Betonbau, der in den Oberschossen mit gelben Klinkern verkleidet wurde.

Einer der Inhaber hatte Frau und Kind und wählte im 3. Obergeschoß des Hauptstraßenteils die Wohnung an der Ecke. So entstand auf dem dreigeschossigen Bauteil eine Dachterrasse mit einem offenen Kamin, die ein Bretterzaun und eine Film-Projektionsleinwand gegen Einblicke abschirmt.

1. View from the side street.
2–5. Floor plans (ground floor, 1st and 2nd floor, 3rd floor, roof terrace).

1. Ansicht von der Seitenstraße.
2–5. Grundrisse (Erdgeschoß, 1. und 2. Obergeschoß, 3. Obergeschoß, Dachterrasse).

FREY

p. 82, 83
6. Detailed view from the main street.
7. View of the courtyard looking towards the
main street.

S. 82, 83
6. Detailansicht von der Hauptstraße.
7. Hofansicht in Richtung Hauptstraße.

8. Furniture store.
9, 10. Apartment and roof terrace of one of the
owners on the 3rd floor and on the roof above.

8. Möbelgeschäft.
9, 10. Wohnung und Dachterrasse eines der
Eigentümer im 3. Obergeschoß und auf dem
darüber liegenden Dach.

Wüstenrot housing development, Karlsruhe-Waldstadt, 1957–61

(with Alfred Fischer and Maria Verena Gieselmann)

This development is one of the first German examples of architecture with resident participation. The one-storey houses were meant to visibly belong together without diminishing the individuality of the residents.

After many discussions with the purchasers of the homes, two types of house were developed: a smaller one with an area of 90 square meters (972 square feet) and a larger one with an area of 120 square meters (1296 square feet), which were varied according to the needs of the residents. Among the variations are not only houses with two-car garages, outbuildings, and finished attics and basements (one of these was used as a small printer's shop and another was even divided into two apartments), but also the rotation of the houses in relation to Stettiner Strasse. The larger connection is achieved by uniform use of color, but also by the walls of the front gardens, shaped like an inverted gable roof. The larger houses have an open fireplace. Instead of a garage the smaller houses have a carport, which has frequently mutated into a garage. It was the wish of the urban planners to protect the woods as much as possible; this is why the original density of the woods in the middle of the development site was maintained.

The unity of the development was unfortunately impaired later on because on one of the three streets, several of the original houses were torn down and replaced by two-storey »villas«, although the zoning laws limited the height of buildings to one storey.

Siedlung Wüstenrot, Karlsruhe-Waldstadt, 1957–61

(mit Alfred Fischer und Maria Verena Gieselmann)

Diese Siedlung ist eines der ersten Beispiele für Mitbestimmungsarchitektur in Deutschland. Die eingeschossigen Häuser sollten sichtbar zusammengehören, ohne daß die Individualität der Bewohner leidet.

Nach vielen Gesprächen mit den Hauserwerbern wurden zwei Haustypen entwickelt, ein kleinerer mit 90 m² und ein größerer mit 120 m² Wohnfläche, die entsprechend den Bedürnissen der Bewohner variiert wurden. Zu den Varianten gehören nicht nur Häuser mit Doppelgaragen, Anbauten sowie Dach- und Kellerausbau (davon diente eine als kleine Druckerei, und eine andere wurde sogar in zwei Wohnungen gesteilt), sondern auch die Drehung der Häuser an der Stettiner Straße. Der große Zusammenhang ist durch die gleichmäßige Farbgebung, aber auch durch die Vorgartenmauern hergestellt, deren Form das Satteldachmotiv auf den Kopf stellt. Die größeren Häuser sind mit einem offenen Kamin ausgestattet. Die kleineren Häuser erhielten statt Garagen einen Carport, der häufig zur Garage mutierte. Dem Wunsch der Stadtplaner, den Wald möglichst zu schonen, wurde durch Erhaltung der ursprünglichen Walddichte in der Mitte des Grundstücks nachgekommen.

Die Einheit der Siedlung wurde leider später durch den Abriß von mehreren Typenhäusern und den Einbau von zweigeschossigen »Villen« gestört, obwohl die Begrenzung der Bauhöhe durch die Bauordnung festgelegt war.

1. Site plan.
2. View from Stettiner Strasse.
3. Type 100 sqm. Floor plan.
4. Type 130 sqm. Floor plan.

1. Lageplan.
2. Ansicht von der Stettiner Straße.
3. Typ 100 m². Grundriß.
4. Typ 130 m². Grundriß.

p. 88, 89
5. View of one of the smaller houses from the garden.
6. View of one of the larger houses with office addition from the garden.
7. Open fireplace in one of the larger houses.

S. 88, 89
5. Ansicht eines der kleineren Häuser vom Garten.
6. Ansicht eines der größeren Häuser mit Büroanbau vom Garten.
7. Offener Kamin in einem der größeren Häuser.

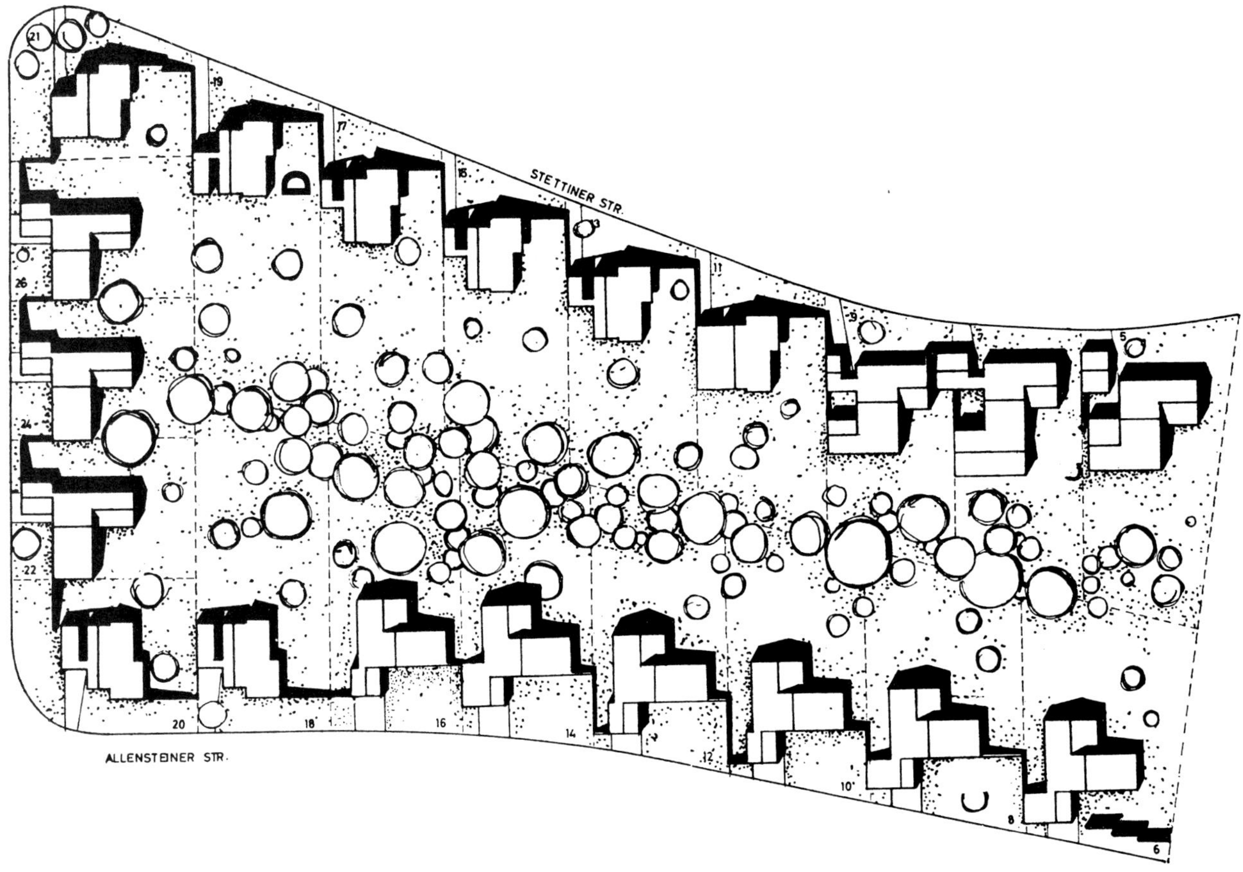

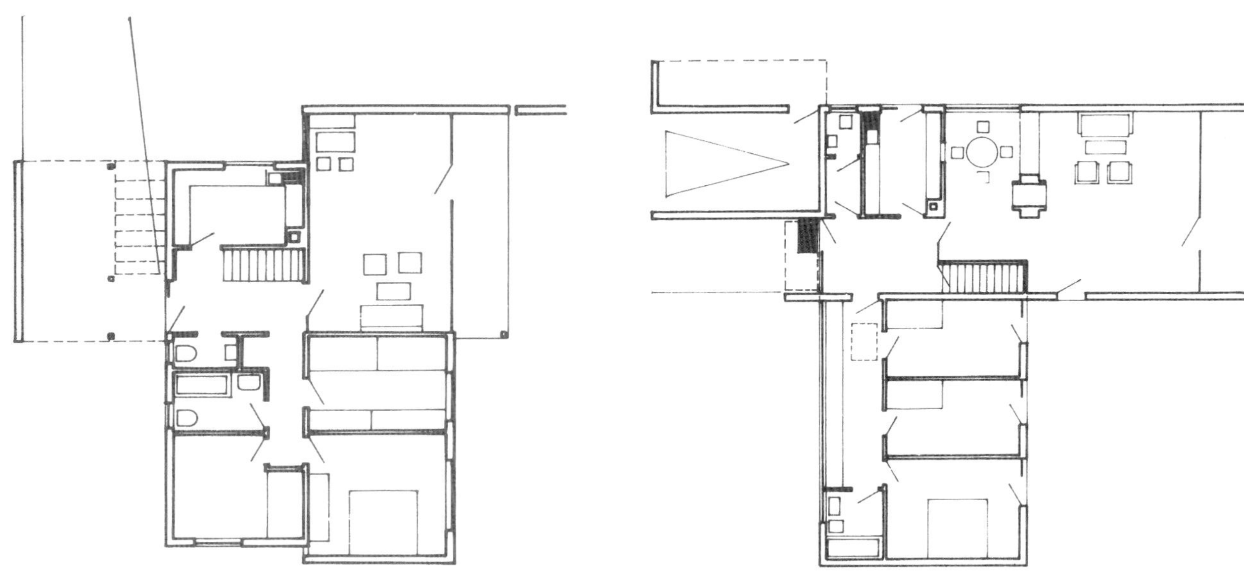

»Carpet-type« housing development in Karlsruhe-Nordweststadt, 1959–62, 1966 to 1969, 1978–80

Into a square with a village linden tree lead one straight and one twisty little street. Located on these streets are twelve semi-atrium-style houses 100 square meters (1080 square feet) in area with partial basements in different-sized gardens whose size is appropriate for urban dwellers. Access to the houses also differs, as does the placement of garages. The only special request was for a physician's practice to be built on to one of the houses.

The houses have double-framed exterior walls, are faced with sand-lime bricks, and have a flat roof with exposed concrete cornices. In order to allow air to pass through the small gardens in the hot summers of the upper Rhine valley, without allowing passersby to look inside, the gardens have screen walls with concrete cornices.

In 1969 a bedroom and a second bathroom were added to all the houses facing west, and a garden storage room, a new entrance, and an enlarged dining room were built in 1980 for the house facing north.

After the experiences with the Waldstadt housing development, the houses and gardens could be completed within a year and then sold by the builder. Comparing this housing development with the Waldstadt housing development described above , it was discovered that it is more economical – both for the builder and the residents – first to live in a prototype house without making alterations to it, then carry out any necessary additions or changes a few years later, rather than make suggestions for changes during the initial planning stage.

Teppichsiedlung in Karlsruhe-Nordweststadt, 1959–62, 1966–69, 1978–80

In einen Platz mit einer Dorflinde münden eine gerade und eine winkelige Gasse. Daran liegen zwölf Semi-Atriumhäuser von 100 m² teilunterkellerter Wohnfläche in verschieden großen Gärten, deren Größe dem Stadtbewohner angemessen ist. Unterscheidbarkeit gibt es auch durch die verschiedenen Zugänge und Anordnungen der Garagen. Als einziger Sonderwunsch wurde an einem Haus eine Arztpraxis angebaut.

Die Häuser haben zweischalige Außenwände mit einer Verblendung aus Kalksandstein, darüber ein Flachdach mit Sichtbetongesimsen. Um die Durchlüftung der kleinen Gärten in dem heißen Sommerklima des Oberrheintals ohne Einblick von außen zu gewährleisten, wurden die Gartenmauern in Lochbauweise mit Sichtbetonattika errichtet.

Alle nach Westen orientierten Häuser wurden 1969 um ein Schlafzimmer und ein zweites Bad erweitert, das nach Norden gerichtete Haus 1980 um einen Gartenabstellraum, einen neuen Eingang und einen vergrößerten Eßraum.

Nach den Erfahrungen mit der Waldstadtsiedlung konnten die Häuser einschließlich der Gärten innerhalb eines Jahres fertiggestellt und danach von dem Bauträger verkauft werden. Beim Vergleich mit der Waldstadtsiedlung stellte sich heraus, daß es – auch für den Bewohner – wirtschaftlicher ist, das Haus zunächst als Typ zu bewohnen und nach ein paar Jahren eventuelle Anbauten oder Änderungen vorzunehmen, als schon bei der Planung mitzubestimmen.

1. View from the north-east.
2. Site plan.
3, 4. Floor plans (original state, present state) of the house in the north corner.

1. Ansicht von Nordosten.
2. Lageplan.
3, 4. Grundrisse (ursprünglicher Zustand, heutiger Zustand) des Hauses in der nördlichen Ecke.

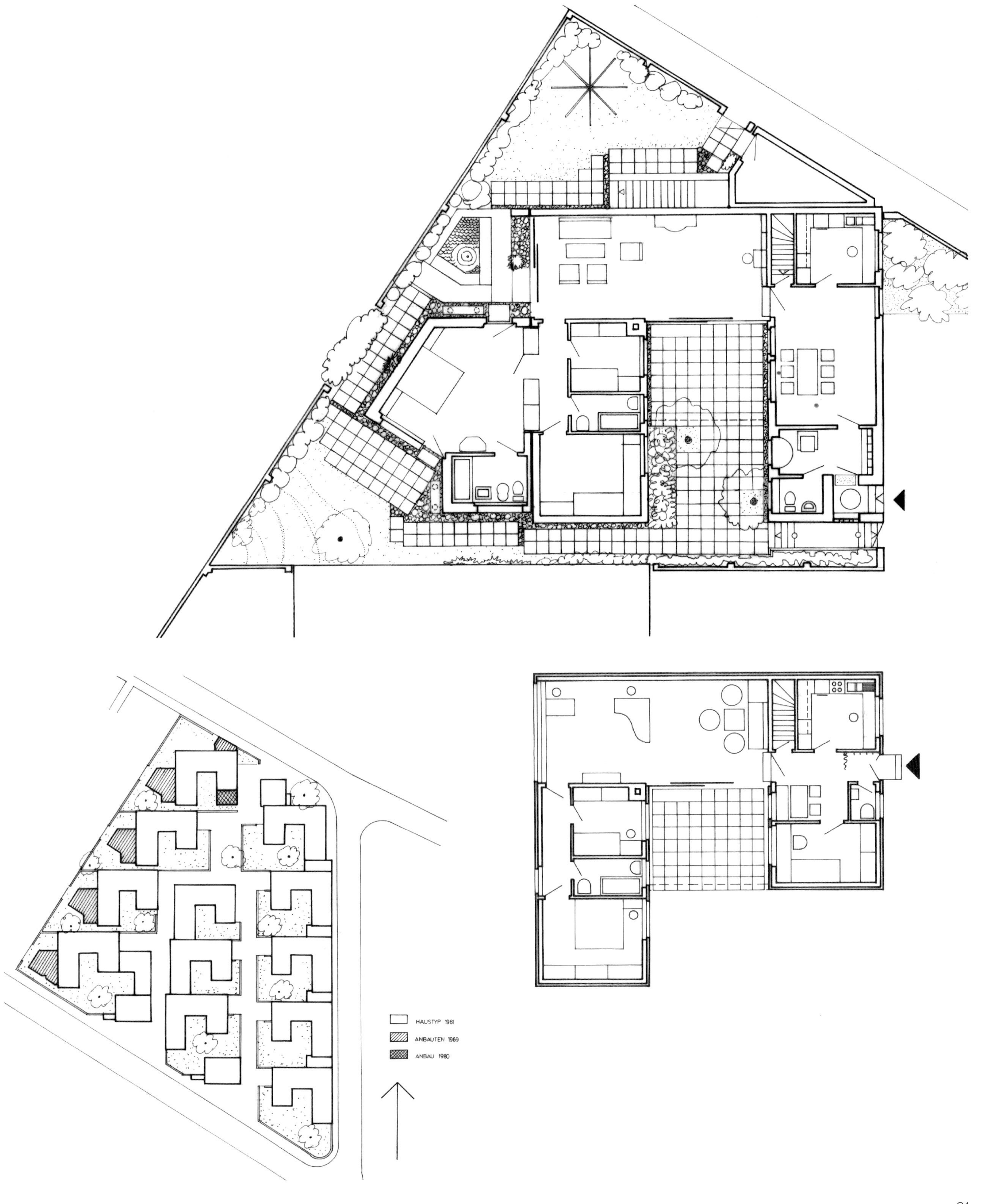

HAUSTYP 1961
ANBAUTEN 1969
ANBAU 1980

5. Aerial view from the north-west.
6. Courtyard of a house.
7. Public space within the housing development.

5. Luftaufnahme von Nordwesten.
6. Wohnhof eines Hauses.
7. Öffentlicher Raum innerhalb der Siedlung.

Gieselmann multi-family house and studio, Karlsruhe-Durlach, 1960–65

The building is located on a slope with varying inclines. Intended to be an »architectonic abstraction« of the slope, seven of the nine levels of the building were provided with a direct exit into the open air. The house is divided into three connected parts. On the left, looking from the street, is the section with three apartments and an entrance shared with the middle section, which consists of a two-storey studio placed above the three garages. From the atelier, by way of the secretary's office, there is access to the architect's workroom. The latter, in turn, is connected by a door with the architect's two-storey apartment, accessed by the entrance stairs of the right-hand section of the building. In the middle of the grounds, at the level of the living room, there is a courtyard, the heart of the building – ideal for warm-weather gatherings of all the residents and staff. This is also where a fountain collects the rainwater from all the roofs. The architect's apartment begins on the 1st floor with a high-ceilinged living area, which has a fireplace, and a terrace in front of it. A freestanding spiral staircase goes up to the library and finally to the 2nd floor where the bedrooms and a walled roof terrace are located. A ladder on the stairwell cylinder goes up to a bench on the roof – a place for moments of reflection.

Mehrfamilien- und Atelierhaus Gieselmann, Karlsruhe-Durlach, 1960–65

Der Bau liegt an einem unterschiedlich geneigten Hang. Als »architektonische Abstraktion« des Hanges gedacht, erhielten sieben von neun Ebenen des Gebäudes einen direktem Ausgang ins Freie. Das Haus ist in drei miteinander verbundene Bauteile gegliedert. Von der Straße aus links liegt der Bauteil mit drei Wohnungen und dem gemeinsamem Eingang zum mittleren Bauteil mit dem zweigeschossigen, über den drei Garagen liegenden Atelier. Dieses hat über das Sekretariat Zugang zum Arbeitsraum des Architekten. Der wiederum ist durch eine Tür zur Eingangstreppe des rechten Bauteils mit der zweigeschossigen Wohnung des Architekten verbunden. In der Mitte der Anlage liegt auf Wohnraumhöhe ein Hof als Herz der Anlage – geeignet für sommerliche Treffen aller Bewohner und Mitarbeiter. Hier fließt auch das Regenwasser aller Dächer in einem Brunnen zusammen. Die Wohnung des Architekten beginnt im 1. Obergeschoß mit einem hohen Wohnteil mit Kamin und vorgelagerter Terrasse. Eine frei stehende Wendeltreppe führt weiter zur Bibliothek und schließlich zum 2. Obergeschoß mit den Schlafräumen und einer ummauerten Dachterrasse. Auf einer Leiter am Treppenhauszylinder kann man bis zur Sitzbank auf dem Dach gelangen – ein Ort für nachdenkliche Momente.

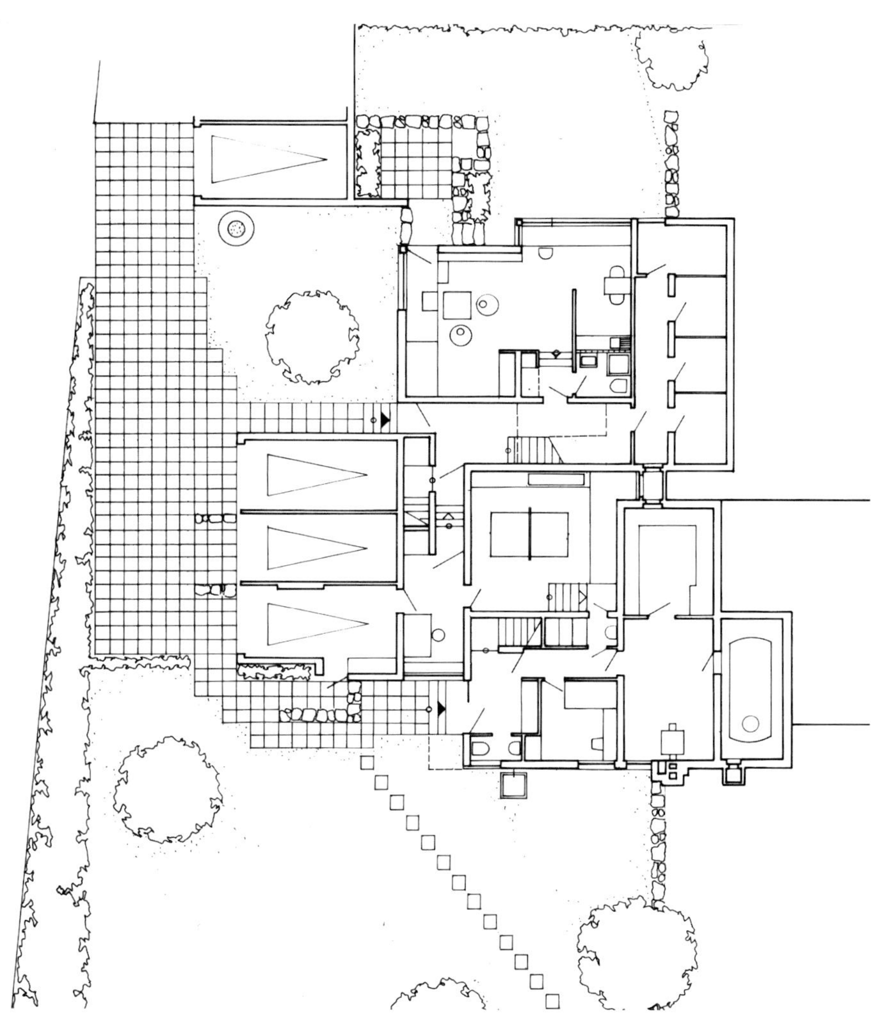

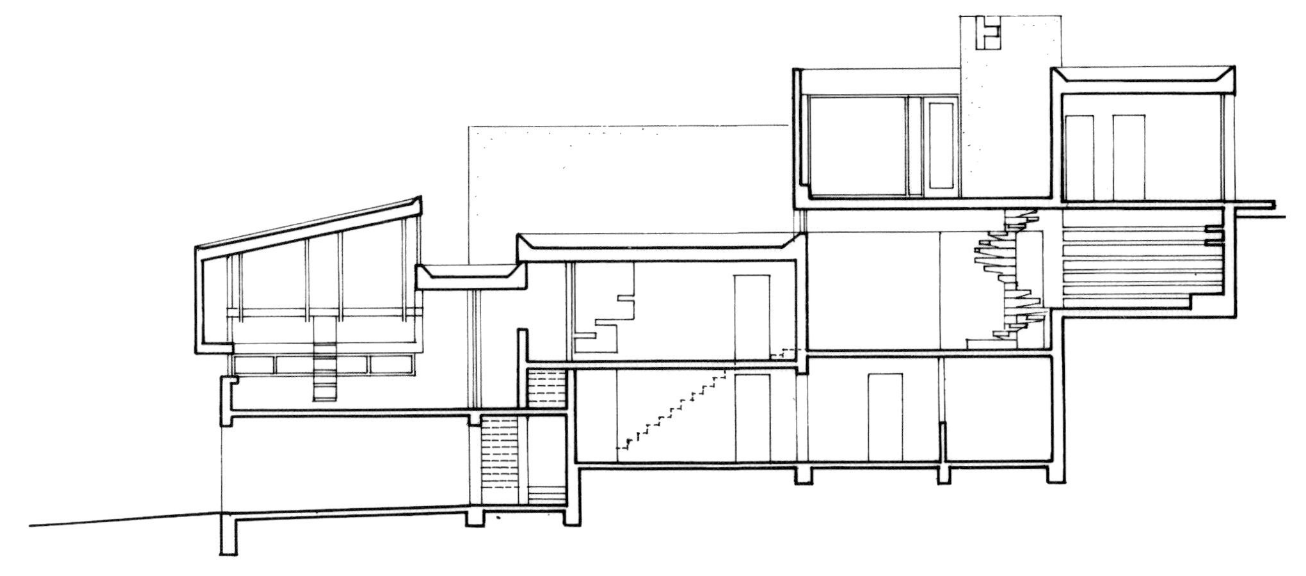

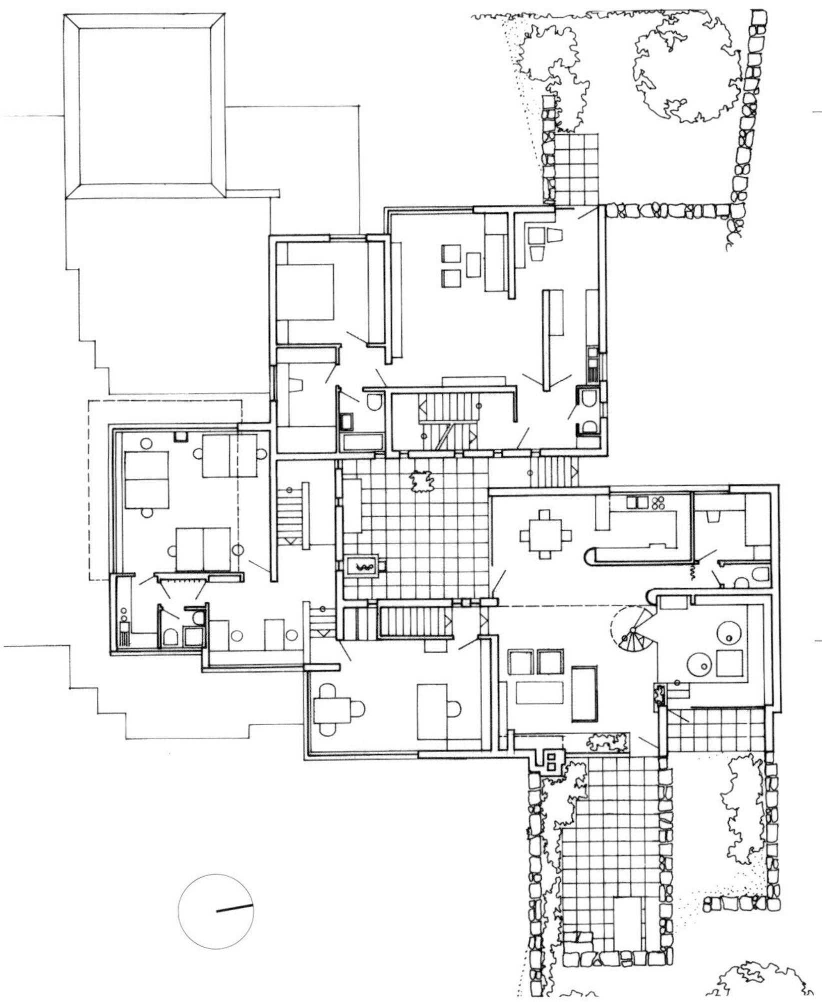

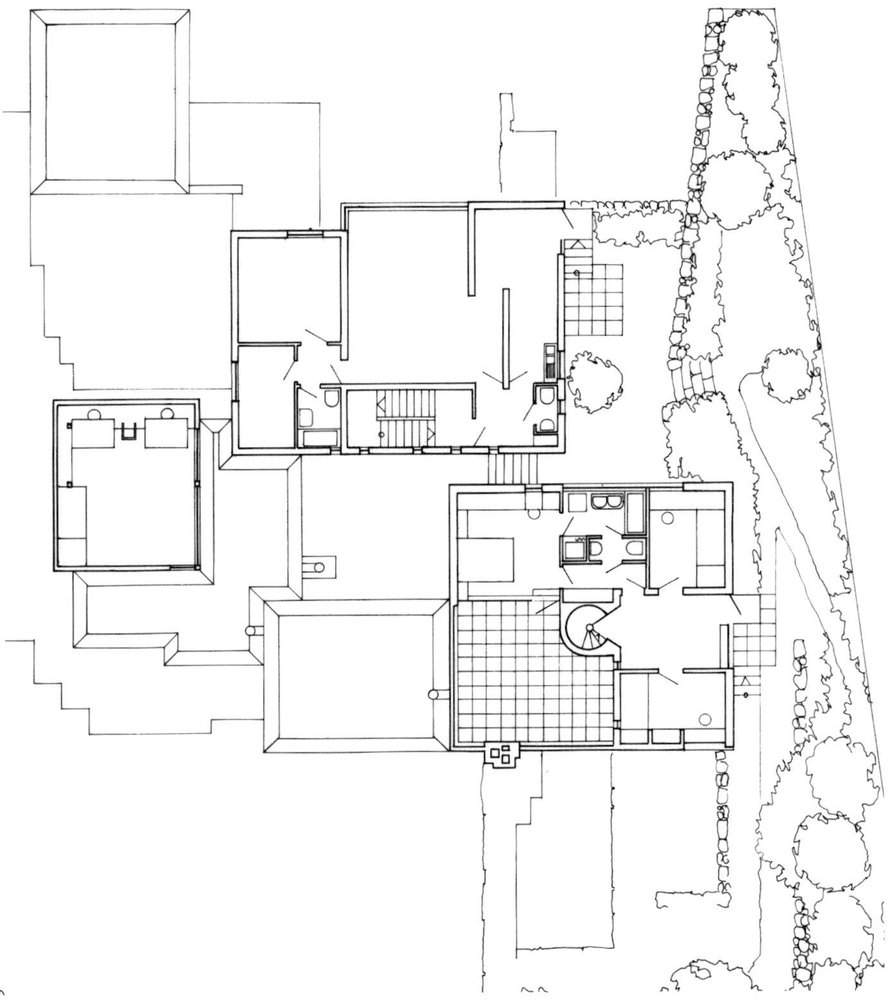

5. View from the east.
6. Detailed view from the east.

5. Ansicht von Osten.
6. Detailansicht von Osten.

7, 8. The architect's writing recess.
9. The architect's studio.

7, 8. Schreibnische des Architekten.
9. Atelier des Architekten.

10. Central courtyard in front of the dining space
in the architect's apartment.
11. Dining space in the architect's apartment.
12. Living room in the architect's apartment.

10. Zentraler Hof vor dem Eßplatz in der Wohnung
des Architekten.
11. Eßplatz in der Wohnung des Architekten.
12. Wohnraum in der Wohnung des Architekten.

Rees multi-family house, Karlsruhe, 1962/63, 1972/73, 1975/76, 1981

The building is located next to the old-age home built in 1967, and is integrated into the development of one of the 100 houses long, late Baroque radial streets of the city. Built in 1820, the main building still had enough usable substance, after being hit by a bomb in World War II: a bead molding was intact, a corbel ledge had been repaired, and there were a red sandstone foundation wall and window jambs. There is a physician's office on the ground floor, followed by a residential floor and a converted attic with rooms for students. Two more storeys first needed to be added to this part of the building.

The original façade was preserved up as far as the corbel ledge. An added full floor above it, with its glass wall, documents our era, and over it is the massive top floor with its flat roof. The façade of this top floor is one of remembrance, since it mirrors the rhythm and the material of the jambs of the historic windows and socle.

Twelve years later the bedrooms in the second-floor apartment located in the garden tract were converted to a two-storey apartment, and their roof was minimally raised. A new spiral staircase now connects the living-room storey with the bedroom one, while another connects the terrace and the garden. The large living/dining area is accentuated by an open, central fireplace. This tract too was given a corbel ledge – as wide as the one of the main building. It was linked with the white plaster surface by round nursery windows. A mural by the architect added interest to the varied bedroom corridor. Between the street and the garden tract there was an inviting area to create a terrace for the apartment on the glass-walled storey of the main building (which has been listed as a historical monument).

Mehrfamilienhaus Rees, Karlsruhe, 1962/63, 1972/73, 1975/76, 1981

Das Gebäude liegt neben dem Altersheim von 1967, eingebunden in die Bebauung einer der 100 Häuser langen Radialstraßen der spätbarocken Stadtgründung. 1820 erbaut, wies das Haupthaus nach einer Kriegsbombe mit einem heilen Astragal- und einem geflickten Konsolgesims, einem roten Sandsteinsockel und ebensolchen Fenstergewänden noch genügend brauchbare Substanz auf. Im Erdgeschoß befindet sich eine Arztpraxis, gefolgt von einem Wohngeschoß und einem ausgebautem Dachgeschoß mit Studentenzimmern. Dieser Bauteil war zunächst um zwei Geschosse aufzustocken.

Die Fassade wurde bis hin zum Konsolgesims erhalten. Eine neues Vollgeschoß darüber dokumentiert mit seiner Glaswand unsere Zeit und trennt ein weiteres, massives Geschoß mit Flachdach ab. Dessen Fassade ist die der Erinnerung – durch Spiegelung des Rhythmus und des Gewändematerials der historischen Fenster und des Sockels.

Zwölf Jahre später wurden die im Gartentrakt der Wohnung im 1. Obergeschoß liegenden Schlafzimmer im Zusammenhang mit einer geringfügigen Aufstockung ihres Daches zu einer zweigeschossigen Wohnung ausgebaut. Eine neue Wendeltreppe verbindet nun das Wohn- mit dem Schlafgeschoß, eine weitere die Terrasse mit dem Garten. Der große Wohn-/Eßraum wird durch einen offenen Kamin in der Mitte akzentuiert. Auch dieser Trakt bekam ein Gesims – so breit wie das des Hauptgebäudes. Es wurde durch runde Kinderzimmerfenster mit der weißen Putzfläche verklammert. Der abwechslungsreiche Schlafzimmerflur erhielt eine Wandbemalung durch den Architekten. Zwischen Straßen- und Gartentrakt blieb noch eine freundliche Fläche für eine Terrasse der Glasgeschoßwohnung im Hauptbau (der unter Denkmalschutz gestellt wurde).

1–6. Floor plans of the house (1st floor, 2nd floor, 3rd floor) before and after conversion.
7. Elevation of the street façade.

1–6. Grundrisse des Hauses (1. Obergeschoß, 2. Obergeschoß, 3. Obergeschoß) vor und nach dem Umbau.
7. Aufriß der Straßenfassade.

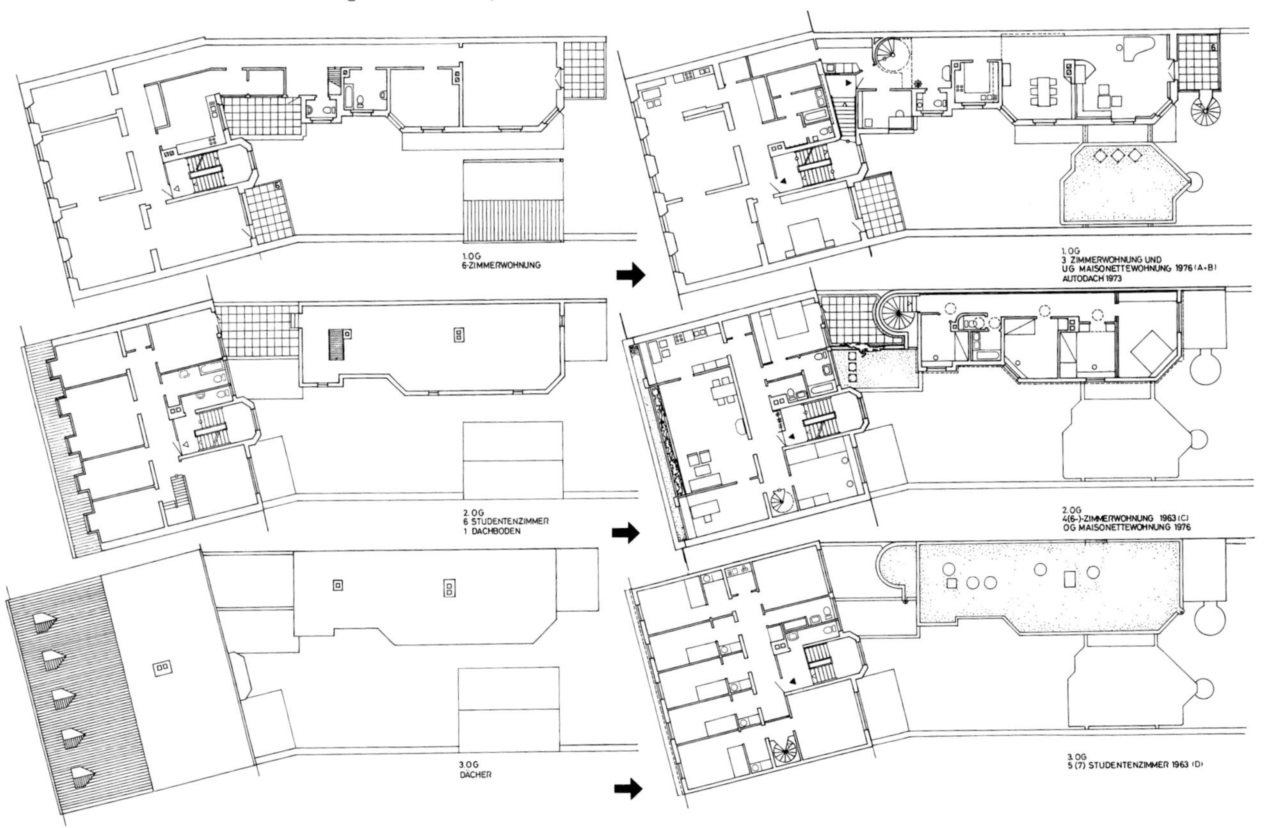

8. The house before conversion.
9. The house after conversion.
10. Living room on the 3rd floor.

8. Das Haus vor dem Umbau.
9. Das Haus nach dem Umbau.
10. Wohnraum im 3. Obergeschoß.

Old-age home of the Deutsches Rotes Kreuz, Karlsruhe, 1962–67

In order to get sunlight even on the courtyard side, which faces north, the rear of the building was rotated slightly toward the west. This created a triangular lobby in the center with light through the ceiling for all five floors – and the corridors became galleries, so that the residents have a view of all floors and the lobby. The two-storey entrance hall with a freestanding elevator tower and a freestanding staircase faces the street with a large articulated glass wall in order to keep the residents in closer contact with what is happening in the outside world. The pillars, which also contain the wiring, connect with the ceiling by means of capitals. One wall is ornamented with a relief, a colorful ceramic work by the painter Karl-Heinz Overkott. A two-level dining hall with a terrace in front of it adjoins the entrance hall. The hallway of the two-storey tract of rooms in the main building is lit by a skylight. The rooms on the courtyard side have small terraces. The roof and terraces of the community rooms in the main building are connected by outside staircases that go up to the roof terrace. At the north end of the grounds there is a one-storey tract with two-room assisted-living apartments.

The façade is underlaid with a grid. Since the loggias and windows on one side mirror those on the other, their positions – in spite of the grid – are individual, and thus it is easier for a resident to recognize his/her room more easily.

Altenheim des Deutschen Roten Kreuzes, Karlsruhe, 1962–67

Um auch auf der nach Norden orientierten Hofseite Sonne zu bekommen, wurde die Rückseite etwas nach Westen abgedreht. Dadurch entstand in der Mitte eine dreieckige Halle mit Licht durch das Dach für alle fünf Geschosse – und die Flure wurden zu Galerien, so daß die Bewohner alle Geschosse und die Halle überblicken können. Die zweigeschossige Eingangshalle mit frei stehendem Aufzugturm und ebensolcher Treppe ist mit einer gegliederten, großen Glaswand auf die Straße gerichtet, um das Erlebnispotential der Bewohner zu stärken. Die Stützen, die auch die Leitungen aufnehmen, schließen mit Kapitellen an die Decke an. Eine Wand ist mit einem Relief geschmückt, zu dem der Maler Karl-Heinz Overkott die farbige Keramik lieferte. Ein Speisesaal auf zwei Ebenen mit vorgelagerter Terrasse schließt sich an die Eingangshalle an. Der Flur des zweigeschossigen Zimmertrakts im Hauptgebäude wird durch ein Oberlicht erhellt. Die hofseitigen Zimmer haben kleine Terrassen. Dach und Terrassen der Gemeinschaftsräume des Hauptgebäudes sind über Außentreppen erreichbar. Im nördlichen Grundstücksbereich befindet sich ein eingeschossiger Trakt mit Zweizimmerwohnungen für selbstversorgende Bewohner.

Die Fassade ist mit einem Raster unterlegt. Da die Loggien und Fenster auch spiegelbildlich verwendet wurden, ergeben sich – trotz Raster – individuelle Positionen von beiden, und damit entsteht für den Bewohner eine leichtere Erkennbarkeit seines Raumes von außen.

p. 108, 109
3. Roofscape on the main building.
4. View of the main building from the courtyard.
5–7. Floor plans (ground floor, upper floors) and section of the main building.

S. 108, 109
3. Dachlandschaft auf dem Hauptgebäude.
4. Ansicht des Hauptgebäudes vom Hof.
5–7. Grundrisse (Erdgeschoß, Obergeschosse) und Schnitt des Hauptgebäudes.

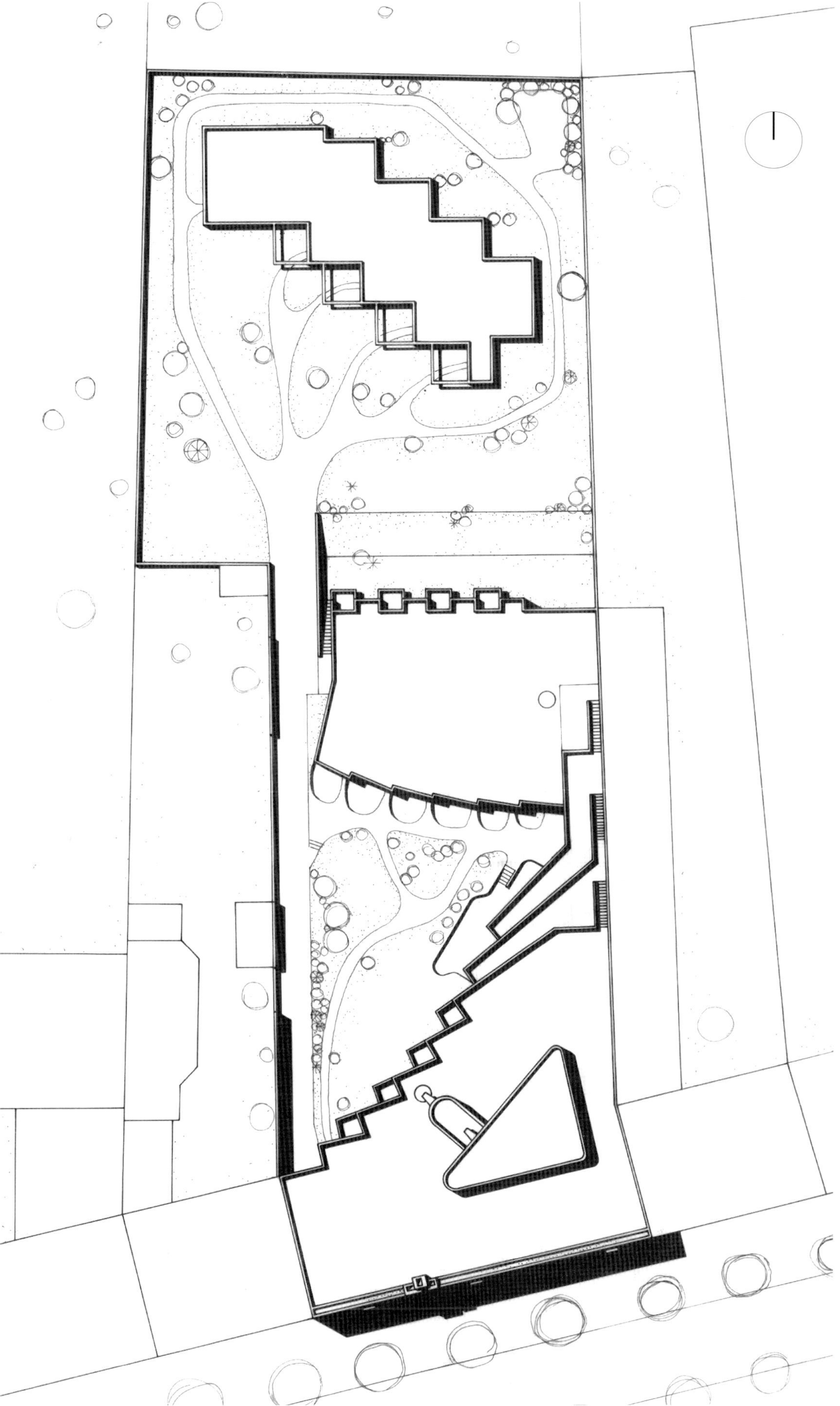

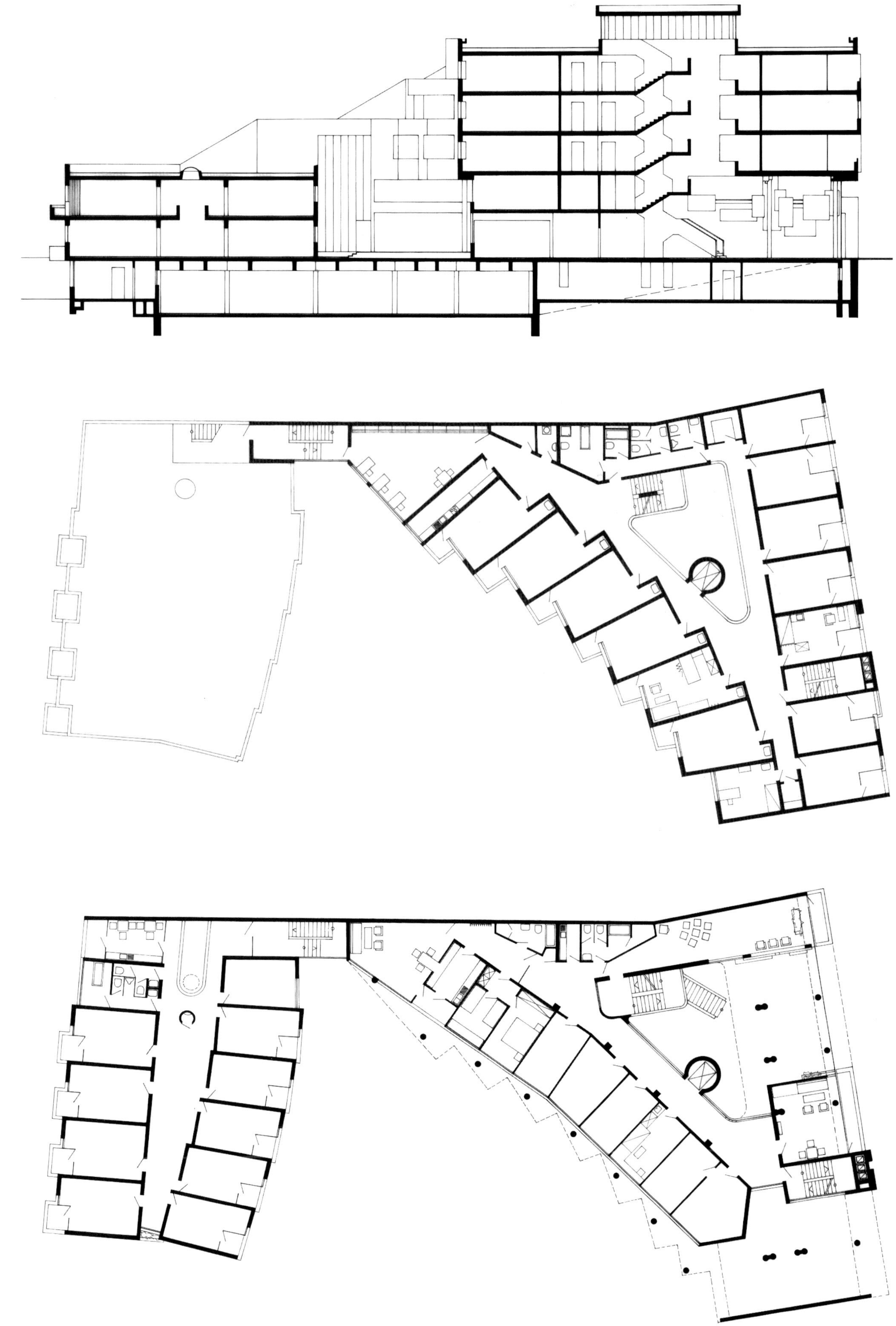

8, 9. Lobby in the main building.

8, 9. Halle im Hauptgebäude.

10, 11. Views of the one-storey tract at the north
end of the grounds.

10, 11. Ansichten des eingeschossigen Trakts am
nördlichen Grundstücksende.

Urban development in Berlin-Frohnau, 1964/65, project

A 1939 development plan, aborted when the war began, had left behind only a grid of banked paths in the forest. With these given, the planning of a dense, one- and two-storey development between large wood lots was begun. In terms of scale (though not typologically) it is integrated in the existing extended three-sided scattered-development neighborhood of single-family homes.

This development of low buildings is screened off by a four- to seven-storey caterpillar-like complex that ascends in four large sweeps, each differently colored. Access roads and parking are from the northeast. The north-south street of the low-rise development ends on a square, in front of the apartment complex, whose ground floor houses the utilities. A ten-floor high-rise for singles accents the northwest corner – the »Landmark Berlin« desired for the east-west superhighway.

For the low-rise development, different types of »growing« houses were developed. As in the life of human beings, individual stages of growth should have an acceptable appearance. The possibilities for variation are then the result of the characteristics of the different stages in construction – not of stylistic chaos, as in neighboring developments.

Stadterweiterung in Berlin-Frohnau, 1964/65, Projekt

Eine Bebauungsabsicht von 1939 hatte wegen des Kriegsbeginns nichts weiter als ein Netz von aufgeschütteten Wegen im Wald hinterlassen. Auf dieser Vorgabe entstand die Planung einer verdichteten, ein- und zweigeschossigen Siedlung zwischen großen Waldparzellen. Sie ordnet sich maßstäblich (nicht typologisch) in die bestehende dreiseitige Nachbarschaft ausgedehnter Einfamilienhaus-Streubebauung ein.

Diese Flachbebauung wird durch eine mit vier bis sieben Geschossen in vier großen, farbig differierenden Schwüngen ansteigende Wohnraupe abgeschirmt. Erschließung und Garagierung erfolgen von der Nordostseite. Die Nord–Süd-Straße der Flachbebauung endet auf einem Platz vor der Wohnraupe, in deren Erdgeschoß die Versorgungseinrichtungen untergebracht sind. Ein zehngeschossiges Hochhaus für Singles akzentuiert die Nordwestecke – die für die Ost–West-Autobahn erwünschte »Landmarke Berlin«.

Für die Flachbebauung wurden verschiedene Typen von »wachsenden« Häusern entwickelt. Wie beim Menschen sollten die einzelnen Wachstumsperioden ein akzeptables Gesicht haben. Die Variationsmöglichkeiten entstehen dann durch Merkmale der verschiedenen Baustufen – nicht durch das stilistische Tohuwabohu wie in den Bebauungen der Nachbarschaft.

1. Model.
2. Site plan.

1. Modell.
2. Lageplan.

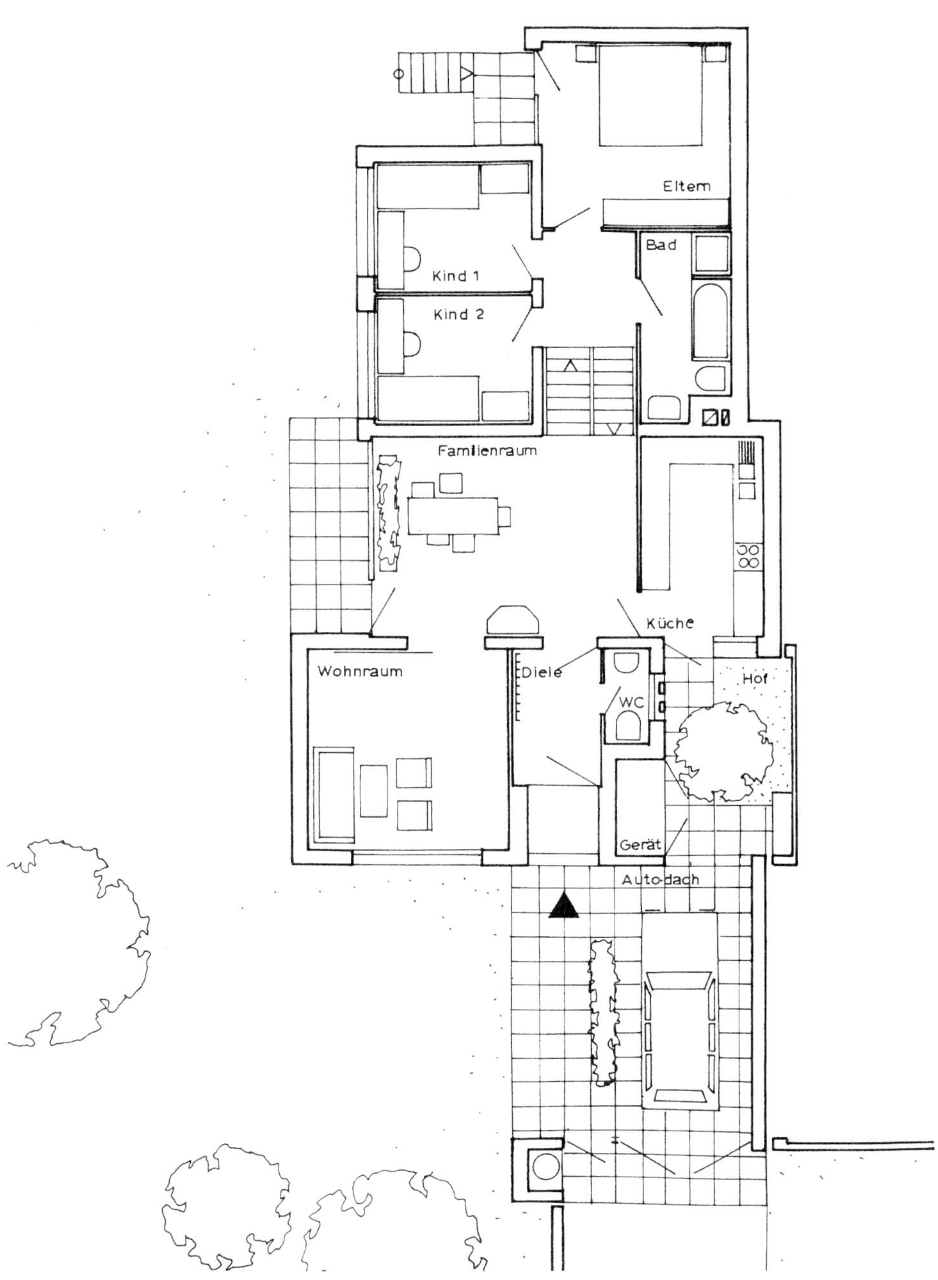

3. Floor plan of type II.
4. Site plan.
5. Sketches by the architect.

3. Grundriß des Typs II.
4. Lageplan.
5. Skizzen des Architekten.

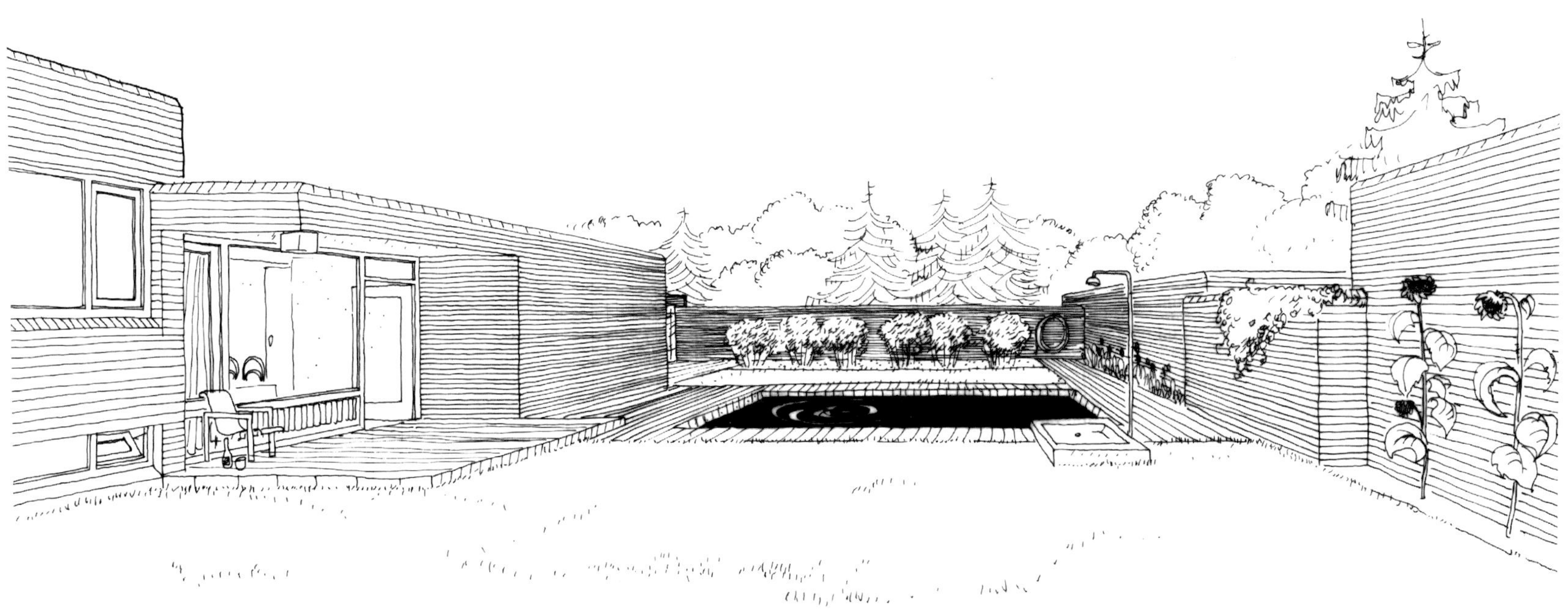

SOS youth home, Müllheim, 1965–68

The project was to build, on the south slope of
an abandoned vineyard, a home for 30 boys who
had outgrown the SOS children's villages. For a
building in this landscape only a one- or two-storey
structure was possible. It consists of a two-storey
staff building located next to the road, and the
main building, both connected by a covered stairwell and by the basement. The entrance is emphasized by a tall heating chimney. The main corridor, which is spatially differentiated, begins with
a mud-room at the entrance and – as a »rue intérieure« with light from different directions, including
the roof – goes past the apartment of the head of
the home on one side and an inner courtyard with
sitting rocks in its center. Located along the courtyard are the hall, a library, and a common room.
The south end of the corridor, which is angled
because of a change in the direction of the slope,
gives access to five two-storey apartments for
groups of six boys each with bedrooms and bathrooms on the top floor and living rooms with small
gardens in front of them below. A side corridor
leads to the infirmary and the apartment of the
head of the home. In the basement, beside the
utility and store rooms, there are a music practice
room and a crafts and hobby workshop.

A towerlike expansion for 24 boys is being
planned adjoining the west balcony.

The building is presently being used as temporary housing for immigrants and regrettably has
badly deteriorated.

SOS-Jugendheim, Müllheim, 1965–68

Auf dem Südhang eines aufgelassenen Weinbergs
sollte ein Heim für 30 Jungen, die den SOS-Kin-
derdörfern entwachsen waren, gebaut werden.
Für einen Bau in dieser Landschaft kam nur eine
ein- bis zweigeschossige Struktur in Frage. Sie
ist gegliedert in einen an der Straße liegenden
zweigeschossigen Personalbau und den Hauptbau, die mit einem gedeckten Treppengang und
durch den Keller verbunden sind. Der Eingang
wird durch einen hohen Heizungskamin betont.
Der räumlich differenzierte Hauptgang beginnt mit
einem Schuhraum am Eingang und führt als »rue
intérieure« mit Licht aus verschiedenen Richtungen – auch aus dem Dach – an der Wohnung
des Heimleiters auf der einen Seite und an einem
Innenhof mit Sitzsteinen in der Mitte vorbei. An
ihm liegen der Saal, eine Bibliothek und ein Ge-
meinschaftsraum. Das Südende des wegen der
anderen Gefällerichtung abgewinkelten Flurs erschließt fünf zweigeschossige Appartements für
je sechs Jungen mit Schlafräumen und Bädern im
Obergeschoß und den Wohnräumen mit vorgelagerten Gärtchen darunter. An einem Nebenflur
liegen die Krankenzimmer und die Wohnung des
Heimleiters. Im Untergeschoß sind außer den
Technik- und Vorratsräumen ein Musikübungs-
raum und eine Bastelwerkstatt untergebracht.

Im Anschluß an den Westbalkon war eine turm-
artige Erweiterung für 24 Jungen geplant.

Der Bau wird heute zur Erstunterbringung von
Einwanderern benutzt und ist leider stark herun-
tergekommen.

1. View from the south.
2. Floor plan (ground floor).

1. Ansicht von Süden.
2. Grundriß (Erdgeschoß).

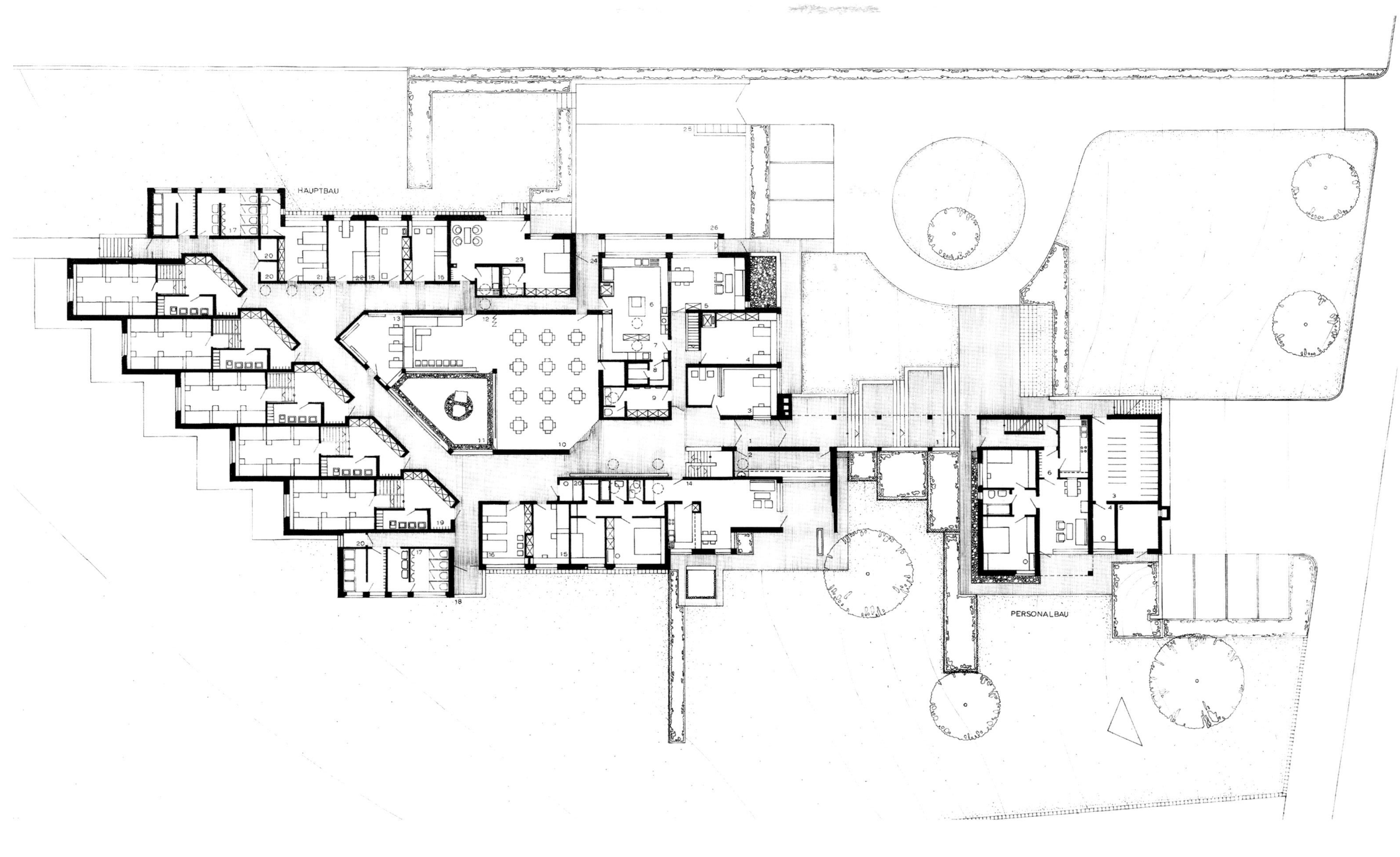

HAUPTBAU
PERSONALBAU

3. View from the north-east.
4. Detailed view from the east.
5. Corridor leading to the apartments for groups
of six boys.
6. Living room of one of the apartments.

3. Ansicht von Nordosten.
4. Detailansicht von Osten.
5. Korridor zu den Appartements für je sechs
Jungen.
6. Wohnraum in einem der Appartements.

BUWOG housing estate in Wien-Döbling, 1969–73

The plan was to build four three-storey apartment houses on the sloping building site between two streets. The buildings were intended for university teachers from out of town. With a cul-de-sac at the eastern edge, it was possible to create the central entrances, 12 garages under the narrow ends of the apartment houses and 13 parking spaces approximately 1.20 meters (4 feet) below the level of the garden courtyards.

As a result of the diagonal slope of the site, a split-level type with two apartments per floor was created for the three upper buildings. Only house No. 4, which is on level ground, has continuous ceilings. A total of 23 three- to six-room apartments were developed. In order to deal with the required variations in apartment size efficiently, the floor plan was divided into an invariable »core« consisting of the rooms necessary in any apartment – hallway, WC, kitchen, storeroom, study, living room with eating area, balcony, and bathroom – and a variable »addition« with up to four bedrooms.

All the rooms – including the bedroom hallway (which can be used as a sewing area) – have windows. The staggering of the ground plans and the resulting corner windows, which face east, allow some sunlight even for the north rooms and a view of the city from east-facing windows or the Wienerwald from west-facing windows. By this means and by the staggering of the buildings it was possible to avoid as much as possible the bleak, monotonous view of the rear of the building next door that meets the eye when rows of apartment buildings are parallel to each other.

The architect believes and hopes that slight variations in the façades will help residents to tell the buildings apart and thus create a sense of belonging.

Wohnanlage der BUWOG in Wien-Döbling, 1969–1973

Stadtplanerisch waren auf dem Hanggrundstück zwischen zwei Straßen vier dreigeschossige Wohnblocks vorgesehen, die auswärtigen Hochschullehrern vorbehalten sein sollten. Mit einer Sackgasse am Ostrand konnten die zentralen Eingänge, 12 Garagen unter den Schmalseiten der Blocks und 13 Einstellplätze etwa 1,20 m unter dem Niveau der Gartenhöfe erschlossen werden.

Angeregt durch das Diagonalgefälle des Hanges, entstand für die drei oberen Häuser ein versetztgeschossiger Zweispännertyp. Nur Haus 4 in ebener Lage hat durchlaufende Decken. Insgesamt ergaben sich 23 Wohnungen mit drei bis sechs Zimmern. Um die verlangten Wohnungsgrößenvarianten rationell zu bewältigen, wurde der Wohnungsgrundriß in einen invariablen »Kern« der in jeder Wohnung notwendigen Räume – Diele, WC, Küche, Abstellraum, Arbeitszimmer, Wohnraum mit Eßplatz, Loggia und Bad – sowie einen variablen »Anbau« mit bis zu vier Schlafzimmern geteilt.

Alle Räume – auch der Schlafzimmerflur (der als Nähplatz genutzt werden kann) – haben Fenster. Die Staffelung der Grundrisse und die daraus abgeleiteten, nach Osten gerichteten Eckfenster ermöglichen auch für die Nordräume etwas Sonne und einen Blick nach Osten auf die Stadt bzw. für die nach Westen gerichteten auf den Wienerwald. Hierdurch und durch die Staffelung der Baukörper ist die bei parallelen Zeilen aufkommende Öde des immer gleichen Blicks auf die Hinterseite des Gegenübers weitmöglichst ausgeglichen.

Die leicht variierten Fassaden könnten zur Unterscheidbarkeit und damit zur Heimatbildung der Bewohner beitragen, glaubt und hofft der Architekt.

1. Site plan.
2, 3. Floor plans with fixed core and variable extensions.

1. Lageplan.
2, 3. Grundrisse mit festem Kern und variablen Anbauten.

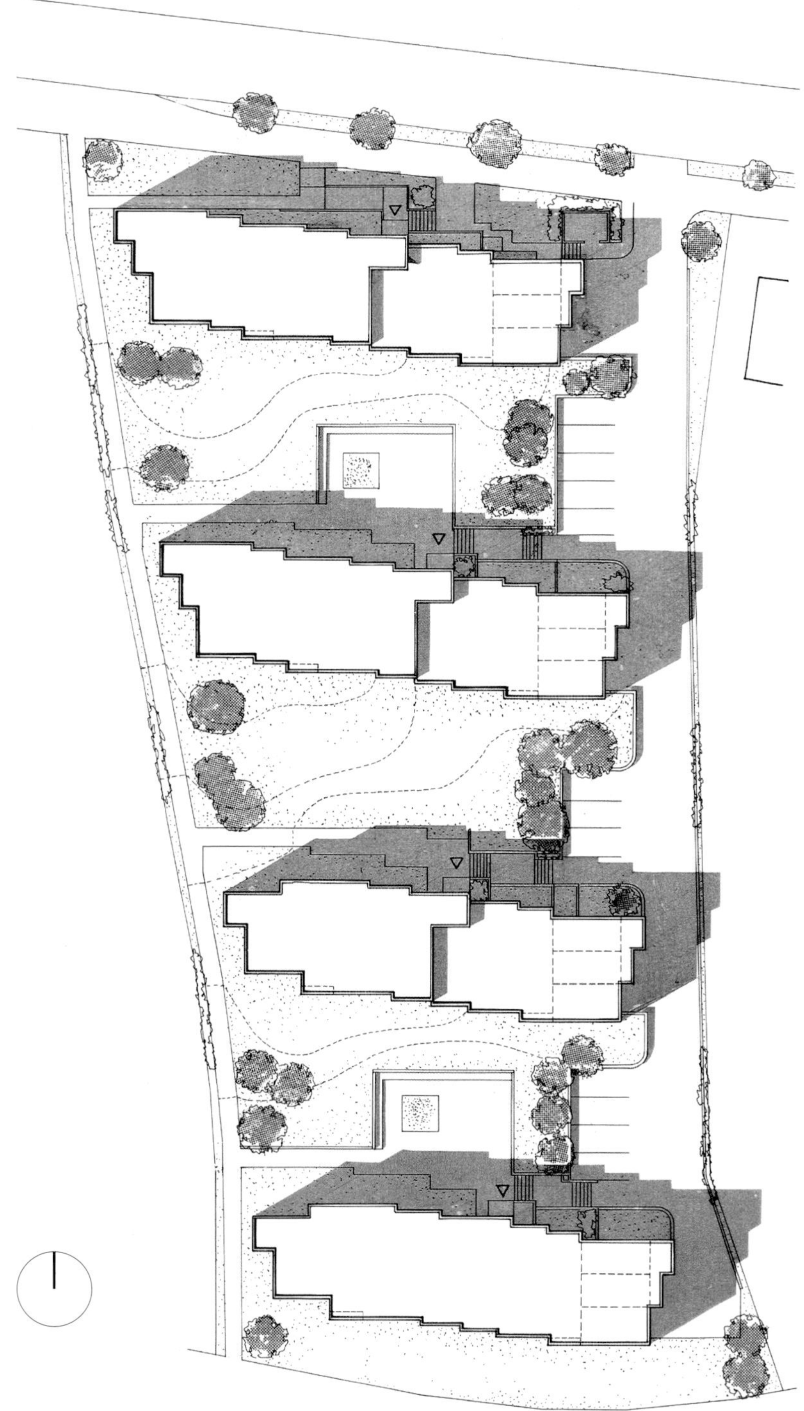

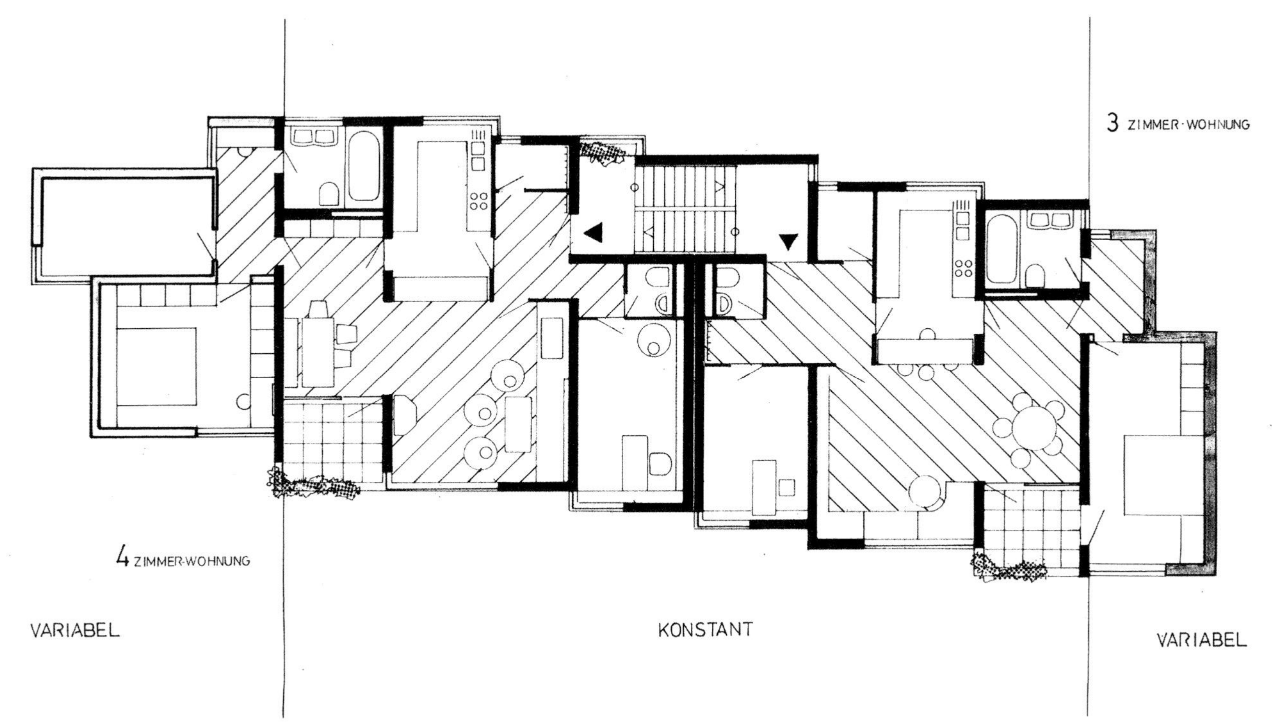

3 ZIMMER·WOHNUNG
4 ZIMMER·WOHNUNG
VARIABEL
KONSTANT
VARIABEL

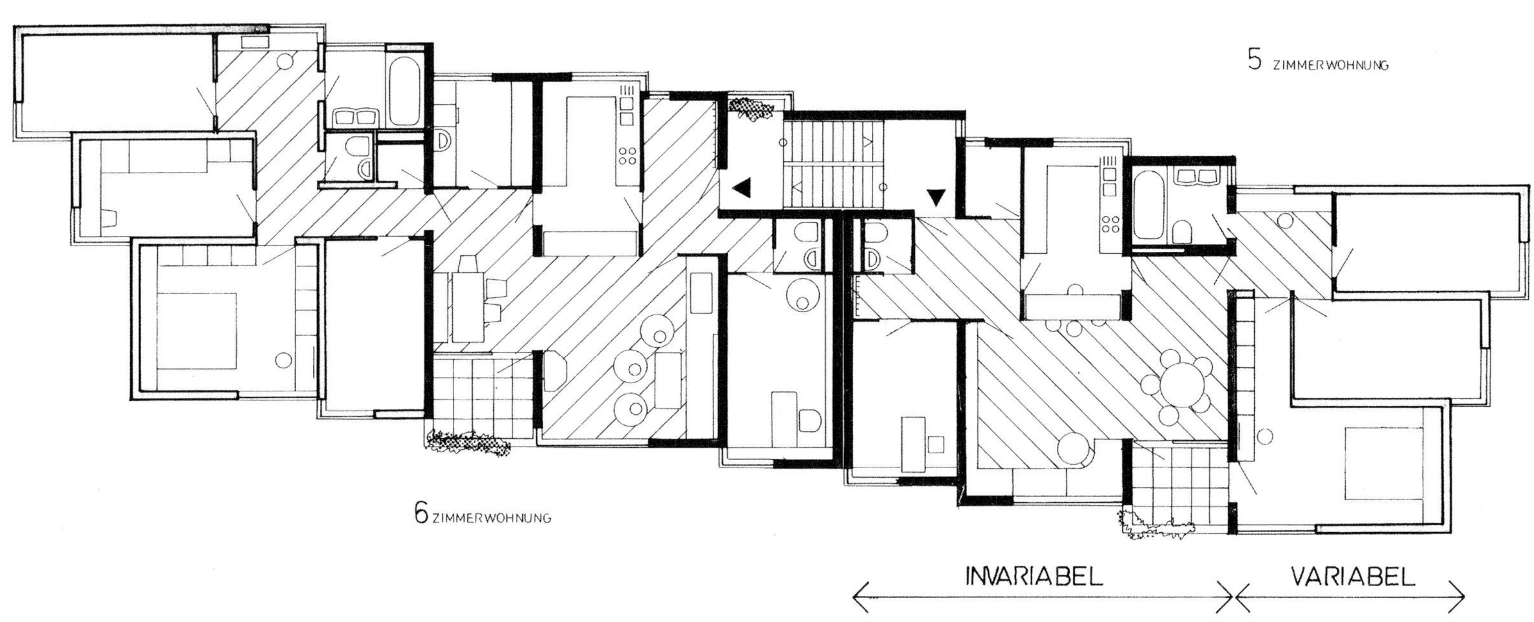

5 ZIMMERWOHNUNG
6 ZIMMERWOHNUNG
INVARIABEL
VARIABEL

4. View from the east.
5. Detailed view from the south.

4. Ansicht von Osten.
5. Detailansicht von Süden.

**Urban renewal at Brigittaplatz, Wien-
Brigittenau, 1975–81**

Four eight-storey rows of houses consisting predominantly of three-room apartments stand perpendicular to Jägerstrasse. The open spaces between the rows of houses were not blocked off
from the street, so that increasing traffic emissions
could penetrate the areas unimpeded.

The goal of planning was therefore to close the
open spaces off toward the street while adding
architectural space. The open spaces became
places that offer residents a sheltered environment. The new six-storey implant buildings are
connected with the existing buildings by means
of narrow building elements without impairing the
view. There is now a more versatile mix of housing
available: one-, two-, and four-room apartments
at three apartments per floor. Only the kitchen
oriels face the street, with terra-cotta balustrades,
echoing the material of the church across the
street.

Along their entire length, the ground floors are
arcaded in front of the stores. The gate in block 2
leads into a connecting pedestrian path between
Brigittaplatz and Gerhardusgasse. This is where
the psychotherapy center and the regional museum were built on. On the street side, the gable
ends of the original buildings now have built-on
wrought-iron balconies covered with vines. These
balconies and the greater height of the buildings
create an encompassing façade rhythm.

The »Tower House« with its stores, doctors'
offices, and apartments is a landmark for east-
west pedestrian traffic to the city center and
north–south traffic to the neighboring marketplace. The »gate house« emphasizes access
from the east. Courtyards 2 and 3 have had underground car parks built under them.

**Stadterneuerung am Brigittaplatz, Wien-
Brigittenau, 1975–81**

Vier achtgeschossige Zeilen mit überwiegend
Dreizimmerwohnungen stehen senkrecht zur
Jägerstraße. Die Freiflächen waren zur Straße hin
offen, so daß die zunehmenden Verkehrsimmis-
sionen voll eindringen konnten.

Ziel der Planung war daher die raumbildende
Abschließung gegen die Straße. Die Freiflächen
wurden zu Freiräumen, die den Bewohnern eine
geborgene Wohnumwelt bieten. Die neuen sechs-
geschossigen Implantatbauten schließen mit
schmalen Bauteilen aussichtsschonend an den
Bestand an. Das Wohnungsangebot findet mit
Ein-, Zwei- und Vierzimmerwohnungen bei drei
Wohnungen pro Geschoß ein variableres Gemen-
ge. Nur die Küchenerker sind auf die Straße gerichtet, mit Brüstungen aus Backstein in Anglei-
chung an das Material der gegenüberliegenden
Kirche.

Die Erdgeschosse sind auf der ganzen Länge
vor den Läden arkadiert. Das Tor in Block 2 erschließt eine Fußgängerverbindung vom Brigittaplatz zur Gerhardusgasse. Hier sind die psycholo-
gische Beratungsstelle und das Bezirksmuseum
angebaut. Die Giebel der Bestandsbauten erhielten zur Straßenseite vorgebaute Balkone in einem
Stahlgerüst, das berankt wird. Damit und durch
die größere Höhe ergibt sich ein übergeordneter
Fassadenrhythmus.

Das »Turmhaus« mit Läden, Arztpraxen und
Wohnungen akzentuiert den ost–westlichen Fuß-
gängerverkehr zur Stadtmitte und den nord–süd-
lichen zum benachbarten Markt. Das »Torhaus«
betont den Zugang von Osten. Die Höfe 2 und 3
wurden mit Tiefgaragen unterkellert.

1. Perspective drawing.
2. Axonometric drawing.

1. Perspektive.
2. Axonometrie.

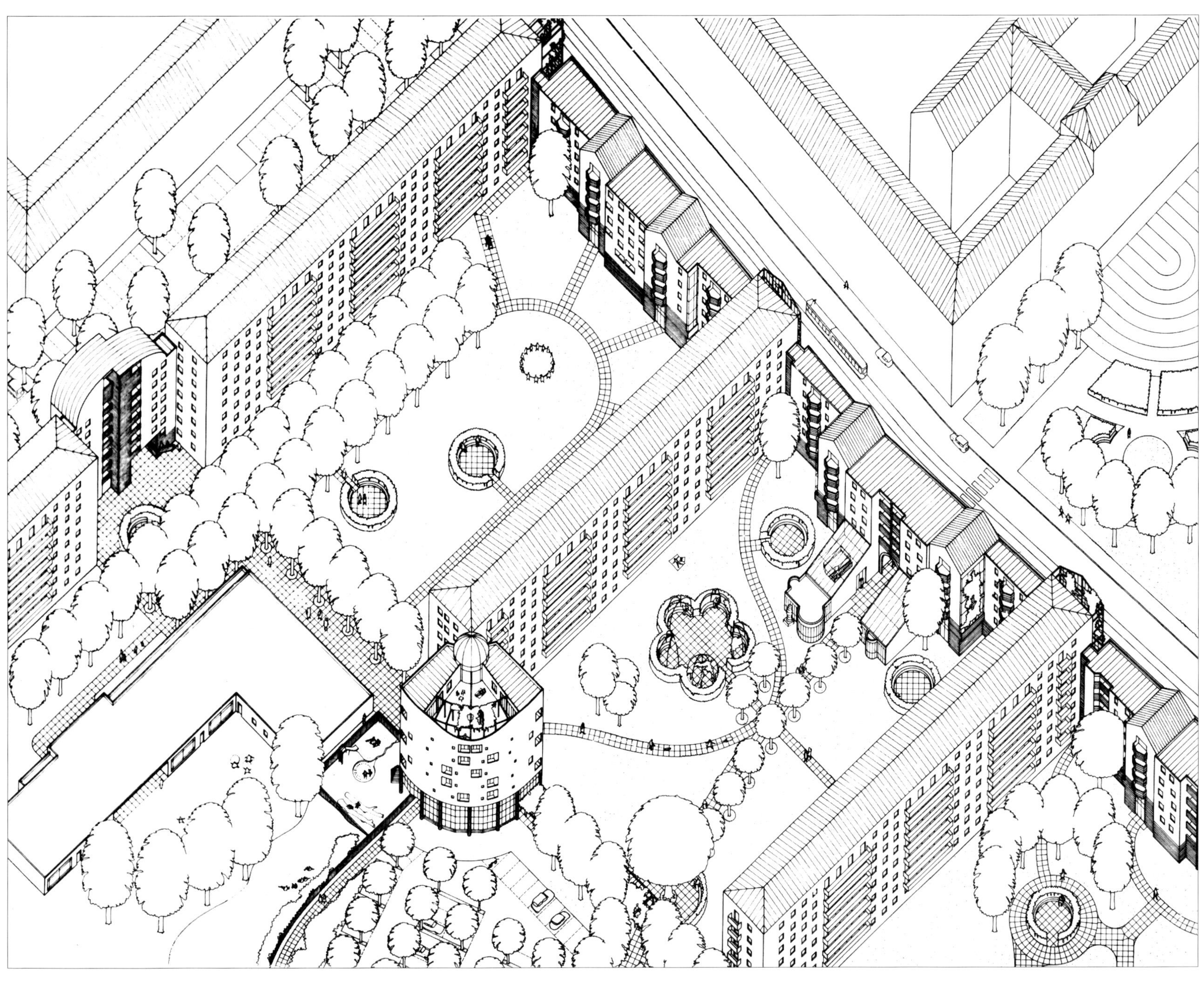

3. Site plan.
4. Floor plans (from bottom to top: standard floor, 1st floor, ground floor, ground floor and 1st floor, 2nd floor and 3rd floor). On top is the »Tower House«.

3. Lageplan.
4. Grundrisse (von unten nach oben: Regelgeschoß, 1. Obergeschoß, Erdgeschoß, Erdgeschoß und 1. Obergeschoß, 2. Obergeschoß und 3. Obergeschoß). Oben das »Turmhaus«.

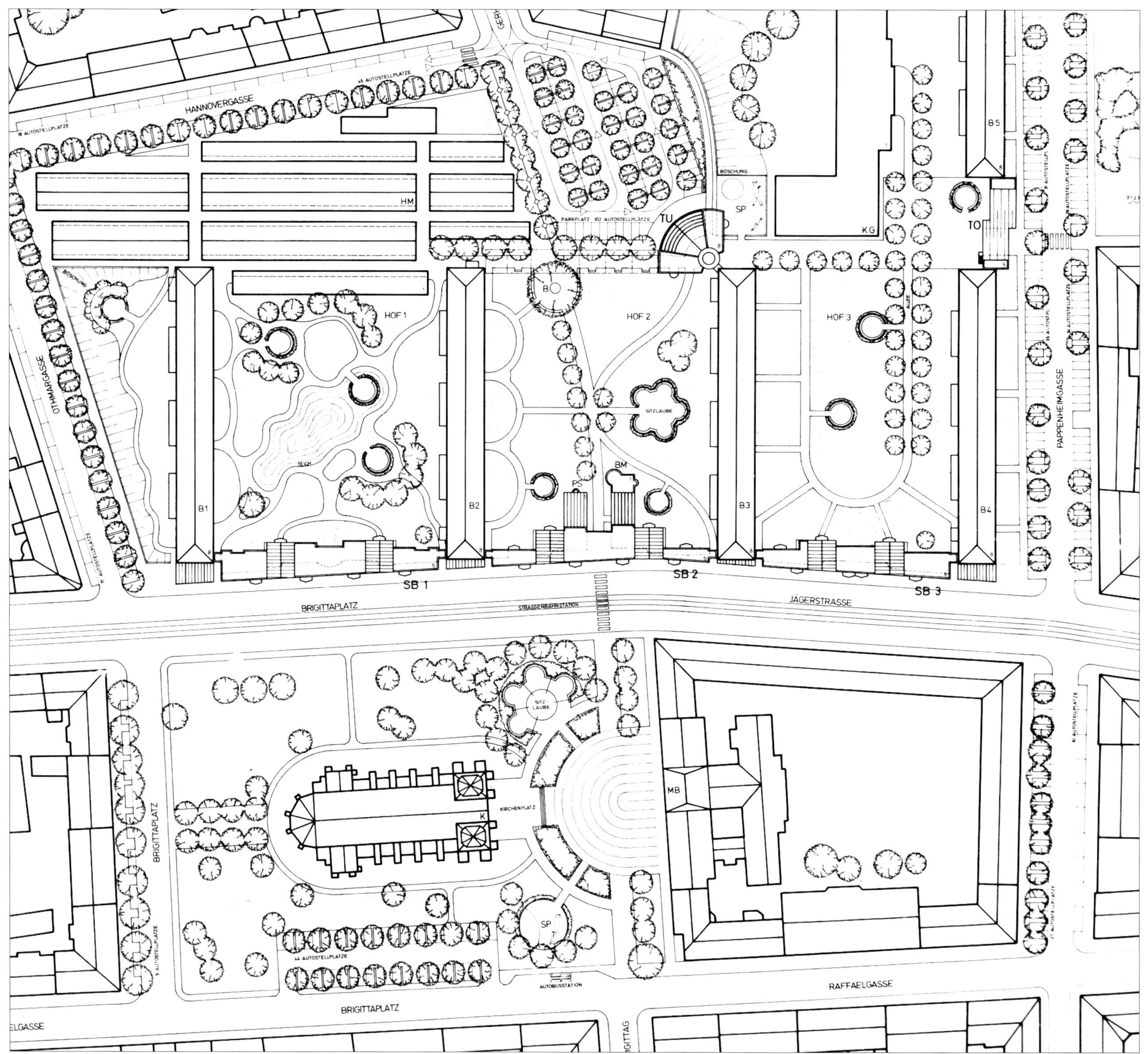

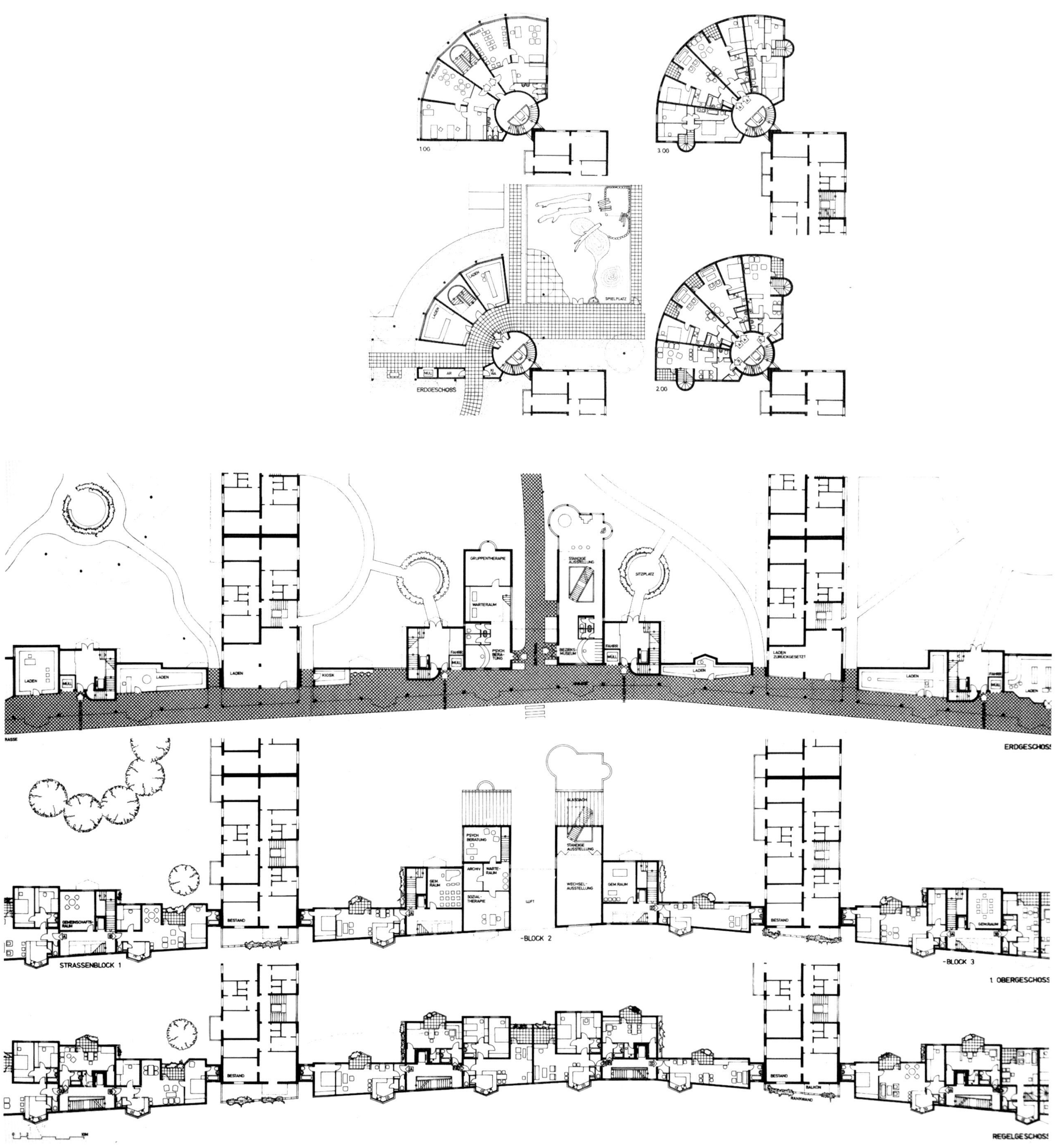

1.OG
3.OG
2.OG
SPIELPLATZ
ERDGESCHOSS
MÜLL
AR
LADEN
GRUPPENTHERAPIE
WARTERAUM
STÄNDIGE AUSSTELLUNG
SITZPLATZ
BEZIRKS MUSEUM
FAHR
MÜLL
LADEN
KIOSK
PSYCH BERATUNG
LADEN ZURÜCKGESETZT
TERRASSE
ERDGESCHOSS
PSYCH BERATUNG
ARCHIV
WARTE RAUM
GEM RAUM
SOZIAL THERAPIE
GLASDACH
STÄNDIGE AUSSTELLUNG
WECHSEL AUSSTELLUNG
GEM RAUM
BESTAND
LUFT
BLOCK 2
STRASSENBLOCK 1
BLOCK 3
1. OBERGESCHOSS
BESTAND
BALKON
REGELGESCHOSS

Leberberg urban expansion, Wien-Simmering, 1981–94

(with Ernst Heiß, Josef Krawina, Ernst Plischke, Michael Wachberger and Fritz Weber)

The urban-planning site, sloping 10 m toward the Danube River, is located between three main traffic arteries and a projected motorway. The project was limited to between five and six floors, thus taking on an intermediary role between the two 12-storey adjacent buildings.

In the middle is the park – bordered by a school and six apartment houses with spacious courtyards. A »ring road«, which has trees on both sides and parking spaces, encircles the buildings and continues northward between the city center, churches, and other apartment buildings, which on the west side are scheduled for a later stage of construction. In the north and south, low buildings adjoin existing, similar structures. Along the heavily traveled west street there are factory buildings, and the Simmering center buildings are planned at the junction with the east-west »link«, which has a streetcar line that connects the three building sites. It was possible to preserve Leberweg – the old pedestrian connection between Kaiserebersdorf and the main cemetery of Vienna. A projected pond in the park was accepted only when it was proposed that rainwater from the roofs of buildings around the park would be discharged into it.

Apartment blocks surrounding a central courtyard were **the** type of residential building preferred in late-19th century Gründerzeit Vienna urban expansions. Though considered capitalistic by the prejudiced, they are popular with residents because of their green, quiet, child-friendly courtyards. In the process of full realization they were, for the most part, replaced by other types of residential buildings.

Stadterweiterung Leberberg, Wien-Simmering, 1981–94

(mit Ernst Heiß, Josef Krawina, Ernst Plischke, Michael Wachberger und Fritz Weber)

Zwischen drei Hauptverkehrsstraßen und einer geplanten Autobahn liegt das zur Donau hin 10 m abfallende Planungsgrundstück. Die Bebauung wurde auf fünf bis sechs Geschosse beschränkt, um eine Mittlerrolle zwischen den beiden zwölfgeschossigen Nachbarbebauungen zu erreichen.

In der Mitte liegt der Park – umrandet von einer Schule und sechs Blockrandbebauungen mit weiträumigen Höfen. Eine zweiseitig baumbepflanzte »Ringstraße« mit Parkplätzen umfaßt die Bebauungen und setzt sich nach Norden zwischen Zentrum, Kirchen und weiteren Wohnbauten fort, die auf der Westseite einem späteren Bauabschnitt vorbehalten bleiben. Im Norden und Süden schließen sich Flachbauten an bestehende, ähnliche Bebauungsformen an. Entlang der stark frequentierten Weststraße sind Gewerbebauten, an der Einmündung der ost–westlich verlaufenden »Spange« – mit der die drei Baugebiete verbindenden Straßenbahn – die Zentrumsbauten geplant. Der Leberweg – die alte Fußgängerverbindung zwischen Kaiserebersdorf und dem Wiener Hauptfriedhof – konnte erhalten werden. Ein Teich im Park war nur mit dem Vorschlag durchzusetzen, das Regenwasser der Dächer der Randbauten einzuleiten.

Die Blockrandbebauung, **der** Wohnbautyp in den Wiener Stadterweiterungen der (vorurteilsbelasteten kapitalistischen) Gründerzeit – doch bei Bewohnern wegen der grünen, ruhigen und kindersicheren Höfe beliebt –, wurde in der Realisierungsphase großenteils durch andere Wohnbautypen ersetzt.

1. Model.
2. Site plan.

1. Modell.
2. Lageplan.

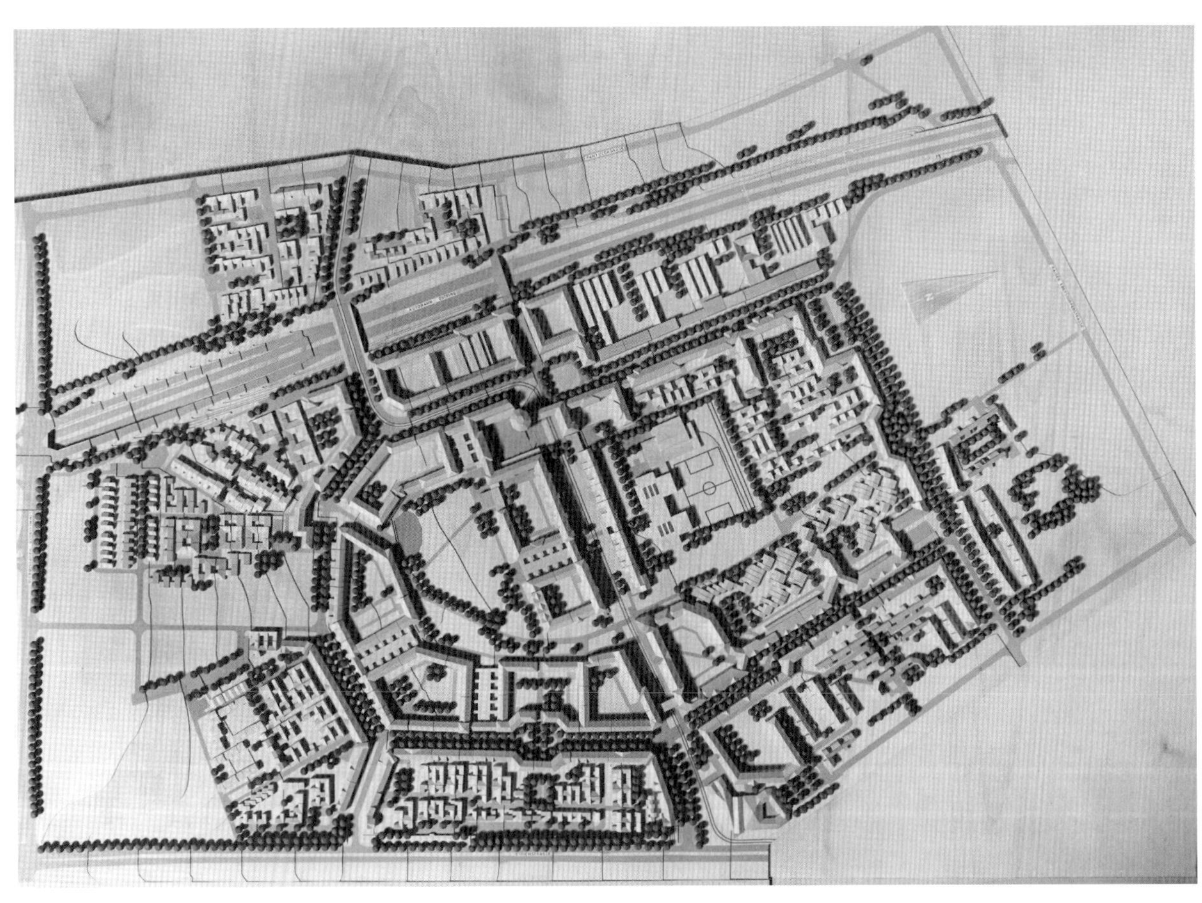

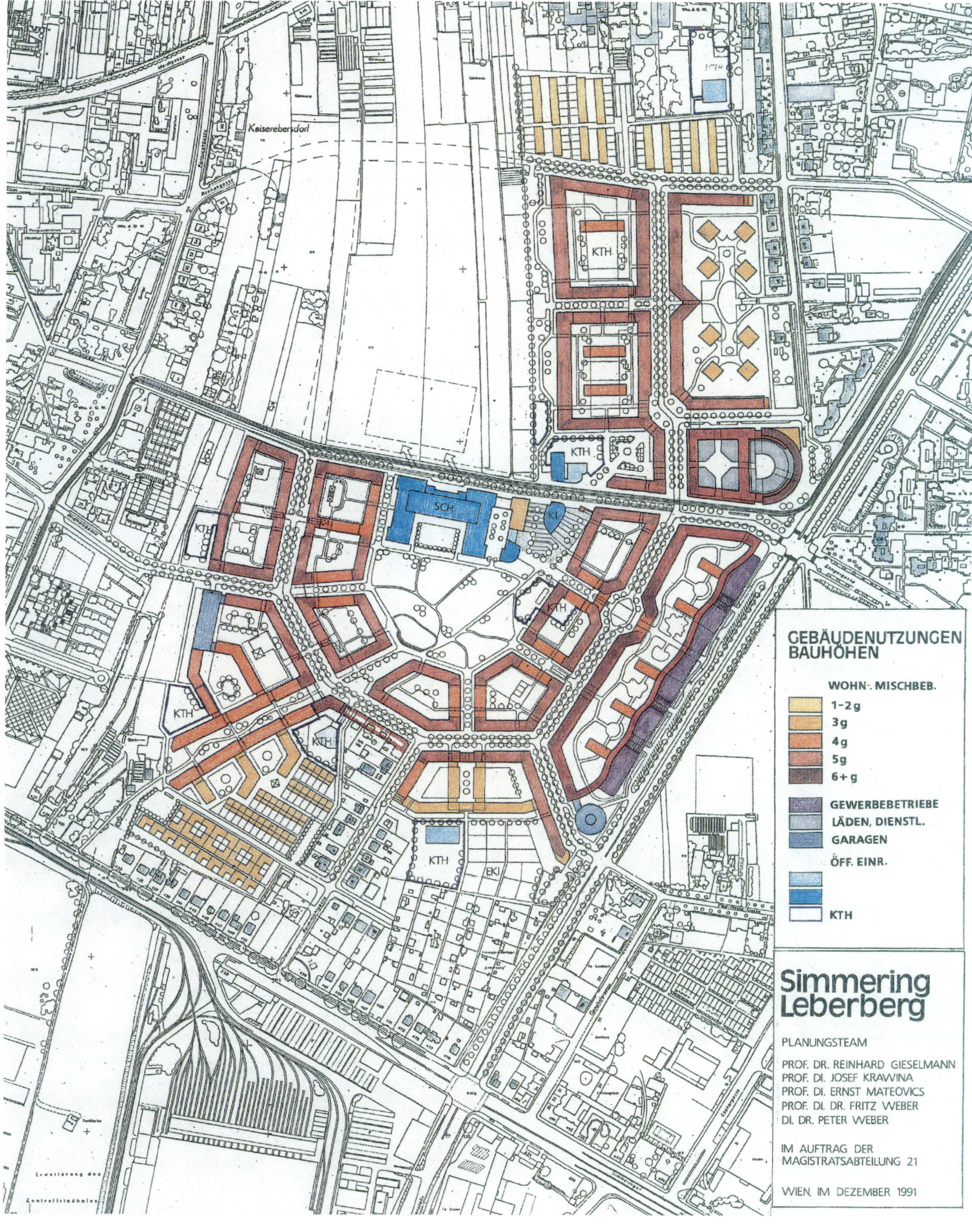

Kaiserebersdorf
KTH
KTH
KTH
KTH
KTH
KTH
KTH
KTH
SCH
KI
EKI

GEBÄUDENUTZUNGEN
BAUHÖHEN

WOHN-, MISCHBEB.
1-2 g
3 g
4 g
5 g
6+ g

GEWERBEBETRIEBE
LÄDEN, DIENSTL.
GARAGEN
ÖFF. EINR.

KTH

Simmering
Leberberg

PLANUNGSTEAM

PROF. DR. REINHARD GIESELMANN
PROF. DI. JOSEF KRAWINA
PROF. DI. ERNST MATEOVICS
PROF. DI. DR. FRITZ WEBER
DI. DR. PETER WEBER

IM AUFTRAG DER
MAGISTRATSABTEILUNG 21

WIEN, IM DEZEMBER 1991

Apartment block and shopping center in the Draschegründe, Wien-Favoriten, 1983–88

U-shaped, three- to four-storey apartment buildings whose courtyards open out into the central, elongated, slightly curved green space (above an underground car park) – this was the urban planning project that was awarded the 1st prize and implemented without cuts (architects: Mayr and Ortner). In the middle of the east side is the shopping center. It was the task of the author, who was awarded the 2nd prize, to implement the latter and the apartment house facing it in the middle of the development, as well as to create a »symbol« for the complex.

The location of the apartment house is characterized by a peaceful green space on the east side and a noisy industrial area with an elevated highway on the west side. The adjacent apartment houses on the north and south side stood in a diverging angle created by a curve in the road. This fact led to the idea of making the west façade slightly concave, which was then livened up by the convex walls of the living rooms. The real reason for this was that the view from the French windows of the living rooms thus bypasses the unpleasant sight of industrial sheds. For the same reason the balconies of the two-sidedly oriented floor plans are situated on the less noisy east courtyard side. The two concave sections of this façade stretch between three projecting buildings. In front of them are the tenants' gardens, slightly above the level of the two halves of the courtyard, one of which is intended for adults and the other for children. The courtyard is only minimally separated from the communal green area by a trellis.

»A palace for the people« was how a Japanese colleague who was familiar with Vienna characterized the building. As a »symbol«, the well house was created with seven pillars and seven tondi for the portraits of the seven architects.

The one-storey shopping center consists of two long buildings with a glass roof covering the central shopping arcade.

Wohnblock und Einkaufszentrum im Gebiet Draschegründe, Wien-Favoriten, 1983–88

U-förmige, drei- bis viergeschossige Wohnbauten, deren Höfe sich zu der mittleren, langgestreckten, leicht gebogenen Grünanlage (über einer Tiefgarage) öffnen – das war die städtebauliche Idee, die mit dem 1. Preis ausgezeichnet und ohne Abstriche realisiert wurde (Architekten Mayr und Ortner). In der Mitte der Ostseite liegt das Einkaufszentrum. Dieses und den ihr gegenüberliegenden Block in der Mitte der Wohnanlage sowie ein »Symbol« der Anlage zu realisieren, war Aufgabe des Verfassers als 2. Preisträger.

Die Lage des Blocks ist gekennzeichnet durch eine ruhige Grünanlage im Osten und ein lautes Industriegebiet mit einer Autobahn in Hochlage im Westen. Der nördliche und der südliche Nachbarblock standen in einem durch die Wegkurve entstehenden divergierenden Winkel. Aus dieser Anregung ergab sich die leichte Konkavität der Westfassade, die dann durch die konvexen Wände der Wohnräume belebt wurde. Dies hatte den realen Grund darin, daß der Blick aus den französischen Fenstern der Wohnräume auf diese Weise an dem unerfreulichen Ausblick auf Industrieschuppen vorbeigehen kann. Aus demselben Grund liegen die Balkone der zweiseitig orientierten Grundrisse auf der ruhigeren östlichen Hofseite. Die beiden konkaven Teile dieser Fassade sind zwischen drei Risalitbauten gespannt – davor die Mietergärten, etwas über dem Niveau der beiden Hofhälften, von denen die eine für Erwachsene und die andere für Kinder vorgesehen ist. Gegen die gemeinsame Grünanlage ist der Hof nur leicht durch eine Pergola abgetrennt.

Als »Schloß für das Volk« charakterisierte ein wienkundiger japanischer Kollege den Bau. Als »Symbol« entstand das Brunnenhaus mit sieben Säulen und sieben Tondi für die Porträts der sieben Architekten.

Das eingeschossige Einkaufzentrum besteht aus zwei langen Baukörpern mit einem die mittlere Passage überdeckenden Glasdach.

1. Perspective drawing.
2–4. Floor plans (ground floor, standard floor, top floor).

1. Perspektive.
2–4. Grundrisse (Erdgeschoß, Regelgeschoß, Dachgeschoß).

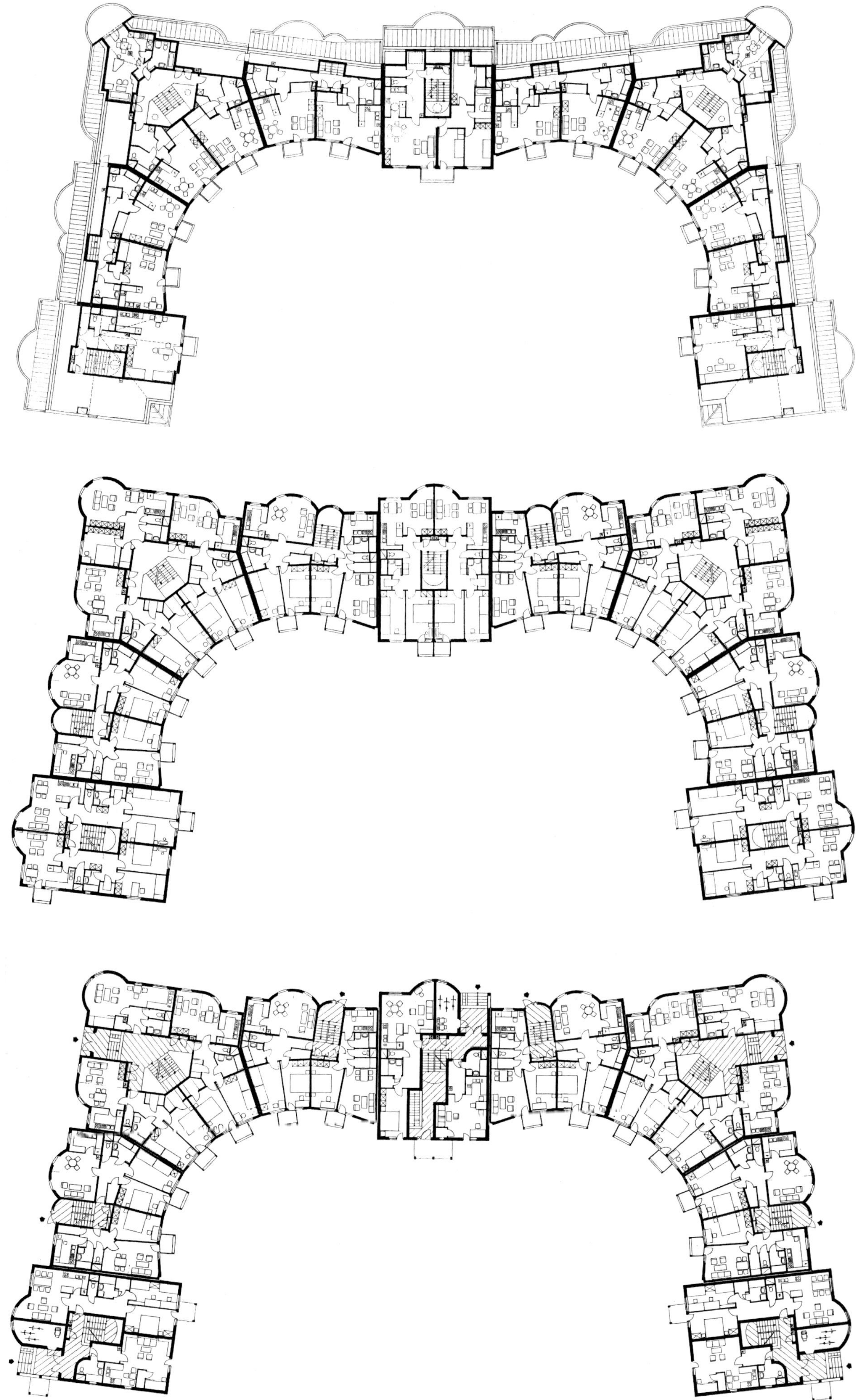

AK
STEMPEL
MARKEN

5. View of the courtyard side.
6. Detailed view of a corner of the building.
7. View of the outer side.

5. Ansicht der Hofseite.
6. Detailansicht einer Gebäudeecke.
7. Ansicht der Außenseite.

Urban renewal in the Karmeliterviertel, Wien-Leopoldstadt, 1984/85, 1989–93

A competition for the regeneration of the Karmeliterviertel in Vienna's 2nd District – known for being »a densely built-up maze of narrow little streets with not a single parking space left« – produced three first prizes – one of them awarded to the author, who incidentally was given the plum job of filling an empty site in one of the narrowest little streets in Vienna. If he kept to the building line – with a taller building across the street on the south side, made possible by previous zoning laws – it was to be expected that there would be a lot of shade. However, if the main building was set 3 meters (10 feet) behind the building line, there would not only be more sun, but also it would be possible not just to build rooms in the attic, but instead to build a complete extra floor. As the building was rotated 90 degrees, the rear of the building also got to have longer hours of sunlight, as well as a greater distance from the house behind it.

The projecting buildings on both sides which were flush with the building line, with their small apartments, create a connection to the equally taller neighboring buildings on the right and left. Behind faux gables are the terraces of the uppermost apartments, from which you can see the tower of the Stephansdom (St. Stephen's Cathedral) in the south.

By moving the building line back, a small front garden was created as well – a welcome accent in the narrow street. On the façade, which is painted red, there is a white trellis for a red climbing rose.

There are a total of eleven apartments on the upper floors, with five types of floor plans. In addition, there are two shops on the ground floor.

Stadterneuerung im Karmeliterviertel, Wien-Leopoldstadt, 1984/85, 1989–93

Aus einem Wettbewerb für die Regeneration des Karmeliterviertels im 2. Wiener Bezirk – bekannt als »dicht verbaut, stark vergasselt und total verparkt« – gingen drei erste Preise hervor – einer davon für den Verfasser, u. a. belohnt mit der Füllung einer Baulücke an einer der schmalsten Gassen Wiens. Die Bauflucht einzuhalten – bei einem wegen einer früheren Bauordnung höheren Gegenüber auf der Südseite – , da war viel Verschattung zu erwarten. Den Hauptbaukörper aber um 3 m hinter die Bauflucht zu setzen, würde außer mehr Besonnung auch zur Folge haben, daß kein Dachausbau, sondern statt dessen ein ganzes Vollgeschoß möglich wäre. Mit einem – darüber hinaus – zum Viertelkreis abgedrehten Baukörper gewann auch die Rückseite länger Sonne und dazu mehr Abstand vom dahinter liegenden Haus.

Die beiderseitig bis auf die Bauflucht vorgezogenen Risalitbauten mit den kleinen Wohnungen stellen den Anschluß an die ebenfalls höheren Nachbarbauten rechts und links her. Hinter Scheingiebeln liegen die Terrassen der obersten Wohnungen, von denen man im Süden den Turm des Stephansdoms sehen kann.

Durch die Zurücknahme der Flucht entstand auch ein kleiner Vorgarten – willkommener Akzent in der schmalen Gasse. Die rot gefärbte Fassade trägt ein weißes Rankgerüst für eine rote Rose.

Insgesamt liegen in den Obergeschossen elf Wohnungen mit fünf Grundrißtypen, dazu kommen im Erdgeschoß zwei Läden.

The built project
1. Floor plans (ground floor, standard floor).
2. View from the street.
3. View from the courtyard.

Das gebaute Projekt
1. Grundrisse (Erdgeschoß, Regelgeschoß).
2. Ansicht von der Straße.
3. Ansicht vom Hof.

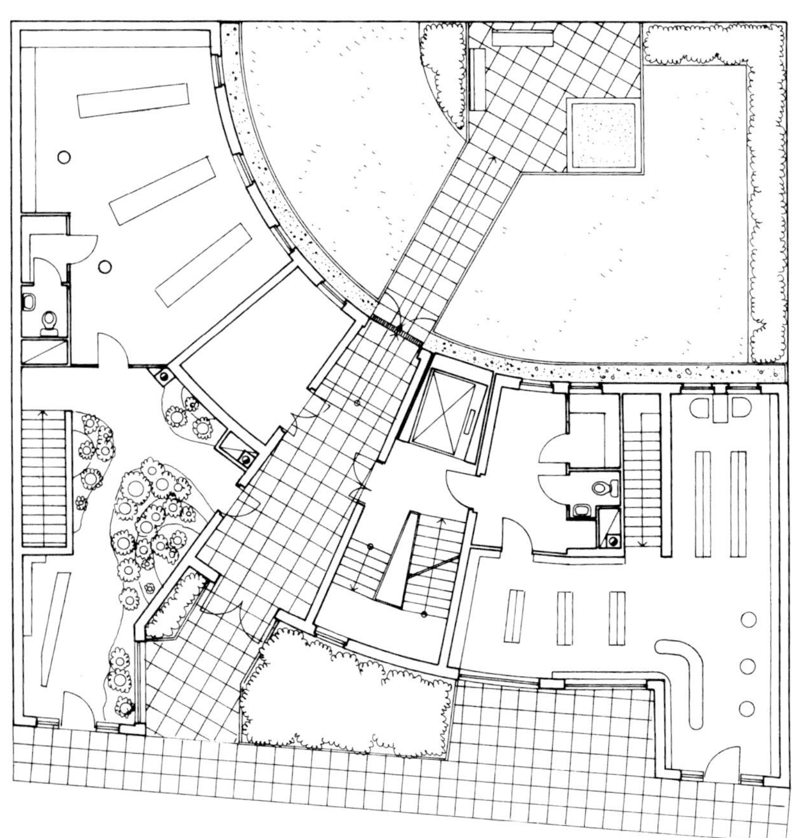

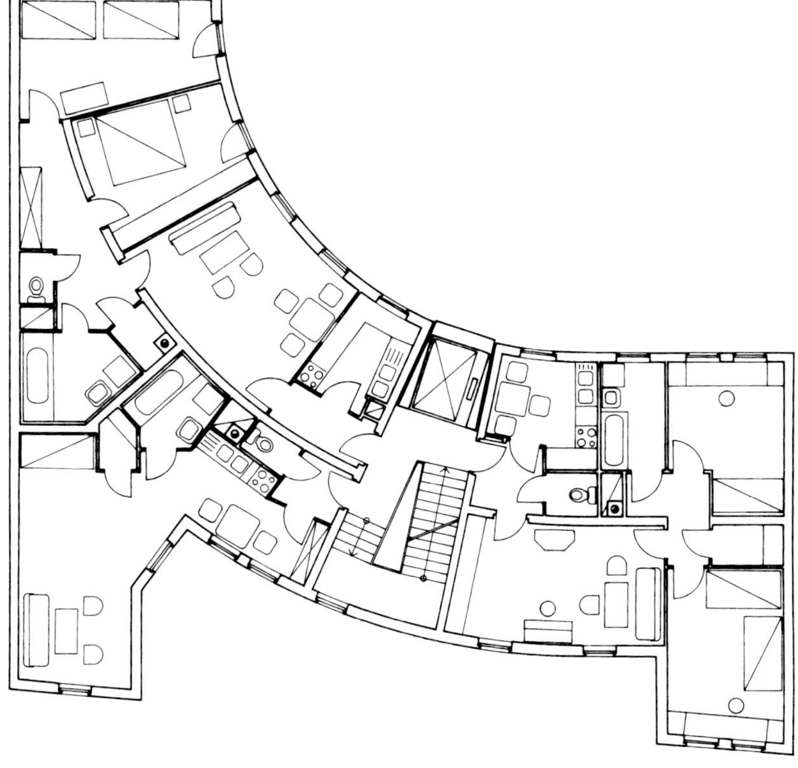

The competition project
4. Perspective drawing.
5. Floor plans, elevations and section.

Das Wettbewerbprojekt
4. Perspektive.
5. Grundrisse, Aufrisse und Schnitt.

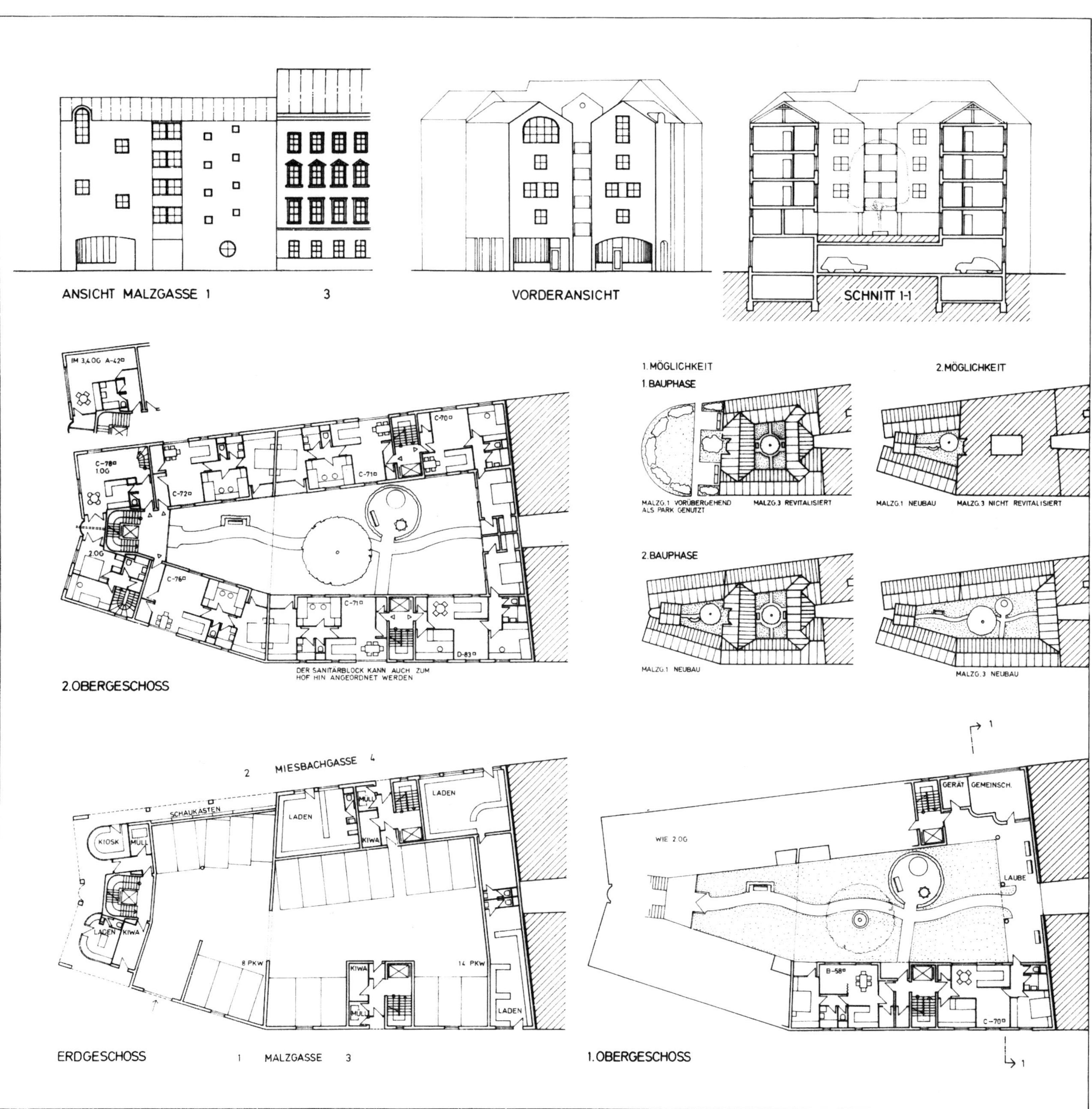

ANSICHT MALZGASSE 1   3
VORDERANSICHT
SCHNITT 1-1
IM 3,4.OG A-42□
C-78□
1.OG
C-72□
C-71□
C-70□
2.OG
C-76□
C-71□
D-83□
DER SANITÄRBLOCK KANN AUCH ZUM
HOF HIN ANGEORDNET WERDEN
2.OBERGESCHOSS
1.MÖGLICHKEIT
1.BAUPHASE
MALZG.1 VORÜBERGEHEND   MALZG.3 REVITALISIERT
ALS PARK GENUTZT
2.BAUPHASE
MALZG.1 NEUBAU
2.MÖGLICHKEIT
MALZG.1 NEUBAU   MALZG.3 NICHT REVITALISIERT
MALZG.3 NEUBAU
2   MIESBACHGASSE   4
SCHAUKASTEN
LADEN
MÜLL
LADEN
KIWA
KIOSK MÜLL
LADEN KIWA
8 PKW
KIWA
MÜLL
14 PKW
LADEN
ERDGESCHOSS   1   MALZGASSE   3
1
GERÄT GEMEINSCH.
WIE 2.OG
LAUBE
B-58□
C-70□
1.OBERGESCHOSS
1

Apartment block in Leberberg, Wien-Simmering, 1993–96
(with Anna Stern and Franz Zeyer)

The architects who were jointly commissioned to work on this building section in the city center, Gieselmann and Pekka Janhunen, were willing to observe the zoning laws. The block was divided, and together the architects worked out the access points, so that, for instance, the entrances of the adult school planned by Janhunen and of Gieselmann's two-storey municipal library could be located at the same street entrance. Incidentally, each architect built according to his own ideas: Janhunen preferred Scandinavian simplicity, while Gieselmann accentuated his street corners with sculptured balconies and, on the »link« building section, built one semicircular and two quadrant-shaped roof superstructures with apartments that tenants could finish themselves. The straight sections of the block have four apartments per floor – each with a partial view of the courtyard. The corner buildings are reserved for smaller and more individual apartments. The Gieselmann share has a total of 74 apartments.

In front of the two apartments for the handicapped and four additional apartments on the ground floor are the tenants' gardens. The courtyard has an area of 2,000 square meters (21,528 square feet) and is directly connected with the public park. Under the courtyard is the underground car park with 134 spaces, accessible from all the stairwells. In view of the adjacent building on the link – a school – a corresponding shop was built on the northeast corner of the block.

A rather practical argument against apartment blocks with central courtyards is that »aggravation« is caused in the corners on the courtyard side when apartments adjoin the courtyard from every side. On this block, such aggravation was avoided by building only one single apartment that filled the corner.

Wohnblock im Gebiet Leberberg, Wien-Simmering, 1993–96
(mit Anna Stern und Franz Zeyer)

Die mit diesem in der Mitte liegenden Bauteil gemeinsam beauftragten Architekten Gieselmann und Pekka Janhunen waren willens, die städtebaulichen Vorgaben auszuführen. Der Block wurde geteilt, die Anschlußstellen wurden gemeinsam erarbeitet, so daß z. B. die Eingänge der von Janhunen eingeplanten Volkshochschule und von Gieselmanns zweigeschossiger Stadtbücherei am gleichen Straßeneingang liegen konnten. Im übrigen baute jeder nach seinen Vorstellungen: Janhunen skandinavisch schlicht, Gieselmann akzentuierte seine Straßenecken mit plastischen Balkonen und setzte dem Bauteil der »Spange« eine halb- und zwei viertelkreisförmige Dachaufbauten mit Wohnungen zum Selbstausbau auf. Die geraden Teile des Blocks haben Vierspännergrundrisse – jeder mit Hofblickanteil. Die Eckbauten sind kleineren und individuelleren Wohnungen vorbehalten. Insgesamt hat der Anteil Gieselmanns 74 Wohnungen.

Den beiden Behinderten- und vier weiteren Wohnungen im Erdgeschoß sind Mietergärten vorgelagert. Der Hof ist 2 000 m² groß und hat direkten Anschluß an den öffentlichen Park. Unter dem Hof liegt die von allen Treppenhäusern zugängliche Tiefgarage mit 134 Plätzen. Angesichts des Nachbargebäudes an der Spange – einer Schule – wurde an der Nordostecke des Blocks ein entsprechender Laden eingebaut.

Ein eher sachliches Argument gegen Blockrandbebauungen ist die »Eckbelästigung« in den hofseitigen Ecken, wenn hier von jeder Seite eine Wohnung angrenzt. Sie wurde in diesem Block durch den Einbau von nur einer die Ecke ausfüllenden Wohnung vermieden.

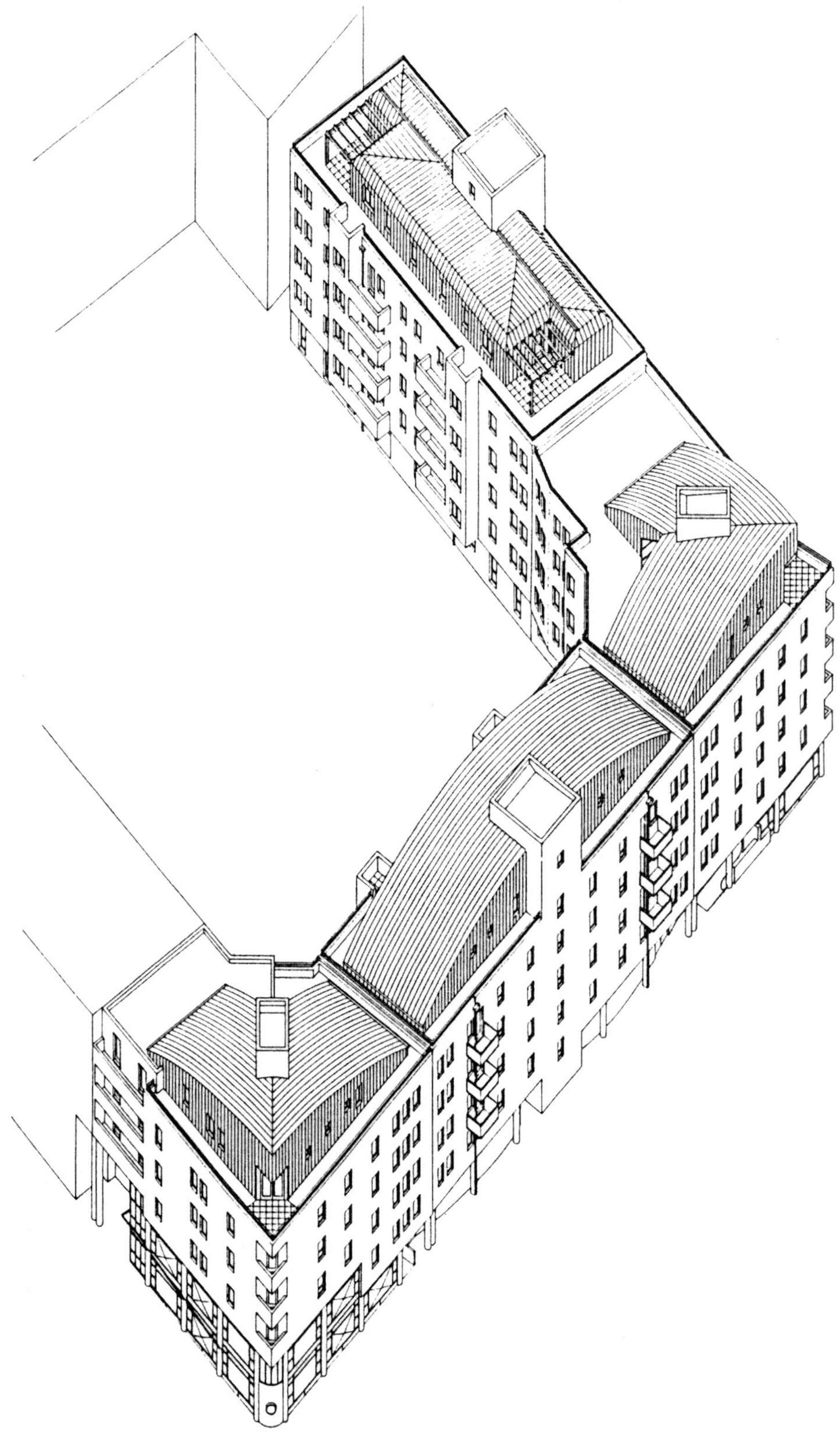

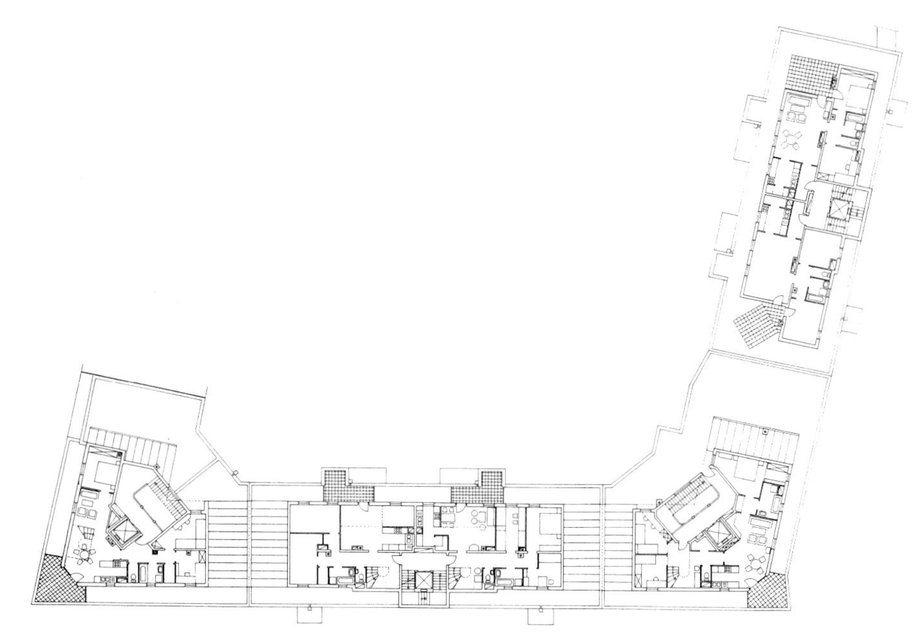

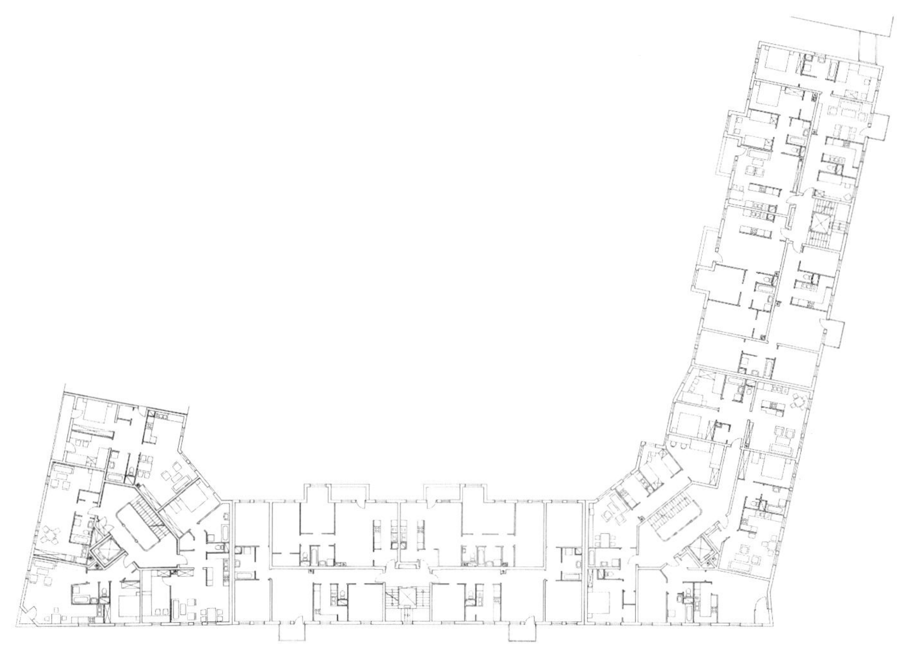

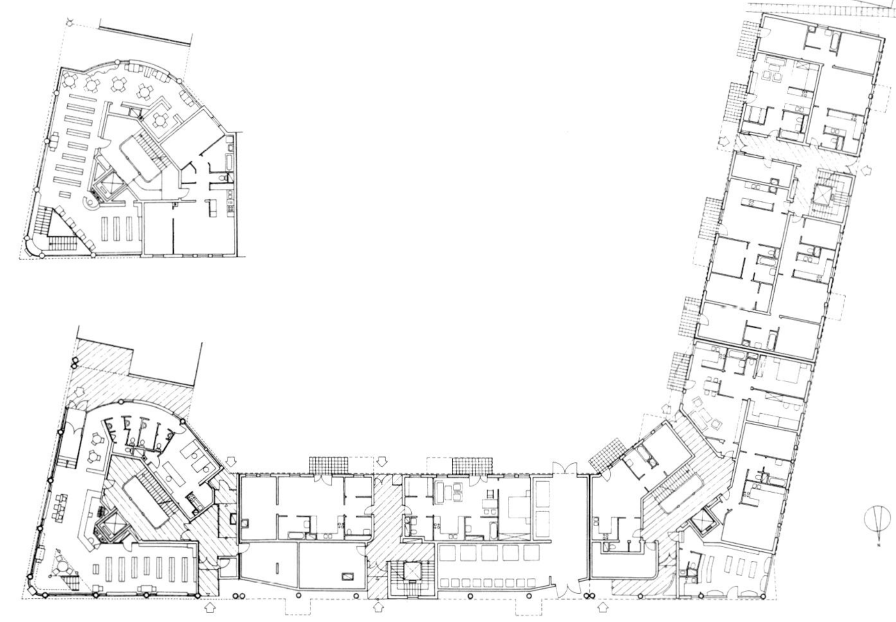

1. Axonometric drawing.
2–4. Floor plans (ground floor, standard floor,
top floor).

1. Axonometrie.
2–4. Grundrisse (Erdgeschoß, Regelgeschoß,
Dachgeschoß).

5. View from the street.
6. View from the courtyard.
7. Detailed view of a corner of the building.
8. Library.

5. Ansicht von der Straße.
6. Ansicht vom Hof.
7. Detailansicht einer Gebäudeecke.
8. Bibliothek.

Library of the Technische Universität Wien, Wien-Wieden, 1978–87
Reinhard Gieselmann (floor plan, interior design, furnishings), Justus Dahinden (façade design), Marchart & Moebius (mechnical engineering, coordination)

The main entrance is located on the street leading to the main building of the Technical University, which is closed to traffic, and is across from the entrance to the university's most important institute building. The lower-lying part of the entrance hall is appropriate for smaller exhibitions. In the background are the checkrooms, the toilets, and the staircase to the winter checkrooms in the basement. Three steps up in the two-storey section are the information desk, the entrances to the lift and the stairwell, the collection of textbooks and the cafeteria, which was put in later. The central point is the fountain with an ornamental spout out of a bronze lion's head. It determines the noise level, which decreases distinctly on the periodical floor one storey higher. In the three floors of stacks above the periodical floor, ceilings and walls are optimally insulated to provide the necessary silence. Group and individual reading tables are lined up along the windows, and a round table with ten computer stations is placed by the rounded corner where there is a bench to relax on while looking at the view outside. The illuminated center of the large room is filled by open-shelf collections of books. On the 5th floor, a lecture room has been partitioned off. The adjacent rooms and installations are arranged along the fire wall. The bookstore on the ground floor can be accessed from the entrance hall and the arcade. Next to it is the staff entrance with a separate stairwell to the 6th (administration) floor. The latter can also be accessed by fire escape from the lower floors. The administration floor houses those staff members who have little if any contact with the public, from the administration to the acquisition department to the bookbindery. The three lower floors include the stockrooms, among others.

Bibliothek der Technischen Universität Wien, Wien-Wieden, 1978–87
Reinhard Gieselmann (Grundriß, Innengestaltung, Möblierung), Justus Dahinden (Fassadengestaltung), Marchart & Moebius (Haustechnik, Koordination)

Der Haupteingang liegt an der verkehrsfreien Straße, die zum Hauptbau der TU führt, und gegenüber dem Eingang zum wichtigsten Institutsgebäude der Hochschule. Der tiefer liegende Teil der Eingangshalle eignet sich für kleinere Ausstellungen, im Hintergrund sind die Garderoben, die WCs und die Treppe zu den Wintergarderoben im Untergeschoß angeordnet. Drei Stufen höher im zweigeschossigen Teil liegen die Auskunftstheke, die Eingänge zum Aufzug und zum Treppenhaus, die Lehrbuchsammlung und die später eingebaute Cafeteria. Mittelpunkt ist der Brunnen mit dem wasserspeienden bronzenen Löwenkopf. Er bestimmt den Lärmpegel, der schon im darüber liegenden Zeitschriftengeschoß deutlich abnimmt. In den drei darüber liegenden Büchergeschossen ist an Decken und Wänden alles für die notwendige Stille getan. Die Gruppen- und Einzellesetische sind entlang den Fenstern gereiht, ein runder Tisch mit zehn Computerplätzen steht bei der abgerundeten Aussichtsecke mit einer Sitzbank zum Ausruhen. Die beleuchtete Mitte des Großraums füllen Bücherregale in Freihandaufstellung. Im 5. Obergeschoß ist ein Vortragsraum abgeteilt. Nebenräume und Installationen sind an der Brandwand angeordnet. Die Buchhandlung im Erdgeschoß ist von der Halle und von der Arkade aus zugänglich. Neben ihr liegt der Personaleingang mit eigenem Treppenhaus zum 6. Obergeschoß der Verwaltung. Über eine Feuertreppe ist diese auch von den Geschossen darunter aus zugänglich. Im Verwaltungsgeschoß sind von der Direktion über die Erwerbungsabteilung bis zur Buchbinderei die Mitarbeiter untergebracht, die kaum Publikumsverkehr haben. In den drei Untergeschossen liegen u. a. die Magazine.

1, 2. Perspective drawing and elevation of Gieselmann's alternative design for the façade which was realized by Justus Dahinden.

1, 2. Perspektive und Aufriß von Gieselmanns Alternativentwurf für die von Justus Dahinden realisierte Fassade.

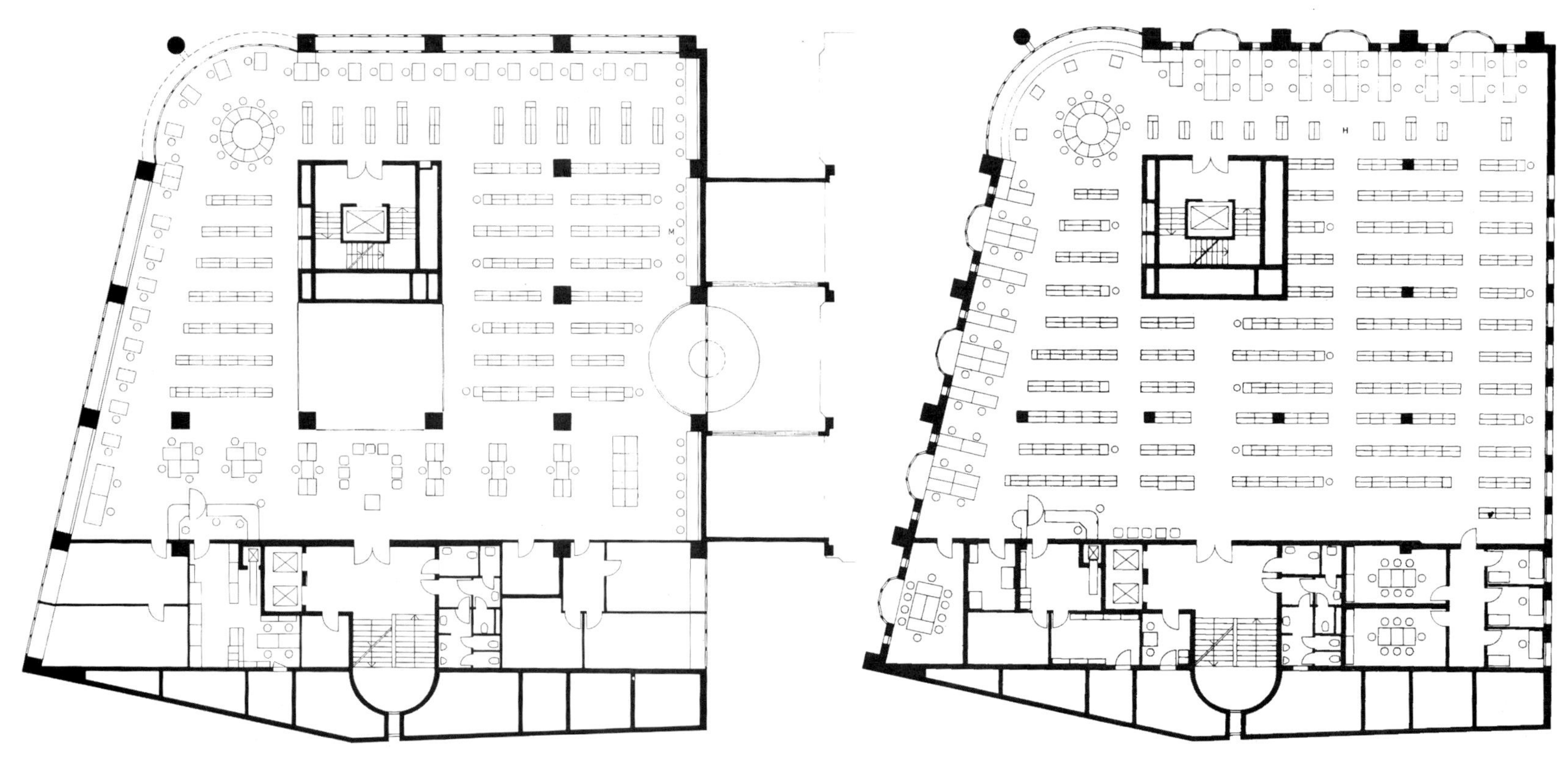
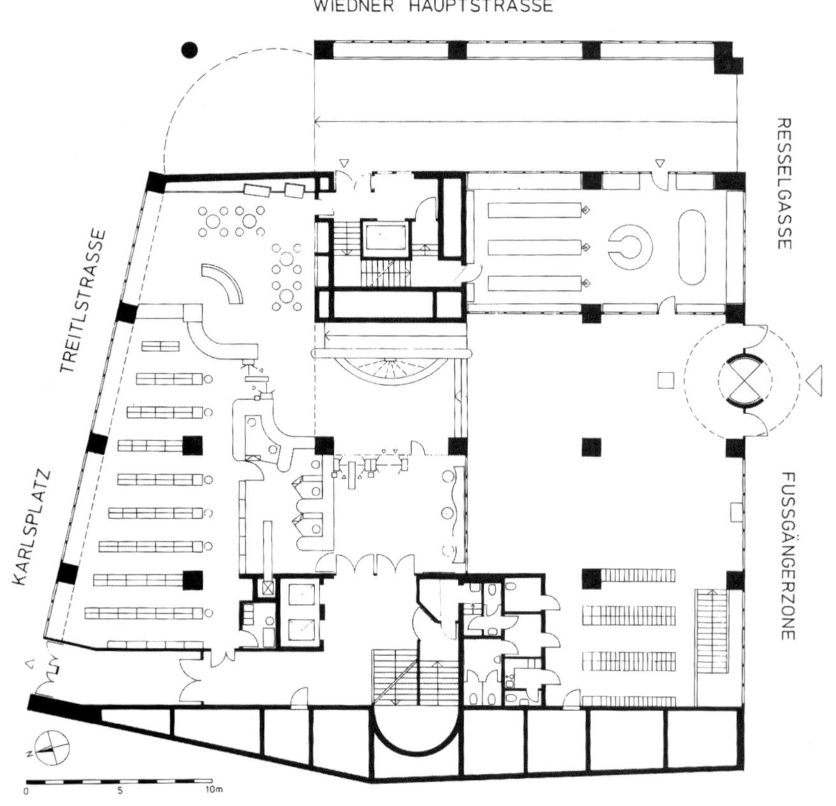

WIEDNER HAÚPTSTRASSE
RESSELGASSE
TREITLSTRASSE
KARLSPLATZ
FUSSGÄNGERZONE
0   5   10m

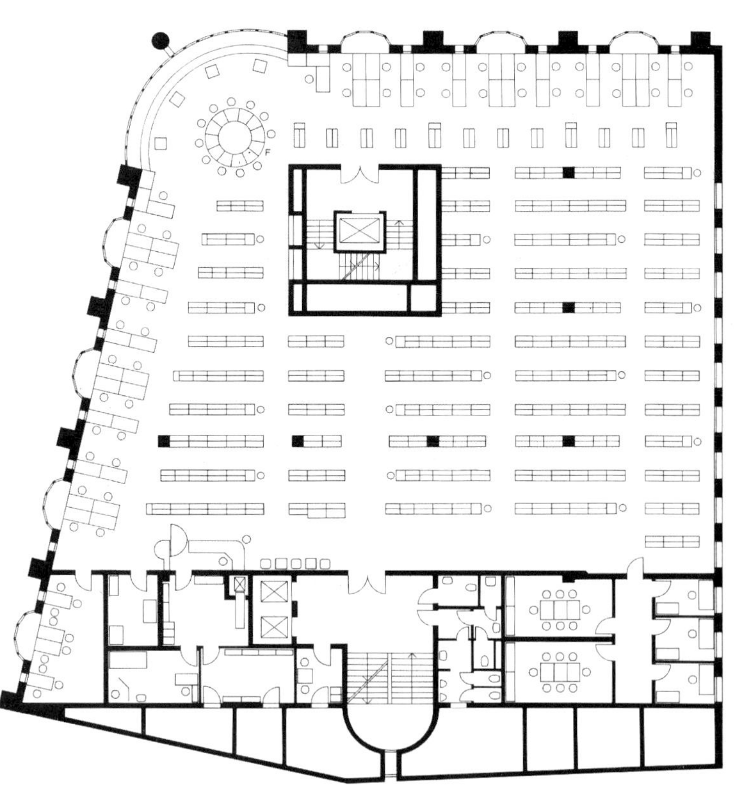

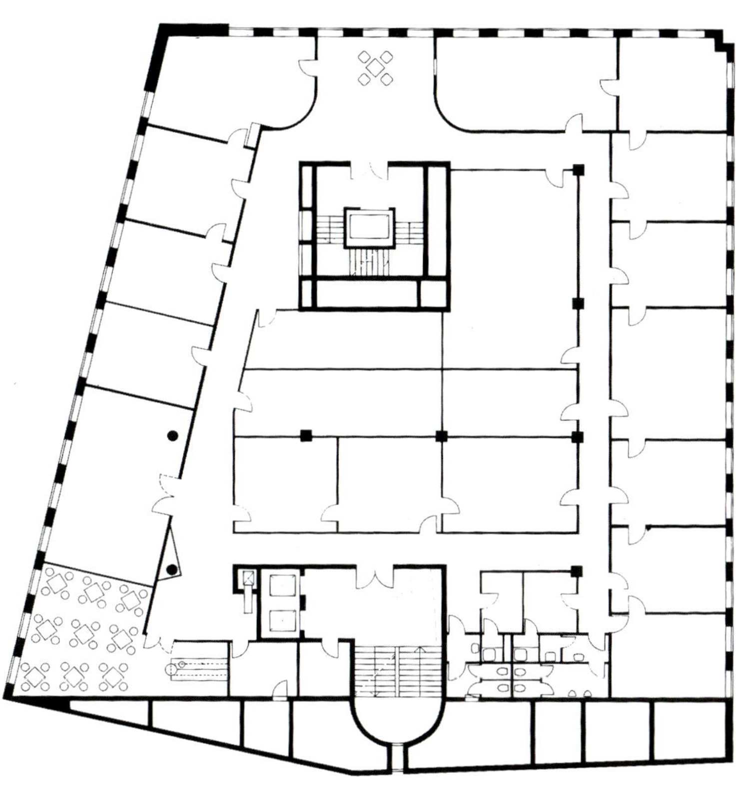

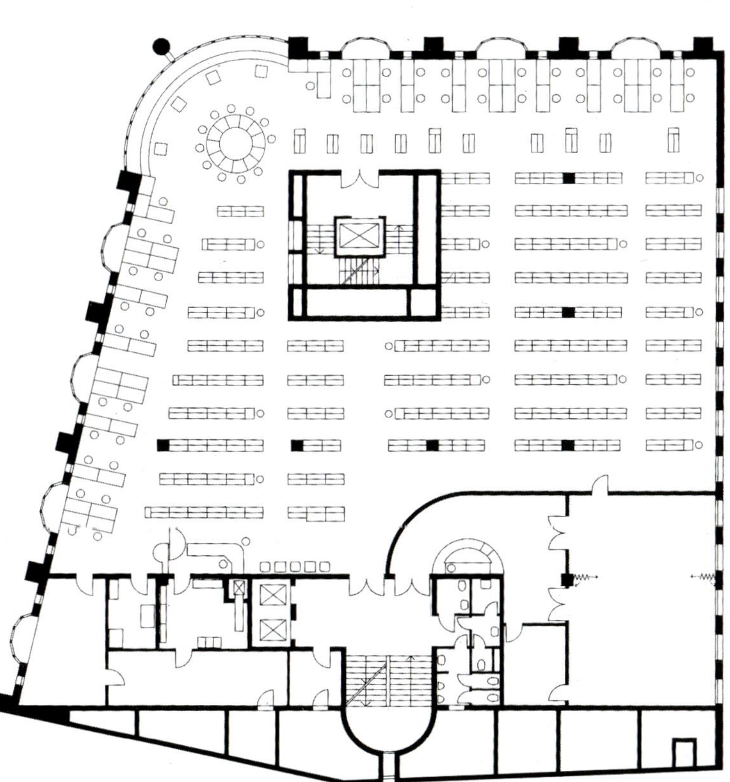

3–8. Floor plans (from bottom to top and from left to right: ground floor, 1st floor, 3rd floor, 4th floor, 5th floor, 8th floor).

3–8. Grundrisse (von unten nach oben und von links nach rechts: Erdgeschoß, 1. Obergeschoß, 3. Obergeschoß, 4. Obergeschoß, 5. Obergeschoß, 8. Obergeschoß).

9–11. Entrance hall with fountain (9, 10) and bookshop right to the entrance (11).

9–11. Eingangshalle mit Brunnen (9, 10) und Buchladen rechts vom Eingang (11).

9–11. Entrance hall with fountain (9, 10) and bookshop right to the entrance (11).

9–11. Eingangshalle mit Brunnen (9, 10) und Buchladen rechts vom Eingang (11).

12. Bookshop.
13. Information desk.
14. Reading room.

12. Buchladen.
13. Informationstheke.
14. Leseraum.

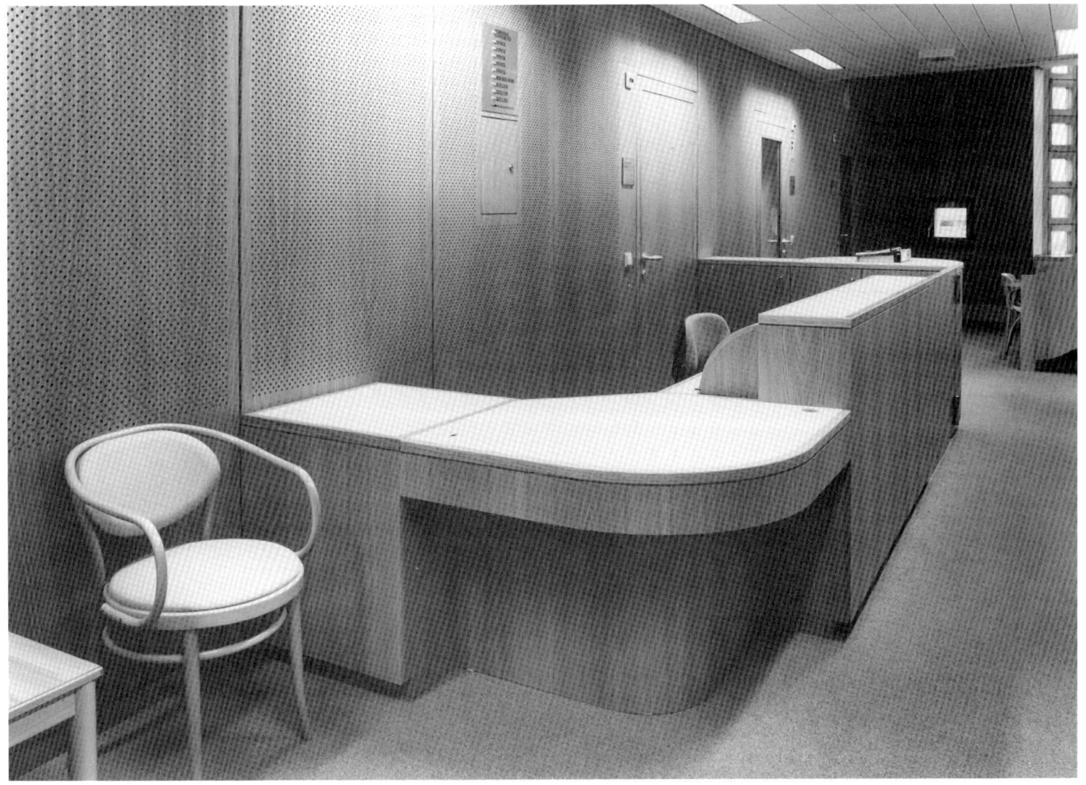

Church of St. Jakobus, Sinsheim, 1961–67, 1994–96

The 1967 church embodies – in new forms – the old, pre-Vatican Council idea of a church. There is a center aisle: a nave open to the altar with the questions of the people, and a chancel opened toward the nave for the answers from the altar. Built on in front is the entrance with a spiral floor plan that gathers and dismisses the worshipers. In the final curve is the baptismal font (baptism = entrance into the Church). The floor of the church is made of earth-colored exposed aggregate concrete; from it, made of the same material, grow the pillars of the gallery, as well as the supports of the benches and the seven steps to the altar. The walls are white and roughcast. In »musical« flourishes, the gallery stretches over the part of the room which narrows toward the back. The tower and sacristy are more or less separated from the nave. Between church and world, the confessionals are inserted in the outside wall. This wall curves at the end for a Lady altar. From the blind arcades grow the spandrels of the vault that overarches the room, which sweeps over it in huge arcs and was manufactured by hand during a cold winter as reed-mat plaster, with built-in light fixtures. Over the altar space, room was left for a skylight. Erich Hauser forged the cover of the baptismal font and the tabernacle, and the painter Franz Dewald ornamented the round and oval window lattices, which were filled with white opal glass.

During renovation (1994–96) the altar was placed lower down and closer to the congregation. The entrance was made smaller and the baptismal font was now made part of the altar space. This made it possible to have a day-to-day chapel. The painter Rafael Seitz created stained-glass church windows to replace the lattices. The walls were painted a pale pink, while the concrete parts are white.

Kirche St. Jakobus, Sinsheim, 1961–67, 1994–96

Die Kirche von 1967 verkörpert – in neuen Formen – die alte, vorkonziliare Idee von Kirche mit Mittelgang: ein zum Altar hin offenes Schiff mit den Fragen der Menschen und ein zum Schiff hin geöffneter Chor für die Antworten des Altars. Vorgebaut ist der Eingang mit sammelndem und entlassendem Spiralgrundriß – in der Endrundung der Taufbrunnen (Taufe = Eintritt in die Kirche). Der Kirchenboden ist aus Waschbeton in der Farbe der Erde; aus ihm wachsen aus dem gleichen Material die Pfeiler der Empore wie die Bankstützen und die sieben Stufen zum Altar. Die Wände sind weiß und rauh verputzt. In »musikalischen« Schwüngen breitet sich die Empore über den sich hinten verengenden Raumteil. Turm und Sakristei sind mehr und weniger vom Schiff abgesetzt. Zwischen Kirche und Welt sind die Beichthäuschen in die Außenwand eingeschoben. Diese krümmt sich am Ende für einen Marienaltar. Aus den Wandvorlagen wachsen die Zwickel des den Raum überspannenden Gewölbes, das sich in großen Bögen über den Raum schwingt und noch als Rohrmattenputz mit eingebauten Leuchten aus Gips in Handarbeit während eines kalten Winters hergestellt wurde. Über dem Altarraum wurde ein Oberlicht ausgespart. Erich Hauser schmiedete den Taufsteindeckel und den Tabernakel, der Maler Franz Dewald ornamentierte die runden und ovalen Fenstergitter, die mit weißem Opalglas ausgefüllt wurden.

Beim Umbau in den Jahren 1994–96 wurde der Altar tiefer und näher an die Gemeinde plaziert. Ein verkleinerter Eingang und der nun dem Altarraum zugeordnete Taufstein machten eine Alltagskapelle möglich. Der Maler Rafael Seitz schuf anstelle der Gitter farbige Kirchenfenster. Die Wände wurden zartrosa, die Betonteile weiß gestrichen.

1. View from the east with bell tower.
2. View from the north-west with the entrance
on the west side.

1. Ansicht von Osten mit Glockenturm.
2. Ansicht von Nordwesten mit dem Eingang auf
der Westseite.

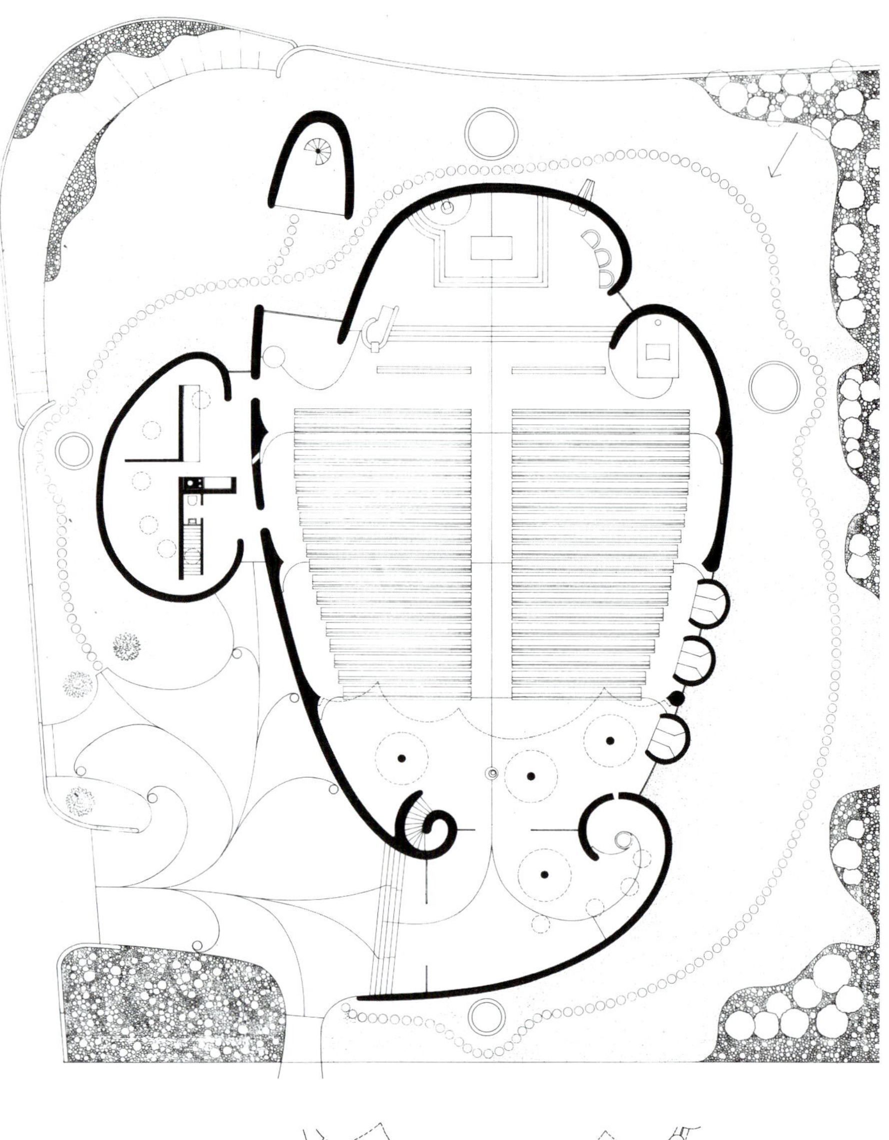

3. Floor plan.
4. Floor plan of the new chapel near the entrance.
5. Perspective drawing of the new chapel.
6. Model of the vault.
7. Interior view towards the altar.
8. Interior view towards the entrance.

3. Grundriß.
4. Grundriß der neuen Kapelle am Eingang.
5. Perspektive der neuen Kapelle.
6. Gewölbemodell.
7. Innenansicht in Richtung Altar.
8. Innenansicht in Richtung Eingang.

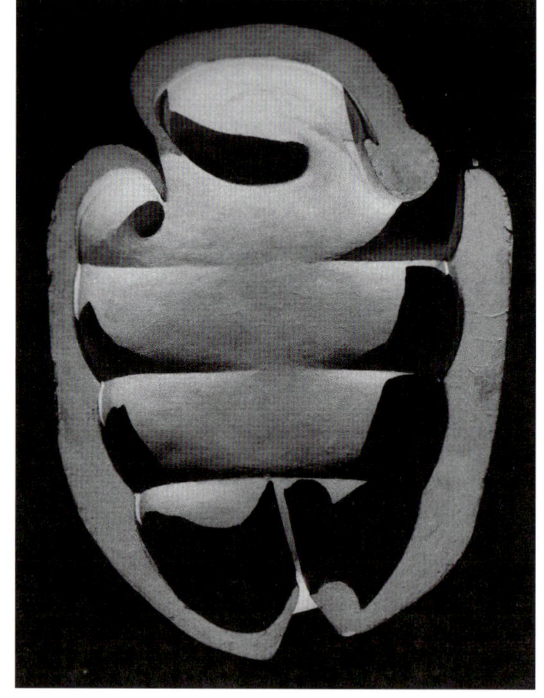

St. Stephanus parish center, Filderstadt-Bernhausen, 1965–75

Surrounded on three sides by houses on the outskirts of the town, and industrial buildings on the fourth side, on the other side of the access road and the overhead approach path to the nearby Stuttgart airport – this project was intended to set something lasting, a place of stillness, against this noisy, everyday environment. Hence the choice of material: concrete – which challenged us to give it vivid, three-dimensional shape – for the walls, tower, and roofs. Something of the spirit of very old churches was to be translated into a modern idiom.

So that all four buildings – church, kindergarten, parish hall, rectory – will harmonize with each other, they have been planned according to the design specification: »The cube which is parallel to the axis penetrates the diagonally positioned cube.« While the individual rooms are arranged parallel to the street, common rooms – the church, the kindergarten classrooms, and the parish hall – are emphasized as fixed corner points by the 45-degree turn. For church festivals a church square – somewhat below street level – and a portal were created between the church and the kindergarten. The tower – the culmination of the street – points the way there. The pre-Vatican Council center aisle leads toward the brightly lit altar zone, an effect that is also created by the increase of light slits in the exterior walls and the rising slope of the roof. The altar shows the realization of a formal mode of design, while the tabernacle stele is a free concrete sculpture. As for the baptismal font, a cube-shaped base penetrates a hemispherical font covered by a rotating lid. The adoration of the Virgin with the stand of votive candles is located in a wall projection.

Next to the kindergarten there are two staff apartments. In the structure of the parish hall the law of form was observed by having diagonal seating and ceiling girders. In the basement are rooms for the parish young people. The one-storey rectory is connected with the parish office and is located opposite the sacristy annex.

Kirchengemeindezentrum St. Stephanus, Filderstadt-Bernhausen, 1965–75

Dreiseitig umgeben von Stadtrandhäusern und Industriegebäuden auf der vierten Seite, jenseits der Zufahrtstraße sowie der Einflugschneise des nahen Stuttgarter Flugplatzes darüber – dieser lauten und alltäglichen Umwelt sollte ein Moment der Dauer und der Stille entgegengesetzt werden. Daher auch die Wahl des Materials: Beton, der dann zu plastischer Gestaltung herausforderte – für die Wände, den Turm und die Dächer. Etwas vom Geist ganz alter Kirchen sollte in die Sprache der Moderne umgesetzt werden.

Damit alle vier Bauten – Kirche, Kindergarten, Saalbau, Pfarrhaus – harmonieren, sind sie nach der Gestaltungsvorgabe: »Der achsparallele Kubus durchdringt den diagonal gestellten Kubus«, entworfen. Während die Einzelräume parallel zur Straße angeordnet sind, werden die Gemeinschaftsräume – Kirche, Kindergartensäle und Gemeindesaal – als Eckfestpunkte durch die 45°-Abdrehung betont. Für die kirchlichen Feste entstand zwischen Kirche und Kindergarten ein gegen die Straße etwas abgesenkter Kirchplatz mit dem Portal. Der Turm – Zielpunkt der Straße – weist den Weg dahin. Der vorkonziliare Mittelgang führt, auch durch Zunahme der Lichtschlitze in den Außenwänden und Ansteigen der Daches, zur hellen Altarzone auf. Der Altar zeigt die Realisierung des formalen Gestaltungsmodus, die Tabernakelstele ist dagegen eine freie Betonplastik. Beim Taufstein durchdringt ein Kubussockel ein Halbkugelbecken, das von einem drehbaren Deckel abgedeckt wird. Die Madonnenanbetung mit dem Lichterhügel liegt in einer Wandausbuchtung.

Neben dem Kindergarten liegen zwei Personalwohnungen. Beim Saalbau ist das formale Gesetz durch diagonale Bestuhlung und Deckenträger nachvollzogen. Im Untergeschoß befinden sich die Jugendräume. Das eingeschossige Pfarrhaus hängt mit dem Pfarrbüro zusammen und liegt gegenüber dem Sakristeianbau.

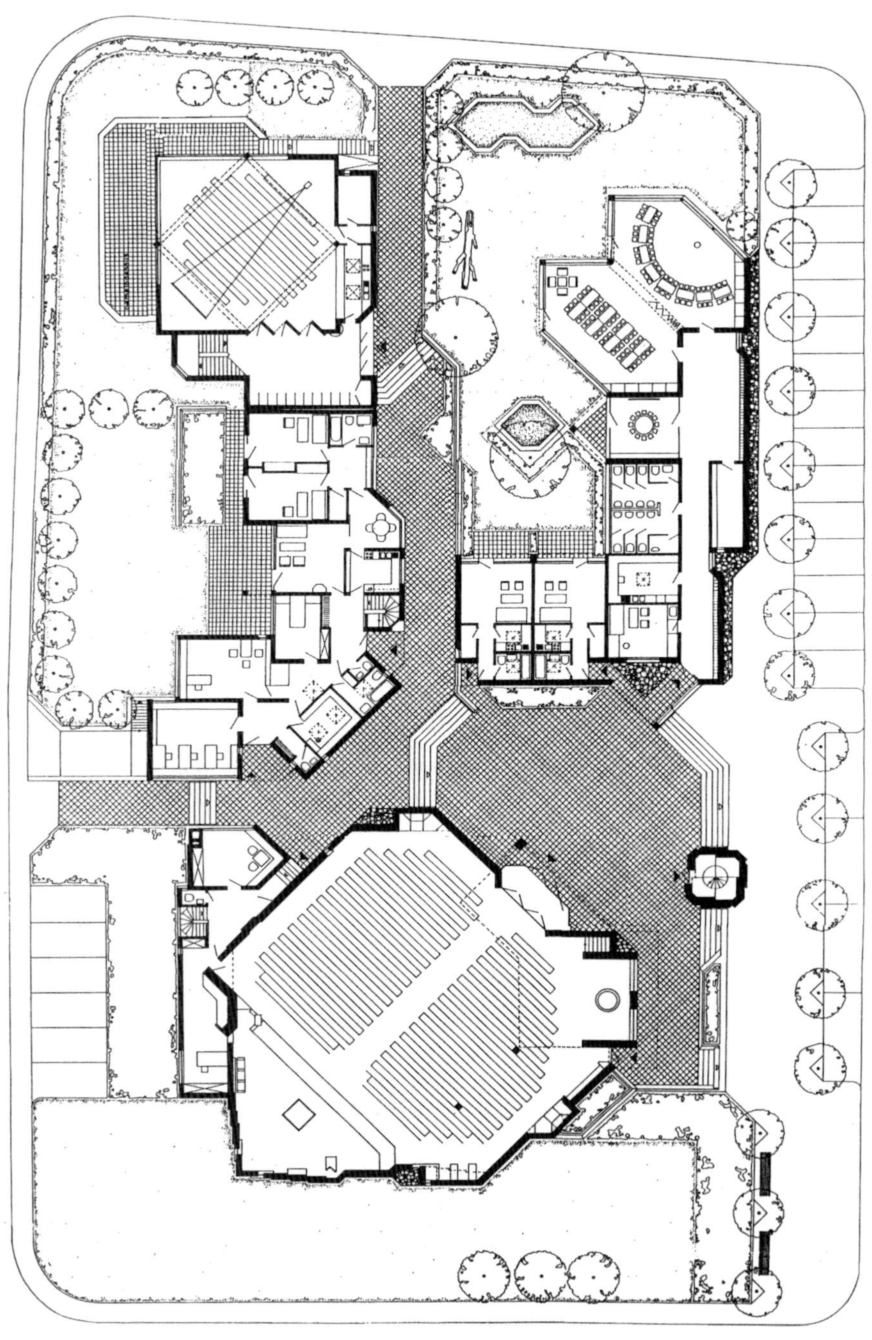

1. Site plan and floor plan.
2. Bell tower.
3. View of the church from the west.

1. Lageplan und Grundriß.
2. Glockenturm.
3. Ansicht der Kirche von Westen.

4. View of the parish hall.
5. Detailed view of the choir.
6. Interior view of the church towards the altar.
7. Baptismal font.

4. Ansicht des Gemeindesaals.
5. Detailansicht des Chors.
6. Innenansicht der Kirche in Richtung Altar.
7. Taufbecken.

**Heilig-Geist-Kirche, Markgröningen,
1977–81**

The church was built by the Brothers of the Holy
Spirit and consecrated in 1297. The architect, Bär,
immortalized himself by depicting a bear in the
tracery of a window.

 At the end of the 1970s all that remained of the
building was the choir, the tower, and the sacristy.
In other words, if this was to become a parish
church, it lacked a nave. In order to add this in an
organic way, the semi-octagon form of the chancel was also used for the new nave, which lay in
the axis. Its light comes from the west through a
Gothic window discovered in the garden. This
area is crossed by the form of the steps opposite,
where the choristers stand, which corresponds to
the rectangular floor plan of the tower. At the point
of the crossing is the altar, and above it is the
main light source of the space – a large glazed
aperture in the roof. The Gothic chancel is now
used as a day-to-day chapel or, during high holy
days when large numbers of people are in atten-
dance, as added space with the altar as its center.
The floor was tiled with red octagonal tiles from
France. The great height of the sacristy made it
possible to install a room for servers. In addition
to the main entrance, there is a second entrance,
from the garden, for choristers. A new organ was
placed on the choristers' platform ten years after
completion of the church, contrary to the original
plan to install it on a gallery built especially for it.

**Heilig-Geist-Kirche, Markgröningen, 1977
bis 1981**

Die Kirche wurde von den Heiliggeistbrüdern erbaut und 1297 geweiht. Der Architekt Bär ver-
ewigte sich durch Darstellung eines Bären im
Maßwerk eines Fensters.

 Ende der 1970er Jahre waren von dem Bauwerk nur noch der Chor, der Turm und die Sakristei übrig. Was also für eine Pfarrkirche fehlte, war
das Schiff. Um dies organisch anzufügen, wurde
die Chorform des halben Achtecks auch für das
in der Achse liegende neue Schiff verwendet. Es
bekommt durch ein im Garten gefundenes goti-
sches Fenster Westlicht. Dieser Zusammenhang
wird gekreuzt durch die dem rechteckigen Turm-
grundriß entsprechende Form der gegenüber liegenden Sängerstufen. Im Kreuzungspunkt steht
der Altar, über ihm die Hauptlichtquelle des Raumes – eine große, verglaste Dachaussparung. Der
gotische Chor dient nun als Alltgskapelle oder bei
hochfestlichem Massenbesuch als Raumerweite-
rung mit dem Altar als Mitte. Auf dem Boden wurden rote, achteckige Fliesen aus Frankreich ver-
legt. Die große Höhe der Sakristei ermöglichte den
Einbau eines Ministrantenraums. Außer dem
Haupteingang gibt es noch einen Sängereingang
vom Garten aus. Eine neue Orgel wurde zehn
Jahre nach der Fertigstellung entgegen dem ursprünglichen Vorhaben, sie auf der eigens errichteten Empore einzubauen, auf dem Sängerpodest
plaziert.

1, 2. Floor plans of the church before and after
conversion.
3. View from the north-west.

1, 2. Grundrisse der Kirche vor und nach dem
Umbau.
3. Ansicht von Nordwesten.

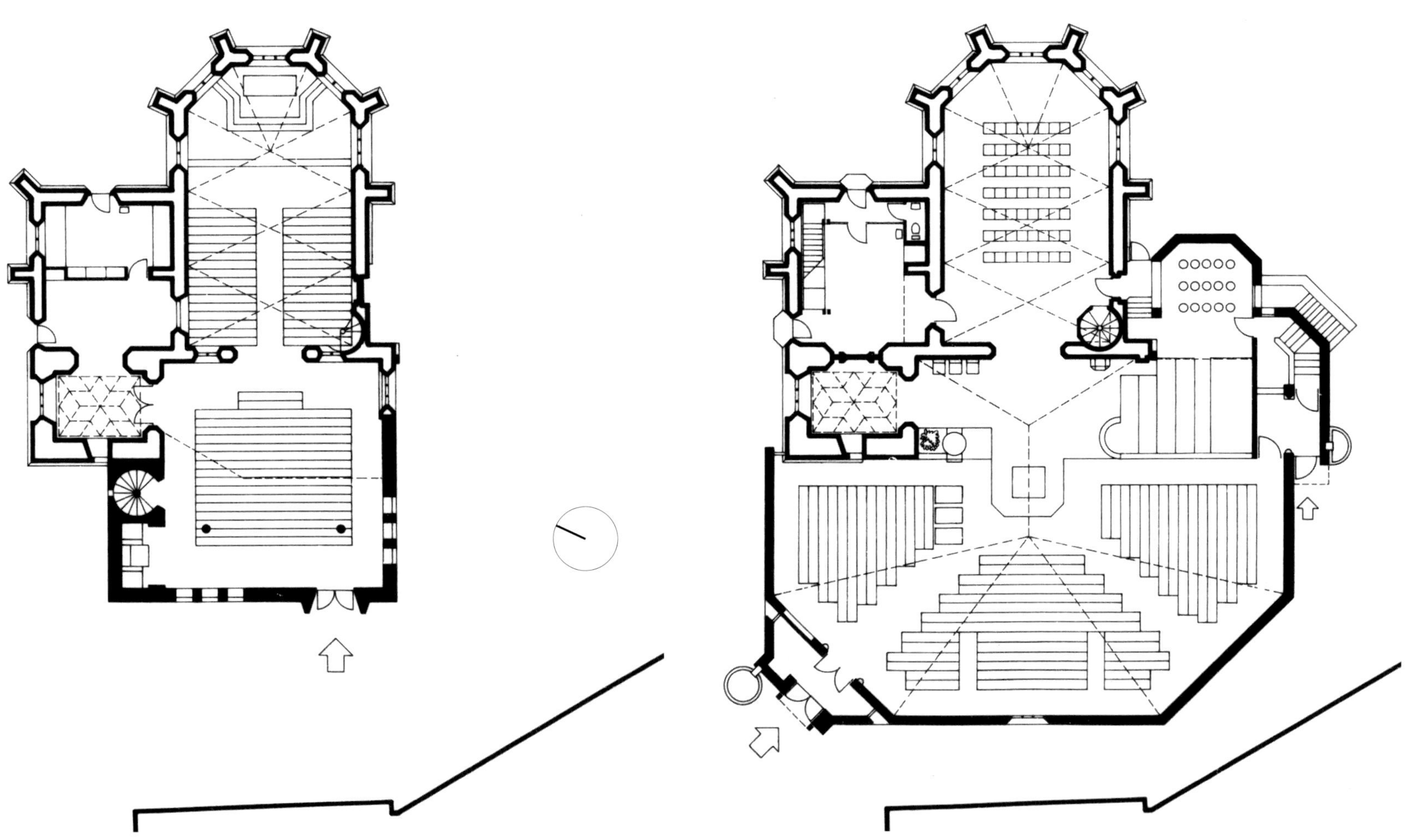

4. View from the north.
5. Lane between the church and the former hospital.
6. View of the choir from the new nave.

4. Ansicht von Norden.
5. Gasse zwischen der Kirche und dem früheren Spital.
6. Blick vom neuen Schiff auf den Chor.

Church of St. Valentin am Forst, Landschach, Lower Austria, 1986–90

The little 13th-century church on the outskirts of the village was rebuilt after the 17th and 18th century Turkish Wars. Before it was rebuilt, it consisted of a nave with a somewhat insensitively built-on Lady chapel, a relatively large, angled chancel, a tower opposite it, and a narrow side aisle with a built-on charnel house (ossuary), whose cellar was still full of bones from the Turkish Wars when construction began.

The old entrance determined the new spatial axis, which made it possible to create a hierarchy of spaces: The side aisle became a two-sided worship space with two altars, the ossuary a confessional, and the former chancel became the day-to-day chapel. The Baroque chapel had to make way for the addition, which is set off from the old building by two floor-to-ceiling windows with depictions of the patron saints; also, the windows of the small chancel, which had been enlarged during the Baroque period, were restored to their original Gothic form. Lastly, the Baroque main altar, which was too high for the space, was moved to the new, much higher chancel wall. The nave holds part of the seats of the added nave. As you walk through between the red pillars Boaz and Jachin, which support the weight of the new double-pitched roof that intersects with the old vault, you see before you, at the end of the center aisle, the new celebration altar and the old high altar behind it in the middle of the widening nave – and above them the glass ridge, which becomes larger toward the altar. The village houses are mirrored in the glass, and the ridge can create an east-west light pendulum effect that lasts as long as a mass.

Materials and colors: The floor is made of Solnhofen slabs, rough and polished, ochre like the earth; old bench ends – lush green, like vegetation; third dimension – blue, like the sky at times.

Kirche St. Valentin am Forst, Landschach, Niederösterreich, 1986–90

Die am Dorfrand gelegene kleine Kirche aus dem 13.Jahrhundert wurde nach den Türkenkriegen im 17. und 18. Jahrhundert wieder aufgebaut. Vor ihrem Umbau bestand sie aus einem Hauptschiff mit einer etwas gefühllos angebauten Marienkapelle, einem relativ großen, abgewinkelten Chor, einem Turm ihm gegenüber sowie einem schmalen Seitenschiff mit angebautem Karner (Beinhaus), dessen Keller bei Baubeginn noch voller Knochen aus den Türkenkriegen war.

Der alte Eingang gab die neue Raumachse vor, die eine Hierarchie der Räume entstehen ließ: Aus dem Seitenschiff wurde ein zweiseitiger Andachtsraum mit zwei Altären, aus dem Karner ein Beichtzimmer und aus dem alten Chor die Alltagskapelle. Dem Zubau, der durch zwei geschoßhohe Fenster mit den Darstellungen der Patronatsheiligen vom Altbau abgesetzt ist, mußte die Barockkapelle weichen, ebenso erhielten auch die im Barock vergrößerten Fenster des kleinen Chores wieder ihre gotische Urform. Schließlich wurde der für den Raum zu hohe barocke Hauptaltar an die neue, viel höhere Chorwand versetzt. Das Hauptschiff nimmt einen Teil der Bänke des Anbauschiffs auf. Geht man zwischen den roten Säulen Boas und Jachym hindurch, mit denen die Last des sich mit dem alten Gewölbe verschneidenden neuen Satteldachs abgefangen wird, hat man am Ende des Mittelgangs den neuen Zelebrationsaltar und dahinter den alten Hochaltar inmitten des sich verbreiterten Schiffes vor sich – und darüber den zum Altar hin vergrößerten gläsernden First, in dem sich die Dorfhäuser spiegeln und der eine Ost–West-Wanderung des Sonnenlichts in der Zeit der Messe erzeugen kann.

Materialien und Farben: Boden Solnhofener Platten, rauh und geschliffen, ockerfarben wie die Erde; alte Bankhäupter sattgrün wie der Bewuchs; dritte Dimension blau wie oft der Himmel.

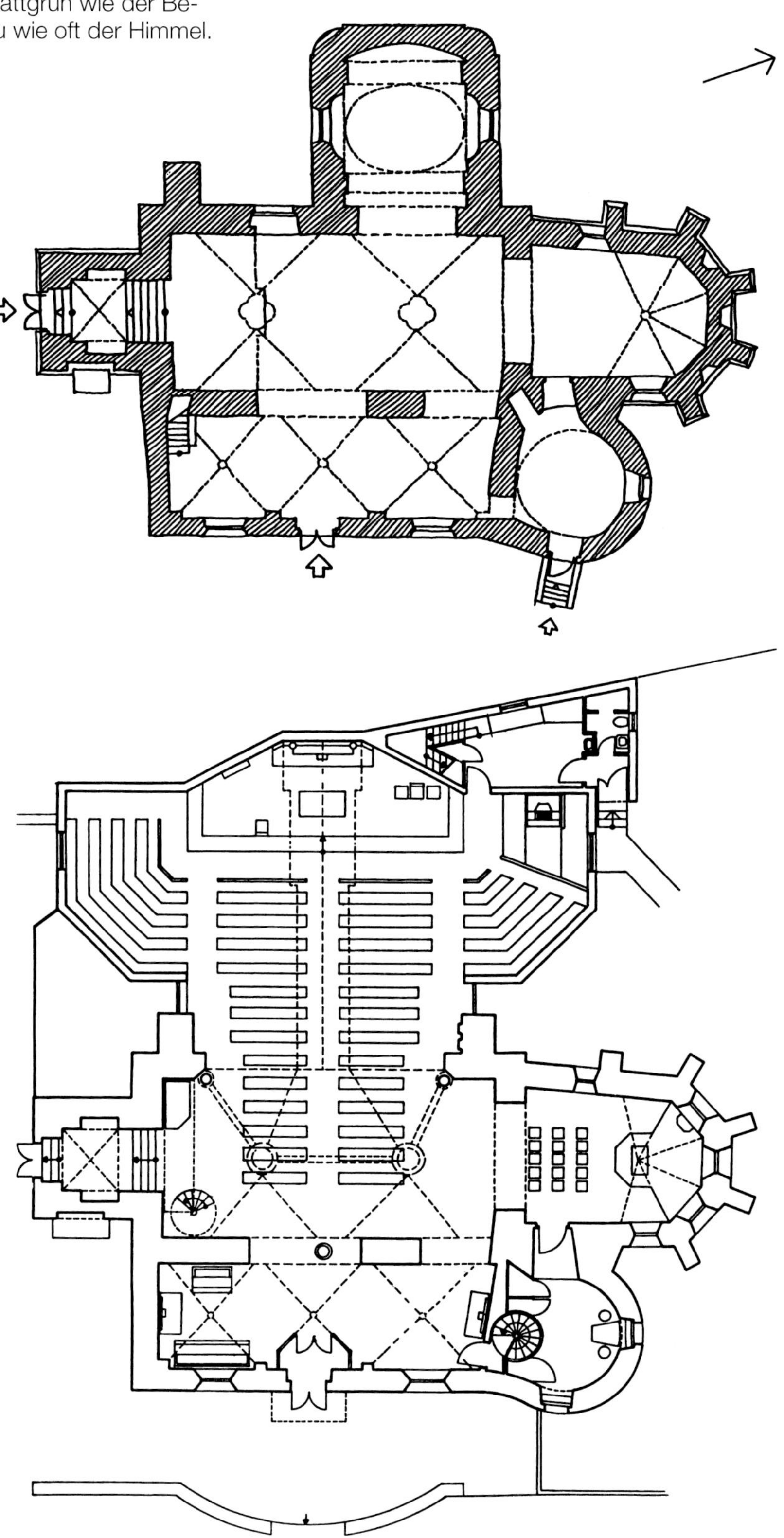

1, 2. Floor plans of the church before and after conversion.
3. View from the south-west.
4. View from the north-east.

1, 2. Grundrisse der Kirche vor und nach dem Umbau.
3. Ansicht von Südwesten.
4. Ansicht von Nordosten.

5. View of the side-chapel on the south side.
6. View of the new nave from the old one.
7. View of the new nave towards the altar.

5. Blick in die Seitenkapelle auf der Südseite.
6. Blick vom alten in das neue Schiff.
7. Blick in das neue Schiff in Richtung Altar.

Convent church of St. Georg am Hang, Maselheim-Heggbach, 1989–93

The convent of which the one-nave Gothic church, built around 1320, is a part, originally belonged to the Cistercian nuns. Today Franciscan sisters run an open institution here, with several houses for the mentally handicapped.

The sanctuary used to be a »space of distance« – not only for the nuns, whose gallery – like the organ gallery located above it – was furthest away from the altar, but also for the handicapped people in the long, narrow nave. Moreover, the location of the entrance through the low gate in the tower meant that people who sat in the back were distracted, and worshipers had long distances to walk.

So that the church could become a »space of closeness« for everyone, furnishings were placed elliptically and transversely – the altar island in the center of the church by the south wall, behind it a light well that comes to life when there are changes in the atmosphere. In front of the altar island, behind the rows of seating, is the new transept-like entrance building with its porch and the pillars that support the new gallery for the organ and choristers, which »floats« free above it. Today, access to the church is by a stairwell existing in the wall and a new passageway. The old entrance was replaced by the Lady chapel. The walls of the chancel rails were removed to create spatial unity. The former mural on the back wall of the chancel was replaced by a memorial for 40 victims of the Nazi regime: a bloodred, floor-to-ceiling slit window is crossed by a recumbent statue of Christ behind glass. On the right and left it is flanked by marble friezes with the names of the dead. Parallel to the benches delicate, curved brass pipes with halogen lamps provide lighting for the room. In analogy to the entrance building on the west side, a sacristy building was added on the east wall.

The architect drew up the designs for the colorful framing of the window glass, the bells at the entrance, the holy water font, the receptacle for donations, and the umbrella stands. The sculptor Hubert Elsässer created the altar, ambo, tabernacle, altar cross, and portal relief.

Klosterkirche St. Georg am Hang, Maselheim-Heggbach, 1989–93

Das Kloster, zu dem die um 1320 erbaute einschiffige gotische Kirche gehört, war ursprünglich im Besitz von Zisterzienserinnen. Heute betreiben hier Franziskanerinnen eine offene Anstalt mit mehreren Häusern für geistig Behinderte.

Der Kirchenraum war ein »Raum der Ferne« – nicht nur für die Nonnen, deren Empore – wie die noch darüber liegende Orgelempore – am weitesten vom Altar entfernt war, sondern auch für die Behinderten im langen, schmalen Schiff. Die Lage des Zugangs durch das niedrige Tor im Turm störte zudem die hinten Sitzenden und erzeugte lange Wege.

Damit die Kirche für alle ein »Raum der Nähe« werden konnte, wurde eine elliptische Quermöblierung gewählt – in der Raummitte an der Südwand die Altarinsel, hinter ihr ein Lichtschacht, der durch Veränderungen in der Atmosphäre belebt wird. Vor ihr liegt hinter den Bankreihen wie ein Querschiff das neue Eingangsgebäude mit dem Windfang und den Stützen, die die frei darüber »schwebende« neue Orgel- und Sängerempore tragen. Der Zugang erfolgt heute über eine in der Wand vorhandene Treppe und einen neuen Steg. Aus dem alten Eingang entstand die Marienkapelle. Die Chorschrankenwände wurden der Raumeinheit zuliebe abgebrochen. An der Chorrückwand wurde das ehemalige Wandbild durch ein Mahnmal für die 40 Opfer des Naziregimes ersetzt: Ein blutrotes, raumhohes Schlitzfenster kreuzt eine liegende Christusplastik in vitro. Sie wird rechts und links von Marmorfriesen mit den Namen der Toten flankiert. Parallel zu den Bänken dienen zarte, gebogene Messingrohre mit Halogenlampen zur Raumbeleuchtung. In Analogie zum Eingangsbau auf der Westseite wurde an die Ostwand ein Sakristeigebäude angebaut.

Vom Architekten stammen die Entwürfe für die farbige Rahmung der Fenstergläser, die Eingangsglöckchen, das Weihwasserbecken, den Spendenbehälter und die Schirmständer. Der Bildhauer Hubert Elsässer schuf Altar, Ambo, Tabernakel, Altarkreuz und Portalrelief.

1. Section through the church after conversion.
2. Floor plan of the church before conversion.
3. View from the north-east.
4. Floor plan of the church after conversion.

1. Schnitt durch die Kirche nach dem Umbau.
2. Grundriß der Kirche vor dem Umbau.
3. Ansicht von Nordosten.
4. Grundriß der Kirche nach dem Umbau.

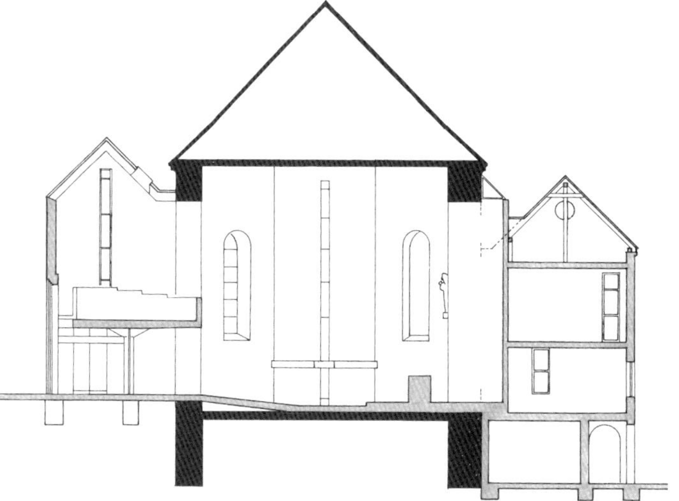

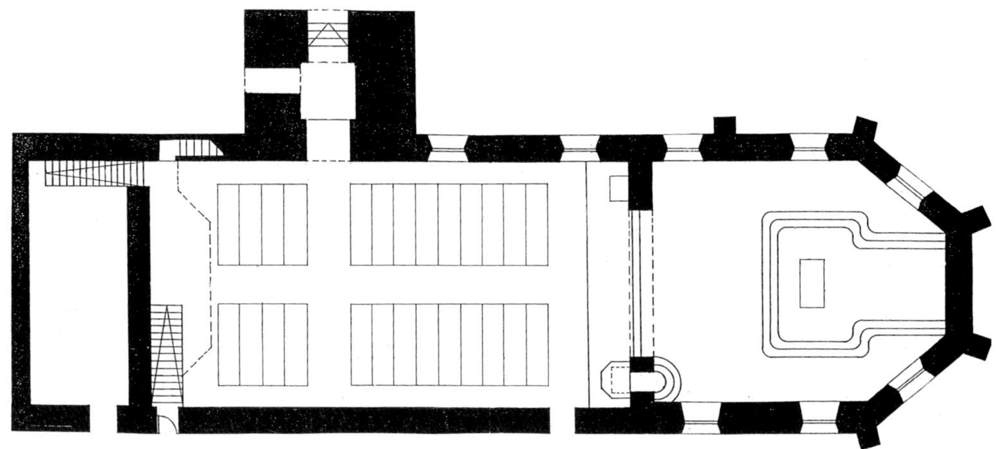

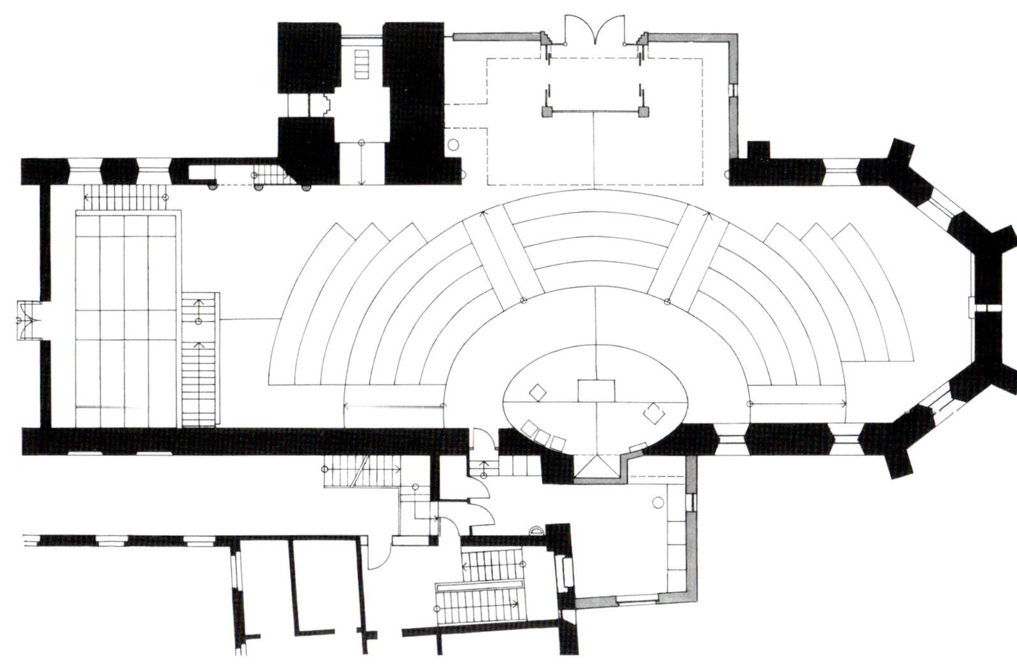

5. View of the nave from the west. The altar is to the right, the organ to the left.
6. Organ.
7. Altar.

5. Blick von Westen in das Schiff. Rechts befindet sich der Altar, links die Orgel.
6. Orgel.
7. Altar.

Church of St. Martinus, Schwaigern, 1994 to 1997
(with Anna Stern)

The entrance of the east-oriented, very high, and overly dark church, which was built in 1963, used to be connected to the rectory (which contains the parish office) by an open, drafty roof. The sacristy was located in the church behind the altar.

Was it a sin against the Holy Spirit to give up the church's east orientation? Yet for the entire complex to be organically connected, it had to happen. When the connecting roof had a sacristy built under it directly next to the church, as well as two offices, WCs, etc., the priest was now in close proximity of the church, and the change brought a new ordinate that fixes the position of the altar island on its west side next to the sacristy. The new gallery has been placed parallel to this, and under it is the main entrance, the confessional room, and – in the altar axis – the day-to-day chapel, and three large round windows over the gallery that face east. When the old gallery was torn down, colored light came from the west side through the glass block wall to the right and left of the altar. The following were added: a statue of St. Martin behind glass which had belonged to the family of the counts of Neipperg on the south wall and a window with a double vesica piscis ornament in the north wall, as well as two tracery windows in the day-to-day chapel. The third dimension needed to be reduced in scale – because the roof now slopes in the wrong direction. It was transformed into a vault, whose wall arches, which rise from the corners of the room – united in four directions – appear to plunge onto the four columns of light and sound that stand around the altar. However, there is a space between the tips of the wall arches and the funnels of the columns. Thus the connection with them is only possible through rays of light, in other words, it is insubstantial – a paraphrase for prayer.

A few much older objects donated by the count's family bring a historical element into the church: the ancient baptismal font, the late Gothic tabernacle, a statue of the Virgin, and a late Gothic crucifix.

Kirche St. Martinus, Schwaigern, 1994 bis 1997
(mit Anna Stern)

Der Eingang der 1963 erbauten, geosteten, sehr hohen und zu dunklen Kirche war durch ein offenes, zugiges Dach mit dem Pfarrhaus – darin das Pfarrbüro – verbunden. Die Sakristei lag in der Kirche hinter dem Altar.

War es eine Sünde wider den Heiligen Geist, wenn man die Ostung aufgab? Doch für einen organischen Zusammenhang des Ensembles mußte es sein. Die Unterbauung des Verbindungsdachs mit der Sakristei gleich neben der Kirche, zwei Büroräumen, WCs usw. brachte nicht nur dem Pfarrer den kurzen Weg dahin, sondern eine neue Ordinate, die die Lage der Altarinsel auf seiner Westseite nächst der Sakristei fixiert. Parallel dazu ist die neue Empore angeordnet, darunter der Haupteingang, das Beichtzimmer, und – in der Altarachse – die Alltagskapelle und über der Empore drei große, nach Osten gerichtete Rundfenster. Durch den Abriß der alten Empore gab es farbiges Licht von der Westseite durch die Betonglaswand rechts und links vom Altar. Dazu kamen aus dem Besitz der gräflichen Familie Neipperg eine Martinusstatue in vitro an der Südwand und ein Zweischneußfenster in der Nordwand sowie zwei Maßwerkfenster in der Alltagskapelle. Die dritte Dimension bedurfte – wegen des Dachanstiegs in der nunmehr falschen Richtung – einer maßstäblichen Reduktion. Sie wurde in ein Gewölbe umgesetzt, dessen aus den Raumecken ansteigende Gurtbögen sich – in vier Richtungen vereinigt – auf die den Altar umstehenden vier Licht- und Schallsäulen zu stürzen scheinen. Ihre Spitzen haben indessen Abstand von deren Trichtern. So wird die Verbindung mit ihnen nur durch Lichtstrahlen möglich, also immateriell – eine Paraphrase für das Gebet.

Ein paar viel ältere, gräflicherseits gestiftete Gegenstände bringen etwas Historizität in den Kirchenraum: das uralte Taufbecken, das spätgotische Sakramentshaus, eine Marienstatue und ein spätgotisches Kruzifix.

1. Perspective view of the converted nave.
2, 3. Floor plans of the church before and after conversion.

1. Perspektive des umgebauten Schiffes.
2, 3. Grundrisse der Kirche vor und nach dem Umbau.

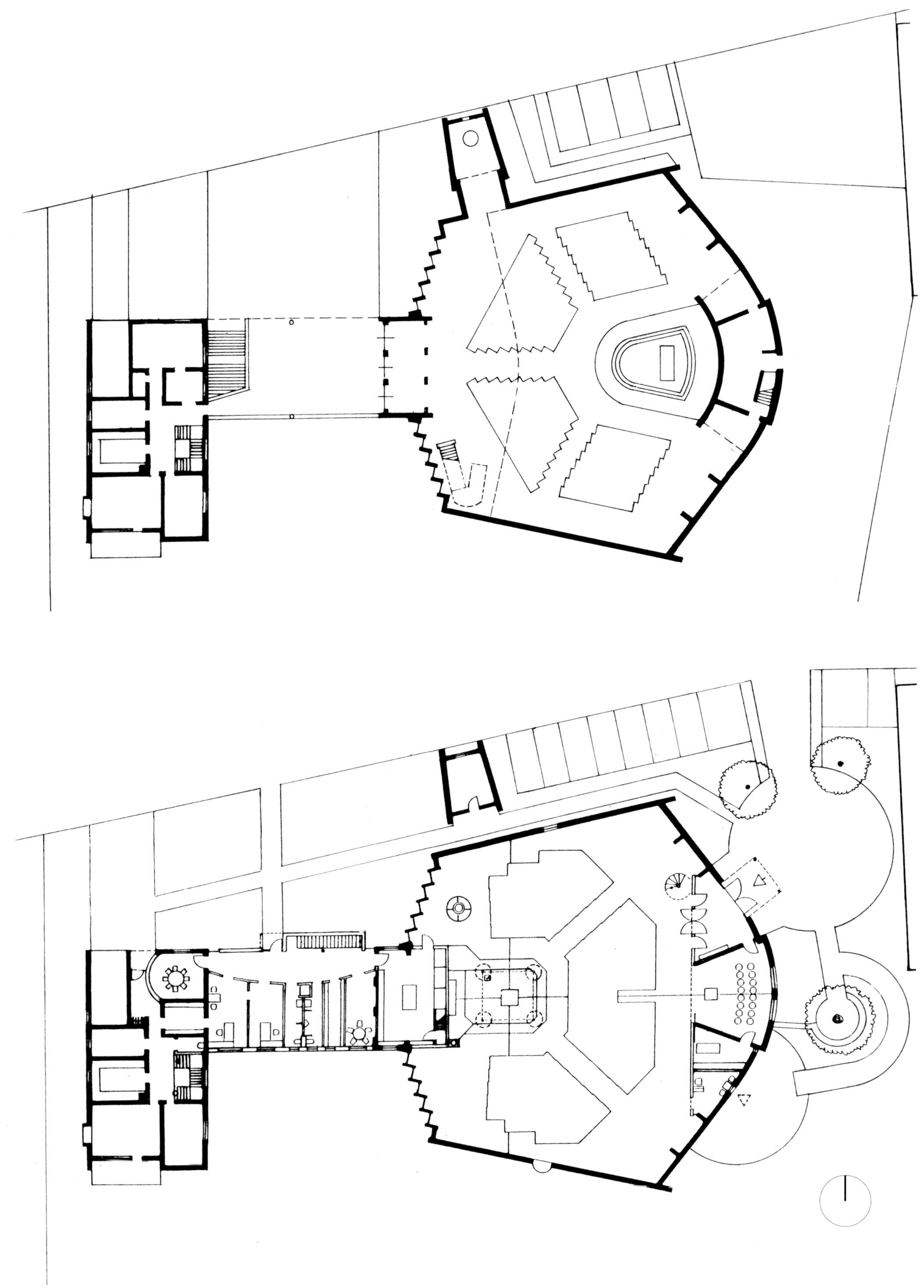

4. View of the nave from the altar.
5. View of the nave towards the altar.
6. View of the nave from the north.

4. Blick vom Altar in das Schiff.
5. Blick in das Schiff in Richtung Altar.
6. Blick von Norden in das Schiff.

Church of St. Michael zu den Wengen, Ulm, 1994–98
(with Anna Stern)

Given the nave of a 1553 Gothic church adapted to be an altar room in 1953, and the addition of a new nave belonging to this church that had few windows and was built in the period style of a »factory of God«, the project was to create a church that could accommodate services with varying numbers of worshipers. The altar space of the Gothic church is government property; while it serves the parish as a chapel, it could not be included in the planning.

The spatial concept is based on the implantation of an altar island as a link between the two rooms. Thus the Gothic nave has been given back its old spatial function. It was furnished semicentrically with groups of chairs oriented toward the new altar island in order to help enlarge the 1953 nave. As a result it was necessary to open the walled-off Gothic entrance and to give the ambo the place from which it is possible to preach in two directions. The (asymmetrical) main entrance of the 1953 nave remained in its former location, while the concrete entrance structure that had been built in front of it was torn down. The longitudinal walls were given five groups of from one to five slit windows arranged in such a way that from the entrance to the altar the number of windows and their brightness increase. Another new addition is a staircase to a new choristers' room and the widened gallery.

The front garden was sacrificed to the dark hall under the church so that a glass-roofed »space of light« could be built in front of it along its whole length.

Kirche St. Michael zu den Wengen, Ulm, 1994–98
(mit Anna Stern)

Aus dem 1953 zum Altarraum adaptierten Schiff einer gotischen Kirche von 1553 und dem fensterarmen Anbau des dazugehörigen neuen Schiffes im damaligen Stil einer »Fabrik Gottes« sollte ein Kirchenraum entstehen, der Gottesdienste mit verschiedenen Besucherzahlen ermöglicht. Der Altarraum der gotischen Kirche ist staatliches Eigentum, dient zwar der Pfarrei als Kapelle, war aber in die Planung nicht einbeziehbar.

Die Raumidee basiert auf der Implantation einer Altarinsel als Gelenk zwischen beiden Räumen. So bekam das gotische Schiff wieder seine alte Raumfunktion. Es wurde semizentrisch mit Stuhlgruppen auf die neue Altarinsel hin möbliert, um zur Erweiterung des Schiffes von 1953 zu dienen. Daraus folgte die Notwendigkeit, den zugemauerten gotischen Eingang zu öffnen und dem Ambo die Stelle zu geben, von der aus in zwei Richtungen gepredigt werden kann. Der (asymmetrische) Haupteingang des Schiffes von 1953 blieb an der alten Stelle, der vorgebaute Eingangsbau aus Beton wurde abgerissen. Die Längswände erhielten je fünf Gruppen von einem bis zu fünf Schlitzfenstern, damit vom Eingang bis zum Altar Anzahl und Helligkeit zunehmen. Neu ist auch eine Treppe zu einem neuen Sängerraum und der verbreiterten Empore.

Dem dunklen Saal unter der Kirche wurde der Vorgarten geopfert, um auf der ganzen Länge einen glasgedeckten »Lichtraum« vorzubauen.

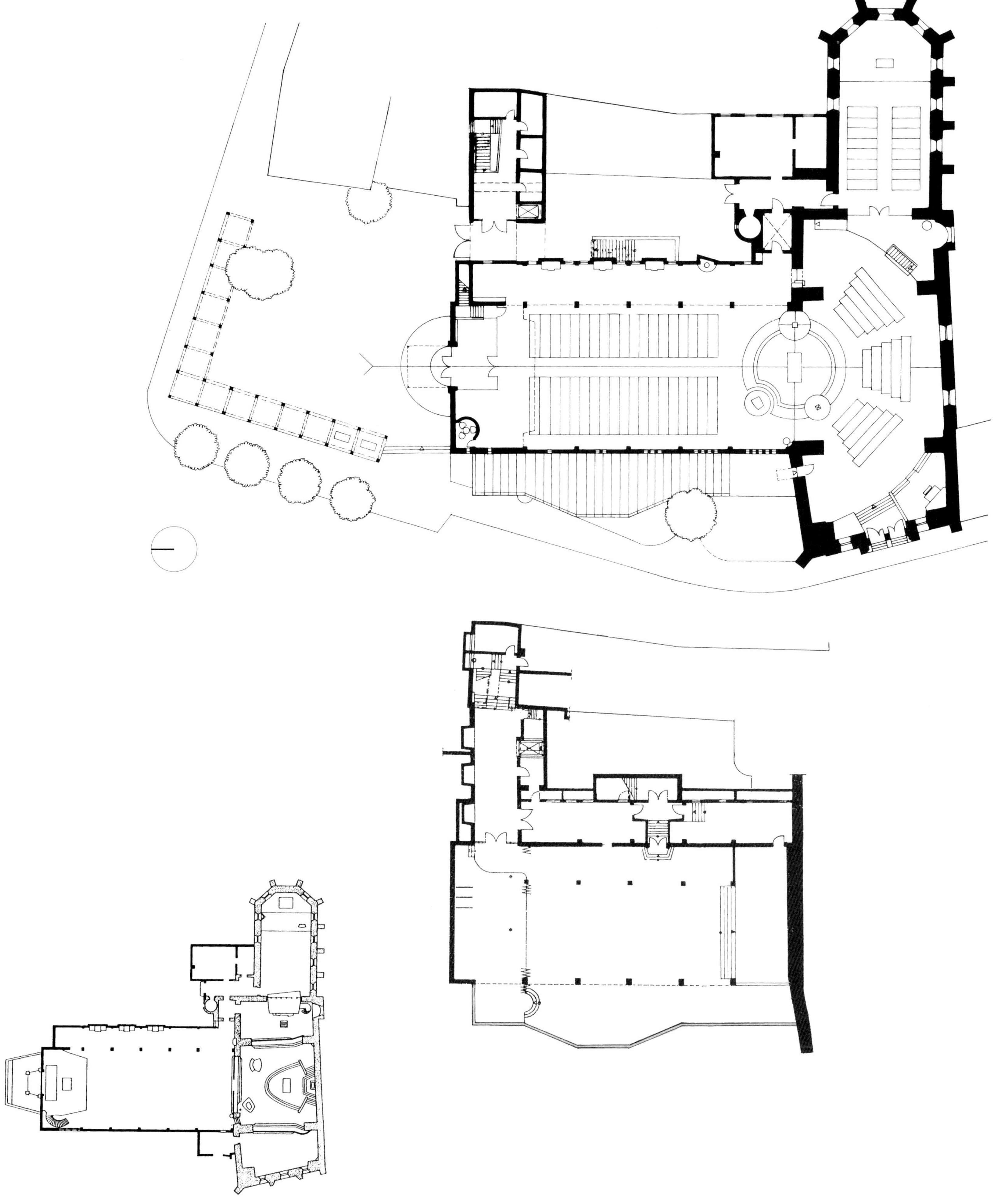

5. View of the main nave from the altar.
6. Altar.
7. Parish hall with glass-roofed »space of light« on
the lower floor.

5. Blick vom Altar in das Hauptschiff.
6. Altar.
7. Gemeindesaal mit glasgedecktem »Lichtraum«
im Untergeschoß.

Furnishings

It all started with an exhibition I was asked to design in 1956, entitled »Furniture, affordable and beautiful«, commissioned by the German Werkbund in Mannheim. The ceiling of the exhibition room was given a coat of black paint; under the ceiling hung a wide-meshed net of boards, painted white, simulating a floor plan structure, with sections of wall standing below it here and there – as a background for the exhibits: in addition to the furniture from furniture stores that fit the theme of the show, there was also a low wooden table with a glass top I had designed and a variable chest of drawers by Oswald Mathias Ungers.

Old ladies do not like to sink into deep, soft easy chairs from which they then have a hard time getting up. So I designed the »granny chair« for my mother, made of bent plywood. Its seat and backrest, which supports the spine, are upholstered with black leather.

When my wife had her first baby, we eventually needed a dining table for three. Consequently it had three pine legs – one leg could potentially be attached to the wall. The pair of legs is connected to a trough for bottles. The table had a black Formica top with a strong edge band.

Later I received a commission to provide furnishings for a new office building of the Münster chamber of commerce. For the head of the organization I designed a striking reverse U-shaped desk made of 36 mm thick pieces of wood with a light ash veneer. A contrasting drawer suspended below the desk was stained black, and the strut that served as a foot rest was also black. Office supplies were kept in a cabinet – also ash.

The managerial staff received desks of the same wood and the same thickness with a cabinet built in under the desk on one side and two connected legs on the other side – somewhat less prestigious but practical.

When the Dewald house in Karlsruhe-Grötzingen was completed, all that was lacking was the furniture. In the bedroom of the lady of the house a built-in cabinet with an adjoining writing area became necessary. As a countermovement to the inclination of the cabinet with the ceiling, the doors are stepped down to table height, and the lowest section merges into the desktop. On the top floor of the owner's studio, a recess had been planned for shelves. This inspired a geometric game with three boxes shifted in relationship to each other; I added two vertical elements, one twice as high as the other, plus four spacious open compartments of the same size. For the living room I designed the seating group Gi1 with frames made of 36 mm thick pinewood with beveled edges – armchairs, a love seat, and a four-seat couch; also a table from the same material with a thick glass top. This prototype was then sold commercially and was later manufactured with blue buffalo leather upholstery. The dining area chairs were of beech wood with caned seats.

When the children left home, the parents took over their ground floor rooms. The head of the owner's bed is framed by shelves, its middle is upholstered – for reading while sitting up in bed – and there is a reading lamp on the side, under it a gap through which the homeowner can see his alarm clock while lying down. Through the window he can see the window of his son's small studio opposite (his son is a frame-maker and gilder). To distinguish it from the many rectangular picture frames that hang inside, the window square has been rotated by 45 degrees. On the right and left one leg each supports a tabletop and a shelf. Between them is the window ledge with a quarry-faced, curved front edge.

The topic of beds continued to preoccupy me. The beds that were commercially available at the time, with their ever-straight, »functional« forms, contrary to expectation, are often far from cozy. The sketch shows the bed designed for the five-cornered bedroom of the Rees house, which was never implemented. It fits precisely into the 45-degree corner, and faces the door. The bed composition, with built-on bedside tables, gives the effect of an »embrace«, as does the wooden headboard with protection for one's shoulders and head if one wants to sit up in bed while ill – surrounded by pictures of children and ancestors, a built-in reading lamp, phone, radio, and television connection, light switch, built-in lights, and small raised projections on the sides and foot of the bed frame to keep one from falling out of bed and to brace one's feet against. An added feature would be the old-timey pull cord for switching on the ceiling light. And finally, there would be a serving cart with bottles of red wine to help one sleep. – The whole thing was too expensive, and re-mained a dream.

To go with the somewhat brutalist style of the German Red Cross old-age home in Karlsruhe, I designed stackable beech-wood chairs with black plywood seats and backs, as well as sturdy tables for four with a central leg, for the dining room. Suitable armchairs with caned seats and backs were produced for the library and other community rooms.

My simplest table for the terrace of my Karlsruhe house consisted of a trapezium-shaped red sandstone slab base quarried locally and a concrete tabletop poured locally that was embedded in the retaining wall opposite. A bench built of quarrystone, with the retaining wall as its back rest, completed the picture – ideal for warm summer days.

For the library of my house I designed a low table between the (white-painted concrete) benches. For the table I chose a white marble slab and a chromium-plated tubular steel frame.

The four-person table, which measures 100 x 100 centimeters (40 x 40 inches) when collapsed, consists of two laminated panels of that size connected by a hinge that rest on two back-to-back molded concrete tubes with an external diameter of 100 centimeters (40 inches). If you take off the tabletop, place the half-tubes 2 meters (6,5 feet) apart, and put two pieces of wood that are rabbeted on both sides on the tubes to the right and left, you can put the unfolded top on these. There is then room for eight to ten persons.

Finally, I designed a cast-iron stove for a national competition in 1963 and was awarded the second prize. The basic prototype, »Karlchen (Charlie)«, was intended for one-room bachelor apartments. Scaled up as »Karl (Charles)«, it could be used by childless couples, while a second, glorified version, »Karl der Große (Charles the Great)« could be marketed to large families. The latter two types are similar in design to old double-deck stoves from the Biedermeier period. Later, though, there was not enough demand for coal stoves.

As an example of lighting fixtures I want to mention the six-branched candelabrum I designed around 1960. It consists of a rectangular steel plate as its base, a thicker steel pipe welded to the base, and six thinner pipes that are welded to this at an angle. Each branch has a holder with a lightbulb and a semicircular copper shade that screens it against the room. The white wall reflects a warm light. In my Karlsruhe house the lamp stood next to the fireplace.

I designed all the lighting fixtures for the library building of the Technische Universität Wien (Vienna University of Technology) – wall lamps, track lighting in half-pipes, hanging lamps for the staff dining room, the lamp for a bulletin board, lamps for reading tables – all in chromium-plated steel and equipped with the same illuminant. I also designed two- and four-person reading tables, circular computer tables for up to eight persons, work tables for floor supervisory staff, shelves for sorting books in the administration department, and the shelves and cashier's island of the bookstore.

In the 1980s I worked on the »Jumbo« group of armchairs made of 36 millimeters (1.4 inches) thick pinewood with glued-in upholstery that extends over the armrests. A development of this was the wing chair.

While working on an interior design project in Vienna, I created the writing place for the lady of the house with a variation on a Thonet-chair.

Möbel

Es begann mit einer Ausstellung, die ich 1956 unter dem Titel »Möbel, billig und schön« im Auftrag des Deutschen Werkbunds in Mannheim zu gestalten hatte. Der Präsentationsraum erhielt einen schwarzen Deckenanstrich, unter diesem ein hängendes, weitmaschiges Netz von weiß lackierten Brettern, das mit da und dort darunter stehenden Wandteilen ein Grundrißgefüge simulierte – als Hintergrund der Ausstellungsstücke: neben den dem Thema entsprechenden Möbeln aus Einrichtungshäusern auch ein von mir entworfener, niedriger Holztisch mit Glasplatte und eine variable Kommode von Oswald Mathias Ungers.

Alte Damen versinken nicht gern in tiefen, weichen Sesseln, aus denen sie dann schlecht wieder herauskommen. Also entwarf ich für meine Mutter den »Omasessel« aus gebogenem Sperrholz. Sitz und Lendenwirbelsäule stützende Lehne sind mit schwarzem Leder bezogen.

Als meine Frau ihr erstes Kind bekam, wurde allmählich ein Eßtisch für drei Personen erforderlilich. Er hat dann auch drei Beine aus Kiefernholz bekommen – eins zur möglichen Befestigung an der Wand. Das Beinpaar ist mit einem Trog für Flaschen verbunden. Der Tisch erhielt eine schwarze Resopalplatte mit starkem Umleimer.

Später kam ein Auftrag für die Möblierung eines neuen Bürogebäudes der Industrie- und Handelskammer in Münster. Dem Chef entwarf ich einen markanten Schreibtisch als umgekehrtes U aus 36 mm starken, mit heller Esche furnierten Platten. Dazu kontrastierten der darunter gehängte, schwarz gebeizte Schubladenkasten und eine ebenso schwarze untere Querstrebe zum Füßeabstellen. Für die Büro-Utensilien diente ein Anstellkasten – ebenfalls in Esche.

Die führenden Mitarbeiter erhielten Schreibtische in dem gleichen Holz und den gleichen Stärken mit untergebautem Kasten auf der einen und zwei verbundenen Füßen auf der anderen Seite – etwas weniger repräsentativ, aber praktisch.

Als das Haus Dewald in Karlsruhe-Grötzingen fertig war, fehlten noch die Möbel. Im Schlafzimmer der Frau des Hausherrn wurde ein Einbauschrank mit anschließendem Schreibplatz notwendig. Als Gegenbewegung zum Anstieg des Kastens mit der Decke treppen sich die Türen bis auf Tischhöhe ab, und die unterste Einteilung geht in die Schreibtischplatte über. Im Obergeschoß des Ateliers des Hausherrn war eine Nische für ein Regal vorgesehen. Das regte zu einem geometrischen Spiel mit drei gegeneinander verschobenen Kästen an, dazu kamen zwei Vertikalelemente, eines doppelt so hoch wie das andere, dazu vier aufnahmefreudige offene Fächer gleicher Größe. Für den Wohnraum entwarf ich die Sitzgruppe Gi1 mit Gestellen aus 36 mm starkem Kiefernholz mit abgefasten Kanten, und zwar als Sessel, als zweisitzige Causeuse und als viersitziges Sofa; dazu einen Tisch aus dem gleichen Material mit einer dicken Glasplatte. Dieser Typ kam dann in den Handel und wurde später auch mit Polstern aus blauem Büffelleder hergestellt. Der Eßplatz bekam Buchenholzstühle mit geflochtenen Sitzen.

Als die Kinder auszogen, übernahmen die Eltern ihre erdgeschossigen Zimmer. Das Bett des Hausherrn wird am Kopfende durch ein Regal gerahmt, die Mitte ist gepolstert – für das Lesen im Sitzen – dazu seitlich die Leuchte, darunter ein Loch, durch das der Hausherr im Liegen seinen Wecker erblickt. Durch das Fenster kann er das Fenster des gegenüberliegenden, kleinen Ateliers seines Sohnes (mit dem Beruf eines Rahmenmachers und Vergolders) sehen. Zur Unterscheidung von den innen herumhängenden vielen Rechteck-Bilderrahmen ist das Fensterquadrat um 45 Grad gedreht. Rechts und links trägt je ein Bein eine Tischplatte und ein Regal. Dazwischen liegt die Fensterbank mit bruchrauh behauener, kurviger Vorderkante.

Das Thema Bett beschäftigte mich weiterhin. Die derzeit im Handel angebotenen Betten in immer geraden, »funktionalen« Formen sind oft von der erwarteten Geborgenheit weit entfernt. Die Skizze zeigt die nicht realisierte Bett-Idee für das Haus Rees in dem fünfeckigen Schlafzimmer. Es paßt genau in die 45-Grad-Ecke mit Blick auf die Tür. Die Bettkomposition mit angebauten Nachtkästchen macht eine »umarmende« Gebärde, auch durch die hölzernen Rückwände mit Schutz für Schultern und Kopf, wenn man bei Krankheit im Bett sitzen will – umgeben von Bildern der Kinder und Ahnen, einer eingebauten Leselampe, Telefon-, Radio- und Fernsehanschluß, Lichtschalter, eingebauten Leuchten und kleinen Erhöhungen der Längs- und Endrahmen gegen Hinausfallen und zum Füßeabstemmen. Zu ergänzen wäre noch die Zugleine aus früheren Zeiten zum Schalten der Deckenleuchte. Dazu käme schließlich ein Rollkasten mit Rotweinflaschen zum besseren Schlafen. – Das Ganze war zu teuer und blieb damals ein Traum.

Passend zum brutalistischen Stil des DRK-Altenheims in Karlsruhe entstanden stapelbare Buchenholzstühle mit schwarzen Sperrholzsitzen und -lehnen, dazu kräftige Vier-Personen-Tische mit Mittelfuß für den Speiseraum. Für die Bibliothek und andere Gemeinschaftsräume wurden dazu passende Sessel mit geflochtenem Sitz und ebensolcher Lehne hergestellt.

Mein einfachster Tisch für die Terrasse meines Karlsruher Hauses bestand aus einer am Ort ausgegrabenen, trapezförmigen roten Sandsteinplatte als Fuß, einer am Ort gegossenen Tischplatte aus Beton, die in die gegenüberliegende Stützmauer eingemauert wurde. Dazu gehörte eine gemauerte Bank aus Bruchstein mit der Stützmauer als Lehne – zum Gebrauch an warmen Sommertagen.

Für die Bibliothek meines Hauses entwarf ich einen niedrigen Tisch zwischen den (betonierten und weiß lackierten) Sitz-/Liegebänken. Ich wählte dazu eine weiße Marmorplatte und ein verchromtes Stahlrohrgestell.

Der in zusammengeklapptem Zustand 100 x 100 cm große Tisch für vier Personen besteht aus zwei mit Scharnier verbundenen, beschichteten Platten dieser Größe, die auf zwei Rücken an Rücken gestellten Schleuderbetonrohren mit einem Außendurchmesser von 100 cm aufliegen. Nimmt man die Platte ab und stellt die Halbrohre im Abstand von 2,00 m sich gegenüber, steckt zwei zweiseitig genutete Holzholme rechts und links auf die Rohre auf, kann man die aufgeklappte Platte auflegen. Man erhält dann Platz für acht bis bis zehn Personen.

Schließlich habe ich für einen nationalen Wettbewerb 1963 einen gußeisernen Ofen entworfen und dafür den zweiten Preis erhalten. Der Grundtyp »Karlchen« war für Junggesellen in Einzimmerwohnungen gedacht. Aufgestockt als »Karl« konnte er kinderlosen Ehepaaren dienen, während die zweite Aufstockung als »Karl der Große« für Großfamilien in Frage kam. Die letzteren beiden Typen nähern sich der Formgebung alter Etagenöfen aus dem Biedermeier an. Später erwies sich allerdings, daß es am Bedarf für Kohleöfen mangelte.

Als Beispiel für Beleuchtungskörper soll der sechsarmige Leuchter erwähnt werden, der um 1960 entstand. Er besteht aus einer rechteckigen Stahlplatte als Fuß, einem darauf aufgeschweißten stärkeren Stahlrohr und sechs dünneren Rohren, die schräg ansteigend daran angeschweißt sind. Sie tragen je eine Fassung mit Glühbirnen und eine sie zum Raum hin abschirmende halbkreisförmige Kupferblende. Die weiße Wand reflektiert ein warmes Licht. In meinem Karlsruher Haus stand die Lampe neben dem Kamin.

Für das Bibliotheksgebäude der Technischen Universität Wien habe ich sämtliche Beleuchtungskörper entworfen – Wandleuchten, Beleuchtungsschienen in Halbrohren, Hängeleuchten für den Eßraum der Angestellten, die Leuchte für ein Anschlagbrett, Lesetischleuchten –, alle in verchromtem Stahl und mit dem gleichen Leuchtmittel bestückt, dazu Lesetische für zwei und vier Personen, kreisrunde Computertische für bis zu acht Personen, Arbeitstische für die Stockwerksaufsicht, Regale für die Büchersortierung der Verwaltung sowie die Regale und die Kasseninsel des Buchladens.

In den 1980er Jahren arbeitete ich an der Sesselgruppe »Jumbo« aus 36 mm starkem Kiefernholz mit eingeklebtem, über die Armlehnen reichenden Polstern. Eine Weiterentwicklung war der Ohrensessel.

Anläßlich eines Innenraumauftrags in Wien entstand der Schreibplatz der Dame des Hauses mit einer Variation eines Thonet-Stuhls.

1. Director's desk for the chamber of industry and commerce in Münster, 1954.
2. Employee's desk for the chamber of industry and commerce in Münster, 1954.
3. Glass table in the Werkbund exhibition »Furniture – affordable and beautiful«, Mannheim, 1956.
4. Shelves in the Dewald house, Karlsruhe, 1957.

1. Chefschreibtisch für die Industrie- und Handelskammer in Münster, 1954.
2. Mitarbeiterschreibtisch für die Industrie- und Handelskammer in Münster, 1954.
3. Glastisch in der Werkbundausstellung »Möbel, billig und schön«, Mannheim, 1956.
4. Regal im Haus Dewald, Karlsruhe, 1957.

5. Sofa and easy chair in the first Gieselmann
house, Karlsruhe, 1964.
6. Dining table and chairs in the old-age home
of the Deutsches Rotes Kreuz, Karlsruhe, 1966.
7, 8. Dining table for four to six persons in the
second Gieselmann house, Vienna, 1974.

5. Sofa und Sessel im ersten Haus Gieselmann,
Karlsruhe, 1964.
6. Eßtisch und Stühle im Altenheim des Deutschen
Roten Kreuzes, Karlsruhe, 1966.
7, 8. Eßtisch für vier bis sechs Personen im zweiten
Haus Gieselmann, Wien, 1974.

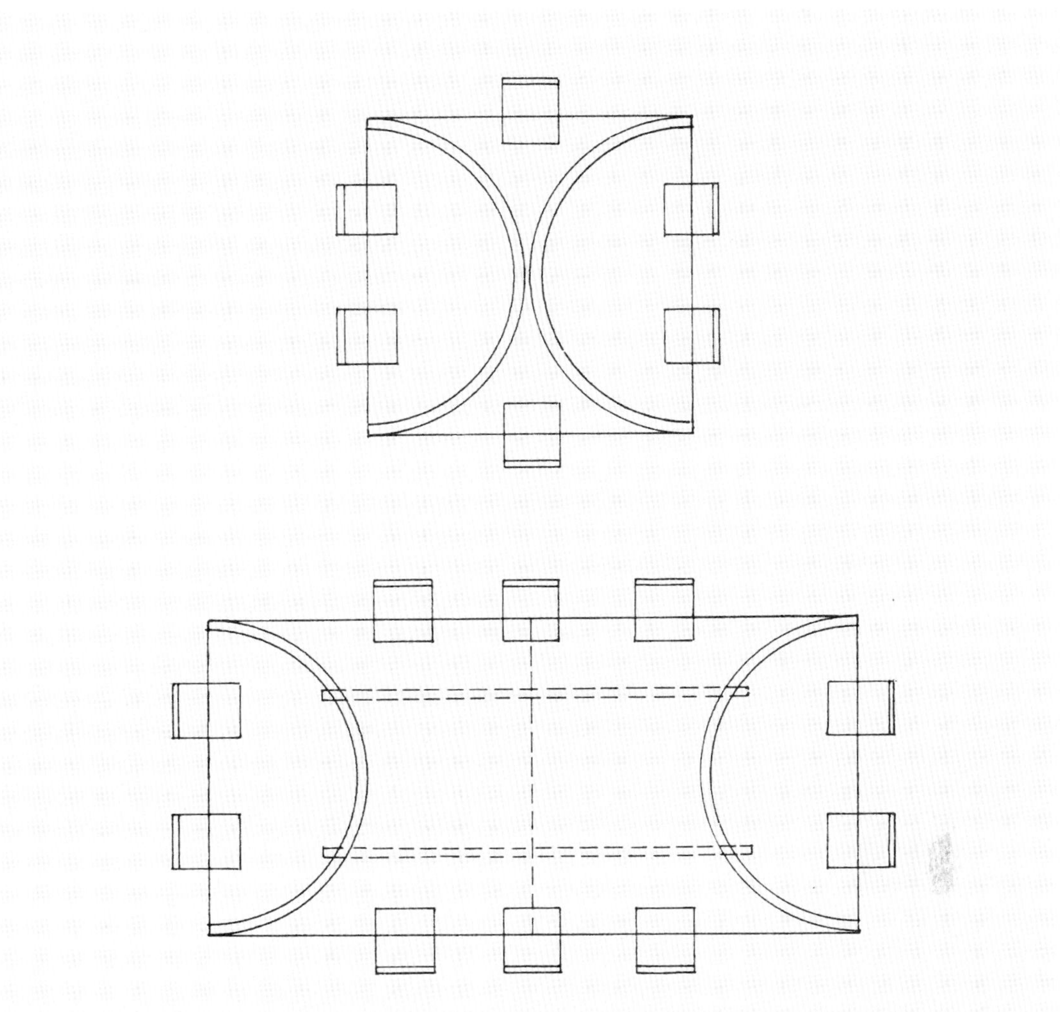

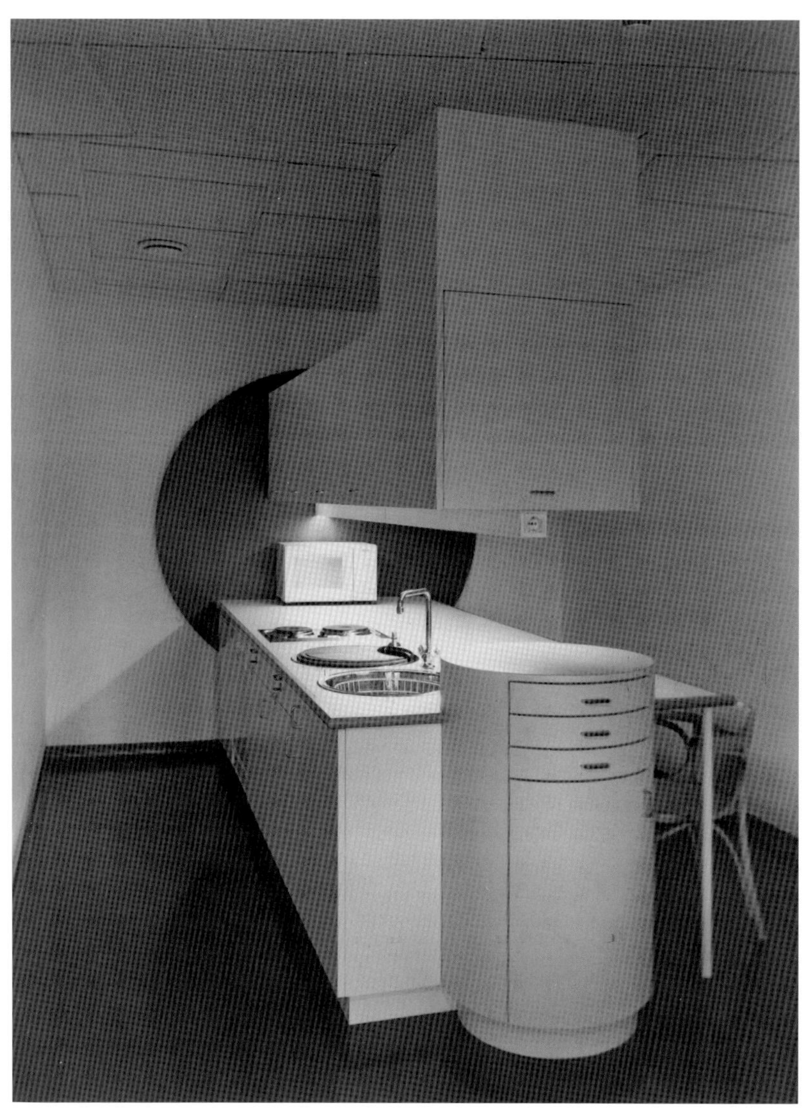

9. Tea kitchen in the library of the Technische Universität Wien, 1985.
10. Reading places in the library of the Technische Universität Wien, 1985.
11, 12. Medicine cabinet in the third Gieselmann house, Karlsruhe, 2000.

9. Teeküche in der Bibliothek der Technischen Universität Wien, 1985.
10. Leseplätze in der Bibliothek der Technischen Universität Wien, 1985.
11, 12. Medikamentenschrank im dritten Haus Gieselmann, Karlsruhe, 2000.

Our style is the search for style

»In welchem Style sollen wir bauen?« (What style shall we build in?) was the title of a book published in 1828 by the Baden architect Heinrich Hübsch. At a later date, when the Vienna opera house had been completed, the Viennese made fun of the architects in a satirical song: »Siccardsburg hasn't any style, and neither does van der Nüll« – whereupon they committed suicide, which goes to show how seriously the architects took their »lack of style«.

Hübsch, a German Romantic among architects, stated in section 2 of his book that »style refers to something general that is inherent in all the buildings of a nation, whether they are intended for divine worship, the administration of the state, teaching, etc.« And he goes on to describe the individual parts of a building that serve to finish and span a room or building. He calls these parts »elements of style, which, depending on their importance, should be ornamented differently, given a more opulent, more economical, etc. shape«.

Nowadays, things are no longer that simple for us, since contemporary usage interprets the term style more broadly. For us, style is not only a question of architecture, but of art in general and even our lifestyle. The term can be used to describe the way one drives, one's table manners, one's aesthetic taste, the way one speaks and writes. Style also means the manner of representation in the arts, but also an artist's form of expression. Meyer-Shapiro draws a further conclusion: »Style is the manifestation of culture as an integral whole« and »a visible characteristic of its unity.« We architects are reluctant to associate the word »fashion« with style – and if we must, then only as the happy-go-lucky and short-lived sister of a more serious brother.

However: is style in our times really more long-lived than fashion? We should hope so, since the pace of changing fashions is dictated primarily by sales. We need to be prepared for the fact that architectural styles are going to change at least with every generation, that they will overlap, pick up older ideas again – while in earlier periods one could count on the Romanesque, Gothic, Renaissance, and Baroque style to last for 200 years, as each developed from an early stage to its zenith. Almost always, this implied a unified conception of the world and a convention as to the development of culture that was supported by those in power and shared by the infrastructure.

Today, there is no longer a unity of style; rather, there is diversity and »heterogeneity« (Foucault) among the stylistic manifestations of the 20th century (art nouveau, de Stijl, neoclassicism, organicism, brutalism, rationalism, constructivism, deconstructivism) – in other words, pluralism, or a number of truths that may be different in every part of the planet but do not exclude the risk of a (technoid) mannerism.

While pluralism does not prevent styles, it does prevent style as such.

Thus we must, it appears, come to the realization – in keeping with our globalized view of the world – that our goal cannot be a single style, but rather the search for one, and consequently the search for culture. The search, if we take it

seriously, i. e., if we avoid the phony junk by the roadside – the search itself allows us to have our pluralistic freedom and creativity. The search is our style. The search, if free of ideology, is the basis for finding architectonic expression.

In this context, the author's standing premises are **time** with its material and intellectual limitations, **place** with its genius loci – if one does not need to be created first – and the **people** for whom we are building, with their need for satisfaction (which is also dependent on whether it is possible for them to be an integral part of the locality) and their material wishes – and finally, based on all three premises, the **technology** that is appropriate to them.

Time is the curved bracket that embraces all the rest – architecture, art, fashions from clothing to auto bodywork – and the buildings, which all occur in lively, though contradictory variations.

Place – which the Romans believed to be the dwelling place of the »genius loci«, the spirit of the place, and to which they therefore ascribed not only a material, but also a spiritual dimension – is a composite of the unique characteristics of the building site and the neighborhood. One can change its form and its spirit simply by leveling the slope of the site. Another example from the practice of a prominent postwar architect: If you try to demolish the steeple, the only remaining part of the church, though damaged by many bomb raids, the people of the neighborhood are suddenly up in arms against you: they demand that you preserve the traditional significance of the place. One can interpret the existing situation by adapting to it or by creating a contrast to it, but one must not ignore the spirit of the place,
if indeed it exists. In this context, I should like to remind readers that the architecture philosopher Sigfried Giedion, in the middle of the 20th century – inspired by the buildings of Alvar Aalto – coined the term »regionalism« to characterize architecture that is adapted to its particular locality.

For architects, **people** should always be the most important point of reference of their work.

How is the **technology** suited to the people, how is it suited to the locality? How cozy is a bedroom on the 13th floor of a high-rise apartment building, a steel-framed structure with curtain walls without balustrades? Don't people sleep better behind insulated brick walls? Or let's say somebody gets to church – a little late – on Sunday morning, sits in the back row and follows the service by monitor and PA system. Here, while the technology is helpful, it is surely out of place, given the significance of the sanctuary.

What I am saying is that the architect needs to understand what constitutes human nature in its broadest sense. Particularly in a highly mechanized age, an architect can do a great deal to create a life-promoting, human architecture. We still have a long way to go before we achieve a »human style«.

The identification of spaces

Phenomena

Identity is being in harmony with oneself. It is the emotional bond with and the striving for another person or another object, linked with the goal of finding oneself. Sigmund Freud defines identification as »establishing the object in the ego«. The reverse of this definition – i.e., establishing the ego in the object – also captures the meaning of the word. Self-identification is the striving for self-realization.

Developing these axioms further, psychology and sociology have now reached a level that claims everyone's interest. They introduce us to a new »difficulté d'être«, as Jean Cocteau says, a difficulty of being, since according to them there is a general loss of identity: identification, they claim, finds its bearings by using false models, obsolete moral concepts, wrongly directed libido, and unsatisfactory collective behavior.

Our age is not characterized by a uniform belief system, ideals or sense of what life is about, but by a pluralistic divertimento of understanding the world. Art movements diverge, Christian denominations multiply and are in a process of transformation. Human existence is about to experience a planetary expansion. In this age when the human brain is no longer equal to the task of coping with the entirety of technological progress, psychologists have determined that progress in self-realization and identification is just about zero.

While the church still occasionally preaches this Western goal of self-realization, sociologists hold up a far clearer, more methodical mirror before us. According to them, we are not able to identify with the spaces we create, and the result is lack of orientation; uniformity produces indifference.

Frustrated contemporaries concur with these judgments: It is easier for them to agree with the scientists' analytical critique than with a critique of architecture as a work of art, whether the explanation is legitimate or only serves as defensive entrenchment.

We architects, on the other hand – and especially those of us who specialize in residential buildings – have realized that we need to use the insights of medicine and sociology in our work in order to build a valid residential environment. Some among us might object that incorporating such scientific insights inhibits intuitive creativity, but this is probably as unlikely as the assertion that the use of computers might be detrimental to architecture.

What does a technology of interdisciplinary collaboration look like? From a purely practical point of view, the collaboration will be predominantly indirect, in other words, it will be the architect's reflection about the sociologists' insights. Here's a practical example: It was the sociologist Alexander Mitscherlich who, as long as thirty years ago, took a stand against the then prevalent idea of urban planners that row houses should be positioned perpendicular to the street »in a green meadow«, and instead demanded that they be positioned parallel to the street. He gave the following reason: »A street that was bordered by houses was enhanced by an additional formal

quality and included the observer in the border-ed area created by its contours.« This is one example illustrating how a sociologist was able to point out to the architects and urban planners that there are benefits to giving inhabitants a sense of identity by structuring the human environment – and incidentally, by using traditional ideas.

Yet how is the need for identification expressed? Young people manifest this need by breaking out of everyday mass-produced traditions and fashions and going against the grain (pop music, hippie- and dropout lifestyles), while older adults emphasize their identity by the type of car they buy, or by partitioning their balcony off from their neighbor's – that's about as far as human risk-taking goes.

This is why I'll add an example from the animal kingdom: sea anemones find an empty shell, grow or stay small – depending on the size of the shell. The space of their housing stimulates their size and thus »gives them identity«. Of course, human beings are not capable of adapting to that extent. The ways our identity is affected by the space we live in are less physically measurable, though space does have an effect on our psyche.

Here is a human example: On the Adriatic side of the Apennines lies the town of Urbino, with the house where Raphael was born. The building is a varied conglomeration of rooms with surprisingly large ground floor halls, richly furnished living spaces, a small, cool inner courtyard with a gallery, many steps and stairs, and so many individual rooms that it is possible to forget one once in a while, only to rediscover it later with a thrill of surprise. Does not this building complete the picture we have of the brilliant Renaissance artist?

Another example, from literature: Marcel Proust, the last novelist before the époque machiniste, in his work *Remembrance of Things Past* – familiar with his parish church in Combrai – at the sight of another small church writes: »But I did not inquire, as I would have in Chartres or Reims, whether a more or less powerful religious feeling is expressed here, but only exclaimed instinctively: ›the church‹!«

No, we are not about to discuss a topic from literary romanticism. On the contrary: Just think of the professor of architecture, appointed to a chair in Berlin, who in his lectures staunchly defends neutral, interchangeable, standardized architecture, but makes every effort to find a spacious apartment in an old building with stuccoed twelve-foot ceilings. Obviously he personally was not satisfied with today's one-dimensional, extroverted, functionalistic residential architecture, which lacked spatial quality. He sought his identification eclectically in an ornamented environment whose spatial quality was superior. I believe this example shows that relatively often, there is a kind of split consciousness – and mistrust whether contemporary residential buildings make emotional expansion possible. »Less is more«, preached Mies van der Rohe to his American students, yet he himself lived in a building in Chicago that dated back to the 1870s.

In the 1970s and '80s a number of architects were working on flexible floor plans and standardized construction in building large-scale public housing, where first-generation renters would have a say in the design, and following generations in the remodeling, of the apartments by moving the walls. It is true that this question has been of interest when building single-family homes – since the first buildings of this type built by Eric Friberger in Göteborg in 1937; however, in an apartment building constant remodeling disturbs the peace of the other residents. And besides, no matter how interesting and inspiring it may be for an architect to work out a project with an individual client, it can be all the more difficult to satisfy several neighboring residents equally.

These concepts of standardization, flexibility, and exchangeability – not only of building elements, but of inhabitants as well – can be traced back to recent architectural history: the 1914 German Werkbund exhibition in Cologne. It was Hermann Muthesius (1861–1927) of all people who, after entering the public sphere with a publication about English country houses that aroused much interest, proclaimed in a discussion, among other things: »Architecture – and that includes the entire sphere of activity of the Werkbund – strives for standardization; only through standardization can it regain the general significance it had in periods when culture was harmonious.« Henry van de Velde (1863–1957) responded: »As long as there are still artists in the Werkbund and as long as they have an influence on the Werkbund's history, they will continue to protest against any suggestion of a canon or of standardization.« Ever since, the controversy has remained virulent. It breaks out again and again under such titles as »Art versus technology« or »Organicism versus function«.

In the »Charter of Athens«, the first program published by the Federation of World Architects (founded in 1928) under the aegis of Le Corbusier, »profitability, efficiency, and standard« are given precedence over all other considerations. The »organicists« – Häring, Scharoun and Aalto – were no longer an issue, and Frank Lloyd Wright was not a member. At the Bauhaus, too, the last director, Hannes Meyer (1889–1954), represented the following school of thought: »Pure construction is the basis and the distinguishing feature of the new world of forms.«

These were and to some extent still are sacrosanct principles of architecture. Until, at one point, it became apparent that the tidy separation of functions or – as Richard Neutra (1892 to 1970) believed, the »analytical way of thinking« – had disastrous consequences, similar to those that befall someone who eats only sterile food. Our »deconcentrated« cities, which have been broken down into separate function areas, not only create more traffic, but prevent the integration of the entity that is a city. The interchangeability of apartments creates neuroses because of their lack of identification (as though Darwin had not proved that the environment influences human beings and even causes them to mutate). It is true that a one-dimensional form of society receives material benefits as a result of the achievements of industrialization, but its psychic needs for expansion are suppressed.

Opportunities for identification

The first and most important opportunity for identification results how it is related to human needs. In order to live in democratic countries people need both privacy and public life. Privacy is the chance to withdraw from the world, to a »retreat« for reflection, to read, write, etc., i. e., an opportunity for every person to have their own room.

The complement to this is public space, i. e., a space where people can be together with others in order to form opinions, or to prepare for participation in public life. Jürgen Habermas defines public as the part of the masses that not only adopts opinions, but also forms its own opinions. For housing this means that the living room is designed to be used as a place where the whole family can be together, not as a room that is meant to give visitors a good impression of the parents. Similarly, schools need a hall where students can meet during breaks to speak what is on their minds, and where – for the first time – they can learn public opinion. Likewise, every large company should have a room where employees can gather during breaks.

Also, schools, old age homes, and other public buildings should not be built in a standardized way; rather, each of these buildings should be given its own unique character – for instance, in response to its special situation – so that everyone who uses the building can say: »This is ›my‹ school« (for example), and does not have to say: »It's just another school!«

This leads to the next opportunity for identification: unmistakability. Thinking in series leads people to strive for uniform elements such as preassembled units, on the principle that a minimal number of different types of preassembled units result in larger series and therefore lower production costs. The end product is a building without distinguishing characteristics whose apartments can be identified from the outside only by counting off the windows. However, it should be possible for people, even if they come home late at night, to find their apartment by its distinguishing features. In reality – just the other way around – here is the way things are now: A person moves to the city, the rationale being: »Nobody knows me there, I can be on my own!« This is not a good precondition for becoming an active member of society.

On the other hand, if architects observed the principle of unmistakability, this contemporary of ours might become an active member of society if he were to spend his working day in an office building in which work stations are laid out in many dissimilar variants. What better way to provoke indifference than by laying out the always identical work stations behind a façade that is always arranged in the same grid or is a wall of glass? What we need are both a living architecture and psychological benefit.

One important condition for improving the organization of housing developments would be a new kind of zoning laws. These should not be limited to laying down individual forms – with the result that there is a large number of uniform types of houses – and prescribed dimensions, but should make possible structural ordering principles, variants, and changeability. For in-

stance, one could lay down the mandatory constants of a certain type of house, while leaving its variables optional. This would assure that permanent factors, such as the kitchens and bathrooms – being ordering elements for the form of the street as far as urban development is concerned – are officially regulated, while anything that has to do with the variables – such as the number of rooms – is left up to the planner's design. Unmistakability would then not be necessary as a demonstration of taste à la Hundertwasser, but would emerge as the architect makes visible the inner process, as life is infused in the standards of urban planners, and as the varied individual needs of the residents are taken into account.

Another issue that is connected with the foregoing one is the building's identification with place, i.e., the way the building harmonizes with its locale, which can turn out to be important for the inhabitants as well. An existing slope should not simply be bulldozed flat, but should be included in the building project, so that the floor plan and the section can be developed from it. No, I am not about to bring up the ideologies of »Blut und Boden« (blood and soil), and of the »Heimatstil«, a style based on locally and regionally rooted building traditions. Rather, what I mean is that the difference in site levels needs to be accepted as a challenge, an element that will give shape to the building. »The land is the simplest form of architecture«, as Frank Lloyd Wright said on the subject. Architecture that is »tied to a locale« means that the building is designed in such a way that it becomes part of the land, that it helps make an arbitrary site into an identified place.

Identification is a psychic process that is nourished by sensual perception. Architects can deaden identification by repeating many uniform elements, irritate it to the point of torture by the exaggerated accumulation of ever new effects, while on the other hand they can produce deep contentment by means of other configurations.

This brings us to the question of beauty. »I do not know what beauty is«, Albrecht Dürer is supposed to have said. Is it the order of the individual elements, such as windows, primary elements, or volumes? No doubt we still expect – even in extreme architecture such as that of Zaha Hadid – that there should be a degree of relationship between interior and exterior design, or at least an indication on the outside of what expects us inside. But even this may quickly become outdated in our times, which are used to pluralism. On the other hand, there is the old goal, which architects still strive for today, whereby the floor plan and façade are of the same order; this will possibly reassure those among us who are older, while it will possibly bore those who are younger. In any case, order is not a priori coordination. Endless rows of church pews all too often bring up associations of marching formations, and endlessly aligned row houses make us think of freight trains, while apartments with long corridors make us think of conveyor belts. Serial coordination here is based on a grossly simplifying intellectual equalization of things that are incommensurable.

In terms of urban planning today, order in our age means the order of dissimilarities. When the inhabitants of Tokyo have to reckon with their city changing its outward appearance every ten years because of ten-year inner city property leases and also because high-rises are demolished and rebuilt, an »order of dissimilarities« might nonetheless remain in effect. It is true that one factor – remembrance of former times, which we Europeans cultivate – could no longer remain in force.

The concept of beauty may possibly take a back seat under these circumstances. The rapid change of styles that is characteristic of pluralism bewilders the inherent human yearning for beauty and sharpens the craving for the sensational. And more and more this yearning for beauty insists on buildings that have been determined to be »historical« rather than »beautiful«. This may be the reason that the »postmodern period« was able to hold on for several years.

Beauty is present whenever we look at a building without prejudice and our aesthetic self accepts it – sometimes after a long scrutiny, sometimes at first sight.

The foregoing is the abbreviated substance of the inaugural lecture the author gave at the Vienna Institute of Technology in 1964. New developments in urban planning make an addition necessary.

The massive advent of high-rise construction has so far been pursued with little consistency as regards urban development. This is true both of the incorporation of high-rise buildings in urban planning as well as of their detailed design. Could it be that in future Europeans, too, will demolish old urban structures and replace them with high-rises? The urban planners of Beijing have already made arrangements for this to happen.

As numerous examples show, high-rises seem to be less of a concern for urban authorities that issue permits involved with design than are single-family houses. And so interchangeable rectangular floor plans with flat roofs predominate, giving the impression that the investor designed them himself. In the Ruhr district the same type of high-rises – encased in glass, cylinder-shaped – can be seen in two different cities. Instead of identification with the locale, the result is confusing interchangeability.

Taking New York as a model in this context, we think primarily of the Chrysler Building, the more modern Seagram Building, or the postmodern AT + T Tower, buildings that contribute to the identification of the city. The destroyed Twin Towers, on the other hand, contributed to identification only by their exceptional height, not their design.

High-rises as three-dimensionally designed groups might even take on a signaling effect in the landscape, like that previously performed by the towers of Gothic cathedrals. The formation of groups would need to be made congruent with the endeavors of individual architects, achieving a vibrant view from several directions and thus contributing to the identification of the city.

Structure and form

It is probably not always that simple: a young man who upon graduating from secondary school decides to study architecture, then acts on his decision. I, at any rate, simultaneously considered the alternatives – becoming a musician or painter. Perhaps the reason for my ultimately choosing architecture was my rage at enemy bombs that had already flattened part of my hometown, Münster: one day, when this nightmare of a government with its lust for war was gone, I would be able to help rebuild my town.

I had gotten my first impressions of architecture in Münster. There were the heavy Romanesque and Gothic churches of light yellow sandstone, which formed striking landmarks in the cityscape. There was the curved façade of the palace of a nobleman built by the Baroque architect Johann Conrad Schlaun, which I passed daily for eight years halfway to school. And there was the Prinzipalmarkt, the marketplace I had to cross just as often – an elongated rectangle, slightly crooked and surrounded by gabled houses, in the center of town. The special charm of this place comes from the arcades that line the entire marketplace under the gables, where people could meet – not just on the many rainy days enjoyed by this region – and go shopping in the stores under the arches.

A wise prince-bishop must have given the townspeople who wanted to build their house here freedom in designing their gabled houses, all approximately equally wide; but at the same time he enjoined them to make available one to two arcade widths for public use. In other words, he allowed them to express their individual taste on the one hand, while on the other hand he expected that they donate space for the market square as their tribute to the community.

As a boy I was initially aware only of form and function. It was not until much later that I found a comparison taken from linguistics in a book by Fernand de Saussure, the precursor of French structuralism. He explains the French word »langue« as »language« – in the sense of a collective system (of communication), and the word »parole« as language spoken by the individual person.

Applied to the houses of the Prinzipalmarkt this means that they share the »langue« of the house type of the arcade buildings, while the individually designed gables speak the »parole«. The use of both, in conjunction with the slightly crooked space of the market street formed by the houses, results in the structure of the complex of buildings.

This is in agreement with Immanuel Kant's statement about the concept of structure as the »relation of individual elements to the common center«. The center here is the space of the market square, formed by the house elements that surround this space.

Claude Lévi-Strauss, the chief proponent of structuralism, declares that »every person must be able to be a definite somebody«. As an architect, I would add that the place where this definite somebody plans to live cannot be arbitrarily standardized, but that every place – over and above the house number – requires its own for-

mal or color definition in order to enable the person to attain his/her definiteness.

What is important for the marketplace is also true of human housing. In architecture, structure can be applied only spatially. A house or an apartment should have a center that stimulates life – the living room in the center, with the individual rooms related to it. A space promotes life when it provides room for the stimulation of community. It must create connection with the individual rooms indoors and public life outside. It must have light, because without light no life can develop. It must make group activities possible and must not be crammed full of furniture. In other words, it has the same function on a small scale as the Prinzipalmarkt does on a large scale.

Buddha says that the center must be empty – only then can it give space to life. This implies that a square filled with volumes can be sufficient only unto itself, or to the objects being exhibited, and yet impedes human activities. Autocrats generally use squares to put up monuments – but for festivals, markets, and protests people need empty space.

The empty center is the place of magic. Here, people can meet with each other. It implies life.

That is why my primary thesis is that fundamental structures must have a lasting character. They signify permanence, identification, image, and home. They convey life. They are the soul of the building and of the city, they can be subjectively grasped.

Forms on the other hand are produced by economic factors, they imply beauty and/or ugliness, they convey emotions. They belong to the finite world, the world of consumption and of objects, they mostly do not last forever and need to be constantly renovated or modified – particularly in our time.

This was precisely what happened in the case of the Prinzipalmarkt: all its gabled houses – except for one – were destroyed by bombs in World War II. Reconstruction could have been accomplished quickly in glass and steel – the »modern-day idiom«. However, city planners preferred to rebuild the houses in their former dimensions, with arcades, and crowned the façades of individual houses each with its uniquely designed gable.

I have said nothing about beauty. And yet I keep hoping that it has the power to endure. No doubt it will if we are capable of experiencing it spontaneously. On the other hand, if beauty becomes the subject of the scientific studies of aestheticians and if we need to translate emotional terms into intellectual ones, we've taken a step away from the paradise of subjectivity into the world of objects.

An architect lives on the borderline between both. As someone who participates in the work of creation, he would do well to respect its laws. If he spends his life trying to fathom and to apply the prerequisites for a structure that promotes growth and creates form, he can hope to make lasting contributions. At the same time, he is constantly aware how relative this human endeavor, too, can be. And how – to our dismay or delight – the eternal recurrence and passing of forms and designs is part of existence.

Time, place, people, and technology in the construction of Catholic churches

In view of the increasing numbers of people who are leaving the Church in the two major religious denominations and the resulting lower number of new churches being built, we could drop the topic entirely. Still, the author wishes to present here the insights he gained while building and renovating seven Catholic churches at the end of the 20th century.

Place

In the beautiful city of Vienna a church was recently built next to a gas station – that is, on a site the planning authorities had intended for »businesses«. This is in contrast with the suggestion of a prominent architect in the 'sixties. He demanded that churches should be placed where the faithful could walk to them in their slippers. Perhaps – now that apartments in many cities are located in high-rises – there will come a day when a worship space will be integrated on the ground floor of a high-rise or – closer to heaven – a church will crown the generally flat roof of one. Not because people want to walk to church in slippers – which would be appropriate for hospital chapels – but because of the absurdity of the scale when a church – such as the neo-Gothic St. Patrick's Cathedral in New York – is set down between high-rises.

Belfries, which once made the location of a church visible from afar – as the bell tower of Ulm Cathedral still does today – are hardly being built anymore. Today the most important prerequisite of the church complex is a square that is accessible to the public – not only as a place to meet after the church service, but large enough to provide sufficient room for the congregation to have a parish fair in summer.

Human needs in our time

Why do people today need a church? Their mindset is predominantly rational, and they are well informed in every respect; they have attained mastery of their gadgets, appliances, and the vehicle they drive. Perhaps, for some reason, they are occasionally assailed by doubts whether their intellect will be able to solve a particular problem, and – though baptized without their own consent – they try an alternative approach by going to church.

What qualities must a sanctuary have for people to be able to discover their soul and open it through meditation? Until recently, theologians have basically looked at church architecture from their own standpoint; here we are going to look at it from the perspective of laypeople.

The church must, first of all, offer visitors a place for silent prayer. Later, when they choose to be part of the congregation, it should be possible for them to follow the church service as well and as directly as possible. If the sanctuary looks like a factory and the pews are arranged like »columns marching to the altar« (as the great church architect Rudolf Schwarz characterized traditional seating in churches), visitors will tend to think of a lecture hall, or even associate church with the open-plan office where they once worked. This will be the case particularly if they happen to sit in the last row of the »marching columns« – that is, the place where the quality of the space deteriorates most. In short, all associations with everyday life must be eliminated. In the center of the seats stands the altar, a few steps higher than these, not to give it monumental importance, but so that the actions and words of the priest can better be seen and heard. How lovely it would be if it were possible to do without the loudspeakers hanging on the walls and the hidden microphones, and if one were addressed by the priest's own voice.

To reiterate, nothing in a church should remind worshipers of their everyday life, the place where they live, their profession, and leisure activities. Church is a space that has its own unique character. This is something that the architect must also make clear to the artists involved in the project. They must be integral to the idea on which the design is based, so that – rather than striving for self-realization, as often happens – they explicitly serve the task at hand, i. e., see their sole purpose as enhancing the religious mission and atmosphere of the sanctuary.

The rapid steel-glass method of construction used in constructing most high-rises and commercial buildings should if possible be avoided in church architecture in order to create a contrast; instead, organic materials such as brick, but also poured concrete, should be used. In less opulent times it must also be possible for there to be rough-cast churches. In contrast to the Gothic style our present ideal is churches that are brightly lit throughout. The altar as a central place – with a maximum of three steps – can be emphasized by more brilliant lighting.

At present there is as yet no one distinctive style that is characteristic of Christian churches. At least one recognizable common trait would be all the more desirable since the mosques being built everywhere now are distinguishable by their – retrospective – style, and signal their function by their respective minarets.

The church of St. Stephen in Karlsruhe – built in the years 1807–16 by Friedrich Weinbrenner – serves as an example here of how a historic building is being used today. The pantheon-like circular space is contained by corner walls, which form a square, and cruciform vestibules. In accordance with this the present development has two intersecting aisles and corresponding furnishings that are only partially oriented toward the altar. In lieu of these, a centralized interior with the altar in the middle under the skylight of the cupola has been proposed, surrounded by four groups of benches placed in a circle. The present altar in the front of the building in the north is replaced by the ambo, and before it in the widest aisle is the baptismal font.

Thus there was an attempt – taking into account the classical style of the sanctuary – to give a physical form, with only marginal changes, to participation in worship that is appropriate for modern-day men and women.

Lasting values and future trends

First, a thesis: The essential quality of that which is lasting can be judged by its symbolic value. In the best stylistic periods the highest intensification of creation became a symbol. Mozart's music is a symbol for music as such, just as the cathedral of Chartres is a symbol for churches as such. How powerful must an epoch be that was able to produce such symbols, and how different are the periods in which (as Ungers says) a multitude of »synthetic« symbols are created – for instance, the initial use of traffic lights as a sign of increasing human submission as machines got to have right of way. Computers produce a similar effect today.

Here are the immaterial values we hope will be lasting:

Among the things that should be lasting in a building are the basic components. A building has always had the function, and should continue to have the function, of protecting and delimiting. The delimitations must allow openings to the social realm and to the open air. We've realized for a long time that space and volume must accordingly be brought into relationship.

Another component is appropriateness, the proper proportions, usefulness, and convenience. We distinguish these terms, which Palladio summed up by one word – »comodità« – as the most important criterion for a house, where the greatest usability results from the proper proportions.

Form, too, is still a true need. It is the way of (re-)presenting the building. In periods of modernity form has been a more or less self-regulating result of the sum of its functions – perhaps a mistake, when we think of the many interchangeable shoebox buildings of the late functionalist period that fill our cities.

Our nostalgia means a lot to us – and so we subject old buildings to our obsession with utility. We can't bear to look at decay and disrepair. We've lost the taste for ruins – understandable in the war generation. Now that we're used to thinking in terms of preassembled units, we fret when we see something unfinished. And so we build many museums and libraries....

One thing that will last – and this is no doubt certain above all else – is natural science. The fund of scientific laws will no doubt remain undisputed. But as immaterial things like art are scientized, it is no longer as easy to find that lasting value. Science has often made our subjective cognitive faculty look small or mistaken. Laypersons cannot comprehend the unassailable position of science, which operates with measurements and analyses, and can only respond with obsequious respect. But science does contribute toward raising the level of general awareness and shapes human progress.

It is well-known that a rise in awareness is connected with the loss of social skills. (The increasing number of singles may be a proof of this.) On the other hand, art historian and social reformer John Ruskin had warned as early as the end of the 19th century against the use of dawning technology and praised manual work and crafts as the source of earthly blessings. For the temptations of encroaching technology were very great even then. People soon discovered that rail travel was more comfortable than travel by horse and carriage, although sensory impressions were not as deep because of the speed of travel. John Ruskin never took a train as long as he lived. His example did no good.

During industrialization, emotional and spiritual matters had to keep a low profile – artists reverted to the Gothic style, which had proven its worth in this respect. Even classicists such as Karl Friedrich Schinkel built neo-Gothic churches. A similar reaction was shown as historicizing postmodernists searched for a style 100 years later – a reaction to »cold« modernity and to a flourishing high-tech-architecture. They used the motifs of classicism, but also of Gründerzeit architecture, which had not been held in high regard until then. Thus, to put it in very general terms, they gradually gave up the scorn the middle of the 20th century had had for the architecture of styles. The postmodern period was over after fifteen years, and the deconstruction that followed was only a variety of high tech.

Mechanization Takes Command was the title of a work published in the 1920s by the architecture philosopher Sigfried Giedion. Today, when you see little preschool boys in the toy stores, standing completely absorbed in front of their computer games, Giedion's prediction is more relevant than ever. That is not the only reason for concluding that high-tech is the coming trend. Technology has become not just a question of convenience, but also of addiction. If we had to give up technology, the withdrawal symptoms would be as severe as those of emotional withdrawal.

If architecture in every era corresponds to that era's zeitgeist, no doubt this is true in our era as well. In our age, rationality is predominant – nothing shows this as clearly as the architecture of reason, expressed primarily in high-tech. It is also reflected in the mentality of the investors who determine the character of large parts of our cities. They are interested not so much in a beautiful cityscape, but rather in economic exploitation, i.e., the density rate of occupancy of their buildings.

The minority of architects who emphasize emotional elements and whom neither their education nor their studies under rational mentors was able to deter from their intention to include emotional features in their work can only hope to find a client who shares their views. The stylistic contrast of the »architecture of feelings« is the only way to save the city they build in from the monotony of an architecture where steel, glass, and concrete grids rule supreme. Will our century, too, revert to the styles of former periods? Who knows?

History teaches us that a genuine style comes about only when there is a fruitful dialogue between the intellect and emotion. In reference to this topic, Goethe once said, »Style is the merging of true objectivity and deepest subjectivity.«

Unser Stil ist die Suche danach

»In welchem Style sollen wir bauen?« betitelte der badische Architekt Heinrich Hübsch sein 1828 erschienenes Buch. Etwas später, als die Wiener Oper fertiggestellt war, sangen die Wiener auf die Architekten den Spottvers: »Siccardsburg und van der Nüll haben beide keinen Styl« – wie ernst die Architekten ihre »Stillosigkeit« nahmen, beweist die Tatsache, daß sie sich deshalb das Leben nahmen.

Hübsch, einer der deutschen Romantiker unter den Architekten, stellte in § 2 seines Buches fest, daß »unter Styl etwas Allgemeines verstanden werde, welches allen Gebäuden eines Volkes zukommt, sie mögen zur Gottesverehrung, zur Staatsverwaltung, zum Unterrichte usw. bestimmt sein«. Und er beschreibt im weiteren die einzelnen Teile des Gebäudes, die der Abschließung und Überspannung eines Raumes oder Gebäudes dienen. Diese Teile bezeichnet er als »Elemente des Styls, die je nach Wichtigkeit verschiedenartig verziert, opulenter, sparsamer usw. gestaltet werden sollten«.

So einfach machen wir es uns heute nicht mehr, da unser Sprachgebrauch den Begriff weiter faßt. Uns ist Stil nicht nur Sache der Architektur, sondern der ganzen Kunst und sogar unserer Haltung im Leben. Mit dem Begriff lassen sich die Art des Autofahrens (»Fahrstil«) wie die Tischmanieren, der ästhetische Geschmack wie auch die Rede- und Schreibweise (»Stilübung«) beschreiben. Mit Stil ist auch die Darstellungsweise in den Künsten, aber auch die der Künstler gemeint. Meyer-Shapiro folgert weiter: »Stil ist die Manifestation der Kultur als Ganzheit« und »sichtbares Merkmal ihrer Einheit.« Wir Architekten möchten das Wort »Mode« nur ungern mit Stil in Verbindung bringen – wennschon, dann als leicht- und schnellebige Schwester eines ernsteren Bruders.

Aber ist Stil in unserer Zeit wirklich langlebiger als Mode? Das ist zu hoffen, da das Tempo des Modenwechsels vor allem vom Umsatz diktiert wird. Wir müssen damit rechnen, daß Architekturstile mindestens mit jeder Generation wechseln, sich überschneiden, Älteres wieder aufgreifen – während man in früheren Zeiten mit 200 Jahren Dauer von Romanik, Gotik, Renaissance und Barock rechnen konnte, die sich jeweils von einem Frühstadium zu ihrer Hochblüte entwickelten. Das bedeutete fast immer ein einheitliches Weltbild und eine von oben protegierte und von unten mitgetragene Konvention für die Entwicklung der Kultur.

Heute gibt es keine Stil-Einheit mehr, sondern Vielfalt und »Heterogenität« (Foucault) und zwischen den Stilerscheinungen des 20. Jahrhunderts (Jugendstil, de Stijl, Neoklassizismus, Organik, Brutalismus, Rationalismus, Konstruktivismus, Dekonstruktivismus) – d. h. also Pluralismus bzw. mehrere Wahrheiten, die an jeder Stelle der Erde anders sein können, aber die Gefahr eines (technoiden) Manierismus nicht ausschließen.

Pluralismus verhindert zwar nicht Stile, aber **den** Stil.

So müssen wir wohl zu der unserem globalisierten Weltbild entsprechenden Erkenntnis kommen, daß nicht ein Stil unser Ziel sein kann, sondern die Suche danach und damit die Suche nach Kultur. Die Suche, wenn wir sie ernst betreiben, d. h., wenn wir die am Wege aufgestellten Attrappen vermeiden, die Suche selbst läßt uns unsere pluralistische Freiheit und Kreativität. Die Suche ist unser Stil. Die (ideologiefreie) Suche ist die Grundlage für das Finden des architektonischen Ausdrucks.

Des Verfassers feststehende Prämissen sind – in diesem Zusammenhang – **die Zeit** mit ihren sachlichen und geistigen Bedingtheiten, **der Ort** mit seinem Genius loci – falls der nicht erst zu schaffen ist – und **die Menschen**, für die wir bauen, mit ihrem Bedarf an Zufriedenheit, die auch von ihrer Integrationsmöglichkeit in den Ort abhängt, und ihren sachlichen Wünschen – und auf Grund aller drei **die Technik**, die dazu paßt.

Die Zeit ist die kurvige Klammer über dem Ganzen – der Architektur, der Kunst, der Moden von der Bekleidung bis zur Autokarosserie – und den Bauten, die alle in lebendigen, aber auch widersprüchlichen Variationen vorkommen.

Der Ort, an dem die Römer den »Genius loci«, den Geist des Ortes, vermuteten und ihm damit nicht nur eine sachliche, sondern auch eine geistige Dimension zuerkannten, ensteht aus den Eigenheiten des Bauplatzes und der Nachbarschaft. Man kann seine Gestalt und seinen Geist verändern, schon wenn man nur sein Gefälle planiert. Ein anderes Beispiel aus der Praxis eines bedeutenden Nachkriegsarchitekten: Wenn man den Kirchturm, das einzige, auch von vielen Bombenangriffen verwundete Relikt der Kirche abbrechen will, hat man plötzlich die anwohnende Bevölkerung gegen sich: Sie verlangt die Erhaltung der traditionellen Bedeutung des Ortes. Man kann den Bestand angleichend oder kontrastierend interpretieren, nur darf man den Geist des Ortes nicht ignorieren, wenn es ihn wirklich gibt. In diesem Zusammenhang mag daran erinnert werden, daß der Architekturphilosoph Sigfried Giedion in der Mitte des 20. Jahrhunderts – angeregt durch die Bauten von Alvar Aalto – den Begriff »Regionalismus« geprägt hat, um die Architektur zu kennzeichnen, die dem jeweiligen Ort angepaßt ist.

Der Mensch sollte für den Planer immer wichtigster Bezugspunkt seiner Arbeit sein.

Wie paßt **die Technik** zum Menschen, wie zum Ort? Wie groß ist der Behaglichkeitsgrad eines Schlafzimmers im 13. Stock eines Wohnhochhauses in Stahlbauweise mit brüstungslosen Fensterwänden? Schläft es sich nicht doch besser hinter wärmegedämmten Backsteinwänden? Oder jemand geht am Sonntag – ein wenig zu spät – in die Kirche, setzt sich in die hinterste Bankreihe und verfolgt die heilige Handlung über Monitor und Lautsprecher. Hier ist die Technik zwar hilfreich, aber sie verfehlt doch wohl die Bedeutung des Ortes.

Es geht um das Verständnis des Architekten für das Humane im weitesten Sinn. Gerade in einer hochtechnisierten Zeit vermag der Architekt, eine Menge für eine lebensfördernde, menschliche Architektur zu tun. Zu einem »Humanstil« fehlt uns noch viel.

Die Identifikation von Räumen

Phämomene

Identität ist die Übereinstimmung mit sich selbst. Sie ist die seelische Bindung an und das Trachten nach einer anderen Person oder einer anderen Sache, verbunden mit dem Ziel, sich selbst zu finden. Sigmund Freud definiert Identifikation als »die Aufrichtung des Objekts am Ich«. Auch die Umkehrung dieser Definition, also die Aufrichtung des Ichs am Objekt, trifft den Wortsinn. Selbstidentifikation ist das Trachten nach Selbstverwirklichung.

Psychologie und Soziologie haben, auf diesen Axiomen aufbauend, einen Stand erreicht, der unser aller Interesse beansprucht. Sie machen uns bekannt mit einer neuen – wie Jean Cocteau sagt – »difficulté d'être«, einer Schwierigkeit zu sein, da nach ihrer Ansicht ein allgemeiner Identitätsverlust festzustellen ist: Die Identifikation orientiere sich an falschen Leitbildern, an verhärteten Moralbegriffen, an falsch gerichteter Libido und an unbefriedigendem Kollektivverhalten.

Unsere Zeit ist nicht gekennzeichnet durch ein einheitliches Bekenntnis, Ideal und Lebensgefühl, sondern durch ein pluralistisches Divertimento des Weltverständnisses. Die Kunstrichtungen divergieren, die christlichen Konfessionen vermehren sich und sind in Umwandlung begriffen. Das menschliche Leben erfährt demnächst eine planetarische Ausweitung. In dieser Zeit, in der das menschliche Gehirn für die Bewältigung des gesamten technischen Fortschritts nicht mehr ausreicht, stellen die Psychologen fest, daß der Fortschritt in Selbstvollendung und Identifikation gegen Null tendiert.

Dieses abendländische Ziel der Selbstvollendung wird uns vielleicht noch von manchen Priestern gepredigt – den ungleich deutlicheren, methodischeren Spiegel halten uns die Soziologen vor Augen. Unsere Raumbildungen seien von mangelnder Identifikationskraft, die Folge sei Orientierungslosigkeit; aus der Gleichförmigkeit resultiere Gleichgültigkeit.

Diesen Urteilen schließt sich der frustrierte Zeitgenosse an: Die wissenschaftlich sezierende Kritik vermag er mit seinem gesteigerten Bewußtsein leichter nachzuvollziehen als die Kritik an der Architektur als Kunstwerk, sei das nun legitime Begründung, oder diene es nur als Verschanzung.

Auf der anderen Seite ist uns Architekten – und besonders den Wohnungsbauspezialisten – bewußt geworden, daß in unsere Arbeit notwendigerweise medizinische und soziologische Anregungen einfließen müssen, um zum Bau einer gültigen Wohnumwelt zu gelangen. Daß die Verarbeitung dieser Wissenschaften zu einer Intuitionshemmung führe, wie manche einwenden könnten, ist wohl so unwahrscheinlich wie die Behauptung, daß der Einsatz des Computers der Architektur Abbruch tun könnte.

Die Frage ist, wie die Technik der interdisziplinären Zusammenarbeit aussehen kann. Rein praktisch wird die Zusammenarbeit überwiegend indirekt sein, also: Reflexion des Architekten über die Erkenntnisse der Soziologen. Daher ein praktisches Beispiel: Es war der Soziologe Alexander Mitscherlich, der sich schon vor 30 Jahren gegen die damalige städtebauliche Idee, Wohnzeilen senkrecht zur Straße »auf der grünen Wiese« an-

zuordnen, äußerte und statt dessen wieder ihre straßenparallele Anordnung verlangte. Er begründete dies damit, daß die »hausbegrenzte Straße eine zusätzliche Gestaltqualität bekäme und den Betrachter innerhalb in die von ihren Konturen geschaffene Begrenzung mit einbezöge«. Ein Beispiel dafür, daß ein Soziologe die Architekten und Stadtplaner auf eine Bereicherung – die Identifizierung der Bewohner durch Gestaltung des menschlichen Umfelds –, auf eine im übrigen altbewährte Weise, hinweisen konnte.

Doch wie äußert sich der Bedarf an Identifikation? Bei der Jugend durch Ausbruch aus den alltäglichen seriellen Bräuchen und Moden durch Konträrverhalten wie Pop-, Hippie- und Gammler-Absonderungen, bei Erwachsenen durch Kenntlichmachung ihres Autotyps, Abtrennung des Balkons zum Nachbarn – viel mehr erlaubt sich die Menschheit nicht.

Deshalb soll ein Beispiel aus der Tierwelt folgen: See-Anemonen suchen sich ein leeres Schneckenhaus, wachsen oder bleiben klein – je nach Schneckenhausgröße. Sie werden vom Gehäuseraum zu ihrem Umfang stimuliert und damit »identifiziert«. So weit reichen die menschlichen Anpassungsfähigkeiten natürlich nicht. Unsere identifikatorischen Ergebnisse beim Umgang mit Raum sind weniger physisch meßbar, eher aber psychisch anregend.

Dazu ein menschliches Beispiel: Auf der adriatischen Seite des Apenninabfalls liegt Urbino mit dem Geburtshaus Raffaels. Das ist ein vielfältiges Raumkonglomerat mit überraschend großen Erdgeschoßhallen, reich ausgestatteten Wohnräumen, einem kleinen, kühlen Innenhof mit Galerie, vielen Stufen und Treppen und so vielen Einzelräumen, daß man schon mal einen vergessen kann, um ihn dann freudig wiederzuentdecken. Vervollständigt es nicht das Bild, daß wir uns von dem genialen Renaissancekünstler machen?

Ein anderes Beispiel aus der Literatur: Marcel Proust, der letzte Romancier vor der Époque machiniste, schreibt in seinem Werk *Auf der Suche nach der verlorenen Zeit* – vertraut mit seiner Pfarrkirche in Combrai – beim Anblick einer kleinen anderen Kirche: »Ich aber habe nicht danach gefragt, wie in Chartres oder Reims, ob sich darin ein mehr oder weniger machtvolles religiöses Gefühl bekundet, sondern rief nur unwillkürlich aus: ›die Kirche‹!«

Nein, wir nähern uns nicht einem Thema literarischer Romantik. Das Gegenteil ist der Fall: wenn wir nur an jenen nach Berlin berufenen Architekturprofessor denken, der in seiner Vorlesung die neutrale, auswechselbare, typisierte Architektur mit aller Überzeugung vertritt, aber alles daransetzte, eine Altbauwohnung mit Stuckdecken und 3,50 m lichter Raumhöhe zu bekommen. Offensichtlich reichte ihm persönlich die eindimensionale, extrovertierte, funktionalistische, raumqualitätsarme heutige Wohnarchitektur denn doch nicht aus. Er suchte seine Identifikation eklektisch in einer ornamentierten und raumqualitätsreicheren Umgebung. Ein, denke ich, relativ häufiges Beispiel, das von einer Art gespaltenen Bewußtseins zeugt – und von dem Mißtrauen in die Möglichkeit emotionaler Expansionskraft zeitgenössischen Wohnbaus. »Less is more«, predigte Mies van der Rohe seinen amerikanischne Studenten und wohnte doch selbst in einem Gründerzeithaus in Chicago.

In den 1970er und 80er Jahren beschäftigten sich manche Architekten mit flexiblen Grundrissen und typisierten Konstruktionen im Massenwohnungsbau, um Mieter der ersten Generation am Entwurf, eine Generationenfolge sodann am Umbau der Wohnungen durch Versetzen der Wände mitbestimmen lassen zu können. So interessant diese Sache beim Bau von Einfamilienhäusern – seit den ersten Bauten dieser Art, die Eric Friberger 1937 in Göteborg realisierte – auch ist, im Wohnungsbau stören die immer wieder einsetzenden Umbauten die Wohnruhe. Außerdem: So interessant und anregend für den Architekten die Erarbeitung des Programms mit einem Einzelbauherrn sein kann, so schwierig kann es sein, mehrere Nachbarbewohner gleichmäßig zufriedenzustellen.

Die Ursprünge zu diesen Vorstellungen von Typisierung, Flexibilität und Austauschbarkeit – nicht nur der Bauelemente, sondern auch der Bewohner – finden wir in der jüngeren Architekturgeschichte anläßlich der Werkbundausstellung 1914 in Köln. Ausgerechnet Hermann Muthesius (1861–1927), der mit einer vielbeachteten Publikation über das englische Landhaus an die Öffentlichkeit getreten war, proklamierte in einer Diskussion u. a.: »Die Architektur und damit das ganze Werkbund-Schaffensgebiet drängt nach Typisierung und kann nur durch sie diejenige allgemeine Bedeutung wieder erlangen, die ihr in Zeiten harmonischer Kultur zu eigen war.« Darauf antwortete Henry van de Velde (1863–1957): »Solange es noch Künstler im Werkbund geben wird und solange diese noch einen Einfluß auf dessen Geschichte haben werden, werden sie gegen jeden Vorschlag des Kanon oder einer Typisierung protestieren.« Seither sind diese gegensätzlichen Auffassungen virulent geblieben. Unter verschiedenen Titeln wie »Kunst gegen Technik« oder »Organik gegen Funktion« brechen sie immer wieder auf.

In der »Charta von Athen«, der ersten Programm-Publikation des 1928 erfolgten Zusammenschlusses der Weltarchitekten unter der Ägide von Le Corbusier, werden allen Überlegungen zur Architektur »Wirtschaftlichkeit, Rationalisierung und Standard« vorangestellt. Die »Organiker« Häring, Scharoun und Aalto wurden ausdiskutiert, Frank Lloydt Wright war nicht Mitglied. Auch am Bauhaus wurde durch den letzten Direktor Hannes Meyer (1889–1954) die Lehrmeinung vertreten: »Die reine Konstruktion ist Grundlage und Kennzeichen der neuen Formenwelt.«

Dies waren und sind teilweise noch unantastbare Grundsätze der Architektur. Bis dann offenbar wurde, daß die reinliche Trennung der Funktionen oder – wie Richard Neutra (1892–1970) fand, die »analytische Denkungsart« – verheerende Folgen hatte, ähnliche Folgen wie bei einem, der nur sterile Nahrung zu sich nimmt. Unsere »entflochtenen« Städte, die in getrennte Funktionsgebiete zerlegt wurden, ergeben nicht nur mehr Verkehr, sondern verhindern die Integration des Gebildes Stadt. Die Verwechselbarkeit der Wohnungen erzeugt Neurosen aufgrund ihrer Identifikationslosigkeit (als ob nicht schon Darwin bewiesen hätte, daß das Milieu den Menschen beeinflußt und sogar zu Mutationen anregt). Die eindimensionale Form der Gesellschaft wird zwar von den Errungenschaften der Industrialisierung materiell gesegnet, doch ihre psychischen Expansionsbedürfnisse werden unterdrückt.

Möglichkeiten der Identifikation

Die erste und wichtigste Möglichkeit der Identifikation resultiert aus ihrer Beziehung auf die Bedürfnisse des Menschen. Zum Leben in demokratischen Ländern braucht er Privatheit und Öffentlichkeit. Privatheit, also die Möglichkeit, sich zurückzuziehen, ein »reduit« zum Nachdenken, Lesen, Schreiben usw., d. h., daß jeder Mensch sein eigenes Zimmer haben sollte.

Das Komplement dazu ist die Öffentlichkei, d. h. für den Menschen ein Raum zum Zusammensein mit anderen, zur Bildung einer Meinung, zur Vorbereitung für Teilnahme im Publikum. Jürgen Habermas definiert Publikum als den Teil der Masse, der nicht nur Meinungen rezipiert, sondern auch selbst Meinungen bildet. Das bedeutet für die Wohnung: den Wohnraum nicht als Repräsentationszimmer der Eltern, sondern für das Zusammensein der ganzen Familie nutzbar zu gestalten. Genauso braucht die Schule eine Pausenhalle, wo sich die Schüler aussprechen können und – erstmals – öffentliche Meinung gelernt werden kann. Entsprechend dazu sollte auch jeder größere Betrieb einen Pausenraum haben.

Man sollte auch Schulen, Altersheime und andere öffentliche Bauten nicht typisiert bauen, sondern jedem dieser Gebäude – zum Beispiel angeregt durch die spezielle Situation – einen eigenen Charakter verleihen, so daß jeder ihrer Nutzer sagen kann: »Dies ist ›meine‹ (beispielsweise) Schule«, und nicht sagen muß: »Dies ist auch so eine Schule!«

Daraus resultiert die nächste Identifikationsmöglichkeit: die Unverwechselbarkeit. Das Denken in Serien verleitet dazu, gleichförmige Elemente – etwa Fertigteile – anzustreben, nach dem Grundsatz: Möglichst wenig verschiedene Fertigteiltypen ergeben größere Serien und daher niedrige Herstellungskosten. Dabei kommt dann ein merkmalloser Bau heraus, dessen Wohnungen von außen nur noch durch Abzählen der Fenster gefunden werden können. Der Mensch müßte aber, auch wenn er nachts spät heimkommt, seine Wohnung an Merkmalen erkennen. In Wirklichkeit ist – genau umgekehrt – der Schluß daraus entstanden: Einer zieht in die Stadt mit dem Argument: »Da kennt mich niemand, da kann ich für mich sein!« Dies ist keine gute Voraussetzung, um ein aktives Mitglied der Gesellschaft zu werden.

Das gegenteilige Prinzip der Unverwechselbarkeit könnte diesen Zeitgenossen aktivieren, wenn er in einem Bürobau arbeiten müßte, in welchem die Arbeitsplätze in vielen ungleichen Varianten angelegt sind. Kann man Gleichgültigkeit besser provozieren, als wenn die immer gleichen Arbeitsplätze hinter der immer gleich dahingerasterten oder total verglasten Fassade angelegt werden? Es geht gleichzeitig sowohl um eine lebendige Architektur als auch um einen psychologischen Gewinn.

Eine wichtige Voraussetzung für eine Gestaltverbesserung von Haussiedlungen wäre eine neue Art von Bauordnungen. Sie dürften sich nicht in der Festlegung von Einzelformen – mit dem Ergebnis der gleichförmigen Haustypen in großer Zahl – und Maßvorgaben erschöpfen, sondern müßten strukturelle Ordnungsprinzipien, Varianten und Veränderbarkeit ermöglichen. Beispielsweise könnte man die Konstanten eines Haustyps zwingend festsetzen, seine Variablen dagegen freilas-

sen. Damit würden die Momente der Dauer – etwa die Räume der Wassereinheit – als ordnende Elemente für die städtebauliche Gestalt der Straße amtlich festgelegt werden, die Anordnung der Variablen – etwa die Zimmerzahl – der Gestaltung des Planers überlassen. Unverwechselbarkeit wäre dann nicht als Geschmacksdemonstration à la Hundertwasser nötig, sondern würde aus architektonischer Sichtbarmachung des inneren Geschehens, aus einer Verlebendigung der städtebaulichen Ansprüche und aus Berücksichtigung des unterschiedlichen individuellen Bedarfs der Anwohner resultieren.

Ein anderer, hiermit zusammenhängender Punkt ist die Ortsidentifikation, also die Übereinstimmung des Baues mit seinem Ort, die auch für die Bewohner wichtig werden kann. Vielmehr ist etwa der vorgefundene Hang nicht einfach flachzuschieben, sondern als Teil der Bauaufgabe einzubeziehen, um daraus Grundriß und Schnitt zu entwickeln. Nein, die Ideologien von »Heimatstil« und »Blut und Boden« sollen nicht wieder aufgewärmt werden. Der Höhenunterschied soll vielmehr als anregendes Element für die Gestalt des Gebäudes akzeptiert werden. »Das Land ist die einfachste Form der Architektur«, hat schon Frank Lloyd Wright dazu gesagt. »Ortsgebundenheit« heißt, den Bau so zu gestalten, daß er dem Ort zugehörig wird, daß er aus der Beliebigkeit eines Platzes einen identifizierten Ort machen hilft.

Identifikation ist ein seelischer Vorgang, der durch die sinnliche Wahrnehmung gespeist wird. Architekten können diese durch die Wiederholung vieler gleichmäßiger Elemente zur Abstumpfung bringen, durch die übertriebene Häufung immer wieder neuer Effekte quälend reizen, durch andere Konstellationen dagegen ein sattes Behagen erzeugen.

Damit steht die Frage nach der Schönheit im Raum. »Was Schönheit ist, das weiß ich nicht«, soll Albrecht Dürer gesagt haben. Ist es die Ordnung der Einzelelemente wie der Fenster, der übergeordneten Elemente oder der Baumassen? Zweifellos erwarten wir immer noch – sogar bei einer Extremarchitektur wie der von Zaha Hadid – einen Verwandtschaftsgrad von Innen- und Außengestaltung oder doch außen einen Hinweis auf das, was einen innen erwartet. Aber auch das kann in unserer pluralismusgewohnten Zeit schnell überholt sein. Das andererseits heute noch angestrebte alte Ziel gleicher Ordnung von Grundriß und Fassade wird die Älteren unter uns womöglich beruhigen, die Jüngeren womöglich langweilen. Ordnung ist jedenfalls nicht a priori Gleichordnung. Zu sehr lassen uns endlos aufgereihte Kirchenbänke mit Marschkolonnen assoziieren und endlos dahingemeterte Reihenhäuser an Güterzüge denken und Wohnungen mit langen Fluren an Fließbändern. Die serielle Gleichordnung basierte hier auf einer stark vereinfachenden gedanklichen Gleichschaltung inkommensurabler Dinge.

Ordnung in unserer Zeit bedeutet – Im Sinne einer heutigen Stadtgestaltung – Ordnung der Ungleichheiten. Wenn die Einwohner von Tokyo damit rechnen müssen, daß ihre Stadt wegen der zehnjährigen Pachtverträge der innerstädtischen Grundstücke alle zehn Jahre ihr Erscheinungsbild – auch hinsichtlich Abriß und Neubau von Hochhäusern – ändert, könnte gleichwohl »Ordnung der Ungleichheiten« gültig bleiben. Das Moment der Erinnerung an frühere Zeiten, das wir Europäer pflegen, könnte allerdings nicht mehr gehegt werden.

Der Begriff Schönheit wird bei diesen Maßnahmen unter Umständen zweitrangig. Der schnelle Wechsel der Stile im Pluralismus verwirrt das immanente menschliche Verlangen nach Schönheit und schärft die Sucht nach Sensationen. Dabei kapriziert sich das erstere immer mehr auf »historisch« als auf »schön« festgelegte Bauten. Das mag der Grund sein, weshalb sich die »Postmoderne« einige Jahre halten konnte.

Schönheit ist dann vorhanden, wenn wir ein Gebäude vorurteilsfrei ansehen und unser ästhetisches Ich es akzeptiert – sei es nach einer langen Auseinandersetzung, sei es auf den ersten Blick.

Soweit der gekürzte Inhalt der Antrittsvorlesung des Verfassers an der Technischen Universität Wien im Jahr 1964. Neue Entwicklungen im Städtebau machen eine Ergänzung notwendig.

Der massive Einzug des Hochhausbaus wurde bisher mit geringer städtebaulicher Konsequenz verfolgt. Dies gilt sowohl für die städtbauliche Einordnung als auch für die Gestaltung im Detail. Könnte es sein, daß es auch europäische Zukunft ist, alte Stadtstrukturen abzubrechen und Hochhäuser an ihre Stelle zu setzen? Die Stadtplaner Pekings haben dies bereits jetzt veranlaßt.

Hochhäuser – das wird an zahlreichen Beispielen deutlich – scheinen den mit Gestaltung befaßten Genehmigungsbehörden eine geringere Sorge zu bereiten als Einfamilienhäuser. So dominieren verwechselbare Rechteckgrundrisse mit Flachdach und machen den Eindruck, als ob der Investor sie selbst entworfen hätte. Im Ruhrgebiet sieht man denselben glasummantelten, zylinderförmigen Hochhaustyp in zwei verschiedenen Städten. Statt Identifikation mit dem Ort entsteht hier Verwechselbarkeit.

Nimmt man das Vorbild New York zu diesem Thema, so denkt man in erster Linie an das Chrysler Building, das modernere Seagram Building oder an den postmodernen AT + T Tower, Gebäude, die zur Identifikation der Stadt beitragen. Die zerstörten Twin Towers dagegen hatten nur durch ihre besondere Höhe, nicht durch Gestaltung zur Identifikation beigetragen.

Hochhäuser als dreidimensional gestaltete Gruppen könnten sogar Signalwirkung in der Landschaft übernehmen, wie sie früher den gotischen Domtürmen zukam. Gruppenbildung müßte mit dem Individualstreben der Architekten zur Deckung gebracht werden, um zu einer lebendigen Ansicht von mehreren Seiten zu gelangen und damit einen Beitrag zur Identifikation der Stadt leisten zu können.

Struktur und Form

Es ist wohl nicht immer so einfach, daß ein junger Mann anläßlich seines Abiturs den Entschluß faßt, Architektur zu studieren, und dieses Vorhaben tatkräftig umsetzt. Ich jedenfalls dachte gleichzeitig an die Alternativen, Musiker oder Maler zu werden. Vielleicht war es die Wut über die feindlichen Bomben, die schon einen Teil meiner Heimatstadt Münster flachgelegt hatten, daß ich schließlich die Architektur wählte, um eines Tages, wenn dieser Spuk einer kriegslüsternen Regierung vorbei wäre, beim Wiederaufbau zu helfen.

Meine ersten Eindrücke von Architektur hatte ich in Münster empfangen. Da waren die schweren romanisch-gotischen Kirchen aus hellgelbem Sandstein, die markante Festpunkte in der Stadt bildeten. Da war die geschwungene Fassade eines Adelspalais des Barockbaumeisters Johann Conrad Schlaun, das auf der Hälfte meines acht Jahre lang gewanderten Schulwegs lag. Und es war der Prinzipalmarkt, den ich ebensooft überqueren mußte – ein langgezogener, mit Giebelhäusern umstandener, leicht abgeknickter Platz in der Mitte der Stadt. Seinen besonderen Reiz erhielt dieser Ort durch die Arkaden, die sich unter den Giebeln um den ganzen Platz herumzogen; hier konnte man sich – auch an den vielen Regentagen in dieser Gegend – treffen und in den unter den Bögen liegenden Läden einkaufen.

Ein kluger Fürstbischof muß den Bürgern, die sich hier ein Haus bauen wollten, Freiheit in der Gestaltung ihrer annähernd gleich breiten Giebelhäuser gelassen, ihnen aber zugleich auferlegt haben, ein bis zwei Arkadenbreiten zum öffentlichen Gebrauch zur Verfügung zu stellen. Er ließ ihnen also die Präsentation ihres individuellen Ausdrucks einerseits und forderte andererseits ihren Beitrag zur Ergänzung des Platzraumes als Tribut an die Öffentlichkeit.

Als Knabe nahm ich zuerst nur die Form und die Funktion wahr. Erst viel später fand ich bei Fernand de Saussure, dem Vorläufer des französischen Strukturalismus, einen Vergleich, der der Linguistik entnommen ist. Er erklärt das französische Wort »langue« als »Sprache« – im Sinne eines kollektiven (Verständigungs-) Systems – und das Wort »parole« als Sprache, wie der einzelne Mensch sie spricht.

Übertragen auf die Prinzipalmarkthäuser bedeutet dies: Gemeinsam ist ihnen die »langue« des Haustyps der Arkadenhäuser, und »parole« sprechen die individuell ausgestalteten Giebel. Beidseitig angewendet ergibt das im Zusammenhang mit dem leicht abgeknickten Platzraum, der von ihnen gebildet wird, die Struktur der Anlage.

Das geht konform mit Immanuel Kants Äußerung über den Begriff der Struktur als der »Zuordnung der einzelnen Elemente auf die gemeinsame Mitte«. Die Mitte ist hier der Platzraum, gebildet durch die diesen Raum umgebenden Haus-Elemente.

Claude Lévi-Strauss, der Hauptvertreter des Strukturalismus, bekennt sich dazu, daß »jeder Mensch ein bestimmter Jemand sein können muß«. Als Architekt füge ich hinzu, daß der Ort, an dem dieser bestimmte Jemand leben will, nicht beliebig typisiert sein kann, sondern daß jeder Ort – über die Hausnummer hinaus – seine eigene Form oder Farbdefinition erfordert, um dem Menschen zu seiner Bestimmtheit zu verhelfen.

Was für den Platz wichtig ist, gilt auch für die Behausung des Menschen. In der Architektur kann Struktur nur räumlich anwendbar sein. Ein Haus oder ein Wohnung sollte ein lebensanregendes Zentrum haben – der Wohnraum in der Mitte, die Einzelzimmer auf ihn bezogen. Ein Raum fördert dann Leben, wenn er Platz bietet zur Stimulation von Gemeinschaft. Er muß Verbindung mit den Einzelräumen innen und der Öffentlichkeit außen herstellen. Er muß hell sein, weil sich ohne Licht kein Leben entwickelt. Er muß gemeinschaftliche Aktivitäten ermöglichen und darf nicht mit Möbeln zugestellt werden. Er hat also im kleinen Maßstab die gleiche Funktion wie der Prinzipalmarkt im großen.

Buddha sagt, daß die Mitte leer sein muß – nur dann könnte sie dem Leben Raum geben. Daraus folgt, daß der mit Volumina angefüllte Platz nur sich selbst bzw. den Ausstellungsobjekten genügen kann, jedoch die Aktionen der Menschen behindert. Autokraten beanspruchen die Plätze gemeinhin für Denkmäler – das Volk braucht aber für Feste, Märkte und Proteste den leeren Raum.

Die leere Mitte ist der magische Ort. Hier begegnen sich Menschen. Er impliziert Leben.

Meine erste These lautet daher: Die grundlegenden Strukturen müssen bleibenden Charakter haben. Sie bedeuten Dauer, Idenitifikation, Image und Heimat. Sie transportieren Leben. Sie sind die Seele des Bauwerks und der Stadt, sie sind subjektiv erfaßbar.

Formen dagegen sind konjunkturell, sie implizieren Schönheit und / oder Häßlichkeit, sie transportieren Emotionen. Sie gehören zu der endlichen Welt, in die Welt des Konsums und der Objekte, sie halten meistens nicht ewig und wollen – gerade in unserer Zeit – immer wieder erneuert oder verändert werden.

Genau dies erlebte der Prinzipalmarkt: Alle seine Giebelhäuser – bis auf ein einziges – wurden im Zweiten Weltkrieg durch Bomben zerstört. Den Wiederaufbau hätte man in Glas und Stahl – als »Sprache unserer Zeit« – schnell vollbringen können. Doch man gab den alten Hausbreiten und den Arkaden den Vorzug und krönte die Straßenansichten der einzelnen Häuser mit individuell gestalteten Giebeln.

Ich habe nichts über Schönheit ausgesagt. Und hoffe doch immer wieder, daß sie die Kraft zum Bleiben hat. Sie wird sie wohl haben, wenn wir in der Lage sind, sie naiv zu empfinden. Wird sie dagegen zum wissenschaftlichen Gegenstand von Ästhetikern und hat sie Übersetzung vom Gefühl in den Verstand nötig, tun wir einen Schritt aus dem Paradies der Subjektivität hinüber in die Welt der Objekte.

Ein Architekt lebt auf der Grenze zwischen beiden. Als Mitarbeiter der Schöpfung tut er gut daran, ihre Gesetze zu achten. Wenn er ein Leben lang versucht, die Voraussetzungen der wachstumsmäßigen, formerzeugenden Struktur zu ergründen und anzuwenden, kann er darauf hoffen, dauernde Beiträge zu schaffen. Dabei bleibt ihm bewußt, wie relativ auch dieses menschliche Tun ist. Und wie – zur Trauer oder zur Freude – das Immer-wieder-Kommende und -Vergehende der Formen und Gestalten dazugehört.

Zeit, Ort, Mensch und Technik im katholischen Kirchenbau

Angesichts der zunehmenden Kirchenaustritte in den beiden großen Konfessionen und dem daraus resultierenden geringeren Bauvolumen neuer Kirchen könnte man das Thema streichen. Dennoch sollen hier Erkenntnisse des Verfassers notiert werden, die ihm bei Bau und Umbau von sieben katholischen Kirchen am Ende des letzten Jahrhunderts gekommen sind.

Ort

In der schönen Stadt Wien wurde kürzlich eine Kirche neben einer Tankstelle gebaut, also auf einem von der Planungsbehörde für »Betriebe« vorgesehenen Grundstück. Das kontrastiert mit der Anregung eines führenden Architekten der sechziger Jahre. Er forderte, Kirchen müßten so plaziert sein, daß die Gläubigen sie in Pantoffeln erreichen könnten. Vielleicht kommen wir – durch die heute in manchen Städten geübte Unterbringung von Wohnungen in Hochhäusern – einmal dazu, in deren Erdgeschoß einen Kirchenraum zu integrieren oder – näher am Himmel – eine Kirche als Bekrönung auf dem im allgemeinen flach gestalteten Dach eines solchen zu bauen. Und das nicht wegen des – eher in Krankenhauskapellen stilgerechten – Gebrauchs von Pantoffeln, sondern wegen der Absurdität des Maßstabs, wenn eine Kirche – wie etwa die neugotische St. Patricks Cathedral in New York – zwischen die Hochhäuser gesetzt wird.

Glockentürme, die früher den Ort der Kirche in der Landschaft weithin sichtbar machten – wie heute noch der Turm des Ulmer Münsters – , werden heute kaum noch gebaut. Zum Ort der Kirche gehört heute vor allem ein öffentlich zugänglicher Platz – nicht nur als Treffpunkt nach dem Gottesdienst, sondern groß genug, um der Gemeinde einen Ort für ein sommerliches Gemeindefest zu bieten.

Der Mensch und seine Zeit

Wozu braucht der heutige Mensch eine Kirche? Er ist überwiegend rational eingestellt und allseits gut informiert, er beherrscht seine Apparate und sein Fahrzeug. Vielleicht drängen sich ihm aus irgendeinem Anlaß einmal Zweifel auf, ob sein Verstand die Lösung eines bestimmten Problems bringen kann, und er macht – wenn schon ohne seinen Willen getauft – einen alternativen Versuch durch einen Gang zur Kirche.

Was muß nun der Kirchenraum an sich haben, daß er seine Seele entdecken und mit einer Meditation öffnen kann? Wenn bisher die Theologen Kirchenbau grundsätzlich von ihrem Standpunkt aus betrachteten, soll dieser hier einmal durch den Betrachtungswinkel eines Laien gesehen werden.

Der Kirchenraum muß ihm zunächst den Ort für ein stilles Gebet bieten. Wenn er dann einmal seinen Platz inmitten der Kirchengemeinde wählt, sollte er den Gottesdienst möglichst gut und direkt verfolgen können. Wenn der Kirchenraum aussieht wie ein Fabrikraum und die Bänke wie »Marschkolonnen zum Altar« (wie der große Kir-

chenarchitekt Rudolf Schwarz die Art der traditionellen Aufstellung kennzeichnete) angeordnet sind, wird der Besucher eher an einen Vortragssaal denken oder sogar das Großraumbüro assoziieren, in dem er einmal gearbeitet hatte. Dies wird besonders dann der Fall sein, wenn er in der letzten Reihe der »Marschkolonne« – also dem Ort mit dem größten Abfall der Raumqualität – zu sitzen kommt. Fazit: Alle Assoziationen an den Alltag müssen verschwinden. In der Mitte der Bänke steht der Altar, einige Stufen höher als diese, nicht wegen einer denkmalhaften Gewichtung, sondern wegen der besseren Sicht- und Hörbarkeit der Aktionen und der Worte des Priesters. Wie schön wäre der Nebeneffekt, wenn man auf die an den Wänden herumhängenden Lautsprecher und die verborgenen Mikrophone verzichten könnte und von der eigenen Stimme des Priester angesprochen würde.

Noch einmal: In der Kirche sollte nichts sein, was an Alltag, Wohnung, Beruf und Freizeit erinnert. Kirche ist ein Raum eigener Prägung. Das muß der Architekt auch den mitbeschäftigten Künstlern klarmachen. Sie sollen in die Entwurfsidee eingebunden werden, damit sie – statt der häufig angestrebten Selbstverwirklichung – eindeutig der Aufgabe dienen, d. h. nichts anderes tun, als die religiöse Sendung und Atmosphäre des Kirchengebäudes zu steigern.

Die schnell zu verarbeitende Stahl-Glas-Bauweise, mit der die meisten Hochhäuser und Geschäftsbauten errichtet werden, sollte – um sich von ihnen abzusetzen – eher vermieden werden; statt dessen sollten organische Materialien wie Backstein, aber auch formbarer Beton zum Einsatz kommen. In ärmeren Zeiten muß es auch verputzte Kirchen geben können. Im Gegensatz zur Gotik streben wir heute eine gleichmäßig helle Beleuchtung des Kirchenraums an. Der Altar als zentraler Ort – mit höchstens drei Stufen – kann durch gesteigerte Lichtqualität hervorgehoben werden.

Ein Stil heutiger christlicher Kirchen zeichnet sich bis jetzt noch nicht ab. Wenigstens eine erkennbare Verwandtschaft wäre um so mehr gefragt, da die nun allerorts entstehenden Moscheen durch ihren – retrospektiven – Stil und signalgebend durch die dazugehörigen Minarette kenntlich werden.

Mit der Kirche St. Stephan in Karlsruhe – in den Jahren 1807–16 von Friedrich Weinbrenner erbaut – soll hier ein Beispiel heutiger Nutzung eines historischen Gebäudes folgen. Der pantheonartige Rundraum wird von quadratbildenden Eckmauern und kreuzformenden Vorbauten gehalten. Dem entspricht die heutige Erschließung mit zwei sich kreuzenden Gängen und entsprechender Möblierung, die nur teilweise auf den Altar ausgerichtet ist. An ihrer Stelle wird ein zentralisierter Innenraum mit dem Altar in der Mitte unter dem Oberlicht der Kuppel vorgeschlagen, umgeben von vier Gruppen kreisförmig aufgestellter Bänke. An der Stelle des jetzigen Altars im nördlichen Vorbau steht der Ambo, davor im breitesten Gang der Taufstein.

So wurde versucht – unter Berücksichtigung des klassizistischen Raumes – mit marginalen Änderungen einer dem heutigen Menschen angemessene Teilhabe am Gottesdienst Gestalt zu geben.

Was bleibt und was kommt

Zunächst eine These: Das Essentielle des Bleibenden ist beurteilbar durch seinen Symbolwert. In den besten Zeiten der Stile wurde die höchste Verdichtung der Gestaltung zum Symbol. Mozarts Musik ist ein Symbol für Musik schlechthin, so wie die Kathedrale von Chartres ein Symbol für Kirchen schlechthin ist. Wie stark muß eine Epoche sein, die solche Symbole hervorbringen konnte, und wie anders gelagert die Zeiten, in denen (nach Ungers) viele »synthetische« Symbole entstehen – beispielsweise der Beginn des Gebrauchs von Verkehrsampeln als Zeichen einer zunehmenden menschlichen Unterwerfung unter die Vorfahrt der Maschine. Mit dem Computer entsteht heute ein ähnlicher Effekt.

Hier die immateriellen Werte, von denen wir uns Dauer versprechen:

Zu dem, was bei einem Gebäude bleiben sollte, gehören die Basiskomponenten. Ein Gebäude sollte immer schon und muß immer wieder abschirmen und abgrenzen. Die Abgrenzungen müssen Öffnungen zur Gesellschaft und zum Freien zulassen. Seit langer Zeit finden wir, daß Raum und Volumen dementsprechend in Beziehung zu setzen sind.

Eine weitere Komponente ist die Angemessenheit, das rechte Maß, der Nutzen und die Bequemlichkeit. Wir unterscheiden diese Begriffe, die Palladio unter dem einen Wort »comodità« zusammenfaßte – als wichtigstes Kriterium für ein Haus, bei dem sich aus dem rechten Maß die größte Nutzbarkeit ergibt.

Auch die Gestalt ist immer noch ein echter Bedarf. Sie ist das Mittel zur (Re-) Präsentation des Gebäudes. In Zeiten der Moderne war die Gestalt ein sich mehr oder weniger selbst regulierendes Ergebnis der Summe der Funktionen – vielleicht ein Irrweg, wenn man an die vielen verwechselbaren Gebäudekisten aus dem Spätfunktionalismus denkt, mit denen unsere Städte angefüllt sind.

Unsere Nostalgie bedeutet uns viel – und so unterwerfen wir die Altsubstanz unserem Nützlichkeitstick. Wir können Verfall nicht mitansehen. Wir haben den Geschmack an Ruinen verloren – verständlich für die Kriegsgeneration. Schon gewohnt, in Fertigteilen zu denken, grämt uns das Unfertige. Also bauen wir viele Museen und Bibliotheken ...

Zum Bleibenden gehört heute – das ist wohl vor allem anderen gewiß – die Wissenschaft. Der Fundus der naturwissenschaftlichen Gesetze wird wohl unangefochten bleiben. Aber bei der Verwissenschaftlichung von Immateriellem wie der Kunst finden wir den Dauerwert nicht so leicht. Sie hat unsere subjektive Erkenntnisfähigkeit oft kleingemacht oder getäuscht. Die Unangreifbarkeit der Wissenschaft, die mit Messungen und Analysen operiert, ist für den Laien nicht nachvollziehbar und erregt nur unterwürfige Anerkennung. Aber sie trägt zur Hebung des allgemeinen Bewußtseinsniveaus bei und prägt den Fortschritt.

Es ist bekannt, daß die Hebung des Bewußtseins mit dem Verlust sozialer Fähigkeiten verbunden ist. (Die zunehmende Zahl der Singles mag das beweisen.) Als Ausgleich hatte schon Ende des 19. Jahrhunderts der Kunstgeschichtler und Sozialreformer John Ruskin vor dem Gebrauch der heraufdämmernden Technik gewarnt und das Handwerk als Quelle irdischen Segens gepriesen. Denn die Versuchungen der platzgreifenden Technik waren schon damals sehr groß. Man hatte bald herausgefunden, daß Reisen mit der Eisenbahn bequemer war als mit dem Pferdefuhrwerk, wenn man auch wegen des Fahrtempos auf tiefergehende Sinneseindrücke verzichten mußte. John Ruskin fuhr niemals in seinem Leben mit der Bahn. Sein Beispiel nützte nichts.

Das Emotionale wie das Spirituelle mußten während der Industrialisierung zurücktreten – man behalf sich mit einem stilistischen Rückgriff auf die in dieser Hinsicht bewährte Gotik. Auch Klassizisten wie Karl Friedrich Schinkel bauten neogotische Kirchen. Eine ähnliche Reaktion zeigte die Stilsuche 100 Jahre später in der historisiernden Postmoderne – eine Reaktion auf die »kühle« Moderne und auf die florierende Hight-Tech-Architektur. Man bediente sich der Motive des Klassizismus, aber auch der bisher wenig geachteten Gründerzeitarchitektur und begann damit auch ganz allgemein, die in der Mitte des Jahrhunderts geübte Mißachtung der Architektur der Stile aufzugeben. Die Postmoderne war nach 15 Jahren am Ende, und die folgende Dekonstruktion war nur eine Spielart von High-Tech.

Mechanisation Takes Command hatte in den 20er Jahren des 20. Jahrhunderts der Architekturphilosoph Sigfried Giedion sein Buch tituliert. Sieht man kleine, noch nicht schulpflichtige Jungen in den Spielzeugläden völlig absorbiert vor ihren Computerspielen stehen, ist heute diese damalige Prognose aktueller denn je. Nicht nur daraus ist zu schließen, daß das, was kommt, High-Tech ist. Technik ist nicht allein zu einer Frage der Bequemlichkeit geworden, sondern auch der Abhängigkeit. Wenn wir auf sie verzichten müßten, würde das Entzugserscheinungen mit sich bringen, die den emotionalen in nichts nachstehen.

Wenn die Architektur in jeder Epoche dem Zeitgeist entspricht, wird das wohl auch in der unsrigen geschehen. Unsere Zeit hat ein rationales Übergewicht – nichts entspricht dem so sehr wie die Architektur des Verstandes, der sich primär in High-Tech äußert. Sie geht auch konform mit der Einstellung der Investoren, die große Teile unserer Stadtgestalt bestimmen. Es geht ihnen nicht so sehr um ein schönes Stadtbild, sondern vielmehr um die wirtschaftliche Ausnutzung, d. h. Belegungsdichte ihrer Bauten.

Die Minderheit der gefühlsmäßig orientierten Architekten, die weder durch ihre Erziehung noch durch ihr Studium bei rationalen Meistern von ihren gefühlsmäßigen Intentionsanteilen abzubringen waren, können nur auf einen Bauherrn gleicher Gesinnung hoffen. Nur dadurch kann geschehen, was die Stadt, in der sie bauen, vor der Einförmigkeit verabsolutierter Stahl-, Glas- oder Betonraster-Bauweise rettet, nämlich der stilistische Kontrast der »Gefühlsarchitektur«. Ob auch unser Jahrhundert darüber hinaus wieder einen stilistischen Rückgriff tun wird – wer weiß?

Die Geschichte lehrt, daß sich ein genuiner Stil nur bei einer fruchtbaren Auseinandersetzung von Verstand **und** Gefühl ergibt. Goethe hat einmal zu diesem Thema gesagt: »Stil ist die Vereinigung wahrhafter Objektivität mit tiefster Subjektivität.«

List of works
edited by Gerhard Kabierske

This chronological list includes all projects, implementations, and submissions to competitions by Reinhard Gieselmann and his studio for which the place and date of origin can be documented. Not included are designs of individual items of furniture.

Source materials such as plans, sketches, photographs, files, and specimen copies of publications are in the Werkarchiv Reinhard Gieselmann of the Süddeutsches Archiv für Architektur und Ingenieurbau Karlsruhe (saai) and in possession of the architect.

Abbreviations:
Gieselmann 1976: *Reinhard Gieselmann. Bauten, Projekte, Schriften*, Vienna 1976 (*Prolegomena. Arbeitsblätter des Instituts für Wohnbau, Technische Universität Wien*, no. 16/17).
Gieselmann 1987: Reinhard Gieselmann, *Architektur ist ein Element für die Sinne. Bauten und Schriften*, Stuttgart 1987.
Gieselmann 1998: Reinhard Gieselmann, *Wohnbau, Entwicklungen. Wohnen, Wohnung, Wohnhaus, Wohnungsbau*, ed. by Anna Stern, Düsseldorf 1998.

Puppet theater
1948/49, student's project
(under Prof. Heinrich Müller, Technische Hochschule Karlsruhe)

Aquarium in the municipal park
1949/50, student's project
(under Prof. Heinrich Müller, Technische Hochschule Karlsruhe)

School in Eppingen
1950, project
Competition
(under Edward Sutt, Karlsruhe)

Schölle house, Karlsruhe-Weiherfeld
Donaustrasse 20
1950

Motel at the autobahn
1950, diploma project
(under Prof. Egon Eiermann, Technische Hochschule Karlsruhe)
Bibliography: Gieselmann 1987, p. 100.

Chamber of crafts in Osnabrück
1950, project
Competition, purchase
(with Ernst August Kroeber, Karlsruhe)

Michaelshof sanatorium, Heidelberg
Philosophenweg
1950, project
(Design work as a collaborator of Lange & Mitzlaff, Mannheim)

Reformist church in Basel
Gellert-Areal
1951, project
(Design work as a collaborator of Otto Senn, Basel)

Curving rows of houses and high-rises in Basel
Gellert-Areal
1951, project
(Design work as a collaborator of Otto Senn, Basel)

Apartment block in Basel
Nasenweg
1951/52
(Design work as a collaborator of Walter Senn, Basel)

Prof. Rein house, Heidelberg-Handschuhsheim
Mühltal
1952
(Design and working drawings as a collaborator of Lange & Mitzlaff, Mannheim)

Office building of the Mannheimer Versicherung, Mannheim
Augustaanlage
1952, project
(Design and working drawings as a collaborator of Lange & Mitzlaff, Mannheim)

Church with parish hall and kindergarten in Weinheim an der Bergstrasse
1952, project
Competition, purchase
(with Carlfried Mutschler, Werner Lang und Peter Haupt, Mannheim)

Roth house and studio, Ludwigshafen-Gartenstadt
Ligustergang 9
1952/53
(with Edward Sutt, Ludwigshafen)
Bibliography: *Baukunst und Werkform*, 7, 1954, no. 7/8, pp. 409–414; *Interieur*, 1957, no. 3, pp. 25–28; *ac Internationale Asbestzement-Revue*, 1959, no. 15, pp. 42–44; Rainer Wolff, *Häuser mit Berufsräumen*, Munich 1960 pp. 76/77; Fritz R. Barran, *Der offene Kamin. Zweite Folge*, Stuttgart 1962, p. 122; *Detail*, 1963, no. 4, p. 472; *Bau*, 1969, no. 6, p. 125; *Kamine und Kachelöfen*, Munich 1967 (*Detail-Bücherei Elemente der Architektur, Beispiele*, 9), p. 49; Gieselmann 1976, pp. 6, 8; Gieselmann 1987, p. 100.
pp. 32–35

»Stöckli« near Suhr, Switzerland
1953, project
(Separate home for the farmer's parents, with Werner Aebli, Basel)

Conversion of a hotel in Braunwald, Switzerland
1953, project
(with Werner Aebli, Basel)

»Ein Beitrag zur Abklärung des Habitat«
1953
(with Werner Aebli, Theo Manz and Beppo Merkle, Basel)
Bibliography: *Werk*, 41, 1954, no. 1, pp. 8–14.

Multi-family house in Münster, Westphalia
1953, project

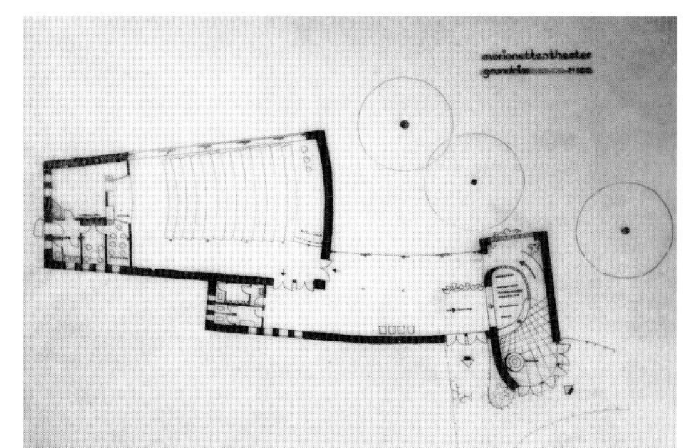

1. Puppet theater.
2. Motel at the autobahn.
3. Michaelshof sanatorium, Heidelberg.
4. Prof. Rein house, Heidelberg-Handschuhsheim.
5. Church with parish center and kindergarten in
Weinheim an der Bergstrasse.

1. Marionettentheater.
2. Motel an der Autobahn.
3. Sanatorium Michaelshof, Heidelberg.
4. Wohnhaus Prof. Rein, Heidelberg-Handschuhsheim.
5. Kirche mit Gemeindehaus und Kindergarten in
Weinheim an der Bergstraße.

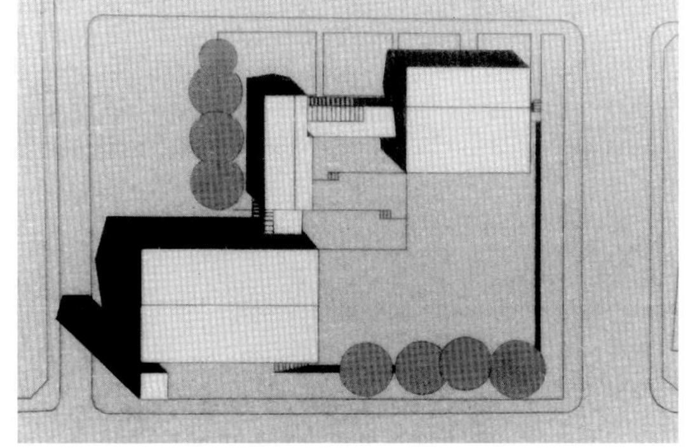

Werkverzeichnis
bearbeitet von Gerhard Kabierske

Das Werkverzeichnis umfaßt in chronologischer
Folge alle mit Ort und Entstehungsdatum nachweis-
baren Projekte, Realisierungen und Wettbewerbs-
beteiligungen von Reinhard Gieselmann und seinem
Büro. Nicht aufgenommen sind Entwürfe für Einzel-
möbel.

Quellenmaterialien, wie Pläne, Zeichnungen,
Phhotographien, Akten und Belegexemplare von
Publikationen, befinden sich im Werkarchiv Reinhard
Gieselmann des Südwestdeutschen Archivs für
Architektur und Ingenieurbau Karlsruhe (saai) sowie
im Besitz des Architekten.

Abkürzungen:
Gieselmann 1976: *Reinhard Gieselmann. Bauten,
Projekte, Schriften*, Wien 1976 (*Prolegomena.
Arbeitsblätter des Instituts für Wohnbau, Techni-
sche Universität Wien*, Nr. 16/17).
Gieselmann 1987: Reinhard Gieselmann, *Architek-
tur ist ein Element für die Sinne. Bauten und
Schriften*, Stuttgart 1987.
Gieselmann 1998: Reinhard Gieselmann, *Wohnbau,
Entwicklungen. Wohnen, Wohnung, Wohnhaus,
Wohnungsbau*, hrsg. von Anna Stern, Düsseldorf
1998.

Marionettentheater
1948/49, Studienentwurf
(bei Prof. Heinrich Müller, Technische Hochschule
Karlsruhe)

Aquarium im Stadtgarten
1949/50, Studienentwurf
(bei Prof. Heinrich Müller, Technische Hochschule
Karlsruhe)

Schule in Eppingen
1950, Projekt
Wettbewerb
(mit Edward Sutt, Karlsruhe)

Wohnhaus Schölle, Karlsruhe-Weiherfeld
Donaustraße 20
1950

Motel an der Autobahn
1950, Diplomentwurf
(bei Prof. Egon Eiermann, Technische Hochschule
Karlsruhe)
Literatur: Gieselmann 1987, S. 100.

Handwerkskammer in Osnabrück
1950, Projekt
Wettbewerb, Ankauf
(mit Ernst August Kroeber, Karlsruhe)

Sanatorium Michaelshof, Heidelberg
Philosophenweg
1950, Projekt
(Entwurfsbearbeitung als Mitarbeiter von Lange &
Mitzlaff, Mannheim)

Reformierte Kirche in Basel
Gellert-Areal
1951, Projekt
(Entwurfsbearbeitung als Mitarbeiter von Otto Senn,
Basel)

Raupen- und Punkthäuser in Basel
Gellert-Areal
1951, Projekt
(Entwurfsbearbeitung als Mitarbeiter von Otto Senn,
Basel)

Wohnblock in Basel
Nasenweg
1951/52
(32 Arbeiterwohnungen, Entwurfsbearbeitung als
Mitarbeiter von Walter Senn, Basel)

**Wohnhaus Prof. Rein, Heidelberg-Handschuhs-
heim**
Mühltal
1952
(Entwurf und Werkplanung als Mitarbeiter von
Lange & Mitzlaff, Mannheim)

**Bürogebäude der Mannheimer Versicherung,
Mannheim**
Augustaanlage
1952, Projekt
(Entwurf und Werkplanung als Mitarbeiter von
Lange & Mitzlaff, Mannheim)

**Kirche mit Gemeindehaus und Kindergarten in
Weinheim an der Bergstraße**
1952, Projekt
Wettbewerb, Ankauf
(mit Carlfried Mutschler, Werner Lang und Peter
Haupt, Mannheim)

**Wohn- und Atelierhaus Roth, Ludwigshafen-
Gartenstadt**
Ligustergang 9
1952/53
(mit Edward Sutt, Ludwigshafen)
Literatur: *Baukunst und Werkform*, 7, 1954, Nr. 7/8,
S. 409–414; *Interieur*, 1957, Nr. 3, S. 25–28; *ac
Internationale Asbestzement-Revue*, 1959, Nr. 15,
S. 42–44; Rainer Wolff, *Häuser mit Berufsräumen*,
München 1960, S. 76/77; Fritz R. Barran, *Der offene
Kamin. Zweite Folge*, Stuttgart 1962, S. 122; *Detail*,
1963, Nr. 4, S. 472; *Bau*, 1969, Nr. 6, S. 125; *Kami-
ne und Kachelöfen*, München 1967 (*Detail-Bücherei
Elemente der Architektur, Beispiele*, 9), S. 49; Gie-
selmann 1976, S. 6, 8; Gieselmann 1987, S. 100.
S. 32–35

»Stöckli« bei Suhr, Schweiz
1953, Projekt
(Altenteil auf einem Bauernhof, mit Werner Aebli,
Basel)

Umbau eines Hotels in Braunwald, Schweiz
1953, Projekt
(mit Werner Aebli, Basel)

»Ein Beitrag zur Abklärung des Habitat«
1953
(mit Werner Aebli, Theo Manz und Beppo Merkle,
Basel)
Literatur: *Werk*, 41, 1954, Nr. 1, S. 8–14.

Mehrfamilienhaus in Münster, Westfalen
1953, Projekt

Gym of the Marienschule, Krefeld
1953/54
(Design, working drawings and site management
as a collaborator of Franz Schlüter-Padberg, Krefeld)
Bibliography: Gieselmann 1987, p. 101.

Dr. Schlüter-Padberg house, Krefeld
Am Immenhof
1953/54
(Design, working drawings and site management as
a collaborator of Franz Schlüter-Padberg, Krefeld)

Kindergarten in Krefeld
1954
(Design, working drawings and site management
as a collaborator of Franz Schlüter-Padberg, Krefeld)

Secondary school in Krefeld
1954, project
Competition, purchase
Bibliography: *Baukunst und Werkform*, 8, 1955,
no. 3, pp. 162/163; *Architektur-Wettbewerbe*, 1963,
vol. 36, pp. 66/67; Gieselmann 1976, p. 6; Gieselmann 1987, p. 100.

Church with shell roof in Krefeld
1954, project
(Design as a collaborator of Franz Schlüter-Padberg, Krefeld)

Apartment block in Krefeld
1954, project
(Design as a collaborator of Franz Schlüter-Padberg, Krefeld)

Office building in Krefeld
1954, project
(Design as a collaborator of Franz Schlüter-Padberg, Krefeld)

Industrial hall in Krefeld
1954, project
(Design as a collaborator of Franz Schlüter-Padberg, Krefeld)

Paulinum grammar school, Münster, Westphalia
1954, project
Competition

Parish centre in Gelsenkirchen-Buer-Hasselt
1954, project
Bibliography: *Streven*, 1955, no. 11/12, pp. 435/
436.

Interior design of the chamber of industry and
commerce in Münster, Westphalia
1954
Bibliography: Gieselmann 1987, p. 101.

BASF polystyrole plant, Ludwigshafen
1954/55

Burger house, Ludwigshafen-Friesenheim
Völklinger Strasse 10
1954–56
(with Willi Zabel, Ludwigshafen)
Bibliography: *Baukunst und Werkform*, 10, 1957,
no. 9, p. 521; Gieselmann 1987, p. 101.

Dr. David two-family house, Markgröningen
Finkenweg 2
1954–56
Bibliography: *ac Internationale Asbestzement-
Revue*, 1959, no. 16, ill. 63/64; *Bauwelt*, 51, 1960,
no. 18, pp. 508/509; *Baumeister*, 60, 1963, no. 6,
pp. 619–621; Gieselmann 1976, p. 6; Gieselmann
1987, p. 102.

Frey residential and commercial building, Ludwigshafen-Mundenheim
Mundenheimer Strasse 18–20
1954–57
Bibliography: *Interieur*, 1958, no. 3, pp. 1–4; *Die
Innenarchitektur*, 6, 1958, no. 5, pp. 300–302;
Bauwelt, 50, 1959, no. 31, pp. 920/921; *Interieur*,
1959, no. 2; *Baumeister*, 58, 1961, no. 3, pp. 204
to 211; *Detail*, 1962, no. 2, p. 151; *Detail*, 1963, no.
3, p. 298; *Bau*, 1969, no. 6, p. 128; Gerda Gollwit-
zer/Werner Wirsing, *Dachgärten und Dachterrassen*, Munich 1962, p. 59; Gieselmann 1976, p. 6;
Gieselmann 1987, pp. 8/9, 102.
pp. 80–85

Attic flat in Prof. Fischer multi-family house,
Karlsruhe
Stephanienstrasse 50–52
1955, extension 1960/61
(with Alfred Fischer and Maria Verena Gieselmann,
Karlsruhe)
Bibliography: *Schöner Wohnen*, 1962, no. 8, pp.
20–23.

Prof. Höffner house, Münster, Westphalia
Rottendorfweg 15
1955/56, extension of an attic floor 1962
Bibliography: *Baukunst und Werkform*, 10, 1957, no.
9, pp. 519/520; Fritz R. Barran, *Der offene Kamin*,
Stuttgart 1957, p. 108; Martin Mittag (ed.), *Kleinsthäuser, Ferienhäuser, Bungalows. 160 Beispiele
kleinerer Eigenheime*, Gütersloh 1959, pp. 230 to
232; *Das Haus*, 1960, no. 6, pp. 2–3; Gieselmann
1976, p. 6; Niels Gutschow/Gunnar Pick, *Bauen in
Münster. Ein Architekturführer*, Münster 1983, p. 84;
Gieselmann 1987, p. 101.

Hebelschule, Karlsruhe
1956, project
Competition, a 1st prize
(with Hubert Reichert, Karlsruhe)
Bibliography: Gieselmann 1976, p. 6.

Dr. Immel house, Ludwigshafen-Friesenheim
Sternstrasse 167
1956/57

Werkbund exhibition »Furniture, affordable and
beautiful«, Mannheim
Wohnberatungsstelle der Stadt Mannheim, N 1, 21
1956/57
Bibliography: Gieselmann 1987, p. 102.

Addition to the Stähler house, Lorch, Württemberg
Götzentalstrasse
1957

Kindergarten in Bammental
1957, project
Bibliography: *Bauwelt*, 51, 1960, no. 10, p. 266; Rolf
Janke, *Architekturmodelle*, Stuttgart 1962 (*Beispiel-*

Turnhalle der Marienschule, Krefeld
1953/54
(Entwurf, Werkplanung und Bauleitung als Mitarbeiter von Franz Schlüter-Padberg, Krefeld)
Literatur: Gieselmann 1987, S. 101.

Wohnhaus Dr. Schlüter-Padberg, Krefeld
Am Immenhof
1953/54
(Entwurf, Werkplanung und Bauleitung als Mitarbeiter von Franz Schlüter-Padberg, Krefeld)

Kindergarten in Krefeld
1954
(Entwurf, Werkplanung und Bauleitung als Mitarbeiter von Franz Schlüter-Padberg, Krefeld)

Realschule in Krefeld
1954, Projekt
Wettbewerb, Ankauf
Literatur: *Baukunst und Werkform*, 8, 1955, Nr. 3,
S. 162/163; *Architektur-Wettbewerbe*, 1963, Bd. 36,
S. 66/67; Gieselmann 1976, S. 6; Gieselmann
1987, S. 100.

Schalenkirche in Krefeld
1954, Projekt
(Entwurf als Mitarbeiter von Franz Schlüter-Padberg, Krefeld)

Wohnblock in Krefeld
1954, Projekt
(Entwurf als Mitarbeiter von Franz Schlüter-Padberg, Krefeld)

Bürogebäude in Krefeld
1954, Projekt
(Entwurf als Mitarbeiter von Franz Schlüter-Padberg, Krefeld)

Industriehalle in Krefeld
1954, Projekt
(Entwurf als Mitarbeiter von Franz Schlüter-Padberg, Krefeld)

Gymnasium Paulinum, Münster, Westfalen
1954, Projekt
Wettbewerb

Kirchenzentrum in Gelsenkirchen-Buer-Hasselt
1954, Projekt
Literatur: *Streven*, 1955, Nr. 11/12, S. 435/436.

Inneneinrichtung der Industrie- und Handelskammer in Münster, Westfalen
1954
Literatur: Gieselmann 1987, S. 101.

Polystyrolfabrik der BASF, Ludwigshafen
1954/55

Wohnhaus Burger, Ludwigshafen-Friesenheim
Völklinger Straße 10
1954–56
(mit Willi Zabel, Ludwigshafen)
Literatur: *Baukunst und Werkform*, 10, 1957, Nr. 9,
S. 521; Gieselmann 1987, S. 101.

Zweifamilienwohnhaus Dr. David, Markgröningen
Finkenweg 2
1954–56
Literatur: *ac Internationale Asbestzement-Revue*,
1959, Nr. 16, Abb. 63/64; *Bauwelt*, 51, 1960, Nr. 18,
S. 508/509; *Baumeister*, 60, 1963, Nr. 6, S. 619
bis 621; Gieselmann 1976, S. 6; Gieselmann 1987,
S. 102.

Wohn- und Geschäftshaus Frey, Ludwigshafen-Mundenheim
Mundenheimer Straße 18–20
1954–57
Literatur: *Interieur*, 1958, Nr. 3, S. 1–4; *Die Innenarchitektur*, 6, 1958, Nr. 5, S. 300–302; *Bauwelt*, 50,
1959, Nr. 31, S. 920/921; *Interieur*, 1959, Nr. 2; *Baumeister*, 58, 1961, Nr. 3, S. 204–211; *Detail*, 1962,
Nr. 2, S. 151; *Detail*, 1963, Nr. 3, S. 298; *Bau*, 1969,
Nr. 6, S. 128; Gerda Gollwitzer / Werner Wirsing,
Dachgärten und Dachterrassen, München 1962,
S. 59; Gieselmann 1976, S. 6; Gieselmann 1987,
S. 8/9, 102.

S. 80–85

Dachwohnung im Mehrfamilienhaus Prof.
Fischer, Karlsruhe
Stephanienstraße 50–52
1955, Erweiterung 1960/61
(mit Alfred Fischer und Maria Verena Gieselmann,
Karlsruhe)
Literatur: *Schöner Wohnen*, 1962, Nr. 8, S. 20–23.

Wohnhaus Prof. Höffner, Münster, Westfalen
Rottendorfweg 15
1955/56, Ausbau des Dachgeschosses 1962
Literatur: *Baukunst und Werkform*, 10, 1957, Nr. 9,
S. 519/520; Fritz R. Barran, *Der offene Kamin*, Stuttgart 1957, S. 108; Martin Mittag (Bearb.), *Kleinsthäuser, Ferienhäuser, Bungalows. 160 Beispiele kleinerer Eigenheime*, Gütersloh 1959, S. 230–232; *Das
Haus*, 1960, Nr. 6, S. 2–3; Gieselmann 1976, S. 6;
Niels Gutschow / Gunnar Pick, *Bauen in Münster.
Ein Architekturführer*, Münster 1983, S. 84; Gieselmann 1987, S. 101.

Hebelschule, Karlsruhe
1956, Projekt
Wettbewerb, ein 1. Preis
(mit Hubert Reichert, Karlsruhe)
Literatur: Gieselmann 1976, S. 6.

Wohnhaus Dr. Immel, Ludwigshafen-Friesenheim
Sternstraße 167
1956/57

Werkbund-Ausstellung »Möbel, billig und
schön«, Mannheim
Wohnberatungsstelle der Stadt Mannheim, N 1, 21
1956/57
Literatur: Gieselmann 1987, S. 102.

Wohnhausanbau Stähler, Lorch, Württemberg
Götzentalstraße
1957

Kindergarten in Bammental
1957, Projekt
Literatur: *Bauwelt*, 51, 1960, Nr. 10, S. 266; Rolf Janke, *Architekturmodelle*, Stuttgart 1962 (*Beispiel-

sammlung moderner Architektur, 1), p. 89; *Zodiac*, 1964, no. 12, p. 197.

Office addition to the garden house of the Prof. Fischer multi-family house, Karlsruhe
Stephanienstrasse 50
1957, conversion 1989

Extension of the Strickwarenfabrik Sieger, Lorch, Württemberg
Götzentalstrasse
1957/58, extensions 1961, 1966
Bibliography: Gieselmann 1976, p. 14; Gieselmann 1987, p. 103.

Prof. Becker house, Karlsruhe-Durlach
1957–59
Bibliography: *Bauwelt*, 51, 1960, no. 38, pp. 1106/1107; *Neue deutsche Architektur 2*, Stuttgart 1962, pp. 26/27; *Detail*, 1963, no. 3, p. 299; *Baumeister*, 61, 1964, no. 1, pp. 40–42; *Zodiac*, 1964, no. 12, p. 198; *Schöner Wohnen*, 5, 1964, no. 3, p. 87; Gieselmann 1976, p. 7; Gieselmann 1987, p. 103.
pp. 36/37

Wüstenrot housing development, Karlsruhe-Waldstadt
Allensteiner Strasse 6–26, Stettiner Strasse 5–21
1957–61
(20 residential buildings, with Alfred Fischer and Maria Verena Gieselmann, Karlsruhe)
Bibliography: *Ziegel Arbeitsblätter*, n. d., no. 3, pp. 19/20; *Ziegel Arbeitsblätter*, n. d. , no. 5, pp. 3–6; *Report, Bauen in unserer Zeit, ed Geschäftsstelle Öffentliche Bausparkassen Stuttgart* n. d., pp. 22/23; *Deutsche Bauzeitschrift*, 9, 1961, no. 2, pp. 157–160; *Mein Eigenheim*, 1960, no. 4, pp. 125 to 127; *Bauwelt*, 52, 1961, no. 22, pp. 630–633; *Byggnads Ingenjoeren, Tidskrift foer internationell byggnadsteknik och byggnadsekonomie*, 19, 1961, no. 4, p. 42; Paul Faerber / Walter Meyer-Bohe, *80 neue Eigenheime und Fertighäuser*, Ludwigsburg 1961 (*Wüstenroter Ratgeber*, 4), pp. 66/67; *Mein Eigenheim*, 1961, no. 4, pp. 120–125; Günther Kühne, *25 neue Kleinhäuser*, Frankfurt a. M. 1962 (Bauwelt-Sonderheft N.S., 50), pp. 9; *Terra*, ed. by Fachverein Ziegelindustrie Hessen, 1962, no. 15, pp. 5–19; *Deutsche Bauzeitung*, 69, 1964, no. 1, pp. 15/16; Karl Krämer, *Einfamilienhäuser in der Gruppe. Eine Beispielsammlung*, Stuttgart 1966, pp. 91–97; *Kamine und Kachelöfen*, Munich 1967 (*Detail-Bücherei Elemente der Architektur, Beispiele*, 9), pp. 60, 97; *Bau*, 1969, no. 6, p. 125; *Aujourd'hui, art et architecture*, 10, 1967, no. 57/58, p. 75; Gieselmann 1976, p. 7; Gieselmann 1987, pp. 11–13, 103; Gieselmann 1998, p. 54.
pp. 86–89

Second Wüstenrot housing development, Karlsruhe-Waldstadt
Elbinger Strasse
1958, project
Bibliography: *Bauwelt*, 49, 1958, no. 26, p. 776.

Higher administrative court in Münster, Westphalia
1958, project
Competition

Choir of the Jesuitenkirche, Coesfeld
1959, project
(with sculptor Walter Goehre, Düsseldorf)
Bibliography: *Bauwelt*, 50, 1959, no. 48, p. 1408.

Row of stores in Karlsruhe-Nordweststadt
Heinrich-Köhler-Platz
1958
(with Alfred Fischer and Maria Verena Gieselmann, Karlsruhe)

Dewald studio, Karlsruhe-Grötzingen
An der Silbergrub 5a
1958/59
Bibliography: *Deutsche Bauzeitung*, 67, 1962, no. 3, pp. 182–185; *Schöner Wohnen*, 1962, no. 9, pp. 66– 69; *Detail*, 1963, no. 4, p. 472; *Zodiac*, 1964, no. 12, p. 196; *Bau*, 1969, no. 6, p. 126; Gerhard Schwab (ed.), *db-Einfamilienhäuser 1–50*, Stuttgart 1962, pp. 217–222; *a+u Architecture and Urbanism*, 1983, no. 154, p. 78; Gieselmann 1976, p. 7, 16/17; Gieselmann 1987, pp. 95–98, 104.

Dr. Stähler office and residence, Münster, Westphalia
Engelstrasse 9
1958–60
Bibliography: *Glasforum*, 11, 1961, no. 4, p. 4; *md möbel interior design*, 10, 1962, no. 6, pp. 272/273; Gieselmann 1976, p. 7; Gieselmann 1987, p. 104.

Extension of the primary school in Bammental
1958–60
(with Alfred Fischer and Maria Verena Gieselmann, Karlsruhe)
Bibliography: *Baumeister*, 59, 1962, no. 2, pp. 108 to 110; *Architektur-Wettbewerbe*, 1963, vol. 36, pp. 24/25; Fritz R. Barran, *Kunst am Bau heute. Wandbild, Relief und Plastik in der Baukunst der Gegenwart*, Stuttgart 1964, p. 40; *Bauwelt*, 55, 1964, no. 46, p. 1280; Gieselmann 1976, p. 12; Gieselmann 1987, p. 104.

Primary school in Mosbach, Baden
1959, project
Competition
Bibliography: *Bauwelt*, 52, 1961, no. 44, p. 1259; Gieselmann 1976, p. 7.

Dr. Hanfmann / Herzer house, Karlsruhe-Durlach
Strählerweg 55
1959–61, addition of an exterior stairway 1962
Bibliography: Klara Trost, *Landhaus und Bungalow. Beispiele moderner Eigenhäuser im In- und Ausland*, Frankfurt a. M. 1961, pp. 152–155; *Bauwelt*, 52, 1961, no. 35, p. 984; *Deutsche Bauzeitung*, 67, 1962, no. 3, pp. 161–165; Gerhard Schwab (ed.), *db-Einfamilienhäuser 1–50*, Stuttgart 1962, p. 193 to 197; *Zodiac*, 1964, no. 12, p. 199; Sherban Cantacuzino, *Modern Houses of the World*, London 1964; *Bau*, 1969, p. 126; Joachim Göricke, *Bauten in Karlsruhe. Ein Architekturführer*, Karlsruhe 1971, no. 676; Gieselmann 1976, pp. 7, 9–11; Siegfried Nagel, *Offene Wohnformen. Ein- und Zweifamilienhäuser, Ferienhäuser*, Gütersloh 1976 (*DBZ-Baufachbücher*, 1), pp. 126/127; Gieselmann 1987, pp. 24–26, 104; Gieselmann 1998, p. 48.
pp. 38–41

12. Extension of the Strickwarenfabrik Sieger,
Lorch, Württemberg.
13. Second Wüstenrot housing development,
Karlsruhe-Waldstadt.
14. Choir of the Jesuitenkirche, Coesfeld.
15. Dr. Stähler office and residence, Münster, Westphalia.
16. Extension of the primary school in Bammental,
Baden.
17. Primary school in Mosbach, Baden.

12. Erweiterung der Strickwarenfabrik Sieger, Lorch,
Württemberg.
13. Zweite Wohnhaussiedlung Wüstenrot, Karlsruhe-Waldstadt.
14. Chor der Jesuitenkirche, Coesfeld.
15. Büro- und Wohnhaus Dr. Stähler, Münster,
Westfalen.
16. Erweiterung der Volksschule in Bammental,
Baden.
17. Volksschule in Mosbach, Baden.

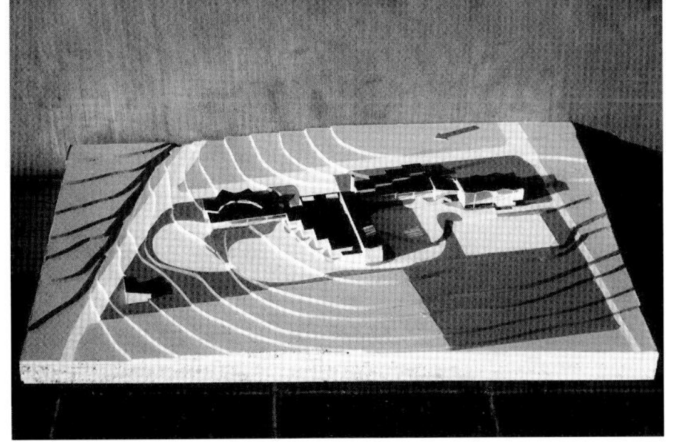

sammlung moderner Architektur, 1), S. 89; *Zodiac*,
1964, Nr. 12, S. 197.

Büroanbau am Gartenhaus des Mehrfamilien-
hauses Prof. Fischer, Karlsruhe
Stephanienstraße 50
1957, Umbau 1989

Erweiterung der Strickwarenfabrik Sieger, Lorch,
Württemberg
Götzentalstraße
1957/58, Erweiterungen 1961, 1966
Literatur: Gieselmann 1976, S. 14; Gieselmann
1987, S. 103.

Wohnhaus Prof. Becker, Karlsruhe-Durlach
1957–59
Literatur: *Bauwelt*, 51, 1960, Nr. 38, S. 1106/1107;
Neue deutsche Architektur 2, Stuttgart 1962,
S. 26/27; *Detail*, 1963, Nr. 3, S. 299; *Baumeister*,
61, 1964, Nr. 1, S. 40–42; *Zodiac*, 1964, Nr. 12,
S. 198; *Schöner Wohnen*, 5, 1964, Nr. 3, S. 87;
Gieselmann 1976, S. 7; Gieselmann 1987, S. 103.
S. 36/37

Siedlung Wüstenrot, Karlsruhe-Waldstadt
Allensteiner Straße 6–26, Stettiner Straße 5–21
1957–61
(20 Wohnhäuser, mit Alfred Fischer und Maria Ve-
rena Gieselmann, Karlsruhe)
Literatur: *Ziegel Arbeitsblätter*, o. J., Nr. 3, S. 19/20;
Ziegel Arbeitsblätter, o. J., Nr. 5, S. 3–6; *Report,
Bauen in unserer Zeit, hrsg. von der Geschäftsstelle
Öffentliche Bausparkassen Stuttgart*, Stuttgart o. J.,
S. 22/23; *Deutsche Bauzeitschrift*, 9, 1961, Nr. 2,
S. 157–160; *Mein Eigenheim*, 1960, Nr. 4, S. 125 bis
127; *Bauwelt*, 52, 1961, Nr. 22, S. 630–633; *Byggnads Ingenjoeren, Tidskrift foer internationell bygg-
nadsteknik och byggnadsekonomie*, 19, 1961, Nr. 4,
S. 42; Paul Faerber / Walter Meyer-Bohe, *80 neue
Eigenheime und Fertighäuser*, Ludwigsburg 1961
(*Wüstenroter Ratgeber*, 4), S. 66/67; *Mein Eigen-
heim*, 1961, Nr. 4, S. 120–125; Günther Kühne, *25
neue Kleinhäuser*, Frankfurt a. M. 1962 (Bauwelt-
Sonderheft N.S., 50), S. 9; *Terra*, hrsg. vom Fachverein Ziegelindustrie Hessen, 1962, Nr. 15, S. 5 bis
19; *Deutsche Bauzeitung*, 69, 1964, Nr. 1, S. 15/16;
Karl Krämer, *Einfamilienhäuser in der Gruppe. Eine
Beispielsammlung*, Stuttgart 1966, S. 91–97; *Kami-
ne und Kachelöfen*, München 1967 (*Detail-Bücherei
Elemente der Architektur, Beispiele*, 9), S. 60, 97;
Bau, 1969, Nr. 6, S. 125; *Aujourd'hui, art et architec-
ture, 10*, 1967, Nr. 57/58, S. 75; Gieselmann 1976,
S. 7; Gieselmann 1987, S. 11–13, 103; Gieselmann
1998, S. 54.
S. 86–89

Zweite Wohnhaussiedlung Wüstenrot, Karls-
ruhe-Waldstadt
Elbinger Straße
1958, Projekt
Literatur: *Bauwelt*, 49, 1958, Nr. 26, S. 776.

Oberverwaltungsgericht in Münster, Westfalen
1958, Projekt
Wettbewerb

Chorgestaltung der Jesuitenkirche, Coesfeld
1959, Projekt
(mit Bildhauer Walter Goehre, Düsseldorf)
Literatur: *Bauwelt*, 50, 1959, Nr. 48, S. 1408.

Ladenzeile in Karlsruhe-Nordweststadt
Heinrich-Köhler-Platz
1958
(mit Alfred Fischer und Maria Verena Gieselmann,
Karlsruhe)

Atelierhaus Dewald, Karlsruhe-Grötzingen
An der Silbergrub 5a
1958/59
Literatur: *Deutsche Bauzeitung*, 67, 1962, Nr. 3,
S. 182–185; *Schöner Wohnen*, 1962, Nr. 9, S. 66
bis 69; *Detail*, 1963, Nr. 4, S. 472; *Zodiac*, 1964,
Nr. 12, S. 196; *Bau*, 1969, Nr. 6, S. 126; Gerhard
Schwab (Hrsg.), *db-Einfamilienhäuser 1–50*, Stutt-
gart 1962, S. 217–222; *a+u Architecture and Ur-
banism*, 1983, Nr. 154, S. 78; Gieselmann 1976,
S. 7, 16/17; Gieselmann 1987, S. 95–98, 104.

Büro- und Wohnhaus Dr. Stähler, Münster,
Westfalen
Engelstraße 9
1958–60
Literatur: *Glasforum*, 11, 1961, Nr. 4, S. 4; *md möbel interior design*, 10, 1962, Nr. 6, S. 272/273; Gieselmann 1976, S. 7; Gieselmann 1987, S. 104.

Erweiterung der Volksschule in Bammental,
Baden
1958–60
(mit Alfred Fischer und Maria Verena Gieselmann,
Karlsruhe)
Literatur: *Baumeister*, 59, 1962, Nr. 2, S. 108–110;
Architektur-Wettbewerbe, 1963, Bd. 36, S. 24/25;
Fritz R. Barran, *Kunst am Bau heute. Wandbild,
Relief und Plastik in der Baukunst der Gegenwart*,
Stuttgart 1964, S. 40; *Bauwelt*, 55, 1964, Nr. 46,
S. 1280; Gieselmann 1976, S. 12; Gieselmann 1987,
S. 104.

Volksschule in Mosbach, Baden
1959, Projekt
Wettbewerb
Literatur: *Bauwelt*, 52, 1961, Nr. 44, S. 1259; Gieselmann 1976, S. 7.

Wohnhaus Dr. Hanfmann / Herzer, Karlsruhe-
Durlach
Strählerweg 55
1959–61, Anbau einer Außentreppe 1962
Literatur: Klara Trost, *Landhaus und Bungalow. Bei-
spiele moderner Eigenhäuser im In- und Ausland*,
Frankfurt a. M. 1961, S. 152–155; *Bauwelt*, 52, 1961,
Nr. 35, S. 984; *Deutsche Bauzeitung*, 67, 1962,
Nr. 3, S. 161–165; Gerhard Schwab (Hrsg.), *db-Ein-
familienhäuser 1–50*, Stuttgart 1962, S. 193–197;
Zodiac, 1964, Nr. 12, S. 199; Sherban Cantacuzino,
Modern Houses of the World, London 1964; *Bau*,
1969, S. 126; Joachim Göricke, *Bauten in Karls-
ruhe. Ein Architekturführer*, Karlsruhe 1971, Nr. 676;
Gieselmann 1976, S. 7, 9–11; Siegfried Nagel, *Offe-
ne Wohnformen. Ein- und Zweifamilienhäuser,
Ferienhäuser*, Gütersloh 1976 (*DBZ-Baufachbücher*, 1),
S. 126/127; Gieselmann 1987, S. 24–26, 104; Gie-
selmann 1998, S. 48.
S. 38–41

Teppichsiedlung in Karlsruhe-Nordweststadt
Eugen-Richter-Straße 10–24, Ludwig-Windthorst-
Straße 5, 5a, 7, 7a
1959–62, Anbauten 1966–69, 1978–80
Literatur: *Bauwelt*, 53, 1962, Nr. 35, S. 976/977;

»Carpet type« housing development in Karls-
ruhe-Nordweststadt
Eugen-Richter-Strasse 10–24, Ludwig-Windthorst-
Strasse 5, 5a, 7, 7a
1959–62, extensions 1966–69, 1978–80
Bibliography: *Bauwelt*, 53, 1962, no. 35, pp. 976/
977; *Schöner Wohnen*, 1963, no. 6, pp. 65 to
68; *Deutsche Bauzeitung*, 69, 1964, no. 1, p. 16;
Baumeister, 61, 1964, no. 9, Entwurfsblätter 68, 71;
Zodiac, 1964, no. 12, pp. 192–195; Ot Hoffmann/
Christoph Repenthin, *Neue urbane Wohnformen.
Gartenhofhäuser, Teppichsiedlungen, Terrassenhäu-
ser*, Berlin 1966, p. 83; Karl Krämer, *Einfamilienhäuser in der Gruppe. Eine Beispielsammlung*, Stuttgart
1966, pp. 60–67; Hubert Hoffmann, *Urbaner Flachbau. Reihenhäuser, Atriumhäuser, Kettenhäuser*,
Stuttgart 1967, pp. 126–129; *Deutsche Bauzeitschrift*, 15, 1967, no. 9, pp. 1465; Siegfried Nagel/
Siegfried Linke (eds.), *Reihenhäuser, Gruppenhäuser,
Hochhäuser. Verdichtete Wohnformen*, Gütersloh
1968, pp. 88–90; *Zuhause*, 1969, no. 9, p. 176;
Bau, 1969, no. 6, p. 128; *Detail*, 1970, no. 3, p.
537; Joachim Göricke, *Bauten in Karlsruhe. Ein
Architekturführer*, Karlsruhe 1971, no. 679; Gieselmann 1976, pp. 12, 15; *Prolegomena, Arbeitsblätter des Instituts für Wohnbau und Entwerfen an
der Technischen Universität Wien*, 1987, no. 56,
p. 32; Gieselmann 1987, pp. 20/21, 105; Friederike
Schneider (ed.), *Grundrißatlas Wohnungsbau*, Ba-
sel/Berlin/Boston 1994 (1st ed.), p. 194; Gieselmann 1998, p. 59.
pp. 90–93

Conversion of the Dewald house, Karlsruhe-
Grötzingen
An der Silbergrub 5a
1959–62, garage extension 1965
Bibliography: *Schöner Wohnen*, 1962, no. 9, pp.
66–69; *Detail*, 1963, no. 4, p. 428; *Zodiac*, 1964,
no. 12, p. 126; *Bau*, 1969, no. 6, p. 126; *a+u Architecture and Urbanism*, 1983, no. 154, p. 78; Gieselmann 1976, pp. 7, 16/17; Gieselmann 1987, pp. 95
to 98, 104.

Grammar school in Eberbach
1960, project
Competition

Town hall and civic center in Achern
1960, project
Competition

Stähler house, Borken, Westphalia
1960, project

Reliefs on the exterior wall of the high-rise dor-
mitory in Karlsruhe-Waldstadt
Insterburger Strasse 2
1960/61
(with Alfred Fischer and Maria Verena Gieselmann,
Karlsruhe)
Bibliography: Joachim Göricke, *Bauten in Karlsruhe.
Ein Architekturführer*, Karlsruhe 1971, no. 616.

Lipp house and studio, Karlsruhe-Waldstadt
Schneidemühler Strasse 3
1960–62
Bibliography: *Deutsche Bauzeitung*, 69, 1964, no.
3, p. 161–163; *Deutsche Bauzeitschrift*, 14, 1966,
no. 5, p. 835–838; Gerhard Schwab (ed.), *db-Einfamilienhäuser 51–100*, Stuttgart 1966, pp. 128 to

133; *Detail*, 1968, no. 4, pp. 685/686; Rainer Wolff,
Das kleine Haus, Munich 1969 (2nd ed), pp. 80/81;
Gieselmann 1976, p. 12; Gieselmann 1987, pp. 18/
19, 105.

Dr. Schnitzler house, Karlsruhe-Durlach
Rittnertstrasse 79
1960–64, project

Gieselmann multi-family house and studio,
Karlsruhe-Durlach
Rittnertstrasse 81
1960–65
Bibliography: *Zodiac*, 1964, no. 12, p. 193; *Bauwelt*,
58, 1967, no. 21/22, pp. 537–539; *Detail*, 1967, no.
2, p. 255; *Aujourd'hui, art et architecture*, 10, 1967,
no. 57/58, p. 74; Werner Weidert, *Einfamilienhäuser international*, Stuttgart 1967, pp. 144–147; *L'Architecture d'Aujourd'hui*, 1968, no. 136, pp. 104/
105; Günther Feuerstein, *New Directions in German Architecture*, New York 1968, pp. 78–80; *Bau*,
1969, no. 6, p. 127; Wolfgang Pehnt, *Neue deutsche Architektur 3*, Stuttgart 1970, pp. 62/63; *Das
Haus*, 1970, no. 12, pp. 14–18; *Ville e Giardini*,
1970, no. 9, pp. 8–12; Joachim Göricke, *Bauten in
Karlsruhe. Ein Architekturführer*, Karlsruhe 1971, no.
673; Fritz R. Barran, *Der offene Kamin, Folge 3*,
Stuttgart 1976, p. 67; Gieselmann 1976, pp. 13,
22–25; Ernst Danz/Axel Menges, *Neue Kamine.
Technik, Material, Form*, Munich/Stuttgart 1979,
p. 101; Gieselmann 1987, pp. 38–41, 107; Gieselmann 1998, p. 110.
pp. 94–101

Tutors' house by the high-rise dormitory in
Karlsruhe-Waldstadt
Schneidemühler Strasse
1961, project

Housing estate in Wattens, Tyrol
1961, project
(with Alfred Fischer and Maria Verena Gieselmann,
Karlsruhe)

School in Gondelsheim
1961, project
Competition
Bibliography: *Bauwelt*, 55, 1964, no. 46, p. 1268;
Gieselmann 1976, pp. 13, 18.

Office for Dr. Stähler, Münster, Westphalia
Engelstrasse 9
1961

Dr. Franz Josef Gieselmann tomb, Münster,
Westphalia
Mauritzfriedhof
1961

Meeting place in Althea, Spain
1961, project

Rosengarten municipal hall, Mannheim
1961, project
Competition
Bibliography: Gieselmann 1976, p. 12; Gieselmann 1987, p. 105.

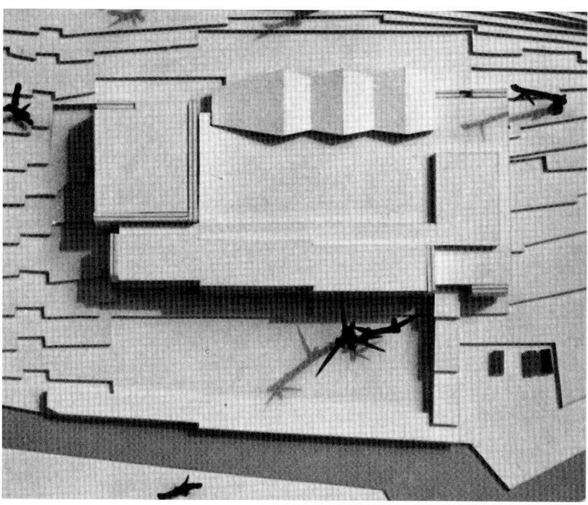

18. Conversion of the Dewald house, Karlsruhe-Grötzingen
19. High school in Eberbach.
20. Reliefs on the exterior wall of the high-rise dormitory in Karlsruhe-Waldstadt.
21. Dr. Franz Josef Gieselmann tomb, Münster, Westphalia.
22. Rosengarten municipal hall in Mannheim.
23. Conversion of a mill in Hontheim, Eifel.

18. Umbau des Hauses Dewald, Karlsruhe-Grötzingen
19. Gymnasium in Eberbach.
20. Außenwandreliefs am Studentenhochhaus in Karlsruhe-Waldstadt.
21. Grabmal Dr. Franz Josef Gieselmann, Münster, Westfalen.
22. Stadthalle Rosengarten in Mannheim.
23. Umbau der Mühle in Hontheim, Eifel.

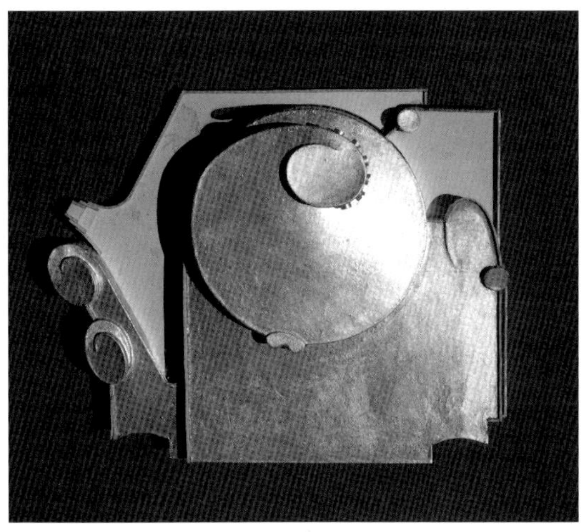

Schöner Wohnen, 1963, Nr. 6, S. 65–68; *Deutsche Bauzeitung*, 69, 1964, Nr. 1, S. 16; *Baumeister*, 61, 1964, Nr. 9, Entwurfsblätter 68, 71; *Zodiac*, 1964, Nr. 12, S. 192–195; Ot Hoffmann/Christoph Repenthin, *Neue urbane Wohnformen. Gartenhofhäuser, Teppichsiedlungen, Terrassenhäuser*, Berlin 1966, S. 83; Karl Krämer, *Einfamilienhäuser in der Gruppe. Eine Beispielsammlung,* Stuttgart 1966, S. 60–67; Hubert Hoffmann, *Urbaner Flachbau. Reihenhäuser, Atriumhäuser, Kettenhäuser*, Stuttgart 1967, S. 126 bis 129; *Deutsche Bauzeitschrift*, 15, 1967, Nr. 9, S. 1465; Siegfried Nagel/Siegfried Linke (Bearb.), *Reihenhäuser, Gruppenhäuser, Hochhäuser. Verdichtete Wohnformen*, Gütersloh 1968, S. 88–90; *Zuhause*, 1969, Nr. 9, S. 176; *Bau*, 1969, Nr. 6, S. 128; *Detail*, 1970, Nr. 3, S. 537; Joachim Göricke, *Bauten in Karlsruhe. Ein Architekturführer*, Karlsruhe 1971, Nr. 679; Gieselmann 1976, S. 12, 15; *Prolegomena, Arbeitsblätter des Instituts für Wohnbau und Entwerfen an der Technischen Universität Wien*, 1987, Nr. 56, S. 32; Gieselmann 1987, S. 20/21, 105; Friederike Schneider (Hrsg.), *Grundrißatlas Wohnungsbau*, Basel/Berlin/Boston 1994 (1. Auflage), S. 194; Gieselmann 1998, S. 59.
S. 90–93

Unmbau des Hauses Dewald, Karlsruhe-Grötzingen
An der Silbergrub 5a
1959–62, Garagenanbau 1965
Literatur: *Schöner Wohnen*, 1962, Nr. 9, S. 66–69; *Detail*, 1963, Nr. 4, S. 428; *Zodiac*, 1964, Nr. 12, S. 126; *Bau*, 1969, Nr. 6, S. 126; *a+u Architecture and Urbanism*, 1983, Nr. 154, S. 78; Gieselmann 1976, S. 7, 16/17; Gieselmann 1987, S. 95–98, 104.

Gymnasium in Eberbach
1960, Projekt
Wettbewerb

Rathaus und Bürgerzentrum in Achern
1960, Projekt
Wettbewerb

Wohnhaus Stähler, Borken, Westfalen
1960, Projekt

Außenwandreliefs am Studentenhochhaus in Karlsruhe-Waldstadt
Insterburger Straße 2
1960/61
(mit Alfred Fischer und Maria Verena Gieselmann, Karlsruhe)
Literatur: Joachim Göricke, *Bauten in Karlsruhe. Ein Architekturführer*, Karlsruhe 1971, Nr. 616.

Wohn- und Atelierhaus Lipp, Karlsruhe-Waldstadt
Schneidemühler Straße 3
1960–62
Literatur: *Deutsche Bauzeitung*, 69, 1964, Nr. 3, S. 161–163; *Deutsche Bauzeitschrift*, 14, 1966, Nr. 5, S. 835–838; Gerhard Schwab (Hrsg.), *db-Einfamilienhäuser 51–100*, Stuttgart 1966, S. 128–133; *Detail*, 1968, Nr. 4, S. 685/686; Rainer Wolff, *Das kleine Haus*, München 1969 (2. Auflage), S. 80/81; Gieselmann 1976, S. 12; Gieselmann 1987, S. 18/19, 105.

Wohnhaus Dr. Schnitzler, Karlsruhe-Durlach
Rittnertstraße 79
1960–64, Projekt

Mehrfamilien- und Atelierhaus Gieselmann, Karlsruhe-Durlach
Rittnertstraße 81
1960–65
Literatur: *Zodiac*, 1964, Nr. 12, S. 193; *Bauwelt*, 58, 1967, Nr. 21/22, S. 537–539; *Detail*, 1967, Nr. 2, S. 255; *Aujourd'hui, art et architecture*, 10, 1967, Nr. 57/58, S. 74; Werner Weidert, *Einfamilienhäuser international*, Stuttgart 1967, S. 144–147; *L'Architecture d'Aujourd'hui*, 1968, Nr. 136, S. 104/105; Günther Feuerstein, *New Directions in German Architecture*, New York 1968, S. 78–80; *Bau*, 1969, Nr. 6, S. 127; Wolfgang Pehnt, *Neue deutsche Architektur 3*, Stuttgart 1970, S. 62/63; *Das Haus*, 1970, Nr. 12, S. 14–18; *Ville e Giardini*, 1970, Nr. 9, S. 8–12; Joachim Göricke, *Bauten in Karlsruhe. Ein Architekturführer*, Karlsruhe 1971, Nr. 673; Fritz R. Barran, *Der offene Kamin, Folge 3*, Stuttgart 1976, S. 67; Gieselmann 1976, S. 13, 22–25; Ernst Danz/Axel Menges, *Neue Kamine. Technik, Material, Form*, München/Stuttgart 1979, S. 101; Gieselmann 1987, S. 38–41, 107; Gieselmann 1998, S. 110.
S. 94–101

Tutorenhaus am Studentenhochhaus in Karlsruhe-Waldstadt
Schneidemühler Straße
1961, Projekt

Siedlung in Wattens, Tirol
1961, Projekt
(mit Alfred Fischer und Maria Verena Gieselmann, Karlsruhe)

Schule in Gondelsheim
1961, Projekt
Wettbewerb
Literatur: *Bauwelt*, 55, 1964, Nr. 46, S. 1268; Gieselmann 1976, S. 13, 18.

Büroeinrichtung Dr. Stähler, Münster, Westfalen
Engelstraße 9
1961

Grabmal Dr. Franz Josef Gieselmann, Münster, Westfalen
Mauritzfriedhof
1961

Begegnungsstätte in Althea, Spanien
1961, Projekt

Stadthalle Rosengarten, Mannheim
1961, Projekt
Wettbewerb
Literatur: Gieselmann 1976, S. 12; Gieselmann 1987, S. 105.

Umbau einer Mühle in Hontheim, Eifel
1961/62
Literatur: *Deutsche Bauzeitschrift*, 15, 1967, Nr. 12, S. 2069–2072, *Detail*, 1971, Nr. 2, S. 268/269; *Hauserneuerung. Bautechnischer Ratgeber für Haus und Wohnung, Organ des Arbeitskreises Althauserneuerung*, 1, 1963, Nr. 1, S. 32–34; *Die Kunst und das schöne Heim*, 61, 1962, Nr. 12, S. 163–169; Jacques Debaigts, *Cheminées et coins de feu*

Conversion of a mill in Hontheim, Eifel
1961/62
Bibliography: *Deutsche Bauzeitschrift*, 15, 1967,
no. 12, pp. 2069–2072, *Detail*, 1971, no. 2, pp.
268/269; *Hauserneuerung. Bautechnischer Ratgeber für Haus und Wohnung, Organ des Arbeitskreises Althauserneuerung*, 1, 1963, no. 1, pp. 32–34;
Die Kunst und das schöne Heim, 61, 1962, no. 12,
pp. 163–169; Jacques Debaigts, *Cheminées et
coins de feu modernes*, Fribourg 1975, pp. 50–53;
Fritz R. Barran, *Der offene Kamin, Folge 3*, Stuttgart
1976, p. 137; Gieselmann 1976, p. 12; Gieselmann
1987, p. 105.

Interior design of the mortuary chapel attached
to the municipal church of St. Stephan, Karlsruhe
1961/62

Dr. Beißwenger two-family house, Karlsruhe-
Waldstadt
Friedländer Strasse 3
1961/62
Bibliography: *Terra*, ed. by Fachverein Ziegelindus-
trie Hessen, 8, 1965, no. 20, pp. 16–19; *Deutsche
Bauzeitschrift*, 14, 1966, no. 8, pp. 1461/1462; Kurt
Hoffmann/Helga Griese, *Mehrfamilienhäuser*, Stutt-
gart 1974, p. 36; Gieselmann 1976, p. 13; Giesel-
mann 1987, p. 106.

Prof. Müller-Lancé house, Umkirch
Mittelweg 4
1961–63; garage extension, 1968/69; conversion
of the upper floor, 1990, project

Church of St. Jakobus, Sinsheim
1961–67, conversion of the interior, 1994–96
Bibliography: *Baumeister*, 64, 1967, no. 12, pp.
1522/1523; *Das Münster*, 20, 1967, no. 12, pp. 480/
481; *Informes de la construcción, revista de información técnica*, 1969, no. 212, pp. 7–13; *Glasforum*,
20, 1970, no. 5, pp. 29/30; Reinhard Gieselmann,
Neue Kirchen, Stuttgart 1972, pp. 19; Hugo Schnell,
*Der Kirchenbau des 20. Jahrhunderts in Deutsch-
land. Dokumentation, Darstellung, Deutung*, Munich
1973, p. 191; Paolo Nestler/Peter M. Bode, *Deutsche Kunst seit 1960, vol. 4, Architektur*, Munich
1976, p. 129; Gieselmann 1976, pp. 30, 44 to 49;
Gieselmann 1987, pp. 28–31, 109.
pp. 152–155

Conversion of the Dr. Rees multi-family house,
Karlsruhe
Stephanienstrasse 78
1962/63; Carport, 1972/73; Aufstockung des Gartentrakts, 1975/76; Gartenkamin und Pergola,
1981, project
Bibliography: *Baumeister*, 71, 1968, no. 9, pp. 996/
997; *Detail*, 1970, no. 3, p. 544; Gieselmann 1976,
p. 14; *Baumeister*, 75, 1978, no. 6, pp. 535/536;
a+u Architecture and Urbanism, 1983, no. 154, pp.
76–78; Gieselmann 1987, pp. 79–81, 107.
pp. 102–105

Dr. Heinz Pietzsch house, Karlsruhe-Durlach
Hahnemannstrasse 8
1962–64

Dr. Nees two-family house, Karlsruhe-Grötzingen
Weingartener Strasse 6
1962–64
Bibliography: Kurt Hoffmann/Helga Griese, *Mehrfamilienhäuser*, Stuttgart 1974, pp. 90/91; *Deutsche
Bauzeitschrift*, 14, 1966, no. 8, pp. 1461/1462;
Gieselmann 1976, pp. 13, 20/21; Gieselmann
1987, p. 106.
pp. 42–45

Old-age home of the Deutsches Rotes Kreuz
(today of the Diakonisches Werk), Karlsruhe
Stephanienstrasse 74–76
1962–67; conversion and extension, 1992–96,
project
Bibliography: *Architektur und Wohnform*, 75, 1967,
no. 7, pp. 458–463; *Aujourd'hui, art et architecture*,
10, 1967, no. 57/58, p. 79; Günther Feuerstein,
New Directions in German Architecture, New York
1968, pp. 33, 36; *L'architettura*, 13, 1968, no. 149,
pp. 744/745; *Bauwelt*, 60, 1969, no. 20, pp. 704/
705; *Bau*, 1969, no. 6, p. 128; *Deutsche Bauzeitung*, 104, 1970, no. 6, p. 448; Joachim Göricke,
Bauten in Karlsruhe. Ein Architekturführer, Karlsruhe
1971, no. 619; *Kenchiku bunka* (Tokyo), 26, 1971,
no. 10, no. 428, p. 67; Antal Reischl, *Lakóépülettervezési tájékoztató*, Budapest 1971, no. 0123;
Konrad Schalhorn, *Wohnungen für alte Menschen.
Altenheime, Wohnstifte, Seniorenzentren*, Munich
1973 (*Entwurf und Planung*, 17), pp. 30/31; Gieselmann 1976, pp. 30, 36–41; *Architektur aktuell*, 14,
1980, no. 79, p. 32; Gieselmann 1987, pp. 46–49,
109.
pp. 106–113

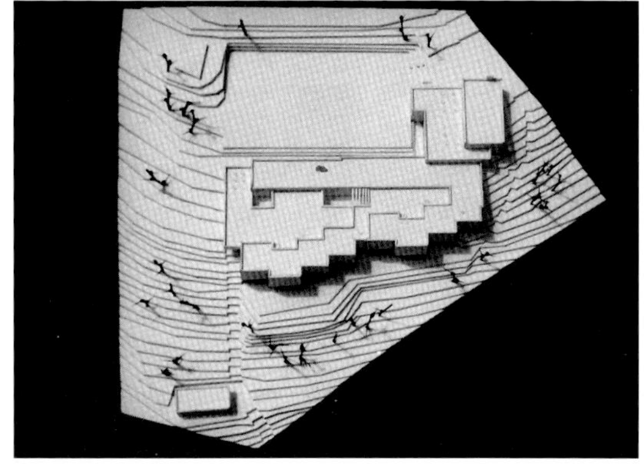

Primary school in Billigheim, Odenwald
1963, project
Competition, 1st prize
Bibliography: *Bauwelt*, 55, 1964, no. 46, p. 1268;
Gieselmann 1976, pp. 13, 19; Gieselmann 1987,
p. 106.

»Modern stoves«
1963, project
Competition, 3rd prize
Bibliography: *md möbel interior design*, 11, 1963,
no. 11, pp. 591/592; *Bauen und Wohnen*, 18, 1963,
no. 9, pp. 42–48; Gieselmann 1976, p. 14; Gieselmann 1987, p. 106.

Badisches Staatstheater, Karlsruhe
Ettlinger-Tor-Platz
1963, project
Competition

St. Hedwig parish center, Karlsruhe-Waldstadt
1963, project
Competition
Bibliography: *Bauwelt*, 56, 1965, no. 3, p. 48.

High school in Bonn
1963, project
Competition

Primary school in Siegelsbach, Kraichgau
1963, project
Competition, acquisition

24. Dr. Beißwenger two-family house, Karlsruhe-Waldstadt.
25. Primary school in Billigheim, Odenwald.
26. St. Hedwig parish center, Karlsruhe-Waldstadt.

24. Zweifamilienhaus Dr. Beißwenger, Karlsruhe-Waldstadt.
25. Volksschule in Billigheim, Odenwald.
26. Kirchenzentrum St. Hedwig, Karlsruhe-Waldstadt.

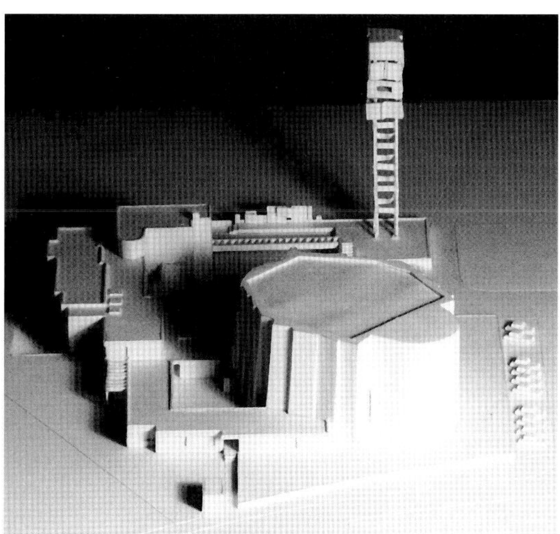

modernes, Fribourg 1975, S. 50–53; Fritz R. Barran, *Der offene Kamin, Folge 3*, Stuttgart 1976, S. 137; Gieselmann 1976, S. 12; Gieselmann 1987, S. 105.

Innengestaltung der Totenkapelle an der Stadtkirche St. Stephan, Karlsruhe
1961/62

Zweifamilienhaus Dr. Beißwenger, Karlsruhe-Waldstadt
Friedländer Straße 3
1961/62
Literatur: *Terra*, hrsg. vom Fachverein Ziegelindustrie Hessen, 8, 1965, Nr. 20, S. 16–19; *Deutsche Bauzeitschrift*, 14, 1966, Nr. 8, S. 1461/1462; Kurt Hoffmann/Helga Griese, *Mehrfamilienhäuser*, Stuttgart 1974, S. 36; Gieselmann 1976, S. 13; Gieselmann 1987, S. 106.

Wohnhaus Prof. Müller-Lancé, Umkirch
Mittelweg 4
1961–63; Garagenanbau, 1968/69; Umbau des Obergeschosses, 1990, Projekt

Kirche St. Jakobus, Sinsheim
1961–67, Umgestaltung des Innenraums, 1994 bis 1996
Literatur: *Baumeister*, 64, 1967, Nr. 12, S. 1522/1523; *Das Münster*, 20, 1967, Nr. 12, S. 480/481; *Informes de la construcción, revista de información técnica*, 1969, Nr. 212, S. 7–13; *Glasforum*, 20, 1970, Nr. 5, S. 29/30; Reinhard Gieselmann, *Neue Kirchen*, Stuttgart 1972, S. 19; Hugo Schnell, *Der Kirchenbau des 20. Jahrhunderts in Deutschland. Dokumentation, Darstellung, Deutung*, München 1973, S. 191; Paolo Nestler/Peter M. Bode, *Deutsche Kunst seit 1960, 4. Bd. Architektur*, München 1976, S. 129; Gieselmann 1976, S. 30, 44–49; Gieselmann 1987, S. 28–31, 109.
S. 152–155

Umbau des Mehrfamilienhauses Dr. Rees, Karlsruhe
Stephanienstraße 78
1962/63; Carport, 1972/73; Aufstockung des Gartentrakts, 1975/76; Gartenkamin und Pergola, 1981, Projekt
Literatur: *Baumeister*, 71, 1968, Nr. 9, S. 996/997; *Detail*, 1970, Nr. 3, S. 544; Gieselmann 1976, S. 14; *Baumeister*, 75, 1978, Nr. 6, S. 535/536; *a+u Architecture and Urbanism*, 1983, Nr. 154, S. 76–78; Gieselmann 1987, S. 79–81, 107.
S. 102–105

Wohnhaus Dr. Heinz Pietzsch, Karlsruhe-Durlach
Hahnemannstraße 8
1962–64

Zweifamilienhaus Dr. Nees, Karlsruhe-Grötzingen
Weingartener Straße 6
1962–64
Literatur: Kurt Hoffmann/Helga Griese, *Mehrfamilienhäuser*, Stuttgart 1974, S. 90/91; *Deutsche Bauzeitschrift*, 14, 1966, Nr. 8, S. 1461/1462; Gieselmann 1976, S. 13, 20/21; Gieselmann 1987, S. 106.
S. 42–45

Altenheim des Deutschen Roten Kreuzes (heute des Diakonischen Werks), Karlsruhe
Stephanienstraße 74–76
1962–67; Umbau und Erweiterung, 1992–96, Projekt
Literatur: *Architektur und Wohnform*, 75, 1967, Nr. 7, S. 458–463; *Aujourd'hui, art et architecture*, 10, 1967, Nr. 57/58, S. 79; Günther Feuerstein, *New Directions in German Architecture*, New York 1968, S. 33, 36; *L'architettura*, 13, 1968, Nr. 149, S. 744/745; *Bauwelt*, 60, 1969, Nr. 20, S. 704/705; *Bau*, 1969, Nr. 6, S. 128; *Deutsche Bauzeitung*, 104, 1970, Nr. 6, S. 448; Joachim Göricke, *Bauten in Karlsruhe. Ein Architekturführer*, Karlsruhe 1971, Nr. 619; *Kenchiku bunka* (Tokyo), 26, 1971, Nr. 10, Nr. 428, S. 67; Antal Reischl, *Lakóépülettervezési tájékoztató*, Budapest 1971, Nr. 0123; Konrad Schalhorn, *Wohnungen für alte Menschen. Altenheime, Wohnstifte, Seniorenzentren*, München 1973 (*Entwurf und Planung*, 17), S. 30/31; Gieselmann 1976, S. 30, 36–41; *Architektur aktuell*, 14, 1980, Nr. 79, S. 32; Gieselmann 1987, S. 46–49, 109.
S. 106–113

Volksschule in Billigheim, Odenwald
1963, Projekt
Wettbewerb, 1. Preis
Literatur: *Bauwelt*, 55, 1964, Nr. 46, S. 1268; Gieselmann 1976, S. 13, 19; Gieselmann 1987, S. 106.

»Der Ofen unserer Zeit«
1963, Entwurf
Wettbewerb, 3. Preis
Literatur: *md möbel interior design*, 11, 1963, Nr. 11, S. 591/592; *Bauen und Wohnen*, 18, 1963, Nr. 9, S. 42–48; Gieselmann 1976, S. 14; Gieselmann 1987, S. 106.

Badisches Staatstheater, Karlsruhe
Ettlinger-Tor-Platz
1963, Projekt
Wettbewerb

Kirchenzentrum St. Hedwig, Karlsruhe-Waldstadt
1963, Projekt
Wettbewerb
Literatur: *Bauwelt*, 56, 1965, Nr. 3, S. 48.

Gymnasium in Bonn
1963, Projekt
Wettbewerb

Volksschule in Siegelsbach, Kraichgau
1963, Projekt
Wettbewerb, Ankauf

Bebauung des Wohngebiets Schälzig, Schwetzingen
1963, Projekt
Wettbewerb, ein 2. Preis

Wohnhaus Dr. Schulte-Frohlinde, Karlsruhe-Grötzingen
Eugen-Wollfarth-Weg 12
1963–66, Erweiterungen, 1977–80, 1983–85
Literatur: *Deutsche Bauzeitschrift*, 18, 1970, Nr. 4, S. 1659–1662; *Ville e Giardini*, 1971, Nr. 40, S. 14/15; Siegfried Nagel (Hrsg.), *Offene Wohnformen. Ein- und Zweifamilienhäuser, Ferienhäuser*, Gütersloh 1976 (*DBZ-Baufachbücher*, 1), S. 126/127; Giesel-

Development of the Schälzig residential area, Schwetzingen
1963, project
Competition, a 2nd prize

Dr. Schulte-Frohlinde house, Karlsruhe-Grötzin-gen
Eugen-Wollfarth-Weg 12
1963–66, extensions, 1977–80, 1983–85
Bibliography: *Deutsche Bauzeitschrift*, 18, 1970, no. 4, pp. 1659–1662; *Ville e Giardini*, 1971, no. 40, pp. 14/15; Siegfried Nagel (ed.), *Offene Wohnformen. Ein- und Zweifamilienhäuser, Ferienhäuser*, Gütersloh 1976 (*DBZ-Baufachbücher*, 1), pp. 126/127; Gieselmann 1976, pp. 30, 42/43; Gieselmann 1987, pp. 42–44, 108.
pp. 46–49

Prof. Häfele house, Karlsruhe-Durlach
Steinlesweg 9
1963–66
Bibliography: *Deutsche Bauzeitung*, 103, 1969, no. 3, pp. 166/167; *Ville e Giardini*, 1971, no. 40, pp. 16/17; Gieselmann 1976, pp. 30, 43; Gieselmann 1987, p. 108.
pp. 50–53

Streit studio, Burrweiler
Im Talacker 3
1963–67
Bibliography: Gieselmann 1976, p. 30.

Lusch house, Karlsruhe-Durlach
Käthe-Kollwitz-Strasse
1964, project

Trenker children's carousel, Karlsruhe
1964, project

Urban development in Berlin-Frohnau
1964/65, project
Competition
Bibliography: *Bauwelt,* 57, 1966, no. 49, pp. 1440 to 1442; *Aujourd'hui, art et architecture*, 10, 1967, no. 57/58, p. 85; *Bau*, 1969, no. 6, p. 129; Gieselmann 1976, pp. 14, 26/27.
pp. 114–117

Prof. Lankheit house, Karlsruhe-Durlach
Erich-Heckel-Strasse 8
1964/65
Bibliography: *Deutsche Bauzeitung*, 103, 1969, no. 3, pp. 168/169; Joachim Göricke, *Bauten in Karlsruhe. Ein Architekturführer*, Karlsruhe 1971, no. 674; *Ville e Giardini*, 1971, no. 40, pp. 18/19; Gieselmann 1976, p. 14; Gieselmann 1987, p. 108.
pp. 54–57

Z. house, Karlsruhe-Durlach
1964–67
Bibliography: *Kamine und Kachelöfen*, Munich 1967 (*Detail-Bücherei Elemente der Architektur, Beispiele*, 9), p. 27; *Deutsche Bauzeitung*, 103, 1969, no. 3, pp. 170/171; *Informes de la construcción, revista de información técnica*, 1969, no. 212, pp. 15–20; *Cement*, 1970, no. 3, n. p.; *Ville e Giardini*, 1970, no. 4, pp. 2–10; *KS – Neues Bauen in Kalksandstein*, 1970, no. 1, n .p.; *The Architectural Review*, 149, 1971, no. 894, p. 123; Joachim Göricke, *Bauten in Karlsruhe. Ein Architekturführer*, Karlsruhe 1971, no. 675; Gieselmann 1976, pp. 31, 58/59;

Ernst Danz/Axel Menges, *Neue Kamine. Technik, Material, Form*, Munich/Stuttgart 1979, pp. 15, 70/71; Gieselmann 1987, pp. 32–35, 110.
pp. 58–63

Conversion of the Schlossplatz, Karlsruhe
1965, project
Bibliography: Gieselmann 1976, pp. 14, 28/29.

Addition to the Prof. Burgholz house, Münster, Westphalia
Allerdinckstrasse 27
1965/66

Prof. Höhler house, Karlsruhe-Bergwald
Heinrich-Weitz-Strasse 27
1965/66

Euratom group of houses for Dr. Benedict, Dr. Lesser, Dr. Ohse, Karlsruhe-Waldstadt
Erasmusstrasse 14–18
1965/66, extension of the Dr. Benedikt house, 1973
Bibliography: Gieselmann 1987, p. 107; Gieselmann 1998, p. 21.

Church of the motherhouse of the Barmherzige Schwestern vom Heiligen Vincenz von Paul, Untermarchtal
1965/66, project
Competition

Temporary buildings for the Bundesgartenschau 1967, Karlsruhe
Schlossgarten and Fasanengarten
1965–67
Bibliography: *Werkkunst*, 29, 1967, no. 2, pp. 6, 25; *ac Internationale Asbestzement-Revue*, 1967, no. 48, pp. 52/53; Gieselmann 1976, pp. 31, 50/51; Gieselmann 1987, p. 109.

SOS youth home, Müllheim, Baden
1965–68
Bibliography: *Detail*, 1969, no. 6, pp. 1283–1290; *Bauwelt*, 60, 1969, no. 7, pp. 216–229; Walter Meyer-Bohe, *Bauten für die Jugend*, Stuttgart 1972, pp. 65–69; Dieter Bilz, *Kinder- und Jugendheime*, Stuttgart 1972, pp. 58–61; Friedemann Wild/Ute Busche-Sievers, *Kinderheime und Kinderdörfer*, Munich 1973 (*Entwurf und Planung*, 16), pp. 38/39; *Deutsche Bauzeitschrift*, 21, 1973, no. 10, pp. 1978/1979; *Architektur aktuell*, 14, 1980, no. 79, p. 33; Gieselmann 1976, pp. 31, 66–69; Gieselmann 1987, pp. 58–62, 110.
pp. 118–121

St. Stephanus parish center, Filderstadt-Bernhausen
1965–75
Bibliography: *Deutsche Bauzeitung*, 102, 1968, no. 12, pp. 936–939; *Bau*, 1969, no. 6, p. 129; Reinhard Gieselmann, *Neue Kirchen*, Stuttgart 1972, pp. 94–97; Hugo Schnell, *Der Kirchenbau des 20. Jahrhunderts in Deutschland. Dokumentation, Darstellung, Bedeutung*, Munich 1973, p. 159; Gottlieb Merkle, *Kirchenbau im Wandel. Die Grundlagen des Kirchenbaus im 20. Jahrhundert und seine Entwicklung in der Diözese Rottenburg. Eine Dokumentation*, Ruit 1973, pp. 216, 231; *Deutsche Bauzeitung*, 109, 1975, no. 12, p. 48; Gieselmann 1976, pp. 31, 52–57; Gieselmann 1987, pp. 52–55, 110.
pp. 156–159

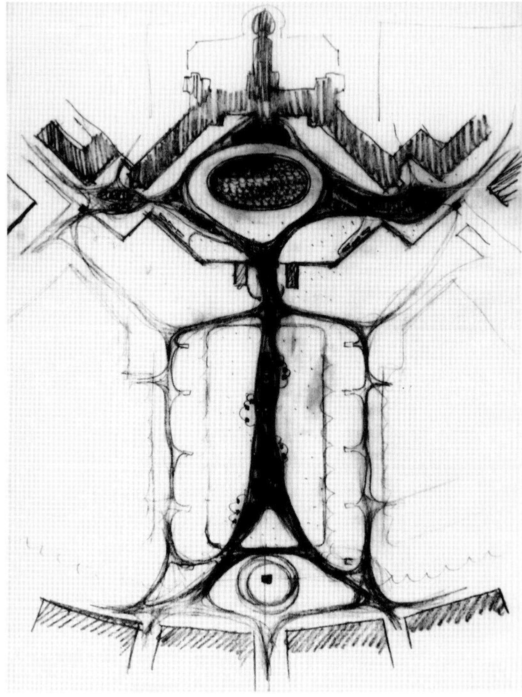

27. Streit studio, Burrweiler.
28. Conversion of the Schlossplatz in Karlsruhe.
29. Euratom group of houses for Dr. Benedict,
Dr. Lesser, Dr. Ohse, Karlsruhe-Waldstadt.
30. Temporary buildings for the Bundesgartenschau
1967, Karlsruhe.
31. Redevelopment of the town center in Hockenheim, Baden.

27. Atelierhaus Streit, Burrweiler.
28. Neugestaltung des Schloßplatzes in Karlsruhe.
29. Euratom-Wohnhausgruppe Dr. Benedict,
Dr. Lesser, Dr. Ohse, Karlsruhe-Waldstadt.
30. Temporäre Bauten der Bundesgartenschau
1967, Karlsruhe.
31. Sanierung des Stadtzentrums in Hockenheim,
Baden.

mann 1976, S. 30, 42/43; Gieselmann 1987, S. 42
bis 44, 108.
S. 46–49

Wohnhaus Prof. Häfele, Karlsruhe-Durlach
Steinlesweg 9
1963–66
Literatur: *Deutsche Bauzeitung*, 103, 1969, Nr. 3,
S. 166/167; *Ville e Giardini*, 1971, Nr. 40, S. 16/17;
Gieselmann 1976, S. 30, 43; Gieselmann 1987,
S. 108.
S. 50–53

Atelierhaus Streit, Burrweiler
Im Talacker 3
1963–67
Literatur: Gieselmann 1976, S. 30.

Wohnhaus Lusch, Karlsruhe-Durlach
Käthe-Kollwitz-Straße
1964, Projekt

Kinderkarusell Trenker, Karlsruhe
1964, Entwurf

Stadterweiterung in Berlin-Frohnau
1964/65, Projekt
Wettbewerb
Literatur: *Bauwelt,* 57, 1966, Nr. 49, S. 1440–1442;
Aujourd'hui, art et architecture, 10, 1967, Nr. 57/58,
S. 85; *Bau*, 1969, Nr. 6, S. 129; Gieselmann 1976,
S. 14, 26/27.
S. 114–117

Wohnhaus Prof. Lankheit, Karlsruhe-Durlach
Erich-Heckel-Straße 8
1964/65
Literatur: *Deutsche Bauzeitung*, 103, 1969, Nr. 3,
S. 168/169; Joachim Göricke, *Bauten in Karlsruhe.
Ein Architekturführer*, Karlsruhe 1971, Nr. 674; *Ville
e Giardini*, 1971, Nr. 40, S. 18/19; Gieselmann 1976,
S. 14; Gieselmann 1987, S. 108.
S. 54–57

Wohnhaus Z., Karlsruhe-Durlach
1964–67
Literatur: *Kamine und Kachelöfen*, München 1967
(*Detail-Bücherei Elemente der Architektur, Beispiele*,
9), S. 27; *Deutsche Bauzeitung*, 103, 1969, Nr. 3,
S. 170/171; *Informes de la construcción, revista de
información técnica*, 1969, Nr. 212, S. 15–20; *Cement*, 1970, Nr. 3, o. S.; *Ville Giardini*, 1970, Nr. 4,
S. 2–10; *KS – Neues Bauen in Kalksandstein*,
1970, Nr. 1, o. S.; *The Architectural Review*, 149,
1971, Nr. 894, S. 123; Joachim Göricke, *Bauten
in Karlsruhe. Ein Architekturführer*, Karlsruhe 1971,
Nr. 675; Gieselmann 1976, S. 31, 58/59; Ernst
Danz / Axel Menges, *Neue Kamine. Technik, Material, Form*, München / Stuttgart 1979, S. 15, 70/71;
Gieselmann 1987, S. 32–35, 110.
S. 58–63

Neugestaltung des Schloßplatzes in Karlsruhe
1965, Projekt
Literatur: Gieselmann 1976, S. 14, 28/29.

**Wohnhausanbau Prof. Burgholz, Münster,
Westfalen**
Allerdinckstraße 27
1965/66

Wohnhaus Prof. Höhler, Karlsruhe-Bergwald
Heinrich-Weitz-Straße 27
1965/66

**Euratom-Wohnhausgruppe Dr. Benedict,
Dr. Lesser, Dr. Ohse, Karlsruhe-Waldstadt**
Erasmusstraße 14–18
1965/66, Erweiterung des Hauses Dr. Benedikt,
1973
Literatur: Gieselmann 1987, S. 107; Gieselmann
1998, S. 21.

**Mutterhauskirche der Barmherzigen Schwestern
vom Heiligen Vincenz von Paul, Untermarchtal**
1965/66, Projekt
Wettbewerb

**Temporäre Bauten der Bundesgartenschau
1967, Karlsruhe**
Schloßgarten und Fasanengarten
1965–67
Literatur: *Werkkunst*, 29, 1967, Nr. 2, S. 6, 25; *ac
Internationale Asbestzement-Revue*, 1967, Nr. 48,
S. 52/53; Gieselmann 1976, S. 31, 50/51; Giesel-
mann 1987, S. 109.

SOS-Jugendheim, Müllheim, Baden
1965–68
Literatur: *Detail*, 1969, Nr. 6, S. 1283–1290; *Bauwelt*, 60, 1969, Nr. 7, S. 216–229; Walter Meyer-
Bohe, *Bauten für die Jugend*, Stuttgart 1972, S. 65
bis 69; Dieter Bilz, *Kinder- und Jugendheime*, Stuttgart 1972, S. 58–61; Friedemann Wild / Ute Busche-
Sievers, *Kinderheime und Kinderdörfer*, München
1973 (*Entwurf und Planung*, 16), S. 38/39; *Deutsche
Bauzeitschrift*, 21, 1973, Nr. 10, S. 1978/1979; *Architektur aktuell*, 14, 1980, Nr. 79, S. 33; Gieselmann
1976, S. 31, 66–69; Gieselmann 1987, S. 58–62,
110.
S. 118–121

**Kirchengemeindezentrum St. Stephanus,
Filderstadt-Bernhausen**
1965–75
Literatur: *Deutsche Bauzeitung*, 102, 1968, Nr. 12,
S. 936–939; *Bau*, 1969, Nr. 6, S. 129; Reinhard
Gieselmann, *Neue Kirchen*, Stuttgart 1972, S. 94
bis 97; Hugo Schnell, *Der Kirchenbau des 20. Jahrhunderts in Deutschland. Dokumentation, Darstellung, Bedeutung*, München 1973, S. 159; Gottlieb
Merkle, *Kirchenbau im Wandel. Die Grundlagen des
Kirchenbaus im 20. Jahrhundert und seine Entwicklung in der Diözese Rottenburg. Eine Dokumentation*, Ruit 1973, S. 216, 231; *Deutsche Bauzeitung*,
109, 1975, Nr. 12, S. 48; Gieselmann 1976, S. 31,
52–57; Gieselmann 1987, S. 52–55, 110.
S 156–159

**Sanierung des Stadtzentrums in Hockenheim,
Baden**
1966, Projekt
Wettbewerb
Literatur: Harald Deilmann / Jörg C. Kirschenmann /
Herbert Pfeiffer, *Wohnungsbau. Nutzungstypen,
Grundrißtypen, Wohnungstypen, Gebäudetypen*,
Stuttgart 1973, S. 114; *Aujourd'hui, art et architec-
ture*, 10, 1967, Nr. 57/58, S. 80; *Baumeister*, 66,
1969, Nr. 1, S. 42/43; Gieselmann 1976, S. 30,
34/35; Gieselmann 1987, S. 108.

Redevelopment of the town center in Hockenheim, Baden
1966, project
Competition
Bibliography: Harald Deilmann / Jörg C. Kirschenmann / Herbert Pfeiffer, *Wohnungsbau. Nutzungstypen, Grundrißtypen, Wohnungstypen, Gebäudetypen*, Stuttgart 1973, p. 114; *Aujourd'hui, art et architecture*, 10, 1967, no. 57/58, p. 80; *Baumeister*, 66,
1969, no. 1, pp. 42/43; Gieselmann 1976, pp. 30,
34/35; Gieselmann 1987, p. 108.

Comprehensive high school and center of the
Märkisches Viertel, Berlin
1966, project
Competition

St. Anna parish centre, Münster, Westphalia
1966, project
Competition
Bibliography: *Architektur-Wettbewerbe*, 1968, vol.
54, p. XVII; Rainer Disse, *Kirchliche Zentren*, Munich
1974 (*Entwurf und Planung*, 24), p. 91.

Old people's home in Karlsruhe-Rintheim
1967, project
Competition

Town hall in Birkenfeld-Gräfenhausen
1967, project
Competition

»Die Stadtstrasse von Morgen«
1967, project
Competition
(Urban planning for the Kaiserstrasse in Karlsruhe,
with Gunnar Martinsson, Karlsruhe)

Redevelopment of the town center in Bruchsal-
Untergrombach
1967–69, project
Competition, first acquisition and revised version
Bibliography: *Baumeister*, 67, 1970, no. 1, pp.
16/17; Gieselmann 1976, p. 31; Gieselmann 1987,
p. 109.

DEGEWO housing estate in Berlin-Frohnau
1967–69, project
Bibliography: Gieselmann 1976, p. 32; Gieselmann 1987, p. 111.

Church extension in Lengerich, Westphalia
1968, project
Competition

Extenson of the church of St. Martin, Starzach-
Bierlingen
1968/69, project
Competition
Bibliography: *Das Münster*, 24, 1971, no. 6, p. 383;
Gieselmann 1976, pp. 32, 61; Gieselmann 1987,
p. 110.

Housing estate in Bietigheim
1968/69, project
Competition, special prize

Rödiger house, Umkirch
Im Schenkenland
1968–71, project
Bibliography: Gieselmann 1976, pp. 32, 72/73;
Gieselmann 1987, p. 111.
pp. 64/65

Terraced housing estate in Müllheim, Baden
Am Zielberg
1968–71, project

School of nursing and students' residents in
Ellwangen (Jagst)
1969, project
Competition
Bibliography: *Baumeister*, 68, 1971, no. 1, p. 42;
Gieselmann 1976, pp. 32, 70; Gieselmann 1987,
p. 111.

BUWOG housing estate in Wien-Döbling
Peter-Jordan-Strasse 145–147
1969–73
Bibliography: Karl Schwanzer (ed.), *Wiener Bauten
1965–1975*, Vienna 1976, no. 187; Gieselmann
1976, pp. 77, 88/89; Gieselmann 1987, p. 112.
pp. 122–125

Urban planning for Wien-Süd
1970, project
Competition
(with Kunibert Gaugusch, Helmut Grasberger, Gernot Nalbach, Othmar Sackmauer, Klaus Semsroth
and Michael Wachberger, Vienna)
Bibliography: Gieselmann 1976, pp. 32, 74.

Redelopment of the old part of Karlsruhe
1970/71, project
Competition
(with Kunibert Gaugusch, Helmut Grasberger, Gernot Nalbach, Othmar Sackmauer, Klaus Semsroth
and Michael Wachberger, Vienna)
Bibliography: *Architekturforum*, 1971, no. 5, pp. 39
to 41; Gieselmann 1976, pp. 32, 75.

Parish centre in Stuttgart-Süd
1970/71, project
Competition
Bibliography: Gieselmann 1976, p. 76.

Dr. Gersuny-Bräkling housing estate, Konstanz
1970–72, project

Conversion of the Institut für Wohnbau at the
Technische Universität Wien
1971

Housing estate in Rastatt
Bahnhofstrasse
1971, project
Bibliography: Gieselmann 1976, pp. 76, 80/81;
Reinhard Gieselmann, *Wohnbau*, Braunschweig /
Wiesbaden 1979, p. 110; Gieselmann 1987, p. 112.

Parish centre in Wien-Stadlau
1971, project
Competition
Bibliography: Gieselmann 1976, pp. 76, 79; Gieselmann 1987, p. 111.

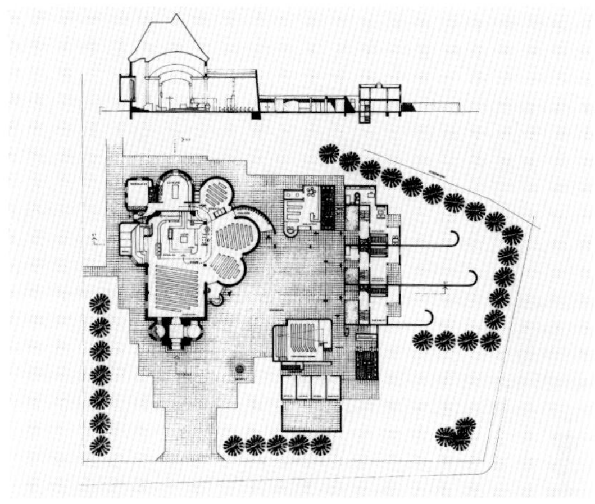

32. Redesign of the city center in Bruchsal-Unter-
grombach.
33. Church extension in Lengerich, Westphalia.
34. Urban-development plan for Wien-Süd.
35. Redeloment of the old part of Karlsruhe.
36. Parish center in Stuttgart-Süd.
37. Conversion of the Institut für Wohnbau at the
Technische Universität Wien.

32. Neugestaltung des Ortszentrums in Bruchsal-
Untergrombach.
33. Kirchenerweiterung in Lengerich, Westfalen.
34. Städtebauliche Planung für Wien-Süd.
35. Altstadtsanierung in Karlsruhe.
36. Kirchenzentrum in Stuttgart-Süd.
37. Umbau des Instituts für Wohnbau an der Technischen Universität Wien.

Gesamtoberschule und Zentrum des Märki-
schen Viertels, Berlin
1966, Projekt
Wettbewerb

Kirchenzentrum St. Anna, Münster, West-
falen
1966, Projekt
Wettbewerb
Literatur: *Architektur-Wettbewerbe*, 1968, Bd. 54,
S. XVII; Rainer Disse, *Kirchliche Zentren*, München
1974 (*Entwurf und Planung*, 24), S. 91.

Altenheim in Karlsruhe-Rintheim
1967, Projekt
Wettbewerb

Rathaus in Birkenfeld-Gräfenhausen
1967, Projekt
Wettbewerb

»Die Stadtstraße von Morgen«
1967, Projekt
Wettbewerb
(Städtebauliche Planung für die Kaiserstraße in
Karlsruhe, mit Gunnar Martinsson, Karlsruhe)

Neugestaltung des Ortszentrums in Bruchsal-
Untergrombach
1967–69, Projekt
Wettbewerb, erster Ankauf und Überarbeitung
Literatur: *Baumeister*, 67, 1970, Nr. 1, S. 16/17;
Gieselmann 1976, S. 31; Gieselmann 1987,
S. 109.

Wohnsiedlung der DEGEWO in Berlin-Frohnau
1967–69, Projekt
Literatur: Gieselmann 1976, S. 32; Gieselmann
1987, S. 111.

Kirchenerweiterung in Lengerich, Westfalen
1968, Projekt
Wettbewerb

Erweiterung der Kirche St. Martin, Starzach-
Bierlingen
1968/69, Projekt
Wettbewerb
Literatur: *Das Münster*, 24, 1971, Nr. 6, S. 383;
Gieselmann 1976, S. 32, 61; Gieselmann 1987,
S. 110.

Wohnanlage in Bietigheim
1968/69, Projekt
Wettbewerb, Sonderpreis

Haus Rödiger, Umkirch
Im Schenkenland
1968–71, Projekt
Literatur: Gieselmann 1976, S. 32, 72/73; Giesel-
mann 1987, S. 111.
S. 64/65

Reihenhauswohnanlage in Müllheim, Baden
Am Zielberg
1968–71, Projekt

Krankenpflegeschule und Schülerinnenwohn-
heim in Ellwangen (Jagst)
1969, Projekt
Wettbewerb
Literatur: *Baumeister*, 68, 1971, Nr. 1, S. 42; Gieselmann 1976, S. 32, 70; Gieselmann 1987, S. 111.

Wohnanlage der BUWOG in Wien-Döbling
Peter-Jordan-Straße 145–147
1969–73
Literatur: Karl Schwanzer (Hrsg.), *Wiener Bauten
1965–1975*, Wien 1976, Nr. 187; Gieselmann
1976, S. 77, 88/89; Gieselmann 1987, S. 112.
S. 122–125

Städtebauliche Planung für Wien-Süd
1970, Projekt
Wettbewerb
(mit Kunibert Gaugusch, Helmut Grasberger, Gernot
Nalbach, Othmar Sackmauer, Klaus Semsroth und
Michael Wachberger, Wien)
Literatur: Gieselmann 1976, S. 32, 74.

Sanierung der Altstadt von Karlsruhe
1970/71, Projekt
Wettbewerb
(mit Kunibert Gaugusch, Helmut Grasberger, Gernot
Nalbach, Othmar Sackmauer, Klaus Semsroth und
Michael Wachberger, Wien)
Literatur: *Architekturforum*, 1971, Nr. 5, S. 39–41;
Gieselmann 1976, S. 32, 75.

Kirchenzentrum in Stuttgart-Süd
1970/71, Projekt
Wettbewerb
Literatur: Gieselmann 1976, S. 76.

Wohnanlage Dr. Gersuny-Bräkling, Konstanz
1970–72, Projekt

Umbau des Instituts für Wohnbau an der Tech-
nischen Universität Wien
1971

Wohnanlage in Rastatt
Bahnhofstraße
1971, Projekt
Literatur: Gieselmann 1976, S. 76, 80/81; Reinhard
Gieselmann, *Wohnbau*, Braunschweig/Wiesbaden
1979, S. 110; Gieselmann 1987, S. 112.

Kirchenzentrum in Wien-Stadlau
1971, Projekt
Wettbewerb
Literatur: Gieselmann 1976, S. 76, 79; Gieselmann
1987, S. 111.

Wohn- und Atelierhaus Gieselmann, Wien-Neu-
stift
Sommerhaidenweg 57
1971–74
Literatur: Yukio Futagawa (Hrsg.), *Houses in Northern Europe*, Tokyo 1972 (Global Interio), S. 142 bis
145; *Baumeister*, 73, 1976, Nr. 6, S. 489–492; *ac
Internationale Asbestzement-Revue*, 1976, Nr. 82,
S. 44/45; Gieselmann 1976, S. 77, 96–98; *Deutsche Bauzeitschrift*, 25, 1977, Nr. 2, S. 175; *Ville e
Giardini*, 1977, Nr. 110, S. 22–27; *Architektur aktuell*,
11, 1977, Nr. 59, S. 32/33; *md möbel interior design*,
23, 1977, Nr. 2, S. 60–63; *Detail*, 1977, Nr. 6, S. 727
bis 729; Ernst Danz/Axel Menges, *Neue Kamine*.

Gieselmann residence and studio, Wien-Neustift
Sommerhaidenweg 57
1971–74
Bibliography: Yukio Futagawa (ed.), *Houses in Northern Europe*, Tokyo 1972 (Global Interior), pp. 142–145; *Baumeister*, 73, 1976, no. 6, pp. 489 to 492; *ac Internationale Asbestzement-Revue*, 1976, no. 82, pp. 44/45; Gieselmann 1976, pp. 77, 96 to 98; *Deutsche Bauzeitschrift*, 25, 1977, no. 2, p. 175; *Ville e Giardini*, 1977, no. 110, pp. 22–27; *Architektur aktuell*, 11, 1977, no. 59, pp. 32/33; *md möbel interior design*, 23, 1977, no. 2, pp. 60–63; *Detail*, 1977, no. 6, pp. 727–729; Ernst Danz / Axel Menges, *Neue Kamine. Technik, Material, Form*, Munich / Stuttgart 1979, pp. 102/103; Paulhans Peters / Ursula Henn, *Einfamilienhäuser*, Munich 1982 (*Entwurf und Planung, Wohnen*), pp. 20/21; Gieselmann 1987, pp. 70–72; *Yapi, a review published monthly by the building and industry center Istanbul*, 1991, no. 119, pp. 61–63.
pp. 66–71

Holiday village in Rohrmoos
1972, project
Bibliography: Gieselmann 1976, pp. 76, 85.

Housing estate in Karlsruhe-Hagsfeld
1972, project

Housing estate in Neustadt an der Weinstrasse
1972, project

Stepped houses in Baden-Baden
Konradin-Kreutzer-Strasse
1972/73, project
Bibliography: Christof Riccabona / Michael Wachberger, *Terrassenhäuser. Natürliche Terrassenbauformen, freie Terrassenbauformen, Terrassen als städtebauliches Element*, Munich 1972 (*Entwurf und Planung*, 14), p. 58; Gieselmann 1976, pp. 76, 86/87; Gieselmann 1987, p. 112.

Housing estate in Pirmasens
Adam-Müller-Strasse
1972/73, project
Bibliography: Gerhard Schwab, *Differenzierte Wohnanlagen. Internationale Beispiele, Informationsdaten in Bild und Text*, Stuttgart 1974, pp. 104–106; Gieselmann 1976, pp. 76, 82–84; Gieselmann 1987, p. 112.

Dr. Ludwig Pietzsch house, Karlsruhe-Durlach
Strählerweg
1972–78, project
Bibliography: Friedemann Wild, *Freistehende Einfamilienhäuser in Stadt, Vorstadt und Dorf*, Munich 1975 (*Entwurf und Planung*, 28), p. 122; Gieselmann 1976, pp. 78, 100–103; Gieselmann 1987, p. 115.

Housing estate in Weiden, Burgenland
1973/74, project

Multi-family house in Wien-Lainz
Versorgungsheimstrasse 15
1973–75

Conversion of an office and multi-family house in Wien-Mariahilf
Hirschengasse 6
1973–75, project
Bibliography: Gieselmann 1976, pp. 77, 90–92; Gieselmann 1987, p. 113.

Urban development of the Donauinsel, Vienna
1974, project
Competition, a prize
(with Günter Lautner, Peter Kopeinigg and Franz Schmid, Vienna)
Bibliography: *Der Aufbau, Fachschrift der Stadtbaudirektion Wien*, 29, 1974, no. 4, pp. 38/39; Gieselmann 1976, pp. 77, 94/95; Gieselmann 1987, p. 113.

Bellavista multi-family house, Wien-Alsergrund
Widerhoferplatz 4
1974, project

Adding a storey to the Haus zum Walfisch, Wien-Innere Stadt
Walfischgasse
1974/75, project
Bibliography: Gieselmann 1976, pp. 77, 93; Gieselmann 1987, p. 113.

Urban redevelopment at Siebenbürgerstrasse, Wien-Kagran
1974/75, project
Bibliography: *Mitteilungen der Heimstätten und Landesentwicklungsgesellschaften 1975*, no. 2, pp. 2–15; Gieselmann 1976, pp. 78, 106–109; Paulhans Peters, *Mehrgeschossige Wohnbauten*, Munich 1978 (*Entwurf und Planung*, 33), pp. 104–107; *Stadt*, 33, 1986, no. 1, pp. 44–47; *Wohnbau*, 1975, no. 4, pp. 20–26; *Beiträge zur Stadterneuerung der Architekten Falkner und Gieselmann*, ed. by Arbeitsgemeinschaft Praktische Stadterneuerung, exhibition catalogue, Vienna 1975, n. p.; *Der Aufbau, Fachschrift der Stadtbaudirektion Wien*, 31, 1976, no. 9–11, pp. 374–376; *Deutsche Bauzeitschrift*, 27, 1979, no. 7, p. 1094; Gieselmann 1987, p. 114.

Urban redevelopment at Eipeldauerstrasse, Wien-Kagran
1974/75, project
Bibliography: *Mitteilungen der Heimstätten und Landesentwicklungsgesellschaften 1972*, no. 2, pp. 2 to 15; *Der Aufbau, Fachschrift der Stadtbaudirektion Wien*, 31, 1976, no. 9–11, p. 377; Gieselmann 1976, pp. 78, 106, 110–115; *Baumeister*, 73, 1976, no. 1, pp. 56–59; Paulhans Peters, *Mehrgeschossige Wohnbauten*, Munich 1978 (*Entwurf und Planung*, 33), pp. 104–107; *Beiträge zur Stadterneuerung der Architekten Falkner und Gieselmann*, ed. by Arbeitsgemeinschaft Praktische Stadterneuerung Wien, exhibition catalogue, Vienna 1975, n. p.; Gieselmann 1987, p. 115.

Urban extension in Neumarkt am Wallersee, Upper Austria
1975, project
Competition
(with Günter Lautner and Peter Kopeinigg, Vienna)
Bibliography: Gieselmann 1976, pp. 78, 104/105; Gieselmann 1987, p. 114.

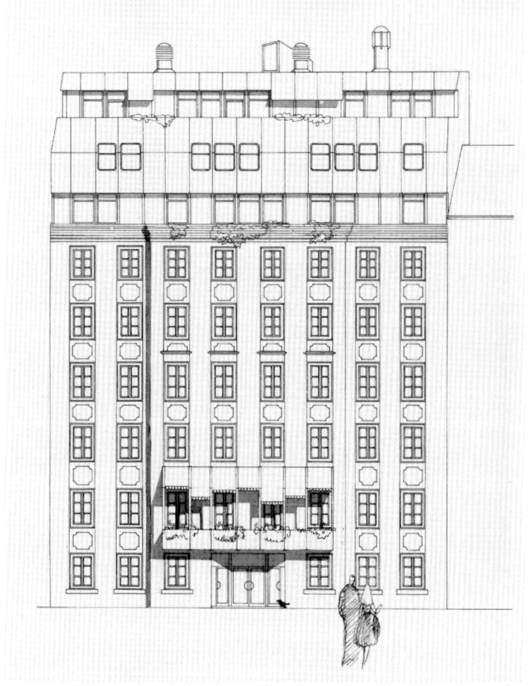

38. Housing estate in Pirmasens.
39. Conversion of an office and multi-family house in Wien-Mariahilf.
40. Adding a storey to the Haus zum Walfisch, Wien-Innere Stadt.
41. Urban redevelopment at Sicbenbürgerstrasse, Wien-Kagran.
42. Urban extension in Neumarkt am Wallersee, Upper Austria.

38. Wohnanlage in Pirmasens.
39. Aufstockung und Umbau eines Büro- und Mehrfamilienhauses in Wien-Mariahilf.
40. Aufstockung des Hauses zum Walfisch, Wien-Innere Stadt.
41. Stadterneuerung an der Siebenbürgerstraße, Wien-Kagran.
42. Ortserweiterung in Neumarkt am Wallersee, Oberösterreich.

Technik, Material, Form, München/Stuttgart 1979, S. 102/103; Paulhans Peters/Ursula Henn, *Einfamilienhäuser*, München 1982 (*Entwurf und Planung, Wohnen*), S. 20/21; Gieselmann 1987, S. 70–72; *Yapi, a review published monthly by the building and industry center Istanbul*, 1991, Nr. 119, S. 61–63.

S. 66–71

Feriensiedlung in Rohrmoos
1972, Projekt
Literatur: Gieselmann 1976, S. 76, 85.

Wohnanlage in Karlsruhe-Hagsfeld
1972, Projekt

Wohnanlage in Neustadt an der Weinstraße
1972, Projekt

Terrassenhäuser in Baden-Baden
Konradin-Kreutzer-Straße
1972/73, Projekt
Literatur: Christof Riccabona/Michael Wachberger, *Terrassenhäuser. Natürliche Terrassenbauformen, freie Terrassenbauformen, Terrassen als städtebauliches Element*, München 1972 (*Entwurf und Planung*, 14), S. 58; Gieselmann 1976, S. 76, 86/87; Gieselmann 1987, S. 112.

Wohnanlage in Pirmasens
Adam-Müller-Straße
1972/73, Projekt
Literatur: Gerhard Schwab, *Differenzierte Wohnanlagen. Internationale Beispiele, Informationsdaten in Bild und Text*, Stuttgart 1974, S. 104–106; Gieselmann 1976, S. 76, 82–84; Gieselmann 1987, S. 112.

Wohnhaus Dr. Ludwig Pietzsch, Karlsruhe-Durlach
Strählerweg
1972–78, Projekt
Literatur: Friedemann Wild, *Freistehende Einfamilienhäuser in Stadt, Vorstadt und Dorf*, München 1975 (*Entwurf und Planung*, 28), S. 122; Gieselmann 1976, S. 78, 100–103; Gieselmann 1987, S. 115.

Wohnhaussiedlung in Weiden, Burgenland
1973/74, Projekt

Mehrfamilienhaus in Wien-Lainz
Versorgungsheimstraße 15
1973–75

Aufstockung und Umbau eines Büro- und Mehrfamilienhauses in Wien-Mariahilf
Hirschengasse 6
1973–75, Projekt
Literatur: Gieselmann 1976, S. 77, 90–92; Gieselmann 1987, S. 113.

Städtebauliche Gestaltung der Donauinsel, Wien
1974, Projekt
Wettbewerb, ein Preis
(mit Günter Lautner, Peter Kopeinigg und Franz Schmid, Wien)
Literatur: *Der Aufbau, Fachschrift der Stadtbaudirektion Wien*, 29, 1974, Nr. 4, S. 38/39; Gieselmann 1976, S. 77, 94/95; Gieselmann 1987, S. 113.

Mehrfamilienhaus Bellavista, Wien-Alsergrund
Widerhoferplatz 4
1974, Projekt

Aufstockung des Hauses zum Walfisch, Wien-Innere Stadt
Walfischgasse
1974/75, Projekt
Literatur: Gieselmann 1976, S. 77, 93; Gieselmann 1987, S. 113.

Stadterneuerung an der Siebenbürgerstraße, Wien-Kagran
1974/75, Projekt
Literatur: *Mitteilungen der Heimstätten und Landesentwicklungsgesellschaften 1975*, Nr. 2, S. 2 bis 15; Gieselmann 1976, S. 78, 106–109; Paulhans Peters, *Mehrgeschossige Wohnbauten*, München 1978 (Entwurf und Planung, 33), S. 104–107; *Stadt*, 33, 1986, Nr. 1, S. 44–47; *Wohnbau*, 1975, Nr. 4, S. 20–26; *Beiträge zur Stadterneuerung der Architekten Falkner und Gieselmann*, hrsg. von der Arbeitsgemeinschaft Praktische Stadterneuerung, Ausstellungskatalog, Wien 1975, o. S.; *Der Aufbau, Fachschrift der Stadtbaudirektion Wien*, 31, 1976, Nr. 9 bis 11, S. 374–376; *Deutsche Bauzeitschrift*, 27, 1979, Nr. 7, S. 1094; Gieselmann 1987, S. 114.

Stadterneuerung an der Eipeldauerstraße, Wien-Kagran
1974/75, Projekt
Literatur: *Mitteilungen der Heimstätten und Landesentwicklungsgesellschaften 1972*, Nr. 2, S. 2–15; *Der Aufbau, Fachschrift der Stadtbaudirektion Wien*, 31, 1976, Nr. 9–11, S. 377; Gieselmann 1976, S. 78, 106, 110–115; *Baumeister*, 73, 1976, Nr. 1, S. 56 bis 59; Paulhans Peters, *Mehrgeschossige Wohnbauten,* München 1978 (*Entwurf und Planung*, 33), S. 104–107; *Beiträge zur Stadterneuerung der Architekten Falkner und Gieselmann*, hrsg. von der Arbeitsgemeinschaft Praktische Stadterneuerung Wien, Ausstellungskatalog, Wien 1975, o. S.; Gieselmann 1987, S. 115.

Ortserweiterung in Neumarkt am Wallersee, Oberösterreich
1975, Projekt
Wettbewerb
(mit Günter Lautner und Peter Kopeinigg, Wien)
Literatur: Gieselmann 1976, S. 78, 104/105; Gieselmann 1987, S. 114.

Umbau und Sanierung eines Biedermeierhauses in Wien-Brigittenau,
Lindengasse 49
1975/76, Projekt
Literatur: Gieselmann 1987, S. 114.

Stadterneuerung am Brigittaplatz, Wien-Brigittenau
1975–81, Projekt
Literatur: *Beiträge zur Stadterneuerung der Architekten Falkner und Gieselmann*, hrsg. von der Arbeitsgemeinschaft Praktische Stadterneuerung Wien, Ausstellungskatalog, Wien 1975, o. S.; *Der Aufbau, Fachschrift der Stadtbaudirektion Wien*, 31, 1976, Nr. 9–11, S. 374–375; Gieselmann 1976, S. 78, 106, 116/117; *Architektur + Wettbewerbe*, 1982, Bd. 112, S. 72/73; *Wohnbau*, 1983, Nr. 9, S. 122–124; Gieselmann 1987, S. 84–86; Friedrich Spengelin/Günter Nagel/Hans Luz, *Wohnen in den Städten*?

Conversion and renovation of a Biedermeier house in Wien-Brigittenau,
Lindengasse 49
1975/76, project
Bibliography: Gieselmann 1987, p. 114.

Urban renewal at Brigittaplatz, Wien-Brigittenau
1975–81, project
Bibliography: *Beiträge zur Stadterneuerung der Architekten Falkner und Gieselmann*, ed. by Arbeitsgemeinschaft Praktische Stadterneuerung Wien, exhibition catalogue, Vienna 1975, n. p.; *Der Aufbau, Fachschrift der Stadtbaudirektion Wien*, 31, 1976, no. 9–11, pp. 374–375; Gieselmann 1976, pp. 78, 106, 116/117; *Architektur + Wettbewerbe*, 1982, vol. 112, S. 72/73; *Wohnbau*, 1983, no. 9, pp. 122–124; Gieselmann 1987, pp. 84–86; Friedrich Spengelin/Günter Nagel/Hans Luz, *Wohnen in den Städten? Stadtgestalt, Stadtstruktur, Bauform, Wohnform, Wohnumfeld*, exhibition catalogue, Berlin 1984, p. 152; *Wiener Wohnbau, Wirklichkeiten*, ed. by the city of Vienna and the Ingenieurkammer für Wien, Niederösterreich und Burgenland, exhibition catalogue, Vienna 1985, p. 279; Karl Ludwig, *Wohnhöfe – Hofräume. Gestaltung, Nutzung, Bepflanzung*, Munich 1987, p. 172; Gieselmann 1987, p. 115.
pp. 126–129

Conversion of the Gieselmann house, Karlsruhe
Stephanienstrasse 50
1976, project

College of technology in Salzburg
1976, project
Competition
(with Günter Lautner and Peter Kopeinigg, Vienna)

Design of the Hameaustrasse pedestrian area, Wien-Neustift
1976, project
Competition, 1st prize
(with Rupert Falkner, Vienna)

Maternushaus archiepiscopal conference center, Cologne
1977, project
Competition, 2nd prize

Extension and redevelopment of the Heilig-Geist-Kirche, Markgröningen
1977–81
Bibliography: *Prolegomena, Arbeitsblätter des Instituts für Wohnbau und Entwerfen an der Technischen Universität Wien*, 1978, no. 26, pp. 39–43; *Baumeister*, 76, 1979, no. 4, pp. 353–355; *Bauwelt*, 73, 1982, no. 37, pp. 1572/1573; *Spitalkirche zum Heiligen Geist Markgröningen von 1297 bis 1981. 45 Jahre Heilig-Geist-Gemeinde 28. Juli 1957 – 28. Juli 1982*, Markgröningen n. d. (1982); *a+u Architecture and Urbanism*, 1983, no. 154, pp. 69–75; *Architektur-Wettbewerbe*, 1983, vol. 115, p. 32; *Deutsche Bauzeitschrift*, 31, 1983, no. 9, pp. 1185–1188; *Architektur aktuell*, 17, 1983, no. 96, pp. 58/59; *Heilige Kunst, Mitgliedsgabe des Kunstvereins der Diözese Rottenburg-Stuttgart, Jahrbuch 21*, 1982/83, pp. 93–95; Kurt Hoffmann/Gretl Hoffmann, *Architekturführer Stuttgart und Umgebung*, Stuttgart 1983 (3rd ed.), no. 229; *Glasforum*, 34, 1984, no. 1, pp. 28–32; *Beton-Prisma*, 1984, no. 46, pp. 16/17; *Kunst und Kirche*, 48, 1985, no. 1, pp. 38/39; Paul Kopf, *Die Entwicklung der Katholischen Kirche im Landkreis Ludwigsburg. Aufbau und Ausbau 1945–1985*, Ludwigsburg 1986, p. 15; Gieselmann 1987, pp. 64–68, 117; Paul Kopf/Wolfgang Urban, *Zeit-Räume. Katholischer Kirchenbau und religiöse Kunst im Landkreis Ludwigsburg 1945–1990*, Ulm 1990, pp. 60/61, 66–69; Heinz Tiefenbacher/Wolfgang Urban/Egon Reiner, *Raum schaffen für Gott. Kirchenbau und religiöse Kunst in der Diözese Rottenburg-Stuttgart*, Ulm 1992, p. 216.
pp. 160–163

Parish center in Tettnang
1978, project
Competition, 1st acquisition
Bibliography: *Prolegomena, Arbeitsblätter des Instituts für Wohnbau und Entwerfen an der Technischen Universität Wien*, 1978, no. 26, pp. 44/45.

Garden of the Cardinal Höffner residence, Cologne
1978/79
Bibliography: Gieselmann 1987, p. 115.
pp. 72–75

Housing estate of the city of Vienna in Wien-Ottakring
Neumayrgasse 7–9, Herbststrasse 13, Schinnaglgasse 8–12
1978–85
Bibliography: Paulhans Peters, *Mehrgeschossige Wohnbauten*, Munich 1978 (*Entwurf und Planung*, 33), pp. 104–107; Peter Marchart, *Wohnbau in Wien 1923–1983*, Vienna 1984, p. 249; *Wiener Wohnbau, Wirklichkeiten*, ed. by the city of Vienna and the Ingenieurkammer für Wien, Niederösterreich und Burgenland, exhibition catalogue, Vienna 1985, p. 254; *Baumeister*, 84, 1987, no. 7, pp. 44–47; Gieselmann 1987, pp. 87–92, 118; *Steinmetz und Bildhauer*, 1989, no. 5, p. 84; *Yapi, a review published monthly by the building and industry center Istanbul*, 1991, no. 115, p. 55.

Library of the Technische Universität Wien, Wien-Wieden
1978–87
(Floor plan, interior design and furniture; design of the façade: Justus Dahinden, Zurich/Vienna; Haustechnik und Koordination: Marchart, Möbius & Partner, Vienna)
Bibliography: *Schul- und Sportstättenbau, Zeitschrift des Österreichischen Institutes für Schul- und Sportstättenbau*, 19, 1983, no. 3, pp. 122–124; *Mitteilungen der Vereinigung Österreichischer Bibliothekare*, 36, 1983, no. 2, pp. 36–43; *Der Aufbau, Fachschrift der Stadtbaudirektion Wien*, 40, 1985, no. 7/8, pp. 456/457; Josef Wawrosch (ed.), *Der Neubau der Universitätsbibliothek der Technischen Universität Wien. Zur festlichen Übergabe des Gebäudes am 17. Dezember 1987*, Vienna 1987; Gieselmann 1987, p. 118; *Bauforum*, 21, 1988, no. 125, pp. 34–38; Josef Wawrosch (ed.), *Festschrift zur Eröffnung des neuen Gebäudes der Universitätsbibliothek der Technischen Universität Wien*, Vienna 1988 (*Biblos-Schriften*, 145), pp. 73–76; *Architektur der DDR*, 38, 1989, no. 12, p. 51; *Steinmetz und Bildhauer*, 1989, no. 12, pp. 9–12; *Baumeister*, 86, 1989, no. 9, pp. 27–31; *Deutsche Bauzeitschrift*, 39, 1991, no. 1, pp. 77–80; *Yapi, a review*

43. Maternushaus archiepiscopal conference center, Cologne.
44. Housing estate of the city of Vienna in Wien-Ottakring.
45. »Landmark«, Melbourne, Australia.

43. Erzbischöfliches Tagungszentrum Maternus-haus, Köln.
44. Wohnanlage der Gemeinde Wien, Wien-Ottakring.
45. »Landmark«, Melbourne, Australien.

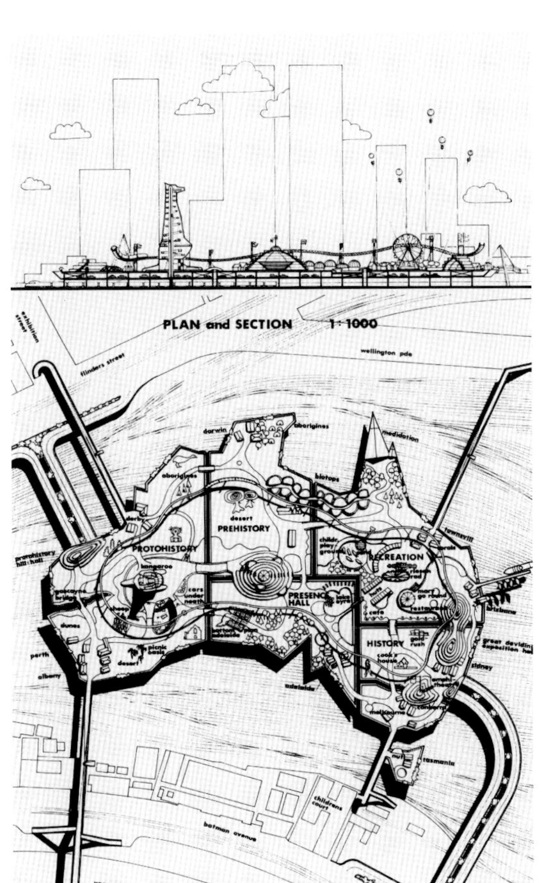

Stadtgestalt, Stadtstruktur, Bauform, Wohnform, Wohnumfeld, Ausstellungskatalog, Berlin 1984, S. 152; *Wiener Wohnbau, Wirklichkeiten*, hrsg. von der Stadt Wien, Geschäftsgruppe Stadterneue-rung und Stadtentwicklung, Magistratsabteilung 19, Stadtgestaltung, und der Ingenieurkammer für Wien, Niederösterreich und Burgenland, Ausstellungska-talog, Wien 1985, S. 279; Karl Ludwig, *Wohnhöfe – Hofräume. Gestaltung, Nutzung, Bepflanzung*, Mün-chen 1987, S. 172; Gieselmann 1987, S. 115.
S. 126–129

Umbau des Gartenhauses Gieselmann, Karls-ruhe
Stephanienstraße 50
1976, Projekt

Höhere Technische Lehranstalt in Salzburg
1976, Projekt
Wettbewerb
(mit Günter Lautner und Peter Kopeinigg, Wien)

Gestaltung der Fußgängerzone Hameaustraße, Wien-Neustift
1976, Projekt
Wettbewerb, 1. Preis
(mit Rupert Falkner, Wien)

Erzbischöfliches Tagungszentrum Maternus-haus, Köln
1977, Projekt
Wettbewerb, 2. Preis

Erweiterung und Sanierung der Heilig-Geist-Kirche, Markgröningen
1977–81
Literatur: *Prolegomena, Arbeitsblätter des Instituts für Wohnbau und Entwerfen an der Technischen Universität Wien*, 1978, Nr. 26, S. 39–43; *Baumeis-ter*, 76, 1979, Nr. 4, S. 353–355; *Bauwelt*, 73, 1982, Nr. 37, S. 1572/1573; *Spitalkirche zum Heiligen Geist Markgröningen von 1297 bis 1981. 45 Jahre Heilig-Geist-Gemeinde 28. Juli 1957 – 28. Juli 1982*, Markgröningen o. J. (1982); *a+u Architecture and Urbanism*, 1983, Nr. 154, S. 69–75; *Architektur + Wettbewerbe*, 1983, Bd. 115, S. 32; *Deutsche Bau-zeitschrift*, 31, 1983, Nr. 9, S. 1185–1188; *Architektur aktuell*, 17, 1983, Nr. 96, S. 58/59; *Heilige Kunst, Mitgliedsgabe des Kunstvereins der Diözese Rot-tenburg-Stuttgart*, Jahrbuch 21, 1982/1983, S. 93 bis 95; Kurt Hoffmann/Gretl Hoffmann, *Architektur-führer Stuttgart und Umgebung*, Stuttgart 1983 (3. Auflage), Nr. 229; *Glasforum*, 34, 1984, Nr. 1, S. 28 bis 32; *Beton-Prisma*, 1984, Nr. 46, S. 16/17; *Kunst und Kirche*, 48, 1985, Nr. 1, S. 38/39; Paul Kopf, *Die Entwicklung der Katholischen Kirche im Land-kreis Ludwigsburg. Aufbau und Ausbau 1945 bis 1985*, Ludwigsburg 1986, S. 15; Gieselmann 1987, S. 64–68, 117; Paul Kopf/Wolfgang Urban, *Zeit-Räume. Katholischer Kirchenbau und religiöse Kunst im Landkreis Ludwigsburg 1945–1990*, Ulm 1990, S. 60/61, 66–69; Heinz Tiefenbacher/Wolf-gang Ur-ban/Egon Reiner, *Raum schaffen für Gott. Kirchenbau und religiöse Kunst in der Diözese Rot-tenburg-Stuttgart*, Ulm 1992, S. 216.
S. 160–163

Kirchenzentrum in Tettnang
1978, Projekt
Wettbewerb, 1. Ankauf
Literatur: *Prolegomena, Arbeitsblätter des Instituts für Wohnbau und Entwerfen an der Technischen Universität Wien*, 1978, Nr. 26, S. 44/45.

Garten der Residenz von Kardinal Höffner, Köln
1978/79
Literatur: Gieselmann 1987, S. 115.
S. 72–75

Wohnanlage der Gemeinde Wien in Wien-Ottakring
Neumayrgasse 7–9, Herbststraße 13, Schinnagl-gasse 8–12
1978–85
Literatur: Paulhans Peters, *Mehrgeschossige Wohn-bauten*, München 1978 (*Entwurf und Planung*, 33), S. 104–107; Peter Marchart, *Wohnbau in Wien 1923–1983*, Wien 1984, S. 249; *Wiener Wohn-bau, Wirklichkeiten*, hrsg. von der Stadt Wien, Ge-schäftsgruppe Stadterneuerung und Stadtentwick-lung, Magistratsabteilung 19, Stadtgestaltung, und der Ingenieurkammer für Wien, Niederösterreich und Burgenland, Ausstellungskatalog, Wien 1985, S. 254; *Baumeister*, 84, 1987, Nr. 7, S. 44–47; Gie-selmann 1987, S. 87–92, 118; *Steinmetz und Bild-hauer*, 1989, Nr. 5, S. 84; *Yapi, a review published monthly by the building and industry center Istanbul*, 1991, Nr. 115, S. 55.

Bibliothek der Technischen Universität Wien, Wien-Wieden
1978–87
(Grundriß, Innengestaltung und Möblierung; Fas-sadengestaltung: Justus Dahinden, Zürich/Wien; Haustechnik und Koordination: Marchart, Möbius & Partner, Wien)
Literatur: *Schul- und Sportstättenbau, Zeitschrift des Österreichischen Institutes für Schul- und Sportstättenbau*, 19, 1983, Nr. 3, S. 122–124; *Mit-teilungen der Vereinigung Österreichischer Bibliothe-kare*, 36, 1983, Nr. 2, S. 36–43; *Der Aufbau, Fach-schrift der Stadtbaudirektion Wien*, 40, 1985, Nr. 7/8, S. 456/457; Josef Wawrosch (Hrsg.), *Der Neu-bau der Universitätsbibliothek der Technischen Uni-versität Wien. Zur festlichen Übergabe des Gebäu-des am 17. Dezember 1987*, Wien 1987; Giesel-mann 1987, S. 118; *Bauforum*, 21, 1988, Nr. 125, S. 34–38; Josef Wawrosch (Hrsg.), *Festschrift zur Eröffnung des neuen Gebäudes der Universitäts-bib-liothek der Technischen Universität Wien*, Wien 1988 (*Biblos-Schriften*, 145), S. 73–76; *Architektur der DDR*, 38, 1989, Nr. 12, S. 51; *Steinmetz und Bildhauer*, 1989, Nr. 12, S. 9–12; *Baumeister*, 86, 1989, Nr. 9, S. 27–31; *Deutsche Bauzeitschrift*, 39, 1991, Nr. 1, S. 77–80; *Yapi, a review published monthly by the building and industry center Istanbul*, 1991, Nr. 115, S. 51; *Yapi, a review published month-ly by the building and industry center Istanbul*, 1991, Nr. 119, S. 70–72.
S. 144–151

»Landmark«, Melbourne, Australien
1979, Projekt
Wettbewerb
Literatur: Gieselmann 1987, S. 116.

published monthly by the building and industry center Istanbul, 1991, no. 115, p. 51; *Yapi, a review published monthly by the building and industry center Istanbul*, 1991, no. 119, pp. 70–72.
pp. 144–151

»Landmark«, Melbourne, Australia
1979, project
Competition
Bibliography: Gieselmann 1987, pp. 116.

Museum in Rottweil
1979, project
Competition

DEGEWO housing estate in Berlin-Buckow
1980, project
Competition
Bibliography: Gieselmann 1987, p. 116.

Conversion of the interior of the church of St. Othmar, Wien-Mödling
1980, project

Dewald studio, Karlsruhe-Grötzingen
An der Silbergrub 5a
1980
Bibliography: Gieselmann 1987, pp. 95–99, 104.

BUWOG multi-family house in Wien-Wieden
Karlsgasse, project
1980
Bibliography: Gieselmann 1987, p. 116.

Parish centre in Heilbronn-Biberach
1981, project
Competition, 2nd prize
Bibliography: *Architektur + Wettbewerbe*, 1983, vol. 115, p. 70; Gieselmann 1987, p. 117.

Anthroposophical old-age home in Wien-Mauer
1981/82, project
Bibliography: *Bauwelt*, 74, 1983, no. 30/31, pp. 1170–1172; Gieselmann 1987, p. 116.

Leberberg urban expansion, Wien-Simmering
1981–94
(with Ernst Heiß, Josef Krawina, Ernst Plischke, Michael Wachberger and Fritz Weber, Vienna)
Bibliography: *Deutsche Bauzeitschrift*, 45, 1997, no. 12, pp. 89–96; Gieselmann 1987, p. 117.
pp. 130/131

»Donaustadt 2000«, Wien-Kagran
1982, project
Competition
(with Dieter Bökermann and Michael Hofstetter, Vienna)

Parish house in Petronell-Carnuntum, Lower Austria
1982/83
Bibliography: *Baumeister*, 81, 1984, no. 11, pp. 58 to 61; *Architektur aktuell*, 18, 1984, no. 100, pp. 34/35; *Deutsche Bauzeitschrift*, 33, 1985, no. 9, pp. 1099–1102; *Bauwelt*, 77, 1986, no. 3, p. 66–69; *a+u Architecture and Urbanism*, 1986, no. 190, p. 63–66; Gieselmann 1987, pp. 74–77, 117.
pp. 76–79

Apartment block and shopping center in the Draschegründe, Wien-Favoriten
1983–88
Competition, 2nd prize
Bibliography: Peter Marchart, *Wohnbau in Wien 1923–1983*, Vienna 1984, p. 262; *Wettbewerbe*, 1985, no. 47/48, pp. 30/31; *Wohnbau*, 1985, no. 7/8, pp. 50/56; *Architektur aktuell*, 24, 1990, no. 135, pp. 55–64; *Yapi, a review published monthly by the building and industry center Istanbul*, 1991, no. 119, pp. 67–69; Gieselmann 1987, p. 118.
pp. 132–135

Conversion of the Dewald house, Karlsruhe-Grötzingen
An der Silbergrub 5a
1984
Bibliography: Gieselmann 1987, pp. 95–98, 104; *Yapi, a review published monthly by the building and industry center Istanbul*, 1991, no. 119, pp. 64–66.

Redesign of the inner courtyards of the Technische Universität Wien, Wien-Wieden
1984, project
Competition, one of five identical prizes
(with Werner Stolfa, Vienna)

Urban renewal in the Karmeliterviertel, Wien-Leopoldstadt
1984/85, project
Competition, a 1st prize
(with Werner Stolfa and Konrad Schermann, Vienna)
Bibliography: *Wettbewerbe*, 1985, no. 47/48, pp. 30/31; *Wohnbau*, 1985, no. 7/8, pp. 50–56; *Der Aufbau, Fachschrift der Stadtbaudirektion Wien*, 40, 1985, no. 7/8, p. 439; *Wiener Wohnbau, Wirklichkeiten*, ed. by the city of Vienna and the Ingenieurkammer für Wien, Niederösterreich und Burgenland, exhibition catalogue, Vienna 1985, pp. 238/239; Gieselmann 1987, p. 118.
pp. 136–139

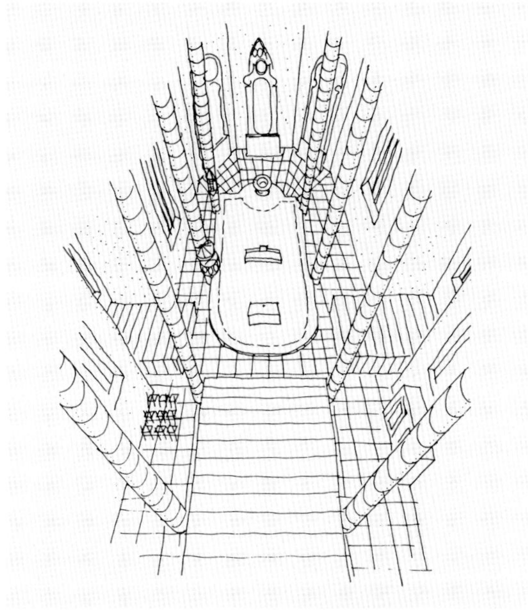

Attic addition for the Anthroposophische Gesellschaft, Wien-Favoriten
Tilgnerstrasse 3
1985, project

Wohnquartier und Bundesamtsgebäude in Wien-Landstrasse
Rennweg
c. 1985, project
Competition
(with Peter Ortner, Vienna)

Conversion of the Doris David house, Markgröningen
Wettegasse 17
1985–87

Extension of the church of St. Valentin am Forst, Landschach, Lower Austria
1986–90
Bibliography: *Deutsche Bauzeitschrift*, 37, 1989, no. 8, p. 1008; *St. Valentin 1990. Festschrift zur Wiedereröffnung der Pfarrkirche St. Valentin nach Erweiterung und Restaurierung und zur Weihe des neuen Altares*, n. p., n. d. (1990); *Architektur aktuell*, 25, 1991, no. 144, pp. 26–28; *Baumeister*, 88, 1991, no. 3, pp. 42–45; *Kunst und Kirche*, 55, 1992, no. 1, pp. 36–39; *Glasforum*, 43, 1993, no. 3, pp. 31–34; *Deutsche Bauzeitschrift*, 46, 1998, no.

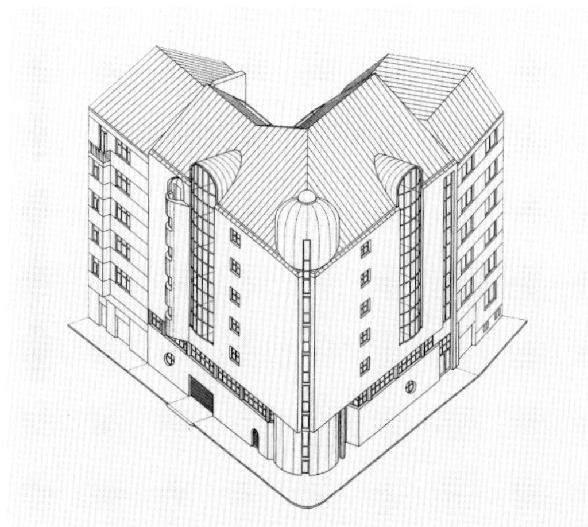

Museum in Rottweil
1979, Projekt
Wettbewerb

Siedlung der DEGEWO in Berlin-Buckow
1980, Projekt
Wettbewerb
Literatur: Gieselmann 1987, S. 116.

**Umgestaltung des Innenraums der Kirche
St. Othmar, Wien-Mödling**
1980, Projekt

Atelierhaus Dewald, Karlsruhe-Grötzingen
An der Silbergrub 5a
1980
Literatur: Gieselmann 1987, S. 95–99, 104.

Mehrfamilienhaus der BUWOG in Wien-Wieden
Karlsgasse, Projekt
1980
Literatur: Gieselmann 1987, S. 116.

Kirchenzentrum in Heilbronn-Biberach
1981, Projekt
Wettbewerb, 2. Preis
Literatur: *Architektur + Wettbewerbe*, 1983, Bd. 115,
S. 70; Gieselmann 1987, S. 117.

Anthroposophisches Altersheim in Wien-Mauer
1981/82, Projekt
Literatur: *Bauwelt*, 74, 1983, Nr. 30/31, S. 1170
bis 1172; Gieselmann 1987, S. 116.

Stadterweiterung Leberberg, Wien-Simmering
1981–94
(mit Ernst Heiß, Josef Krawina, Ernst Plischke,
Michael Wachberger und Fritz Weber, Wien)
Literatur: *Deutsche Bauzeitschrift*, 45, 1997, Nr. 12,
S. 89–96; Gieselmann 1987, S. 117.
S. 130/131

»Donaustadt 2000«, Wien-Kagran
1982, Projekt
Wettbewerb
(mit Dieter Bökemann und Michael Hofstetter, Wien)

**Pfarrhof in Petronell-Carnuntum, Niederöster-
reich**
1982/83
Literatur: *Baumeister*, 81, 1984, Nr. 11, S. 58–61;
Architektur aktuell, 18, 1984, Nr. 100, S. 34/35;
Deutsche Bauzeitschrift, 33, 1985, Nr. 9, S. 1099
bis 1102; *Bauwelt*, 77, 1986, Nr. 3, S. 66–69; *a+u
Architecture and Urbanism*, 1986, Nr. 190, S. 63
bis 66; Gieselmann 1987, S. 74–77, 117.
S. 76–79

**Wohnblock und Einkaufszentrum im Gebiet
Draschegründe, Wien-Favoriten**
1983–88
Wettbewerb, 2. Preis
Literatur: Peter Marchart, *Wohnbau in Wien 1923
bis 1983*, Wien 1984, S. 262; *Wettbewerbe*, 1985,
Nr. 47/48, S. 30/31; *Wohnbau*, 1985, Nr. 7/8,
S. 50/56; *Architektur aktuell*, 24, 1990, Nr. 135,
S. 55–64; *Yapi, a review published monthly by the
building and industry center Istanbul*, 1991, Nr. 119,
S. 67–69; Gieselmann 1987, S. 118.
S. 132–135

**Umbau des Hauses Dewald, Karlsruhe-Grötzin-
gen**
An der Silbergrub 5a
1984
Literatur: Gieselmann 1987, S. 95–98, 104; *Yapi,
a review published monthly by the building and
industry center Istanbul*, 1991, Nr. 119, S. 64–66.

**Neugestaltung der Innenhöfe der Technischen
Universität Wien, Wien-Wieden**
1984, Projekt
Wettbewerb, einer von fünf gleichen Preisen
(mit Werner Stolfa, Wien)

**Stadterneuerung im Karmeliterviertel, Wien-
Leopoldstadt**
1984/85, Projekt
Wettbewerb, ein 1. Preis
(mit Werner Stolfa und Konrad Schermann, Wien)
Literatur: *Wettbewerbe*, 1985, Nr. 47/48, S. 30/31;
Wohnbau, 1985, Nr. 7/8, S. 50–56; *Der Aufbau,
Fachschrift der Stadtbaudirektion Wien*, 40, 1985,
Nr. 7/8, S. 439; *Wiener Wohnbau, Wirklichkeiten*,
hrsg. von der Stadt Wien, Geschäftsgruppe Stadterneuerung und Stadtentwicklung, Magistratsabteilung 19, Stadtgestaltung, und der Ingenieurkammer
für Wien, Niederösterreich und Burgenland, Ausstellungskatalog, Wien 1985, S. 238/239; Gieselmann
1987, S. 118.
S. 136–139

**Dachausbau für die Anthroposophische Gesell-
schaft, Wien-Favoriten**
Tilgnerstraße 3
1985, Projekt

**Wohnquartier und Bundesamtsgebäude in
Wien-Landstraße**
Rennweg
um 1985, Projekt
Wettbewerb
(mit Peter Ortner, Wien)

Umbau des Hauses Doris David, Markgröningen
Wettegasse 17
1985–87

**Erweiterung der Kirche St. Valentin am Forst,
Landschach, Niederösterreich**
1986–90
Literatur: *Deutsche Bauzeitschrift*, 37, 1989, Nr. 8,
S. 1008; *St. Valentin 1990. Festschrift zur Wiedereröffnung der Pfarrkirche St. Valentin nach Erweite-
rung und Restaurierung und zur Weihe des neuen
Altares*, o. O., o. J. (1990); *Architektur aktuell*, 25,
1991, Nr. 144, S. 26–28; *Baumeister*, 88, 1991,
Nr. 3, S. 42–45; *Kunst und Kirche*, 55, 1992, Nr. 1,
S. 36–39; *Glasforum*, 43, 1993, Nr. 3, S. 31–34;
Deutsche Bauzeitschrift, 46, 1998, Nr. 6, S. 121–124;
*10 Jahre. Beispiele aus der Denkmalpflege von
1986 bis 1996*, Wien 1996 (*Denkmalpflege in Niederösterreich*, 17), S. 47; *Umbauten, Zubauten*,
St. Pölten 1997 (*Denkmalpflege in Niederöster-
reich*, 19), S. 24.
S. 164–167

Gestaltung des Bahnhofvorplatzes in Salzburg
1987, Projekt
Wettbewerb
Literatur: *Architektur + Wettbewerbe*, 1987, Bd. 132,
S. 50/51.

6, pp. 121–124; *10 Jahre. Beispiele aus der Denkmalpflege von 1986 bis 1996*, Vienna 1996 (*Denkmalpflege in Niederösterreich*, 17), p. 47; *Umbauten,
Zubauten*, St. Pölten 1997 (*Denkmalpflege in Nie-
derrösterreich*, 19), p. 24.
pp. 164–167

Design of the railway-station square in Salzburg
1987, project
Competition
Bibliography: *Architektur + Wettbewerbe*, 1987, vol.
132, pp. 50/51.

Episcopal museum in the Karmeliterkirche,
Rottenburg am Neckar
1988, project
Competition, 1st prize ex aequo

Conversion of the interior of the cathedral of
St. Eberhard, Stuttgart
1988, project
Competition

Heilig-Kreuz-Kirche, Ravensburg-Sonnen-
büchel
1989, project
Competition, purchase

Multi-family house of the city of Vienna in
Wien-Leopoldstadt
Im Werd 4
1989–93
Bibliography: Ernst Helmar Zwick (ed.): *Entwürfe
für Wien 1989. Architektur zu aktuellen Stadtfragen*, exhibition catalogue, Vienna 1989, pp. 46/47;
*Wohnbau aktuell, Jahresbericht 1992, Geschäfts-
gruppe Wohnbau und Stadterneuerung, Magistratsabteilung 24, Städtischer Wohnhausbau*, Vienna
1993, pp. 98/99; *Architekturjournal Wettbewerbe*,
17, 1993, no. 125/126, pp. 67–72; Friederike Schneider (ed.), *Grundrißatlas Wohnungsbau*, Basel 1997
(2nd ed.), p. 88.
pp. 136–139

Conversion and extension of the convent church
of St. Georg am Hang, Maselheim-Heggbach,
Upper Svabia
1989–93
Bibliography: *Heilige Kunst, Mitgliedsgabe des
Kunstvereins der Diözese Rottenburg-Stuttgart*,
Jahrbuch 25, 1992/1993, pp. 186–193; *Deutsche
Bauzeitschrift*, 46, 1998, no. 6, pp. 125/126.
pp. 168–171

Extension of the parish church of St. Blasius,
Maselheim, Upper Svabia
1990, project
Competition

Catholic church with presbytery and urban-
development plan for a residential area in
Mössingen, Württemberg
1990, project
Competition

Multi-family house of the city of Vienna in Wien-
Leopoldstadt
Große Schiffgasse 32
1990/91
Bibliography: *Wohnbau aktuell, Jahresbericht 1992,
Geschäftsgruppe Wohnbau und Stadterneuerung,*

Magistratsabteilung 24, Städtischer Wohnhausbau,
Vienna 1993, pp. 94/95.

Multi-family house of the city of Vienna in Wien-
Leopoldstadt
Große Schiffgasse 30
1991–93
Bibliography: *Wohnbau aktuell, Jahresbericht 1992,
Geschäftsgruppe Wohnbau und Stadterneuerung,
Magistratsabteilung 24, Städtischer Wohnhausbau*,
Vienna 1993, pp. 96/97; *Architekturjournal Wettbe-
werbe*, 17, 1993, no. 125/126, pp. 67–72.

Conversion of the Dr. Haas house, Wien-Neustift
Sommerhaidenweg 59
1991–94
Bibliography: *Trend, das österreichische Wirtschaftsmagazin. Spezial, Der beste Weg zum Haus*, 1995,
no. 1, pp. 34/35.

Leberberg Catholic church, Wien-Simmering
1992/93, project
(with Anna Stern and Franz Zeyer, Stuttgart)

Dylla house, Stuttgart-Heslach
Pfaffenweg 37
1993, project

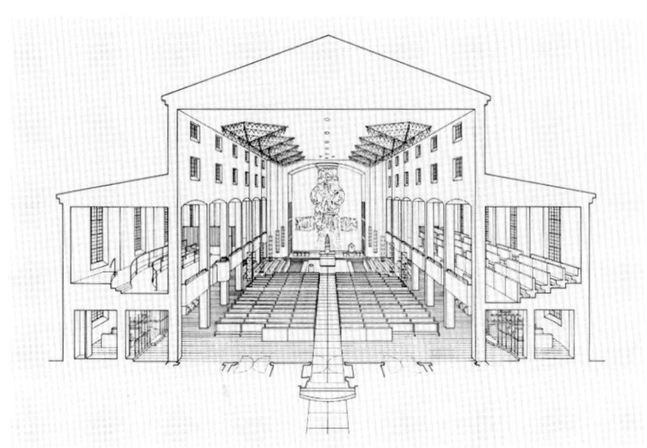

Apartment block in Leberberg, Wien-Simmering
Leberberg, Block 9D
(with Anna Stern and Franz Zeyer, Stuttgart)
1993–96
Bibliography: *Deutsche Bauzeitschrift*, 45, 1997, no.
12, pp. 89–96; *Wohnbau aktuell, Jahresbericht
1995/1996, Geschäftsgruppe Wohnbau und Stadterneuerung, Magistratsabteilung 24, Städtischer
Wohnhausbau*, Vienna 1997, pp. 26/27; *Architekturjournal Wettbewerbe*, 22, 1998, no. 173–174, pp.
138/139.
pp. 140–143

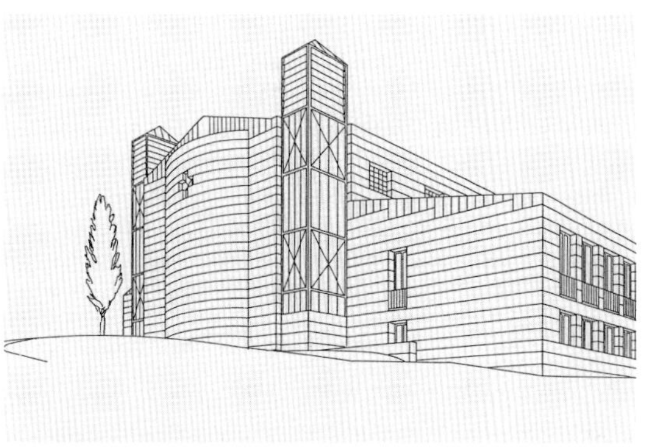

Conversion and extension of the church of
St. Martinus, Schwaigern
1994–97
(with Anna Stern, Stuttgart)
Bibliography: *Deutsche Bauzeitschrift*, 46, 1998, no.
6, p. 121; *Heilige Kunst, Mitgliedsgabe des Kunstvereins der Diözese Rottenburg-Stuttgart*, *Jahrbuch
31*, 1999/2000, p. 243.
pp. 172–175

Conversion and extension of the church of
St. Michael zu den Wengen, Ulm
(with Anna Stern, Stuttgart)
1994–98
Bibliography: *Heilige Kunst, Mitgliedsgabe des
Kunstvereins der Diözese Rottenburg-Stuttgart*,
Jahrbuch 30, 1997/98, p. 173; *Heilige Kunst, Mitgliedsgabe des Kunstvereins der Diözese Rottenburg-Stuttgart*, *Jahrbuch 31*, 1999/2000, S. 243;
*St. Michael zu den Wengen. Kirche in der Mitte
der Stadt*, ed. by Katholische Kirchengemeinde
St. Michael zu den Wengen, Ulm 2004.
pp. 176–179

51. Episcopal museum in the Karmeliterkirche, Rottenburg am Neckar.
52. Conversion of the interior of the cathedral of St. Eberhard, Stuttgart.
53. Heilig-Kreuz-Kirche, Ravensburg-Sonnen-büchel.
54. Multi-family house of the city of Vienna in Wien-Leopoldstadt.

51. Diözesanmuseum in der Karmeliterkirche, Rottenburg am Neckar.
52. Umgestaltung des Innenraums der Domkirche St. Eberhard, Stuttgart.
53. Heilig-Kreuz-Kirche, Ravensburg-Sonnen-büchel.
54. Mehrfamilienhaus der Gemeinde Wien in Wien-Leopoldstadt.

Collaborators / Mitarbeiter 1954–98

Gerd Bauer, Stanley Bertheaud, Alfred Bosch, Martin Botsch, Berthold Bubner, Robert Bundy, Ortrud Bürk, Rosemarie Burkhardt, Hanno Chef, Wolfgang Döring, Horst Elsässer, Peter Fritz, Josef Fürstl, Cosmas Gozali, Wolfgang Graeser, Josef Grösswang, Werner Hackermüller, Peter Hass, Sabine Hengge, Gerald Holy, Peter Huber, Peter Hudritsch, Ulf Hüttner, Adam Kanner, Herbert Keck, Peter Kielinger, Hans Kollhoff, Peter Kopeinigg, Thomas Krämer, Günter Lautner, Friedrich Lehmann, William John Marshall, Johannes Matern, Zlatan Medugorac, Klaus Müllner, Takekazu Murayama, Gernot Nalbach, Albert Nikolaus, Gottfried Nobl, Peter Ortner, Gottfried Pasour, Horst Raabe, Ernest Reichert, Hugo Reißner, Hans Sachsse, Albrecht Scherer, Konrad Schermann, Franz Schmid, Meinrad Schnurr, Robert Schranz, Karl-Georg Schreck, Waltraud Schreck, Michael Schreger, Hubert Schultheiß, Walter Schulz, Peter Skowronek, August Steinlesberger, Werner Stolfa, Klaus Sye, Ute Sye-Kirchner, Josef Tasar, Paolo Tenaglia, Peter Treitl, Ivo Vañhamme, Svetislav Velkov, Hans-Peter Waldenberger, Friedrich Waltz, Peter Wiedemair, Dagmar Wörn, Monika Zanik

Diözesanmuseum in der Karmeliterkirche, Rottenburg am Neckar
1988, Projekt
Wettbewerb, 1. Preis ex aequo

Umgestaltung des Innenraums der Domkirche St. Eberhard, Stuttgart
1988, Projekt
Wettbewerb

Heilig-Kreuz-Kirche, Ravensburg-Sonnen-büchel
1989, Projekt
Wettbewerb, Ankauf

Mehrfamilienhaus der Gemeinde Wien in Wien-Leopoldstadt
Im Werd 4
1989–93
Literatur: Ernst Helmar Zwick (Hrsg.): *Entwürfe für Wien 1989. Architektur zu aktuellen Stadtfragen*, Ausstellungskatalog, Wien 1989, S. 46/47; *Wohnbau aktuell, Jahresbericht 1992, Geschäftsgruppe Wohnbau und Stadterneuerung, Magistratsabteilung 24, Städtischer Wohnhausbau*, Wien 1993, S. 98/99; *Architekturjournal Wettbewerbe*, 17, 1993, Nr. 125/126, S. 67–72; Friederike Schneider (Hrsg.), *Grundrißatlas Wohnungsbau*, Basel 1997 (2. Auflage), S. 88.
S. 136–139

Umbau und Erweiterung der Klosterkirche St. Georg am Hang, Maselheim-Heggbach, Oberschwaben
1989–93
Literatur: *Heilige Kunst, Mitgliedsgabe des Kunstvereins der Diözese Rottenburg-Stuttgart, Jahrbuch 25*, 1992/1993, S. 186–193; *Deutsche Bauzeitschrift*, 46, 1998, Nr. 6, S. 125/126.
S. 168–171

Erweiterung der Pfarrkirche St. Blasius, Maselheim, Oberschwaben
1990, Projekt
Wettbewerb

Katholische Kirche mit Pfarrhaus und städtebauliche Planung für ein Wohngebiet in Mössingen, Württemberg
1990, Projekt
Wettbewerb

Mehrfamilienhaus der Gemeinde Wien in Wien-Leopoldstadt
Große Schiffgasse 32
1990/91
Literatur: *Wohnbau aktuell, Jahresbericht 1992, Geschäftsgruppe Wohnbau und Stadterneuerung, Magistratsabteilung 24, Städtischer Wohnhausbau*, Wien 1993, S. 94/95.

Mehrfamilienhaus der Gemeinde Wien in Wien-Leopoldstadt
Große Schiffgasse 30
1991–93
Literatur: *Wohnbau aktuell, Jahresbericht 1992, Geschäftsgruppe Wohnbau und Stadterneuerung, Magistratsabteilung 24, Städtischer Wohnhausbau*, Wien 1993, S. 96/97; *Architekturjournal Wettbewerbe*, 17, 1993, Nr. 125/126, S. 67–72.

Umbau des Hauses Dr. Haas, Wien-Neustift
Sommerhaidenweg 59
1991–94
Literatur: *Trend, das österreichische Wirtschaftsmagazin. Spezial, Der beste Weg zum Haus*, 1995, Nr. 1, S. 34/35.

Katholische Kirche Leberberg, Wien-Simmering
1992/93, Projekt
(mit Anna Stern und Franz Zeyer, Stuttgart)

Haus Dylla, Stuttgart-Heslach
Pfaffenweg 37
1993, Projekt

Wohnblock im Gebiet Leberberg, Wien-Simmering
Leberberg, Block 9D
1993–96
(mit Anna Stern und Franz Zeyer, Stuttgart)
Literatur: *Deutsche Bauzeitschrift*, 45, 1997, Nr. 12, S. 89–96; *Wohnbau aktuell, Jahresbericht 1995/1996, Geschäftsgruppe Wohnbau und Stadterneuerung, Magistratsabteilung 24, Städtischer Wohnhausbau*, Wien 1997, S. 26/27; *Architekturjournal Wettbewerbe*, 22, 1998, Nr. 173–174, S. 138/139.
S. 140–143

Umbau und Erweiterung der Kirche St. Martinus, Schwaigern
1994–97
(mit Anna Stern, Stuttgart)
Literatur: *Deutsche Bauzeitschrift*, 46, 1998, Nr. 6, S. 121; *Heilige Kunst, Mitgliedsgabe des Kunstvereins der Diözese Rottenburg-Stuttgart, Jahrbuch 31*, 1999/2000, S. 243.
S. 172–175

Umbau und Erweiterung der Kirche St. Michael zu den Wengen, Ulm
1994–98
(mit Anna Stern, Stuttgart)
Literatur: *Heilige Kunst, Mitgliedsgabe des Kunstvereins der Diözese Rottenburg-Stuttgart, Jahrbuch 30*, 1997/1998, S. 173; *Heilige Kunst, Mitgliedsgabe des Kunstvereins der Diözese Rottenburg-Stuttgart, Jahrbuch 31*, 1999/2000, S. 243; *St. Michael zu den Wengen. Kirche in der Mitte der Stadt*, hrsg. von der Katholischen Kirchengemeinde St. Michael zu den Wengen, Ulm 2004.
S. 176–179

Publications by Reinhard Gieselmann

Books

Kirchenbau, Zurich 1960 (with Werner Aebli).
Neue Kirchen, Stuttgart / London 1972.
Wohnbau, Braunschweig / Wiesbaden 1979.
Architektur ist ein Element für die Sinne. Bauten und Schriften, Stuttgart 1987.
Sanierungshandbuch Wohnungsbau. Probleme, Lösungen, Kosten, Düsseldorf 1994 (ed. by Reinhard Gieselmann, Anna Stern and Franz Zeyer). Based on a research work, realized by Anna Stern.
Wohnbau, Entwicklungen. Wohnen, Wohnung, Wohnhaus, Wohnungsbau, ed. by Anna Stern, Düsseldorf 1998.

Research reports

Organisationsformen und Strategien der Stadterneuerung, commissioned by Österreichisches Bundesministeriums für Bauten und Technik, Vienna 1973 (with Klaus Becker, Hans Grasberger, Heinz Tesar).
Analyse des Wohnbaus, commissioned by Krupp-Stahlbau, Berlin 1975 (with Michael Wachberger).
Prolegomena, Arbeitsblätter des Instituts für Wohnbau und Entwerfen an der Technischen Universität Wien, Vienna 1972–92 (publication of 60 issues and 3 special issues with the collaboration of the assistants of the institute).

Texts on architecture (selection)

»Diskussion um Frank Lloyd Wright, Brief an den Herausgeber«, *Baukunst und Werkform*, 5, 1952, no. 6/7, pp. 82/83.
»Zu Bruce Goff, Brief an den Herausgeber«, *Baukunst und Werkform*, 6, 1953, no. 9, pp. 447/448.
»Die Lehre vom Afunktionalismus«, *Baukunst und Werkform*, 7, 1954, no. 6, p. 323.
»X. Triennale Mailand. Ein Bericht von Reinhard Gieselmann und Oswald Mathias Ungers«, *Baukunst und Werkform*, 7, 1954, no. 10, pp. 589–595.
»Ein Beitrag zur Abklärung des Habitat« (with Werner Aebli, Theo Manz, Beppo Merkle, Basel), *Werk*, 41, 1954, no. 1, pp. 8–14.
»Reise zu Alvar Aalto«, *Bauen und Wohnen*, 9, 1954, no. 3, pp. 119–124.
»Nieuwe Kerkbouw in Duitsland«, *Streven*, 1955, no. 11/12, pp. 430–436.
»Parallele Entwicklungen?«, *Baukunst und Werkform*, 9, 1956, no. 2, p. 58.
»Das heiße Eisen«, *Baukunst und Werkform*, 9, 1956, no. 9, pp. 463/464.
»Gestern heute morgen«, *Bauwelt*, 51, 1960, no. 11, p. 287.
»Ein Werkstattbericht«, *Bauwelt*, 51, 1960, no. 14, p. 369.
»Gegen den Akademismus in der Architektur«, *Bauwelt*, 52, 1961, no. 2, pp. 29, 32.
»Für eine lebendige Baukunst«, *Bauwelt*, 52, 1961, no. 22, pp. 621, 624.
»Zu einer neuen Architektur« (with Oswald Mathias Ungers), *Der Monat*, no. 174, März 1963, p. 96.

»Vom Geist des lebendigen Gestaltens«, *Werk und Zeit*, 12, 1963, no. 11/12, p. 4.
»Arroganz auf höherer Ebene«, *Deutsche Bauzeitung*, 68, 1963, no. 11, pp. 919/920.
»›Mobiler‹ Städtebau«, *Bauwelt*, 54, 1963, no. 7, pp. 182, 198.
»Zum Thema Hallenschulen«, *Bauwelt*, 55, 1964, no. 46, pp. 1268/1269.
»Manifest zu einer neuen Architektur«, in: Ulrich Conrads (ed.), *Programme und Manifeste zur Architektur des 20. Jahrhunderts*, Gütersloh / Berlin / Munich 1964 (*Bauwelt Fundamente*, 1), pp. 158/159.
»Städtebau in der Krise«, *Deutsche Bauzeitung*, 70, 1965, no. 3, p. 170.
»Zu einer Tagung des Deutschen Werkbunds in Baden-Württemberg«, *Bauwelt*, 57, 1966, no. 32, pp. 914/915.
»Für eine strukturelle Bauordnung«, *Bauwelt*, 57, 1966, no. 49, pp. 1439–1442.
Review of Ot Hoffmann und Christoph Repenthin, *Neue urbane Wohnformen. Gartenhofhäuser, Teppichsiedlungen, Terrassenhäuser*, Berlin 1966, *Deutsche Bauzeitung*, 102, 1968, no. 1, p. 60.
Review of Karl Wilhelm Schmitt, *Mehrgeschossiger Wohnbau*, Stuttgart 1966, *Deutsche Bauzeitung*, 102, 1968, no. 1, p. 64.
»Eine Kirche ist eine Kirche«, *Architektur-Wettbewerbe*, 1968, vol. 54, pp. XVII–XVIII
»Hommage à Billing«, *Bauen und Wohnen*, 24, 1969, no. 7, pp. VII, 3–4.
»Die Welt ist voller neuer Farben, Reflexionen«, *I-Punkt Farbe*, 1969, no. 4, pp. 63/64.
»Architektur ist ein Element für die Sinne«, *Werk und Zeit*, 18, 1969, no. 8, p. 4.
»Die Identifikation von Räumen«, Vienna 1969 (*Antrittsvorlesungen der Technischen Hochschule in Wien*, 9).
»Bauten der Weltausstellung in Osaka«, *Detail*, 1970, no. 5, pp. 1019–1023.
»So baut man heute für die Zukunft«, *Die Presse* (Vienna), April 2, 1971.
»Wohnbau für Wien und Krems«, *Informationen, Technische Hochschule Wien*, 2, 1971, no. 1, pp. 40–42.
»Architektur als Basis – Anmerkungen zu Änderung und Dauer des Architektenberufs, Einführungsvorlesung«, *Detail*, 1972, no. 5, pp. 907/908.
»20 Jahre Wohnbau in Mitteleuropa«, *Der Aufbau, Fachschrift der Stadtbaudirektion Wien*, 27, 1972, no. 9/10, pp. 362–365.
»Imagination, Inspiration, Intuition«, *Prolegomena, Arbeitsblätter des Instituts für Wohnbau und Entwerfen an der Technischen Universität Wien*, 1973, no. 4, p. 37.
»Beyond beauty«, *Prolegomena, Arbeitsblätter des Instituts für Wohnbau und Entwerfen an der Technischen Universität Wien*, 1973, no. 5, p. 2.
»Die Stelle der Technologie – Provokante Marginalien«, *Porös, Arbeitsblätter des Lehrstuhls für Baukonstruktion 2, Architekturabteilung, Technische Hochschule Aachen*, 1, 1974, no. 0, p. 6.
»Grundsatzüberlegungen zum Heimbau«, *Der Architekt*, 23, 1974, no. 5, pp. 114–117.
»Institut für Wohnbau und Entwerfen 3«, *Österreichische Hochschulzeitung*, 25, 1973, no. 14, pp. 28 to 30.
»Des Kaisers neue Kleider«, *Kunst und Kirche*, 36, 1973, no. 3, pp. 150–153.

Review of Gottlieb Merkle, *Kirchenbau im Wandel*, *Das Münster*, 26, 1973, no. 3, pp. 217 to 218, and *Kunst und Kirche*, 27, 1974, no. 3, p. 162.
»Die Sendung der Kirche«, *Kunst und Kirche*, 28, 1975, no. 3, p. 21.
»Architektenausbildung an der TU Wien«, *Architektur aktuell*, 9, 1975, no. 45, pp. 38/39.
»Relative Architektur«, *Prolegomena, Arbeitsblätter des Instituts für Wohnbau und Entwerfen an der Technischen Universität Wien*, 1975, no. 15, pp. 4–7.
»Römerbergecke«, *Baumeister*, 72, 1975, no. 8, pp. 680/681.
»Junge Architekten sollen Gründerzeitviertel retten«, *Wohnbau*, 1975, no. 5, pp. 16–23.
»Ein Nachwort zu Habitat«, *Konstruktiv, Zeitschrift der Bundes-Ingenieurkammer*, 1976, no. 36, pp. 16/17.
»Leitideen des städtischen Wohnbaus«, *Österreichische Hochschulzeitung*, 29, 1977, no. 7/8, pp. I–V.
»Sponsionsrede für die Diplomanden der Studienrichtung Bauingenieurwesen an der TU Wien«, *Der Architekt*, 25, 1976, no. 1, p. 8.
»Beiträge zur Stadterneuerung«, *Der Aufbau, Fachschrift der Stadtbaudirektion Wien*, 31, 1976, no. 1/2, pp. 2/3.
»Ein Berufungsverfahren an der TU Wien«, *Der Architekt*, 26, 1977, no. 3, p. 6.
»Begräbnis erster Klasse, Gutachten im Auftrag der Stadtgemeinde Klagenfurt«, *Wohnbau*, 1977, no. 7, pp. 28–30.
»Ein Flakturm in Architektur verpackt«, *Wohnbau*, 1977, no. 1, pp. 18–26.
»Erotik und Architekten«, *Der Architekt*, 26, 1977, no. 6, p. 231.
»Architektonische Entwicklung des Kommunalen Wohnhausbaus im Wien der Zweiten Republik«, in: Karl Mang (ed.), *Kommunaler Wohnbau in Wien*, exhibition catalogue, Vienna 1978, pp. 7–16.
»Leitideen des Wohnungsbaues«, *Deutsche Bauzeitschrift*, 26, 1978, no. 6, pp. 811–814.
»Spielarten nach funktionaler Architektur«, *Konstruktiv, Zeitschrift der Bundes-Ingenieurkammer*, 1978, no. 52, p. 4.
»Nur wer es besser kann, werfe den ersten Stein«, *Bauwelt*, 69, 1978, no. 13, p. 501.
»Ai Margini della Citta«, *Ville e Giardini*, 1979, no. 3, pp. 12–17.
»Wohnen heute, eine Bestandsaufnahme mit Folgerungen«, *Bau im Spiegel, Architektur und Bau, Installation*, 8, spring / summer 1979, pp. 10 to 16.
»Prolegomena-Preis 1979, Rede von Prof. Dr. Reinhard Gieselmann«, *Architektur aktuell*, 1979, no. 75, p. 6.
»Wohnbau in Wien von Otto Wagner bis heute« (with Günter Lautner, Rudolf Szedenik), *Deutsche Bauzeitschrift*, 27, 1979, no. 7, pp. 1087–1097.
»Die Entwicklung der Wiener Stadtgestalt, *Architektur aktuell*, 14, 1980, no. 77, pp. 27–32.
»Stadterneuerung«, *Bau im Spiegel, Architektur und Bau, Installation*, 9, spring / summer 1980, pp. 11–22.
»Europa Nostra 1980, Kongreß – auch über Verwendungsmöglichkeiten alter Gebäude«, *Der Aufbau, Fachschrift der Stadtbaudirektion Wien*, 35, 1980, no. 11, pp. 352/353.

»Kirchenbaugeschichte nach 1945«, in: Rainer Bürgel (ed.): *Bauen mit Geschichte*, Gütersloh 1980 (*Dokumentation über den evangelischen Kirchenbautag*, 17), pp. 36–48.

»Viyana'da konut mimarisi, Otto Wagner, den günnümüze« (with Günter Lautner, Rudolf Szedenik), *Yapi, a review published monthly by the building and industry center Istanbul*, 1980, no. 37, pp. 42 to 48.

»Die Fassade als neue Aufgabe«, *Bau im Spiegel, Architektur und Bau, Installation*, 10, spring/summer 1981, pp. 45–50.

»Über Bruno Taut«, *Der Aufbau, Fachschrift der Stadtbaudirektion Wien*, 36, 1981, no. 10, pp. 377/378.

»Solides Design«, *Architektur aktuell*, 15, 1981, no. 86, p. 15.

»Fassaden-Entwicklungen«, *Deutsche Bauzeitschrift*, 30, 1982, no. 7, pp. 1003–1006.

»Bericht eines Deutschen aus Wien«, *Bauwelt*, 73, 1982, no. 3, pp. 92/93.

»Yeni bir Görv olarak Cephe« (Fassade – eine neue Disziplin), *Yapi, a review published monthly by the building and industry center Istanbul*, 1982, no. 46, pp. 23/24, 30–38.

»Wohnbau heute«, *Modul, Werkbericht Atelier Architekt Prof. Karl Schwanzer*, 1983, no. 17, pp. 2/3.

»Entwicklungstendenzen des modernen Kirchenbaues, *Architektur + Wettbewerbe*, 1983, vol. 115, pp. 3–7.

»Ricardo Bofill«, *Der Aufbau, Fachschrift der Stadtbaudirektion Wien*, 38, 1983, no. 9/10, p. 396.

»Moderne Architektur in Japan«, *Deutsche Bauzeitschrift*, 32, 1984, no. 9, pp. 1167–1171.

»Defilee im Abteil. Die besondere Betreuung bei einer Bahnreise nach Budapest«, *Die Zeit*, no. 23, 1. 6. 1984, p. 51.

»Ricardo Bofill oder die Toleranz«, *Glasforum*, 34, 1984, no. 1, p. 7.

»Neue Entwicklungen im Wiener Wohnbau«, in: Viktor Hufnagl/Erich Schlöss (ed.), *Reflexionen und Aphorismen zur österreichischen Architektur*, Vienna 1984, pp. 367/368.

»Aus Vorträgen, Vorlesungen und Veröffentlichungen«, in: Viktor Hufnagl/Erich Schlöss (ed.), *Reflexionen und Aphorismen zur österreichischen Architektur*, Vienna 1984, pp. 582–587.

»Höherer Wohnwert durch bauliche und funktionale Nutzung«, in: Friedrich Spengelin/Günter Nagel/Hans Luz, *Wohnen in den Städten? Stadtgestalt, Stadtstruktur, Bauform, Wohnform, Wohnumfeld*, exhibition catalogue Akademie der Künste, Berlin 1984, p. 152.

»Architektur – ihre Zukunft in Europa«, *Der Architekt*, 34, 1985, no. 1, p. 15.

»Tadao Ando, Architekt des Minimalismus«, *Architektur aktuell*, 19, 1985, no. 105, pp. 46–47.

»Zum Entwurf des Stadtentwicklungsplans Wien vom November 1984«, *Der Aufbau, Fachschrift der Stadtbaudirektion Wien*, 1985, no. 5/6, pp. 330/331.

»Stadterneuerung«, *Deutsche Bauzeitschrift*, 33, 1985, no. 10, pp. 1299–1305.

»Stadterneuerung – Blickwinkel Wien«, *Stadt*, 1986, no. 1, pp. 44–47.

»Innerstädtischer Wohnbau in Wien« (with Werner Stolfa), *Architektur + Wettbewerbe*, 1986, vol. 126, pp. 2–4.

»Anarchisches Bauen – Anarchische Architektur«, *Deutsche Bauzeitschrift*, 35, 1987, no. 11, pp. 1413–1417.

»Auf der Suche nach Stil«, *Prolegomena, Arbeitsblätter des Instituts für Wohnbau und Entwerfen an der Technischen Universität Wien*, 1987, no. 57, pp. 3–25.

»Stadterweiterung und Stadtreparatur nach dem Zweiten Weltkrieg«, in: Karl Mang/Peter Marchart (ed.), *Wohnen in der Stadt, Ideen für Wien*, Vienna 1989, pp. 37–47.

»Kirchenbau – der Stand der Dinge«, *Deutsche Bauzeitschrift*, 37, 1989, no. 8, pp. 1007–1013.

»Wohnbau in Göteborg 1990«, in: Magistrat der Stadt Linz, Baurechtsamt und Planungsamt (ed.), *Stadterneuerung, Methoden und Beispiele*, Linz n. d. (1991), pp. 26–33.

»Käse mit Löchern. Interview von Christoph Mandl«, *Solidarität*, 1990, no. 712, pp. 13–16.

»Erich Boltenstern 1896–1991«, *Architektur aktuell*, 25, 1991, no. 145, pp. 11/12.

»Metamorphosen des Fertigteilbaues«, *Deutsche Bauzeitschrift*, 39, 1991, pp. 77–80.

»Zo pacht Zweden de systeembouw aan«, *De Bouwwereld*, 87, 1991, no. 21, pp. 36–38.

»Experimenteller Wohnbau in Bayern«, *Architekturjournal Wettbewerbe*, 1991, no. 103/104, pp. 162 to 165.

»Wiener Stil«, *Deutsche Bauzeitschrift*, 40, 1992, no. 9, pp. 1285–1289.

»Der Pluralismus als Gestaltungsprinzip. Reinhard Gieselmann im Gespräch mit Patricia Zacek«, *Architektur & Bauforum*, 1992, no. 152, pp. 86 to 91.

»Kelch und Mikrophon«, in: Heinz Tiefenbacher/Wolfgang Urban/Egon Reiner, *Raum schaffen für Gott, Kirchenbau und religiöse Kunst in der Diözese Rottenburg-Stuttgart*, Ulm 1992, pp. 114 to 125.

»Die Wand – Versuch über ein Architekturelement«, *Deutsche Bauzeitschrift*, 42, 1994, no. 3, pp. 93 to 104.

»Entwicklung des Wohnungsgrundrisses, die Organisation der Wohnung, Grundrißidee«, in: Friederike Schneider (ed.), *Grundrißatlas Wohnungsbau*, Basel/Boston/Vienna, 1994, pp. 13–25.

»Zur Sanierung von Wohnanlagen«, *Deutsche Bauzeitschrift*, 43, 1995, no. 7, pp. 137–143.

»Grenzgänge der Architektur. Ein Aufsatz über die Grenzen der Erfaßbarkeit«, *Deutsche Bauzeitschrift*, 44, 1996, no. 8, pp. 99–105.

Review of Peter Faller, *Der Wohnungsgrundriß. Entwicklungslinien 1920–1990. Schlüsselprojekte, Funktionsstudien*, Stuttgart 1996, *Kursiv, Literaturblatt der Bauwelt*, 1996, no. 28, S. 12.

Review of Gert Kähler (ed.), *Geschichte des Wohnens, vol. 4, 1918–1945. Reform, Reaktion, Zerstörung*, Stuttgart 1996, *Kursiv, Literaturblatt der Bauwelt*, 1996, no. 28, pp. 16–17.

»Modernisierung von Kirchen«, *Deutsche Bauzeitschrift*, 46, 1998, no. 6. pp. 121–126.

»Was ist Baukunst?«, *Raumeister*, 99, 2002, no. 12, p. 4.

Publikationen von Reinhard Gieselmann

Buchveröffentlichungen

Kirchenbau, Zürich 1960 (mit Werner Aebli).
Neue Kirchen, Stuttgart / London 1972.
Wohnbau, Braunschweig / Wiesbaden 1979.
Architektur ist ein Element für die Sinne. Bauten und Schriften, Stuttgart 1987.
Sanierungshandbuch Wohnungsbau. Probleme, Lösungen, Kosten, Düsseldorf 1994 (hrsg. von Reinhard Gieselmann, Anna Stern und Franz Zeyer). Basierend auf einer Forschungsarbeit, durchgeführt von Anna Stern.
Wohnbau, Entwicklungen. Wohnen, Wohnung, Wohnhaus, Wohnungsbau, hrsg. von Anna Stern, Düsseldorf 1998.

Forschungsberichte

Organisationsformen und Strategien der Stadterneuerung, im Auftrag des Österreichischen Bundesministeriums für Bauten und Technik, Wien 1973 (mit Klaus Becker, Hans Grasberger, Heinz Tesar).
Analyse des Wohnbaus, im Auftrag der Firma Krupp-Stahlbau, Berlin 1975 (mit Michael Wachberger).
Prolegomena, Arbeitsblätter des Instituts für Wohnbau und Entwerfen an der Technischen Universität Wien, Wien 1972–1992 (Herausgabe von 60 Heften und 3 Extraheften unter Mitarbeit der Institutsassistenten).

Texte zur Architektur (Auswahl)

»Diskussion um Frank Lloyd Wright, Brief an den Herausgeber«, *Baukunst und Werkform*, 5, 1952, Nr. 6/7, S. 82/83.
»Zu Bruce Goff, Brief an den Herausgeber«, *Baukunst und Werkform*, 6, 1953, Nr. 9, S. 447/448.
»Die Lehre vom Afunktionalismus«, *Baukunst und Werkform*, 7, 1954, Nr. 6, S. 323.
»X. Triennale Mailand. Ein Bericht von Reinhard Gieselmann und Oswald Mathias Ungers«, *Baukunst und Werkform*, 7, 1954, Nr. 10, S. 589–595.
»Ein Beitrag zur Abklärung des Habitat« (mit Werner Aebli, Theo Manz, Beppo Merkle, Basel), *Werk*, 41, 1954, Nr. 1, S. 8–14.
»Reise zu Alvar Aalto«, *Bauen und Wohnen*, 9, 1954, Nr. 3, S. 119–124.
»Nieuwe Kerkbouw in Duitsland«, *Streven*, 1955, Nr. 11/12, S. 430–436.
»Parallele Entwicklungen?«, *Baukunst und Werkform*, 9, 1956, Nr. 2, S. 58.
»Das heiße Eisen«, *Baukunst und Werkform*, 9, 1956, Nr. 9, S. 463/464.
»Gestern heute morgen«, *Bauwelt*, 51, 1960, Nr. 11, S. 287.
»Ein Werkstattbericht«, *Bauwelt*, 51, 1960, Nr. 14, S. 369.
»Gegen den Akademismus in der Architektur«, *Bauwelt*, 52, 1961, Nr. 2, S. 29, 32.
»Für eine lebendige Baukunst«, *Bauwelt*, 52, 1961, Nr. 22, S. 621, 624.
»Zu einer neuen Architektur« (mit Oswald Mathias Ungers), *Der Monat*, Nr. 174, März 1963, S. 96.

»Vom Geist des lebendigen Gestaltens«, *Werk und Zeit*, 12, 1963, Nr. 11/12, S. 4.
»Arroganz auf höherer Ebene«, *Deutsche Bauzeitung*, 68, 1963, Nr. 11, S. 919/920.
»›Mobiler‹ Städtebau«, *Bauwelt*, 54, 1963, Nr. 7, S. 182, 198.
»Zum Thema Hallenschulen«, *Bauwelt*, 55, 1964, Nr. 46, S. 1268/1269.
»Manifest zu einer neuen Architektur«, in: Ulrich Conrads (Hrsg.), *Programme und Manifeste zur Architektur des 20. Jahrhunderts*, Gütersloh / Berlin / München 1964 (*Bauwelt Fundamente*, 1), S. 158/159.
»Städtebau in der Krise«, *Deutsche Bauzeitung*, 70, 1965, Nr. 3, S. 170.
»Zu einer Tagung des Deutschen Werkbunds in Baden-Württemberg«, *Bauwelt*, 57, 1966, Nr. 32, S. 914/915.
»Für eine strukturelle Bauordnung«, *Bauwelt*, 57, 1966, Nr. 49, S. 1439–1442.
Besprechung von Ot Hoffmann und Christoph Repenthin, *Neue urbane Wohnformen. Gartenhofhäuser, Teppichsiedlungen, Terrassenhäuser*, Berlin 1966, *Deutsche Bauzeitung*, 102, 1968, Nr. 1, S. 60.
Besprechung von Karl Wilhelm Schmitt, *Mehrgeschossiger Wohnbau*, Stuttgart 1966, *Deutsche Bauzeitung*, 102, 1968, Nr. 1, S. 64.
»Eine Kirche ist eine Kirche«, *Architektur-Wettbewerbe*, 1968, Bd. 54, S. XVII–XVIII.
»Hommage à Billing«, *Bauen und Wohnen*, 24, 1969, Nr. 7, S. VII 3–4.
»Die Welt ist voller neuer Farben, Reflexionen«, *I-Punkt Farbe*, 1969, Nr. 4, S. 63/64.
»Architektur ist ein Element für die Sinne«, *Werk und Zeit*, 18, 1969, Nr. 8, S. 4.
»Die Identifikation von Räumen«, Wien 1969 (*Antrittsvorlesungen der Technischen Hochschule in Wien*, 9).
»Bauten der Weltausstellung in Osaka«, *Detail*, 1970, Nr. 5, S. 1019–1023.
»So baut man heute für die Zukunft, *Die Presse* (Wien), 2. April 1971.
»Wohnbau für Wien und Krems«, *Informationen, Technische Hochschule Wien*, 2, 1971, Nr. 1, S. 40–42.
»Architektur als Basis – Anmerkungen zu Änderung und Dauer des Architektenberufs, Einführungsvorlesung«, *Detail*, 1972, Nr. 5, S. 907/908.
»20 Jahre Wohnbau in Mitteleuropa«, *Der Aufbau, Fachschrift der Stadtbaudirektion Wien*, 27, 1972, Nr. 9/10, S. 362–365.
»Imagination, Inspiration, Intuition«, *Prolegomena, Arbeitsblätter des Instituts für Wohnbau und Entwerfen an der Technischen Universität Wien*, 1973, Nr. 4, S. 37.
»Beyond beauty«, *Prolegomena, Arbeitsblätter des Instituts für Wohnbau und Entwerfen an der Technischen Universität Wien*, 1973, Nr. 5, S. 2.
»Die Stelle der Technologie – Provokante Marginalien«, *Porös, Arbeitsblätter des Lehrstuhls für Baukonstruktion 2, Architekturabteilung, Technische Hochschule Aachen*, 1, 1974, Nr. 0, S. 6.
»Grundsatzüberlegungen zum Heimbau«, *Der Architekt*, 23, 1974, Nr. 5, S. 114–117.
»Institut für Wohnbau und Entwerfen 3«, *Österreichische Hochschulzeitung*, 25, 1973, Nr. 14, S. 28 bis 30.
»Des Kaisers neue Kleider«, *Kunst und Kirche*, 36, 1973, Nr. 3, S. 150–153.

Besprechung von Gottlieb Merkle, *Kirchenbau im Wandel*, *Das Münster*, 26, 1973, Nr. 3, S. 217 bis 218, und *Kunst und Kirche*, 27, 1974, Nr. 3, S. 162.
»Die Sendung der Kirche«, *Kunst und Kirche*, 28, 1975, Nr. 3, S. 21.
»Architektenausbildung an der TU Wien«, *Architektur aktuell*, 9, 1975, Nr. 45, S. 38/39.
»Relative Architektur«, *Prolegomena, Arbeitsblätter des Instituts für Wohnbau und Entwerfen an der Technischen Universität Wien*, 1975, Nr. 15, S. 4–7.
»Römerbergecke«, *Baumeister*, 72, 1975, Nr. 8, S. 680/681.
»Junge Architekten sollen Gründerzeitviertel retten«, *Wohnbau*, 1975, Nr. 5, S. 16–23.
»Ein Nachwort zu Habitat«, *Konstruktiv, Zeitschrift der Bundes-Ingenieurkammer*, 1976, Nr. 36, S. 16/17.
»Leitideen des städtischen Wohnbaus«, *Österreichische Hochschulzeitung*, 29, 1977, Nr. 7/8, S. I–V.
»Sponsionsrede für die Diplomanden der Studienrichtung Bauingenieurwesen an der TU Wien«, *Der Architekt*, 25, 1976, Nr. 1, S. 8.
»Beiträge zur Stadterneuerung«, *Der Aufbau, Fachschrift der Stadtbaudirektion Wien*, 31, 1976, Nr. 1/2, S. 2/3.
»Ein Berufungsverfahren an der TU Wien«, *Der Architekt*, 26, 1977, Nr. 3, S. 6.
»Begräbnis erster Klasse, Gutachten im Auftrag der Stadtgemeinde Klagenfurt«, *Wohnbau*, 1977, Nr. 7, S. 28–30.
»Ein Flakturm in Architektur verpackt«, *Wohnbau*, 1977, Nr. 1, S. 18–26.
»Erotik und Architekten«, *Der Architekt*, 26, 1977, Nr. 6, S. 231.
»Architektonische Entwicklung des Kommunalen Wohnhausbaus im Wien der Zweiten Republik«, in: Karl Mang (Hrsg.), *Kommunaler Wohnbau in Wien*, Ausstellungskatalog, Wien 1978, S. 7 bis 16.
»Leitideen des Wohnungsbaues«, *Deutsche Bauzeitschrift*, 26, 1978, Nr. 6, S. 811–814.
»Spielarten nach funktionaler Architektur«, *Konstruktiv, Zeitschrift der Bundes-Ingenieurkammer*, 1978, Nr. 52, S. 4.
»Nur wer es besser kann, werfe den ersten Stein«, *Bauwelt*, 69, 1978, Nr. 13, S. 501.
»Ai Margini della Citta«, *Ville e Giardini*, 1979, Nr. 3, S. 12–17.
»Wohnen heute, eine Bestandsaufnahme mit Folgerungen«, *Bau im Spiegel, Architektur und Bau, Installation*, 8, Frühjahr / Sommer 1979, S. 10–16.
»Prolegomena-Preis 1979, Rede von Prof. Dr. Reinhard Gieselmann«, *Architektur aktuell*, 1979, Nr. 75, S. 6.
»Wohnbau in Wien von Otto Wagner bis heute« (mit Günter Lautner, Rudolf Szedenik), *Deutsche Bauzeitschrift*, 27, 1979, Nr. 7, S. 1087–1097.
»Die Entwicklung der Wiener Stadtgestalt«, *Architektur aktuell*, 14, 1980, Nr. 77, S. 27–32.
»Stadterneuerung«, *Bau im Spiegel, Architektur und Bau, Installation*, 9, Frühjahr / Sommer 1980, S. 11–22.
»Europa Nostra 1980, Kongreß – auch über Verwendungsmöglichkeiten alter Gebäude«, *Der Aufbau, Fachschrift der Stadtbaudirektion Wien*, 35, 1980, Nr. 11, S. 352/353.

»Kirchenbaugeschichte nach 1945«, in: Rainer Bürgel (Hrsg.), *Bauen mit Geschichte*, Gütersloh 1980 (*Dokumentation über den evangelischen Kirchenbautag*, 17), S. 36–48.

»Viyana'da konut mimarisi, Otto Wagner, den günnümüze« (mit Günter Lautner, Rudolf Szedenik), *Yapi, a review published monthly by the building and industry center Istanbul*, 1980, Nr. 37, S. 42 bis 48.

»Die Fassade als neue Aufgabe«, *Bau im Spiegel, Architektur und Bau, Installation*, 10, Frühjahr / Sommer 1981, S. 45–50.

»Über Bruno Taut«, *Der Aufbau, Fachschrift der Stadtbaudirektion Wien*, 36, 1981, Nr. 10, S. 377/378.

»Solides Design«, *Architektur aktuell*, 15, 1981, Nr. 86, S. 15.

»Fassaden-Entwicklungen«, *Deutsche Bauzeitschrift*, 30, 1982, Nr. 7, S. 1003–1006.

»Bericht eines Deutschen aus Wien«, *Bauwelt*, 73, 1982, Nr. 3, S. 92/93.

»Yeni bir Görv olarak Cephe« (Fassade – eine neue Disziplin), *Yapi, a review published monthly by the building and industry center Istanbul*, 1982, Nr. 46, S. 23/24, 30–38.

»Wohnbau heute«, *Modul, Werkbericht Atelier Architekt Prof. Karl Schwanzer*, 1983, Nr. 17, S. 2/3.

»Entwicklungstendenzen des modernen Kirchenbaues, *Architektur + Wettbewerbe*, 1983, Bd. 115, S. 3–7.

»Ricardo Bofill«, *Der Aufbau, Fachschrift der Stadtbaudirektion Wien*, 38, 1983, Nr. 9/10, S. 396.

»Moderne Architektur in Japan«, *Deutsche Bauzeitschrift*, 32, 1984, Nr. 9, S. 1167–1171.

»Defilee im Abteil. Die besondere Betreuung bei einer Bahnreise nach Budapest«, *Die Zeit*, 23, 1.6.1984, S. 51.

»Ricardo Bofill oder die Toleranz«, *Glasforum*, 34, 1984, Nr. 1, S. 7.

»Neue Entwicklungen im Wiener Wohnbau«, in: Viktor Hufnagl/Erich Schlöss (Hrsg.), *Reflexionen und Aphorismen zur österreichischen Architektur*, Wien 1984, S. 367/368.

»Aus Vorträgen, Vorlesungen und Veröffentlichungen«, in: Viktor Hufnagl/Erich Schlöss (Hrsg.), *Reflexionen und Aphorismen zur österreichischen Architektur*, Wien 1984, S. 582–587.

»Höherer Wohnwert durch bauliche und funktionale Nutzung«, in: Friedrich Spengelin/Günter Nagel/Hans Luz, *Wohnen in den Städten? Stadtgestalt, Stadtstruktur, Bauform, Wohnform, Wohnumfeld*, Ausstellungskatalog Akademie der Künste, Berlin 1984, S. 152.

»Architektur – ihre Zukunft in Europa«, *Der Architekt*, 34, 1985, Nr. 1, S. 15.

»Tadao Ando, Architekt des Minimalismus«, *Architektur aktuell*, 19, 1985, Nr. 105, S. 46–47.

»Zum Entwurf des Stadtentwicklungsplans Wien vom November 1984«, *Der Aufbau, Fachschrift der Stadtbaudirektion Wien*, 1985, Nr. 5/6, S. 330/331.

»Stadterneuerung«, *Deutsche Bauzeitschrift*, 33, 1985, Nr. 10, S. 1299–1305.

»Stadterneuerung – Blickwinkel Wien«, *Stadt*, 1986, Nr. 1, S. 44–47.

»Innerstädtischer Wohnbau in Wien« (mit Werner Stolfa), *Architektur + Wettbewerbe*, 1986, Bd. 126, S. 2–4.

»Anarchisches Bauen – Anarchische Architektur«, *Deutsche Bauzeitschrift*, 35, 1987, Nr. 11, S. 1413 bis 1417.

»Auf der Suche nach Stil«, *Prolegomena, Arbeitsblätter des Instituts für Wohnbau und Entwerfen an der Technischen Universität Wien*, 1987, Nr. 57, S. 3–25.

»Stadterweiterung und Stadtreparatur nach dem Zweiten Weltkrieg«, in: Karl Mang/Peter Marchart (Hrsg.), *Wohnen in der Stadt, Ideen für Wien*, Wien 1989, S. 37–47.

»Kirchenbau – der Stand der Dinge«, *Deutsche Bauzeitschrift*, 37, 1989, Nr. 8, S. 1007–1013.

»Wohnbau in Göteborg 1990«, in: Magistrat der Stadt Linz, Baurechtsamt und Planungsamt (Hrsg.), *Stadterneuerung, Methoden und Beispiele*, Linz o. J. (1991), S. 26–33.

»Käse mit Löchern. Interview von Christoph Mandl«, *Solidarität*, 1990, Nr. 712, S. 13–16.

»Erich Boltenstern 1896–1991«, *Architektur aktuell*, 25, 1991, Nr. 145, S. 11/12.

»Metamorphosen des Fertigteilbaues«, *Deutsche Bauzeitschrift*, 39, 1991, S. 77–80.

»Zo pacht Zweden de systembouw aan«, *De Bouwwereld*, 87, 1991, Nr. 21, S. 36–38.

»Experimenteller Wohnbau in Bayern«, *Architekturjournal Wettbewerbe*, 1991, Nr. 103/104, S. 162 bis 165.

»Wiener Stil«, *Deutsche Bauzeitschrift*, 40, 1992, Nr. 9, S. 1285–1289.

»Der Pluralismus als Gestaltungsprinzip. Reinhard Gieselmann im Gespräch mit Patricia Zacek«, *Architektur & Bauforum*, 1992, Nr. 152, S. 86–91.

»Kelch und Mikrophon«, in: Heinz Tiefenbacher/Wolfgang Urban/Egon Reiner, *Raum schaffen für Gott, Kirchenbau und religiöse Kunst in der Diözese Rottenburg-Stuttgart*, Ulm 1992, S. 114 bis 125.

»Die Wand – Versuch über ein Architekturelement«, *Deutsche Bauzeitschrift*, 42, 1994, Nr. 3, S. 93 bis 104.

»Entwicklung des Wohnungsgrundrisses, die Organisation der Wohnung, Grundrißidee«, in: Friederike Schneider (Hrsg.), *Grundrißatlas Wohnungsbau*, Basel/Boston/Wien, 1994, S. 13–25.

»Zur Sanierung von Wohnanlagen«, *Deutsche Bauzeitschrift*, 43, 1995, Nr. 7, S. 137–143.

»Grenzgänge der Architektur. Ein Aufsatz über die Grenzen der Erfaßbarkeit«, *Deutsche Bauzeitschrift*, 44, 1996, Nr. 8, S. 99–105.

Besprechung von: Peter Faller, *Der Wohnungsgrundriß. Entwicklungslinien 1920–1990. Schlüsselprojekte, Funktionsstudien*, Stuttgart 1996, *Kursiv, Literaturblatt der Bauwelt*, 1996, Nr. 28, S. 12.

Besprechung von Gert Kähler (Hrsg.), *Geschichte des Wohnens, Bd. 4, 1918–1945. Reform, Reaktion, Zerstörung*, Stuttgart 1996, *Kursiv, Literaturblatt der Bauwelt*, 1996, Nr. 28, S. 16–17.

»Modernisierung von Kirchen«, *Deutsche Bauzeitschrift*, 46, 1998, Nr. 6. S. 121–126.

»Was ist Baukunst?«, *Baumeister*, 99, 2002, Nr. 12, S. 4.

Photo credits / Photonachweis

Architekturmuseum der TU München 25.34
Martin Botsch, Bremen 20.23, 37.2, 204.20
Richard Einzig, London 47.3, 48.4, 49.5, 49.6,
    59.2, 61.6, 62.7
Joachim Feist, Pliezhausen 176.1, 178.5, 179.6,
    179.7
Maria Gieselmann, Karlsruhe 19.22
Moritz Gieselmann, Vienna/Wien 124.4
Peter Gössel, Gabriele Leuthäuser, *Architektur des
    20. Jahrhunderts*, Cologne/Köln 1990 14.14
Günther Hamm, Klosterneuburg 185.8
Gerhard Kabierske, Karlsruhe 26.36, 213.41
Margherita Krischanitz, Vienna/Wien 165.3, 165.4,
    166.5, 166.6, 167.7
Bruno Krupp, Freiburg 105.10
Joachim Langner, Ludwigshafen 37.2, 206.24
*Le Corbusier. Chapelle Notre Dame du Haut, Ron-
    champ, France. 1950–54*, Tokyo 2000 23.30
Monika Lenzner 24.31, 58.5
Thilo Mechau, Karlsruhe 8.6, 25.33, 30.42, 42.1,
    43.2, 44.3, 98.7, 99.9, 100.10, 100.11, 106.1,
    108.3, 108.4, 111.9, 112.12, 113.11, 121.5, 121.6,
    184.5, 184.6, 187.11, 187.12
Hans-Jürgen Meier-Menzel, Murnau 31.44
Beppo Merkle, Basel 15.16, 16.18, 33.3, 34.4,
    35.6, 35.7
Karl-Siegfried Mühlensiep, Neu-Ulm 169.3, 170,5,
    171.6, 171.7
Gernot Nalbach, Berlin 210.34, 211.35
Sigrid Neubert, Munich/München 6.2, 8.5, 9.8,
    63.8, 63.9, 67.2, 67.3, 69.7, 70.8, 71.9, 97.6,
    98.8, 101.12, 158.4, 158.5
Oswald Mathias Ungers. Architektur 1951–1990,
    Stuttgart 1991 18.21
Otto Senn. Raum als Form, Basel 1990 13.13
Wolfgang Pehnt, *Neue deutsche Architektur 3*,
    Stuttgart 1970 9.7
Artur Pfau, Mannheim 18.20, 62.6, 63.7
Walter Schmidt, Karlsruhe 22.27, 87.2
S. Schwingenschlögl, Vienna/Wien 76.1, 78.4,
    78.5, 79.6, 79.7, 134.5, 135.6, 135.7
Margherita Spiluttini, Vienna/Wien 28.38, 29.41,
    137.3, 137.4, 142.5, 142.6, 143.7, 143.8, 148.9,
    148.10, 149.11, 150.12, 151.13, 151.14, 166.5,
    166.6, 167.7, 186.9, 186.10, 214.44
Friedhelm Thomas, Hamburg 38.1, 40.4, 41.5,
    88.5, 92.5, 93.7, 183,4
Peter Walser, Stuttgart 29.40, 55.2, 56.4, 152.1,
    153.2, 155.7, 155.8, 157.2, 157.3, 159.6, 161.3,
    162.4, 162.5, 163.6, 174.4, 175.5, 175.6
Werk, 1954, 1 15.16